HERE'S WHAT A FEW FAMOUS BROOKLYN RESIDENTS AND FANS TOLD THE AUTHOR:

"I invite everyone to explore and enjoy the many interesting neighborhoods and exciting cultural landmarks that Brooklyn has to offer."

—Howard Golden,
Brooklyn Borough President

"Brooklyn is homes and neighborhoods with caring, loyal people who proudly take their Brooklyn roots with them wherever they go. It's mostly a quiet place where you can see the sky, travel on wide, tree-lined streets, hear the sounds of life, and smell the culinary diversity."

—Franklin Thomas,
Past President, The Ford Foundation

"Brooklyn, there really are great restaurants there. And with deep-dish apple pie and (Gage & Tollner's) Miss Edna, I may never go back to Virginia."

—Willard Scott

"You can take the kid out of Brooklyn, but you can't take Brooklyn out of the kid. Kickin' the can. Ring-a-leevio. Stoop ball. Potsy. Punch ball! Playing marbles along the curb. Hearing my mother call me from the third-floor window telling me it was time to eat. Brooklyn! The cosmos!"

—Julius La Rosa

"If I'm gonna live in the city, Brooklyn is where I'd live forever. When I saw it I flipped. It's very unpretentious—nobody cares who you are until you can shoot a basketball. Until I scored three points in a game the cats in the neighborhood wouldn't speak to me. When I moved here the only thing I wanted to do was find Ebbets Field. At least the wall was left. BAM is a beautiful place, my favorite place to play. It sounds great and the decor is fantastic."

—Branford Marsalis

• Brooklyn Best Bets •

- Walk over the **Brooklyn Bridge** (but don't buy it!).
- Wander through the world-class **Brooklyn Museum of Art**.
- Live like a Brooklynite: Race slot cars at **Buzz-a-rama**. Get a haircut at the Sinatra-era **Park Slope Barbershop**. Chow down at **Brennan & Carr**. Ice skate at **Wollman Rink.** Patronize **Brooklyn Brewery**.
- See the new SoHo: **Williamsburg.** Visit the galleries. Eat at **Oznot's** or **Plan Eat Thailand**.
- Experience different ethnic neighborhoods, from Italian **Bensonhurst** to Hasidic **Borough Park**.
- Take a guided tour of historic **Greenwood Cemetery** and **Clinton Hill**.
- Walk through prosperous **landmarked districts** in **Park Slope** and **Brooklyn Heights**.
- Check out newly trendy **Smith Street** with its slew of funky boutiques and eateries, such as **Patois**.
- Go kayaking at the **Sebago Kayak Club** and horseback riding at **Jamaica Bay Riding Academy**.
- Enjoy the **Brooklyn Botanic Garden,** especially at tulip, lilac, or cherry blossom time.
- In **Greenpoint,** get a kielbasa or babka to take home; visit **St. Stanislaus Kostka Church.**
- Go vintage shopping at **Domsey's, Grassroots, Ladybird,** or **Hooti Couture.**
- Take in a jazz concert at **Arts at St. Ann's,** a landmarked church with famous stained-glass windows.
- Stroll the **Promenade,** eat at **Henry's End,** see **Plymouth Church,** a stop on the underground railroad.
- Gaze at the Manhattan skyline from the tiny **Empire Fulton Ferry State Park** in arty **"DUMBO."**
- In season: View the Christmas lights in **Dyker Heights;** shop at **Park Slope stoop sales.**
- Stay overnight in a local brownstone **bed & breakfast,** or the new **Brooklyn Marriott.**
- Take a **house tour** in elegant **Prospect Park South.**

- See how matzoh is really made at the **Schmura Matzoh** factory, open seasonally.
- "Do" the fairs and carnivals: the **International African Arts Festival, Mermaid Parade, West Indian American Day Parade, BARC Dog Parade, Park Slope Halloween Parade.**
- Have a sunset picnic with your kids, spouse or lover at remote **Coffey Pier.**
- Attend a Next Wave performance at **BAM;** dine at **BAM Café** or nearby **New City Café .**
- Play at the **Brooklyn Children's Museum, Prospect Park Zoo,** and the **Carousel.**
- Visit **UrbanGlass** studios to watch as contemporary art glass is blown, poured, and molded.
- Attend a concert at the floating **Bargemusic.** Dine at the upscale **River Café** or the operatic **Tin Café .**
- Tour the historic free-black community of **Weeksville** and African-American **Bedford-Stuyvesant.**
- Fly a kite in **Prospect Park** or **Shore Parkway.**
- Buy quality, buy discount: a hat at **Larisa's,** undies at **UnderWorld Plaza,** kids' clothes at **Rachel's.**
- Have a day at the ocean side: Visit the **New York Aquarium, Coney Island,** and **Manhattan Beach.**
- In multiethnic Sunset Park, visit a mosque, stock up at **Hong Kong Supermarket,** try on Mexican cowboy boots at **Zapateria II**, and dine at **Nyonya Malaysian** restaurant.
- Learn about efforts to revitalize the still-grungy, industrial **Gowanus Canal** area; take a **BCUE** boat tour.
- Bike down the **Ocean Parkway bike path** to Russian **M&I International** or **Caffe Cappuccino.**
- Hit golf balls at **Gateway Recreation Center,** or play a round at the **Marine Park Golf Course.**
- Along **Atlantic Avenue,** go to **Sahadi's** for Middle Eastern foods; check out **BARK** and **Brawta.**
- Argue about who makes better pizza: **Patsy Grimaldi's** or **Totonno's.**

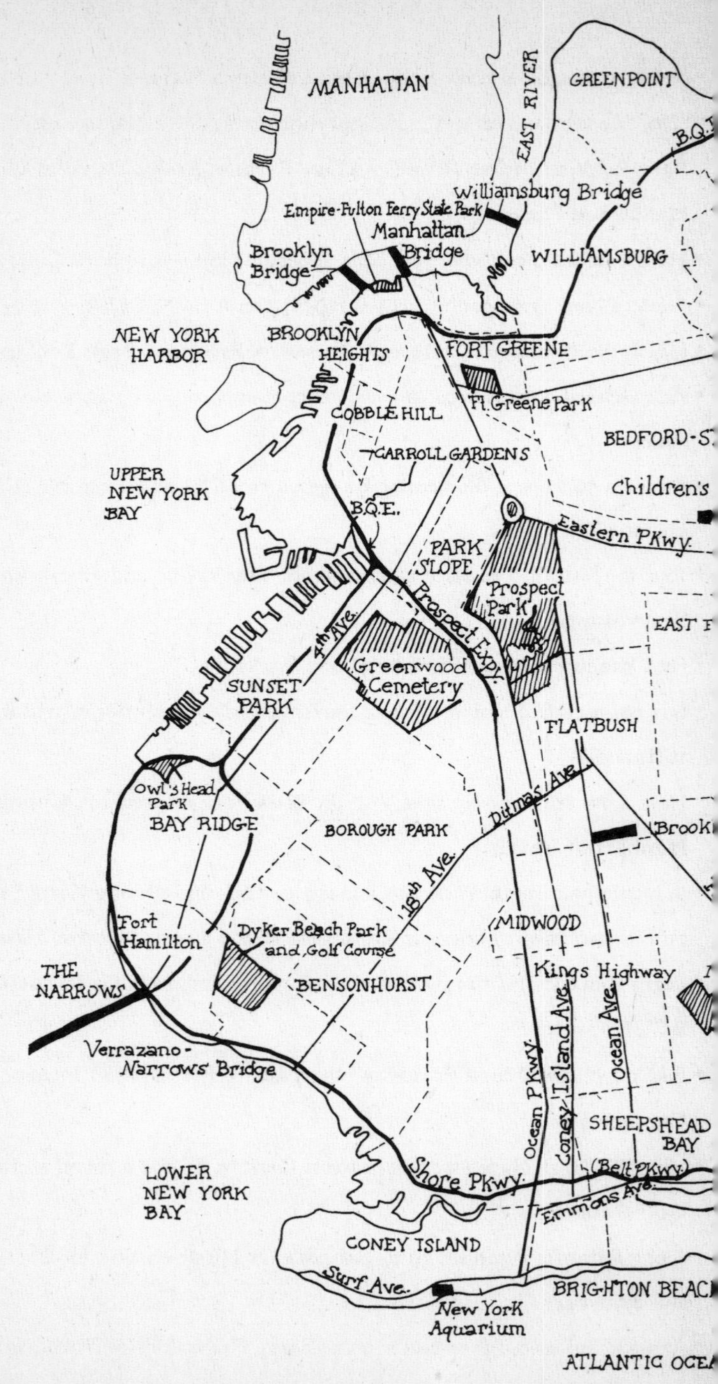
MANHATTAN
EAST RIVER
GREENPOINT
B.Q.E.
Williamsburg Bridge
Empire-Fulton Ferry State Park
Manhattan Bridge
Brooklyn Bridge
WILLIAMSBURG
NEW YORK HARBOR
BROOKLYN HEIGHTS
FORT GREENE
Ft. Greene Park
COBBLE HILL
CARROLL GARDENS
BEDFORD-S
UPPER NEW YORK BAY
Children's
B.Q.E.
Eastern PKwy.
PARK SLOPE
Prospect Park
Prospect Expy.
7th Ave.
EAST F
Greenwood Cemetery
SUNSET PARK
FLATBUSH
Ditmas Ave.
Owl's Head Park
BAY RIDGE
BOROUGH PARK
18th Ave.
MIDWOOD
Fort Hamilton
Dyker Beach Park and Golf Course
Kings Highway
THE NARROWS
BENSONHURST
Verrazano-Narrows Bridge
Ocean PKwy.
Coney Island Ave.
Ocean Ave.
SHEEPSHEAD BAY
(Belt PKwy.)
Shore PKwy.
LOWER NEW YORK BAY
Emmons Ave.
CONEY ISLAND
Surf Ave.
BRIGHTON BEAC
New York Aquarium
ATLANTIC OCE

Brooklyn!

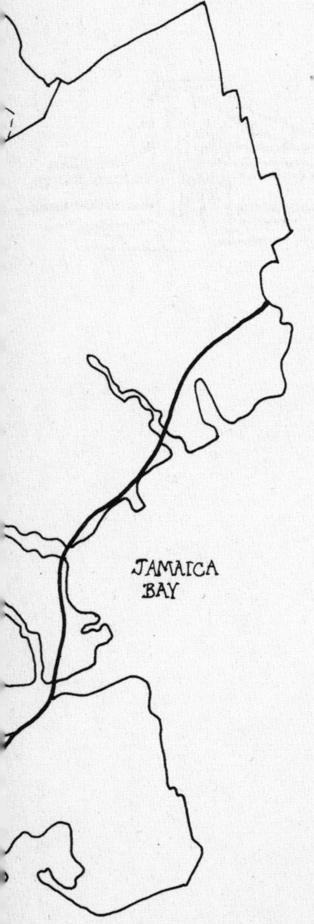

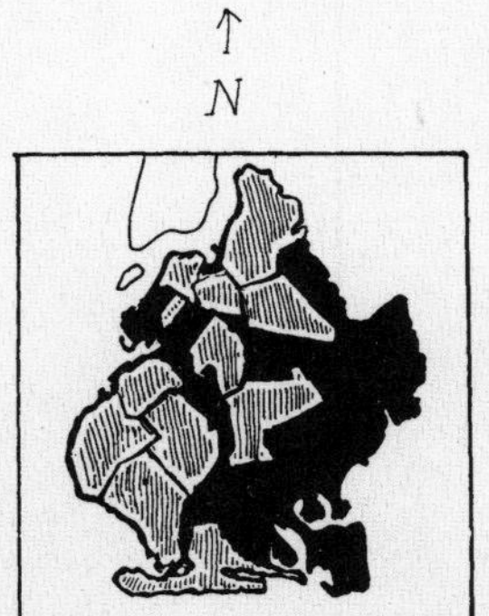

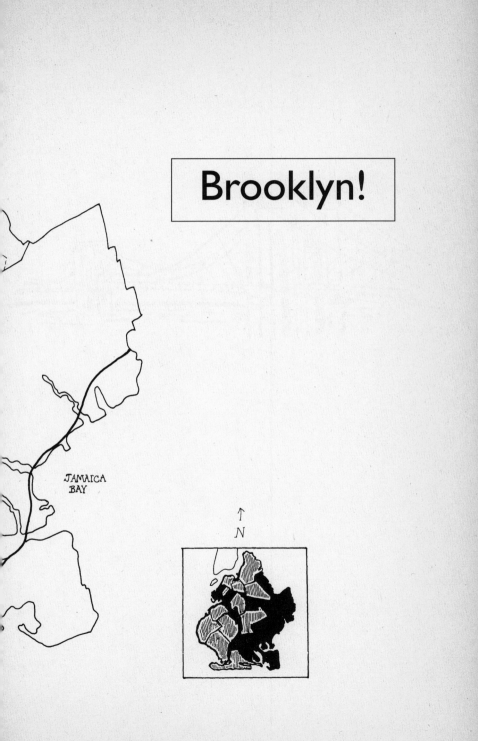

Brooklyn!

A Soup-to-Nuts Guide to Sights, Neighborhoods, and Restaurants

Ellen Freudenheim

St. Martin's Griffin
New York

To Daniel, David, and Anna

Editor: Greg Cohn
Book design by Ellen R. Sasahara

Brooklyn Bridge line art by Michael Storrings

ISBN: 0-312-20446-9

10 9 8 7 6 5 4 3

Books are available in quantity for promotional or premium use. Write to Director of Special Sales, St. Martin's Press, 175 Fifth Avenue, New York, NY 10010, for information on discounts and terms, or call toll-free (800)221-7945. In New York, call (212) 674-5151 (ext. 645).

Contents

Acknowledgments

Many people helped create this second edition of our Brooklyn guidebook. First thanks are due to the hundreds of Brooklyn residents, shopkeepers, restaurant owners, and artists who cooperated by sharing their stories and answering our questions. Special acknowledgments are due to Hal Cohn and Andy Gerstig, who researched and wrote most of the Carroll Gardens/Cobble Hill and Brighton Beach chapters, respectively, and to Joe Hagan, Howard Pritsch, Andrea Askowitz, and Sue Fox for their excellent contributions to the Williamsburg, Fort Greene, and Park Slope chapters. A hearty thanks is due to people who reviewed parts of the manuscript, including Florence Neal, Christine Mark, Lyn Stallworth, and Jean Halloran, and to Hee Jin Kang, whose research was impeccable. The lovely maps were drawn by Florence Neal, and the cover designed by Scott Levine. And, thanks again to Borough President Howard Golden and the celebrities whose quotes capture bits of the essence of Brooklyn.

Brooklyn Bridge magazine was an excellent source for news about Brooklyn, and the magazine's editors were generous in providing both references and back issues. Other publications which were helpful included the *AIA Guide to New York, Guide to New York City Landmarks, The Encyclopedia of New York City,* BRIC calendars and brochures, Ed Levine's *New York Eats,* and the Brooklyn Chamber of Commerce publications *Brooklyn Eats* and *Brooklyn@tlas*. This guidebook builds on our first edition, called *Brooklyn: Where to Go, What to Do, How to Get There,* which in turn utilized helpful source material from the Fund for the Borough of Brooklyn.

Insights into Brooklyn's burgeoning art scene and art neighborhoods were contributed by Joe Amrhein of Pierogi 2000, Joy Glidden of the DUMBO Art Center, Kathy and Jim Hartzler, Charolotta Kotik of the Brooklyn Museum of Art, Terrance Lindall and Yuko Nii of the Williamsburg Art and Historical Society, sculptors Deborah Masters and Boaz Vaadia, various members of the Brooklyn Waterfront Artists Coalition and Brooklyn Arts Council, and many others, to whom we also extend a thank you.

Thanks also to Carolina Gonzalez, Pat Olmstead, Jim Yardley, and the Park

Slope Food Coop staff for swapping information and sharing ideas, to Brooklyn "food spy" Cynthia Cohen Congress, to Vinnie, Anthony, and Sandra at BQE Pet Supply for their impromptu tour around Williamsburg, and to neighbors Sharon Golden, Lisa Robins, and to eleven-year olds Anna Wiener and Sophie Pauze for helping out with research. St. Martin's editorial staff, including Ann Savarese, and especially Greg Cohn and Kim Walker deserve credit for their professional and timely contributions.

Kudos are due to David Wiener, age fourteen, for photocopying management, Daniel Wiener for his organizational genius, and a special thanks to our friends at EnTrust Capital Inc. for their gracious, if unanticipated, last-minute assistance in manuscript preparation. To Joan Rizzo, Sam Wiener, and Maureen Gaffney a special hug for being great family hosts during busy weeks.

Finally, to my wonderful family—Anna, David and Daniel—a loving thank you for your patience and moral support through many long hours of work.

Introduction: Falling in Love with Brooklyn

Brooklyn's back. It's hip. And it's hot. Exploring Brooklyn is an experience you won't soon forget.

New York City's most interesting, most human-scaled borough, Brooklyn is bubbling over with creative energy. And that ain't hype. Here's proof:

- Brooklyn restaurants, architecture, food emporia, vintage shops, innovative art and music performances, and human-interest stories are making headlines in *The New York Times*, the *Daily News* and *New York Post, Time Out New York, New York Magazine,* and international newspapers.
- In less than a decade, Brooklyn's got a spanking, brand-new hotel, new movie theaters, new shopping malls, new university endowments, new waterfront parks, its own Brooklyn brewery, *Brooklyn Bridge* magazine which covers its every nook and cranny, a Brooklyn Youth Chorus that has performed at venues from the White House to European capitals, a spiffy Metro Tech office complex—and lots of new refugees from rising Manhattan real estate prices.
- Brooklyn is having a love affair with young artists—and vice versa. Williamsburg is being transformed into an art and music center. Red Hook and DUMBO may follow suit. Most Brooklynites don't even know this, but on the Richter scale of the art world, Brooklyn's got the reputation of being the "epicenter" of a hot young generation of new and emerging artists, not just in the USA but internationally.
- New, hip neighborhoods are popping up faster than zucchini in a Vermont August; suddenly Smith Street, Columbia Street, Park Slope's Fifth Avenue, the Gowanus, Little Pakistan, Chinatown in Sheepshead Bay, and other sleepy backwaters are flowering into interesting neighborhoods, pockets of small-town friendliness and commerce embedded in the big bad Apple.

- European visitors flock to Brooklyn to see how "real New Yorkers" live. Some even settle here, in places such as Brooklyn Heights, Williamsburg, and Greenpoint, attracted by the small scale and old-worldliness of these old neighborhoods.

Brooklyn's not stuck in the past anymore. It was for awhile associated only with the Brooklyn Dodgers, Ralph Kramden, and the old Coney Island amusement park, all long gone. Brooklyn, for years, was the place where people both came from and left—Woody Allen, George Gershwin, Walt Whitman, and even Spike Lee.

Why is Brooklyn "happening" now? As one young man said, "I moved here from Manhattan only because I had to, and after awhile I grew to love it. Just like everybody else." The interesting thing about Brooklyn in the late 1990s is not that people are moving here (they always have). It's that people are falling in love with Brooklyn.

Brooklyn is "hot" because the architecture is great, its history is colorful, the neighborhoods are mini-hotbeds of ethnically authentic cultures, restaurants are cheap, and transportation is easy. And it is livable; from many places, you can see the sky, the water, and the incredible silhouette of Manhattan.

Brooklyn is "hip" because there's a critical mass of artists, musicians, writers, producers, actors, and other creative types now living in the borough, and the Brooklyn Academy of Music and Brooklyn Museum of Art are pathbreaking cultural institutions. Its small streets filled with mom-and-pop stores are a welcome antidote to highly commercial, chain-store merchandising. And there are pockets of urban adventure, particularly in Red Hook and the Gowanus Canal, where dreamers and pioneers are trying to transform dead waterfronts and abandoned nineteenth-century warehouses into public piers, waterfront parks, artists lofts, and galleries.

And, Brooklyn is "back" because, despite past ups and downs, it is a spirited place that attracts up-and-comers. And it's the one place you are sure to find *Brooklynites*. Traveling the neighborhoods you will rapidly cross invisible boundaries, streets representing cultural worlds: Italian to Russian, Chinese to Latino, yuppie American to Hasidic. While the nation struggles with questions of how to "do" diversity, most Brooklynites *live* it every day. Brooklyn is probably one of the most diverse population centers in the United States. Professionals, hipsters, businesspeople, families with kids, urban refugees, writers, performers, theater folks, recent college graduates; Jewish, black; Asian folks; immigrants from Mexico and the Dominican Republic; from Russia, China, Hong Kong, Malaysia and other parts of Asia; from Pakistan and the Middle East, Italy, and even Canada live in Brooklyn. Within a half mile you will find people who depend on welfare, and people who own not one, but several, half-million dollar homes, all in the same area. Yet residents have that peculiar thing in common, that *Brooklyn* thing—a can-do attitude, a practical outlook, an unpretentious urbanity. The cultural currency here is not about money, nor power, though of course both exist. In a borough where people actually know their neighbors, the glue that binds is a sense of community—and the need to get along. Brooklyn's mixed population is a good strong stock, and it's astonishing diversity breeds tolerance, adaptability—and humor.

This Brooklyn guidebook lists more than 950 shops, restaurants, parks, playgrounds, movie theaters, museums, historic places, official landmarks, and the little things that everyone knows about their own neighborhood. It was written for just about anybody interested in what goes on today in Brooklyn's many and different neighborhoods. If you live here, the authors bet a nickel (or, more appropriately, a pickle) that you'll discover something that you never knew about the borough, like why Park Slope smells like roasting coffee and where you can take sailing lessons. If you live in Manhattan, you'll discover why it is that people rarely move back from Brooklyn once they get here. If you grew up and Brooklyn, and left, you'll be sorry, or at least nostalgic. And if you are from out of town, or from another country, you will quickly understand that Brooklyn is a livable, affordable, neighborly counterpoint to Manhattan.

You can't beat the Brooklyn Museum of Art, Brooklyn Botanic Garden, BAM, or the Children's Museum for culture and entertainment. Where else can you listten to chamber music on a barge, and gaze at the famous Manhattan skyline? There is enough left of historic Brooklyn for good reminiscing: Peter Luger's, Junior's, the boardwalk, Gargiulo's, Alba's, Gage & Tollner, and more. If you want, you can eat huge strawberry pancakes for breakfast, Middle Eastern couscous chicken for lunch, and Polish potato pirogi for dinner, while shopping for designer clothing at blue-jeans prices. And you'll still have time to take a ride on Coney Island's famous roller coaster, the Cyclone, visit the nation's first children's museum, or play nine holes of golf.

Brooklyn has a population of 2.3 million—which would make it the fourth largest city in the U.S.—and it is having a renaissaince. If Manhattan is the swelling heart of New York City, then Brooklyn is its soul. People are falling in love with Brooklyn. The reason why—the quality of life here—can be found in the pages of this book.

A word from the author

Brooklyn! A Soup-to-Nuts Guide to Sights, Neighborhoods, and Restaurants is a second edition of this guidebook. The original version, published in 1991 with my co-author and husband Daniel Wiener, was the first nationally distributed guidebook to Brooklyn in more than fifty years.

We discovered Brooklyn because we had to. Ex-Manhattanites with two small children, we went in search of discount furniture, that elusive knish, and a great place to take the kids on a rainy day. Our guide was our neighbor, Sharon Golden, who tossed off suggestions that we visit a hitherto unknown "Avenue J" or "McDonald Avenue" as though they were as familiar as Madison or Fifth. To our astonishment, it was impossible, short of word of mouth, to find out about Brooklyn.

In 1991, people thought it was laughable to write a guidebook to Brooklyn. ("You're kidding, who wants to know about *Brooklyn*?", they'd say, rolling their eyes.) Well, we've had the last laugh. Brooklyn has again been "discovered," and it is undergoing a major renaissance. In 1991, ours was one of about three books concerning Brooklyn to be found in big bookstores; by 1999, there are whole sections with books detailing Brooklyn recipes, featuring photos of Coney Island, describing in detail how the Brooklyn Bridge was built, and documenting the history of Brooklyn's neighborhoods. So welcome to a happening place. We've tried to capture the best of Brooklyn on the cusp of the new millennium, and so *Brooklyn!* includes hundreds of new listings. And yes, after fifteen years, we still live here.

How to Use This Book

There are several ways to tour Brooklyn.

Pick a neighborhood. The introductions to each chapter will highlight what you can expect to find there. Then set your priorities—food, fun, or fashion—and take it from there.

Or, use the Where to Find It index (see page 348) to pinpoint the particular cuisine, shop, cultural or historical site, or entertainment you want. Then consider the surrounding neighborhoods yours to explore.

Parents can turn directly to the Brooklyn's Best Bets for Children section (page 322) or the Kidstuff section in each chapter. "Brooklyn Best Bets" are indicated by the icon ✪ which signifies points of particular interest.

Transportation

Cabs. Yellow cabs are rare on Brooklyn streets. A reliable and slightly cheaper alternative are the numerous neighborhood car services, licensed by the Taxi and Limousine Commission. Several are listed in each neighborhood section, but almost any car service will take you wherever you wish to go. If the local car service is busy, try calling one based in an adjoining neighborhood. Prices are set by a dispatcher instead of registering on a meter. When you call a car service, the dispatcher should give you a price for your trip before sending a car for you. Expect to wait about ten minutes for a car, or longer during rush hour or in bad weather. Car services are a good way to get around Brooklyn or to get from Brooklyn back to Manhattan.

Unbeknownst to many Manhattanites, car services are also considerably cheaper than yellow cabs when going from Manhattan to Brooklyn, particularly when you are headed for distant points. Call at least a half hour in advance and most services will pick you up in Manhattan for a flat fee of about $20 or less.

Subways. The subways that run to Brooklyn from Manhattan are the 2, 3, 4, 5, and the A, B, C, D, F, G, J, L, M, N, Q, and R. Three stations where many lines intersect are Borough Hall in Brooklyn Heights and Atlantic Avenue and DeKalb Avenue near Fort Greene. For information on the subway and bus routes, call the hotline operated from 6 A.M. to 9 P.M. daily by the New York City Transit Authority at (718) 330-1234. Be prepared to wait a few minutes to get through.

LIRR. The Long Island Railroad stops at the Atlantic Avenue station, at the intersection of Atlantic and Flatbush avenues. The terminal, just a stone's throw from the Brooklyn Academy of Music, connects with a number of subway lines.

Maps

The maps preceding each chapter should be adequate for most casual expeditions in Brooklyn. Or you can pick up a detailed street map of Brooklyn in bookstores, many drugstores, and often from sidewalk book merchants. A subway map, free at token booths, is also helpful.

Neighborhood Newspapers

Did you know that Walt Whitman got his start as a Brooklyn newspaperman? Cyberspace notwithstanding, the locals are still a great way to get the gossip and news about your neighborhood, be it the police precinct crime blotter, information on retail stores, or quotable quotes from Brooklyn politicians about the Mayor. Most are weekly and most (but not all) are freebies; you'll find them piled in the dry cleaners, butchers, supermarket, pharmacy, etc. Different papers serve Brooklyn Heights, Park Slope, Sheepshead Bay, Bay Ridge, and many other neighborhoods.

Safety and Style

The neighborhoods listed in this book are, we feel, friendly to visitors. Still, since this is New York City, you should make sure to pack your street smarts. A few tips: Wandering around during the day is always better than a nighttime stroll. Two is always safer than one (it's more fun to bring a friend anyway). Brooklyn is a practical place; you generally are better off dressing down in casual clothes. All but the fanciest restaurants will seat and serve anyone who looks presentable, regardless of whether the men are wearing jackets and ties or the women fancy clothes.

Phone Numbers and Web Sites

All of the phone numbers listed here are in the 718 area code unless otherwise noted. Several key web sites are listed in the index.

Bay Ridge

Where it is: 65th Street to 101st Street, Belt Parkway to Fort Hamilton Parkway.

What's nearby: Bath Beach, Bensonhurst, Borough Park, Dyker Heights, Sunset Park, and Staten Island.

How to get there:

By car: Take the Brooklyn-Queens Expressway (BQE) to the Gowanus Expressway toward Staten Island. Exit at 86th Street (and 7th Avenue). If you arrive at the Verrazano-Narrows Bridge, you've gone too far.
By subway: R train to 86th Street (at 4th Avenue).
Cab services: About $24 to Grand Central Station; $15 to Brooklyn Heights. Apple Car Service (363-9000) or Harborview Car Service (748-8800).

Special Events: Norwegian Constitution Day Parade (first Sunday after May 17); Ragamuffin Parade and Third Avenue Festival (first weekend in October). Call 836-6700 for information.

How it got its name: Known first as Yellow Hook for the yellow clay in its soil; the infelicitous name was changed in 1853 after New York City suffered a bout of yellow fever. The spectacular views from a ridge overlooking the entrance to New York Bay gave Bay Ridge its current name.

Official landmarks: 8200 Narrows Avenue House and Fort Hamilton Officers Club.

ABOUT THE NEIGHBORHOOD

It would be impossible to take in all of Bay Ridge in one visit. The neighborhood is just too big. You'll find large name-brand shops along 86th Street and smaller, intimate family-run shops on 5th Avenue. Third Avenue is restaurant row, with many good eateries along a twenty-five-block stretch.

Bay Ridge is not a fancy place. Its shops, restaurants and community

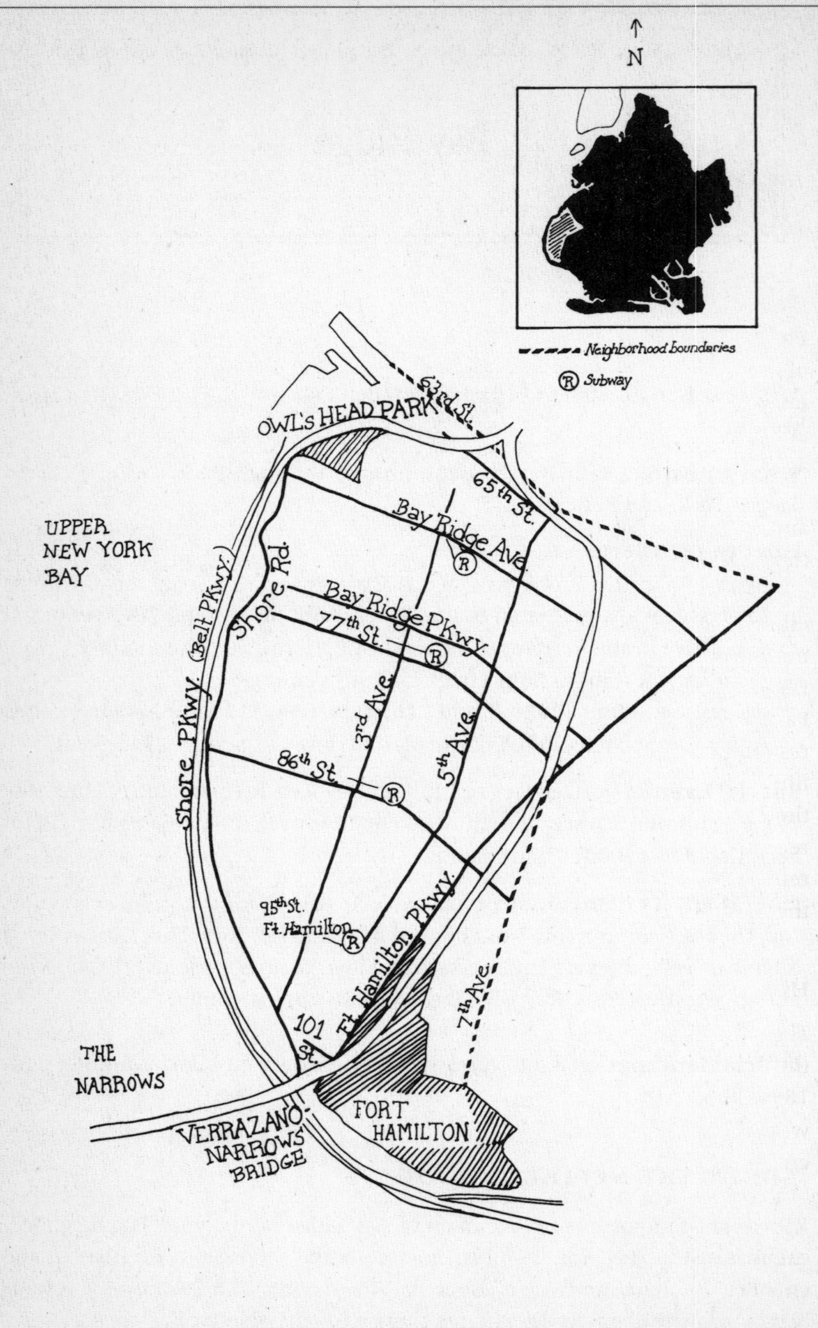
N
Neighborhood boundaries
Subway
OWL's HEAD PARK
63rd St.
65th St.
Bay Ridge Ave.
Bay Ridge Pkwy.
77th St.
Shore Rd.
Shore Pkwy. (Belt Pkwy.)
UPPER NEW YORK BAY
3rd Ave.
5th Ave.
86th St.
95th St. Ft. Hamilton
Ft. Hamilton Pkwy.
7th Ave.
101 St.
THE NARROWS
VERRAZANO-NARROWS BRIDGE
FORT HAMILTON

events reflect the solid middle-class family values of the local populace. The community-sponsored **Narrows Botanical Gardens** is testimony to the spirit of the neighborhood. Many stores sell good, moderately priced home furnishings, from country-style **Grassroots** to upscale **The Hutch**, punctuated by several unusual shops such as **John Johnston's Jukebox Classics**, and **A&J Police Equipment**. There's plenty of clothing for women, including trendy stores such as **Threadz**.

The range of restaurants offering moderately priced, satisfying meals is unparalleled in all of Brooklyn. The choices vary, from exotic dishes at **India Passage** to great Italian food at **Areo** and **Tuscany Grill**, to huge portions of barbecue chicken and ribs at **Short Ribs**, to classy French at **St. Michel**, music and dancing with dinner at **T. J. Bentley**, and an earthy Polish meal at **Polonica**. In addition, there are cafés and a few outstanding bakeries such as **Pierrot**.

Waves of immigrants have moved here—the Irish, Muslims from Yemen and Lebanon, Poles, Asians from China and Hong Kong, and, most recently, thousands of Russian immigrants.

The shops, restaurants, and community events in Bay Ridge celebrate its ethnic diversity. The early Scandinavian settlers' presence is still felt in the neighborhood bakeries and food shops. The annual Norwegian Constitution Day Parade culminates with the crowning of Miss Norway in Leif Ericson Park. The sizable Italian population is reflected in the many excellent Italian restaurants and cappuccino and espresso cafés. At Christmas, fourth- and fifth-generation Italians in the Dyker Heights section of Bay Ridge bedeck their homes with thousands of lights and decorations. The Irish, and more recently the Asian, Polish, Russian, Greek, Lebanese, and Syrian, presence is reflected in small specialty shops that sell food, clothing, and gift items from the old country.

Historical Notes

The area now called Bay Ridge was purchased from the Nyack Indians by the Dutch West India Company in 1652. A rural farming area until the late 1890s, Bay Ridge, like Brooklyn Heights, was developed as a retreat for wealthy Manhattanites. The spectacular views from a ridge overlooking the entrance to New York Bay gave Bay Ridge its name and attracted a number of industrialists who built summer estates along the bluffs of Shore Road. But with the extension of the 4th Avenue Subway in 1915, the exclusivity of the area was destroyed. The neighborhood's population changed as Manhattan workers seeking more suburban surroundings began to settle in the area.

The long history of Bay Ridge remains visible in its homes and churches.

Elegant turn-of-the-century houses more typical of Westchester than Brooklyn line Colonial Road and Shore Road between 80th and 83rd streets. The land on which Fort Hamilton was built played a role in George Washington's failed Battle of Long Island against the British in 1776. Nearby Saint John's Episcopal Church at 99th Street and Fort Hamilton Parkway, known as the "church of the generals," was frequented by such military leaders as Stonewall Jackson and Robert E. Lee.

Visitors love looking at the so-called **Gingerbread House**, with a mock thatched roof, located at the corner of 82nd Street and Narrows Avenue. Local legend suggests that it was built as a country getaway for a young homesick British bride. It is a New York City landmark building, known officially as **8200 Narrows Avenue House**, erected for a successful shipping magnate in an Arts and Crafts design. The home at the intersection of Colonial Road and Wakeman Place is also a point of local historical interest. It was on the estate known as Owl's Head, belonging to Henry Murphy, the first editor of the *Brooklyn Eagle* newspaper, that the construction of the Brooklyn Bridge was authorized.

Standing guard over the neighborhood's one- and two-family homes and dominating many of the views is the **Verrazano-Narrows Bridge**. Named after Giovanni da Verrazano, first explorer of New York Harbor, the bridge's opening in 1964 linked Brooklyn to Staten Island and New Jersey. At that time it was the world's longest suspension bridge.

Shopping Areas

There are three main shopping areas: 3rd Avenue, 5th Avenue, and 86th Street.

86th Street: Major chain stores. This two-lane street between 4th and 6th avenues is home to many national and regional retail chains, including Benetton, Lane Bryant, Lerner's, and Century 21.

5th Avenue: Specialty retail. From 75th to 88th streets, the stretch of specialty stores, ethnic delis, gift shops (such as the top-notch **The Hutch**), and cafés is "Main Street" for the families in the adjacent neighborhood of tree-lined streets and two-story homes. The block from 82nd to 83rd Street could be called the "wedding center" of Brooklyn. Along with a number of bridal boutiques, this is the home of **Kleinfeld's**, New York City's most famous prenuptial retail operation.

3rd Avenue: Restaurant row. Bay Ridge has so many good restaurants, it's hard to know when to stop eating. (See listings from page 9–15.)

Kidstuff

The two-and-a-half mile stretch known as **Shore Road Park** along the waters of upper New York Bay is a favorite spot for kite flying, fishing, and biking. **Owl's Head Park**, overlooking the harbor, is great for picnics. Visit the **Narrows Botanical Gardens** in the springtime to smell flowers in bloom. For kids interested in things military, a visit to the **Harbor Defense Museum** is a must (call ahead to check the hours). Sports fans will find gear aplenty in this neighborhood at **Royale Sporting Goods** and specialty items at **Panda Sports. Novel Idea Bookstore** is less overwhelming than the chain bookstores, and has a manageable children's selection and warm, friendly staff.

ENTERTAINMENT

Cineplex Odeon Alpine Theater. 6900 5th Avenue, at 69th Street, 748-4200.

A small, friendly, seven-screen first-run movie theater located at the beginning of the 5th Avenue commercial strip in Bay Ridge. Walk two blocks through a residential area to lots of great restaurants on Third Avenue. There's easy local parking and bargain matinees.

Kings Squares Square Dancing. At Redeemer St. John Lutheran Church, 939 83rd Street, between Seventh and 10th avenues, 336-1650. First and third Sundays, 7:30–10:00 P.M.

Join a lively set ranging in age from 18- to 50-somethings for old-fashioned square dancing fun. You may have to take some classes first, but once you know your do-si-do from your promenade calls, you'll find yourself twirling through the evening. People say they enjoy the alcohol-free atmosphere and hearty fun. This is one of a half-dozen such American folk dancing clubs in New York City, and it's been in business for over twenty years.

Lee Mark Lanes. 423 88th Street, between 4th and 5th avenues, 745-3200. Daily, 9 A.M.–6 P.M. No credit cards.

This two-floor, thirty-six-lane renovated bowling alley is a popular neighborhood spot for birthday parties and league play. Baby-sitting is available. If you're going to have a children's party, you can arrange for inflatable bumpers to be installed so that every ball stays in the lane.

PARKS AND PLAYGROUNDS

5th Avenue Playground. 84th Street, on 5th Avenue.

This is your basic urban playground, complete with swings and other necessary equipment. Nothing fancy, but it is conveniently located near 5th Avenue shopping. For a greener setting, check out the 79th Street and 95th Street playgrounds on the other side of Bay Ridge (see listing below).

Leif Ericson Park. 4th Avenue, between 66th and 67th streets.

Reflecting the neighborhood's early Scandinavian roots, this sixteen-acre park is the site of the annual crowning of Miss Norway during Bay Ridge's Norwegian Constitution Day Parade in May. (See calendar page 331.)

Narrows Botanical Gardens. Shore Road between 69th and 72nd streets, May to November.

This lovely four-and-a-half acre garden is known for its flowers, tranquility, and great views of the Narrows, the Statue of Liberty, and the Verrazano-Narrows Bridge. Come in the spring to enjoy the rose gardens, a native plant area with lady slipper orchids, and a miniature bog and pond. It's all tended and paid for by volunteers who transformed it from a grubby piece of untended land. To quote one, "The lily pond in an old sandbox is the best thing you've ever saw." Lovely for young children in particular.

✪ **Owl's Head Park** and **Shore Road Park.** Shore Road, between 68th Street and Colonial Road, 965-6524.

With almost thirty acres of lovely green space on a bluff overlooking the harbor, this breezy point is a popular place for family picnics. Get here early to watch the Tall Ships sailboat flotilla on the fourth weekend in July, or enjoy the summer concerts sponsored by the Brooklyn arts association, BACA (see page 205). At 69th Street a footbridge crosses the Belt Parkway to the waterside promenade, where the walking, jogging, and biking path starts. The 97th Street ball fields are popular for amateur baseball games. Nearby there are two playgrounds, lots of open space, and tennis courts (call 965-8993 for permit information). Take a stroll along the sidewalk from 100th Street back down to 69th Street for fresh breezes, views of the Verrazano-Narrows Bridge, and some lovely old homes. At John Paul Jones Park, at 4th Avenue and 101st Street, adjacent to the entrance to **Fort Hamilton**, there are frequent summer concerts.

Russell Pederson Playground. Colonial Road, at 84th Street.

A nice-sized playground located in one of the neighborhood's wealthiest residential sections, this is a lovely place to stop with little ones on a fine day.

79th and 95th Street playgrounds. Along Shore Road, 965-6528.

Here are two lovely, breezy playgrounds. The 79th Street Playground is only a few long blocks from the heart of Bay Ridge's 3rd Avenue restaurant area. The 95th Street Playground, also pleasant, is near a popular ball field at 97th Street.

Shore Parkway Promenade. From Owl's Head Park at 69th Street to Bensonhurst Park at Bay Parkway.

Running along Brooklyn's westernmost edge, this long, narrow band of asphalt and benches between the Belt Parkway and the water connects Owl's Head Park at 68th Street to Bensonhurst Park and passes under the Verrazano-Narrows Bridge. Bikers, joggers, and walkers love this stretch on warm days. You can cross over the Belt Parkway at the exits or stop and park in one of the parking areas just to the side of the parkway. When you get near the bridge, keep your eyes open—you might see some of the peregrine falcons that nest in its superstructure.

POINTS OF CULTURAL INTEREST

Brooklyn Public Library. 73rd Street, between 3rd Avenue and Ridge Boulevard, 748-3042. Call to check hours.

Located at the edge of a lovely residential area off tree-lined Ridge Boulevard, this large, pleasant library has a children's room on the second floor with a wide selection for preschoolers through teens. There are occasional movies and special programs for youngsters. For Brooklynites: any book you borrow here can be returned to your local Brooklyn branch library.

Fontbonne Hall Academy. 9901 Shore Road, corner of 99th Street.

Life was tough for the industrial barons of the nineteenth century, as you can see from this extraordinarily lovely mansion, built as a getaway from the noise and bustle of Manhattan. Lore has it that this home, the sole remnant of a district once filled with gracious plantation houses and mini-castles, was purchased by Diamond Jim Brady for Lillian Russell. Party guests would boat down to this bucolic retreat—which sure would beat the subway! Today the halls are filled not with party guests but with young female students. No tours are available.

"Gingerbread House." 82nd Street, near Narrows Avenue.

Thatched cottages in England dating back to the 1600s were considered so quaint by the turn of the twentieth century that some whimsical wealthy folks used the thatched cottage as a theme for their second (or third) homes. This house dates from the era when Brooklyn was full of rolling green hills, meadows, and the sounds of nature. It is a private home, so no tours are available.

✪ **Harbor Defense Museum at Fort Hamilton.** Fort Hamilton Parkway at 101st Street, almost under Verrazano-Narrows Bridge, 630-4349. Take the B63 bus or B16 bus and ask the driver for the stop nearest the fort, which is some distance from commercial Bay Ridge. Open some weekday afternoons and some Saturdays. Call for hours. Group tours can be arranged.

It seems incongruous that you'd find a military institution smack in the middle of contemporary Brooklyn, but the sign at the entrance stating "you are entering a military base" is no fake. The base houses about two thousand military personnel and their families who follow rules of conduct emanating directly from, you guessed it, the Pentagon.

A self-guided walking tour takes you past a block of cannons, Robert E. Lee's house (posted here as chief engineer from 1841 to 1846), the barracks, stable, and commissary, as well as the old Officers Club, now a popular venue for wedding receptions. Pick up the brochure at the Harbor Defense Museum (see below).

✪ **The Harbor Defense Museum** is one of only four dozen Army base museums in the U.S. Located in a 160-year-old, wedge-shaped stone structure called a *caponier*, the building was once used to protect Fort Hamilton from a rear-guard attack. Inside, the museum chronicles the defense of New York Harbor, with exhibits of guns, mines, cannons and missiles, as well as weapons captured during the Gulf War. Kids may enjoy the exhibit of G.I. Joe figures.

Both the museum building and officer's club are listed in the National Register of Historic Places.

Poly Prep Country Day School. 92nd Street, corner of 7th Avenue, 836-9800.

Poly Prep is nestled in a vast greenbelt of a campus, complete with duck ponds, swimming pools, and tennis courts. Founded in Brooklyn Heights in 1854, today it is a highly regarded private school.

✪ **Verrazano-Narrows Bridge.** Shore Parkway and Fort Hamilton Parkway.

Visible from many Brooklyn neighborhoods, the Verrazano-Narrows Bridge celebrates Giovanni da Verrazano, the first European to see Staten Island (in 1524). Designed in 1964, the steel bridge is 4,260 feet long and is the starting point for the New York City Marathon each fall. The bridge connects Brooklyn with Staten Island and is a quick route to southern New Jersey and Pennsylvania. Driving across it toward Staten Island will cost you $7; the return trip is free.

NOTABLE RESTAURANTS

There are many good restaurants in Bay Ridge. For tips on where to find quick snacks and ice-cream parlors, see the separate listing at the end of this section.

✪ **Areo Ristorante Italiano.** 8424 3rd Avenue, corner of 85th Street, 238-0079. Open for lunch and dinner. Closed Mondays. Reservations are recommended.

It's easy to see why Areo is such a popular spot—modern decor, big windows, usually busy, always noisy, with excellent Italian fare. The antipasti are superb, as are specials such as sliced filet mignon marsala, *zuppa di pesce,* and spinach with garlic. All this doesn't come cheap, though; dinner for two with a couple of drinks comes to about $75.

✪ **Arirang Hibachi Steak House and Sushi Bar.** 8814 Fourth Avenue, between 88th and 89th streets, 238-9880. Mon.–Thurs., 5–10:30 P.M.; Fri., 5 P.M.–1 A.M.; Sat., 4:30 P.M.–1 A.M.; Sun., 3–10 P.M.

Food as fun: the kids will love the showy, twirling tricks that the waiters perform while cooking your food over a tabletop hibachi. The Korean–Japanese seasonings are good, and the steak is excellent.

Baci. 7107 3rd Avenue, near 71st Street, 836-5536. Tues.-Thurs,. 5–11 P.M.; Fri.–Sat., 5 P.M.–midnight; Sun., 4–10 P.M. Valet parking on weekends. Reservations are recommended.

Some locals rave about this sparse, Italian restaurant with the French doors opening onto the sidewalk, while others find the food "sometimes great, sometimes fair." Baci runs about $30 per person for an average meal.

Bally Bunion, an Irish house. 9510 3rd Avenue, near 95th Street, 833-280. Daily, 11 A.M.–11 P.M.

This informal restaurant/bar serves up a bit of Irish schmaltz with songs by the bar, a dreamy open fireplace, and lots of warm feelings. Skip the burgers and go for bangers and mash, and maybe an Irish whiskey cake. Prices are moderate.

✪ **Canedo's.** 7316 3rd Avenue, between 73rd and 74th streets, 748-1908. Mon.–Fri., noon–3:30 P.M.; Sat., 4 P.M.–midnight; Sun., lunch 2–10 P.M. and dinner 4–10 P.M. Reservations are recommended.

Ssshhhh. This great Italian restaurant has somehow escaped the crowds. An elegant wooden façade and framed turn-of-the-century posters and mirrors are matched by excellent Northern Italian food. Try shrimp and artichoke in white sauce, stuffed mushrooms and artichokes, or veal fiorentino. The service is good and dress is casual. Dinner entrées hover around $18.

Casa Pepe. 114 Bay Ridge Avenue, off Colonial Road, 833-8865. Daily, noon–11 P.M.

A fireplace in the winter, and garden in fine weather make Casa Pepe a local favorite for fans of Spanish and Mexican cuisine. The seafood and tacos are reliably good. Come hungry; the food is a bit heavy.

Casablanca. 6744 5th Avenue, off 67th Street, 491-0105. Daily, 11 A.M.–9 P.M. Cash only.

Surely Lawrence of Arabia would have enjoyed this simple, from-the-desert fare: harira, a Moroccan soup; shish kebabs, and flavorful couscous. For under $8 for an entrée you also get a map of Morocco on the back of your menu, just in case you are feeling lost.

✪ **Chadwick's.** 8822 Third Avenue, between 88th and 89th streets, 833-9855. Daily, 11: 30 A.M.–10:30 P.M.

A Chicago-style meat lovers' restaurant, Chadwick's serves what our waitress described to us as a "meal for a man"—big portions of steak and potatoes. Expect a wide variety of beef dishes with few surprises except for the extremely good Beef Wellington, a Saturday night special. Vegetarians will be satisfied with the pasta. Entrées cost about $18.

Chianti's. 8530 Third Avenue, at 86th Street, 921-6300. Daily 11:30 A.M.–10:30 P.M. Early bird dinner, Mon.–Fri, 5–6 P.M.

If you've just run a marathon or are feeding a crowd, come here for large portions of inexpensive, decent Italian fare. Some people rave about the eggplant dishes, others about the veal.

Pocketbook tips: You can eat two-for-the-price-of-one because the "family style" portions are so big; the antipasti can be a meal in themselves. And the early bird dinner is a particular bargain.

✪ **Embers.** 9519 3rd Avenue, near 95th Street, 745-3700. Lunch, Mon.–Fri., noon–3 P.M.; dinner, Mon.–Thurs., 5–10:30 P.M., Sat., 4:30–midnight, Sun. 2–9:30 P.M. Reservations accepted weekdays only.

Embers is a family restaurant and is run by the folks who own the meat market next door. It's crowded and noisy, and the fresh steaks and chops arrive in big portions; locals like to say it's Bay Ridge's response to Peter Luger. You'll get great food, excellent value, and friendly service. The casual atmosphere is great for kids. Entrées start at $12.

Goodfella's Brick Oven Pizza. 9606 Third Avenue, corner 96th Street, 833-6200. Mon.–Sat., 1: 30 A.M.–11 P.M.; Sun., 2–11 P.M. Valet parking.

Award-winning, thin-crusted pizza rolls out of Goodfella's, and you have a choice of such toppings as fresh garlic, black olives, and other vegetables. If you like vodka sauce you'll be pleased to learn it's the house special.

Karam. 8519 4th Avenue, between 85th and 86th streets, 745-5227. Daily, 6–1 A.M. No credit cards.

If you call this Lebanese restaurant to ask the special of the day, and they say "lima beans," don't fret. The lamb-lima bean stew happens to be delicious, but so is the chicken schwarma with garlic sauce, baba ghanoush, tabbouleh, hummus, and protein-perfect rice and lentil imm' jadarara. For dessert, have baklava or a homemade pudding. The ambience is "hole in the wall," but surprisingly fresh, authentic food makes up for it. Cheap at under $10 per person.

✪ **India Passage.** 7407 3rd Avenue, between 74th and 75th streets, 833-2160. Daily, noon–11 P.M.

Faruk, the owner of India Passage, one of the borough's best Indian restaurants, serves up traditional northern Indian favorites from the clay oven as well as Bengal shrimp and some southern Indian specialties. Kids will love the tandoori chicken, which falls off the bone into your mouth. The decor at India Passage is classy, the prices are reasonable, and the food is terrific.

101. 10033 4th Avenue, near 101st Street, at the foot of the Verrazano Bridge, 833-1313. Sun.–Wed., noon–midnight; Thurs.–Sat., noon–1 A.M. Cash, AmEx only.

Young customers love the hopping bar scene at snazzy 101, with its leopard-skin bar stools. Restaurant 101 serves Italian fare, such as simple pastas and meat or seafood entrées. The views are impressive in the winter when the leaves have fallen, revealing an expanse of New York Harbor. It costs about $45 for dinner for two, including a drink.

✪ **Mambo Italiano.** 8803 Third Avenue, near corner of 88th Street, 833-3891. Tues.–Thurs., noon–11 P.M.; Fri.–Sat., noon–midnight; Sun., 2–10 P.M.; closed Mon.

Wildly popular with families and young folks, Mambo is decorated to the hilt. With good food, live music, funny decorations, and a party atmosphere, Mambo's is one of the local favorites in Bay Ridge. We won't say any more; go and check this out for yourself!

Mezzanotte. 8408 Third Avenue, between 84th and 85th streets, 238-5000. Daily, noon–3 P.M. and 5:30–11 P.M.

Mezzanotte makes hearty (some say superior) Italian food. From baked clams oreganata to fried calamari to the linguine with seafood and the zesty grilled veal chop, this Bay Ridge restaurant is a place to sit back, loosen your belt, and dig in.

Mr. Tang. 7523 3rd Avenue, near 76th Street, 748-0400. Mon.–Thurs., noon–10:30 P.M.; Fri.–Sun., noon–12:30 A.M.

Mr. Tang features a broad menu with a lot of Cantonese and Szechuan dishes, and seems to do best with seafood dishes. Tang has two other restaurants by the same name on Coney Island Avenue and on Avenue X. All offer reasonably good Chinese food in an Americanized setting.

✪ **New Corner Restaurant.** 7201 8th Avenue, near 72nd Street, 833-0800. Daily, noon–11 P.M.

You won't find New Corner just around the corner; it's tucked away in a residential section. But it's worth finding, particularly if you've never had out-of-this-world lobster fra diavolo or French-fried broccoli. The portions are beyond huge: one bowl of minestrone is a full meal. Sambuca liqueur is automotically served with coffee. The menu is à la carte, and most entrées run $13 to $15. Weekend reservations are recommended.

Pearl Room. 8203 Third Avenue, near 82nd Street, 833-6666. Mon.–Thurs., 5–11 P.M.; Fri.–Sat., 5 P.M.–12:30 A.M.; Sun., 2–10 P.M. Valet parking on weekends.

This promising seafood joint is the latest incarnation in a location that has seen other restaurants come and go. It's crowded and noisy, but fans say the seafood preparation is excellent (and there are pasta and meat dishes as well). Entrées average about $15.

Peggy O'Neal. 8121 5th Avenue, between 81st and 82nd streets, 748-1400. Daily, 11–4 A.M. AmEx only.

Stainte! ("Cheers!" in Irish). A favorite among New York's finest, this pub draws police officers from all over the city. The Irish chef turns out shepherd's pie, potato-leek soup, corned beef and cabbage, and fish and chips as well as lots of Italian dishes. Entrées run about $12 to $18.

Pho Hoai. 8616 4th Avenue, between 86th and 87th streets, 745-1640. Daily, 10:30 A.M.–10:30 P.M.

Pho Hoai began on Avenue U and was hailed by an area newspaper as having "some of the best, straightforward Vietnamese food in New York," so expectations for this newcomer are high. The food is subtly spiced, fresh and tasty. Try the Beef Balls Noodle Soup, Grilled Chicken with Rice, or Shrimp with Little Salt (gotta love those translations), or one of the excellent vegetable dishes. Inexpensive, at under $10 per person.

✪ **Polonica.** 7214 3rd Avenue, between 72nd and 73rd streets, 630-5805. Mon., 3–11 P.M.; Tues.–Sun., 11 A.M.–11 P.M. No credit cards.

Pretty red tablecloths with pink lampshades and authentic Polish food give the feel of a country cottage here. Choose from among peach, strawberry, or cherry blinis, thick soulful barley soup, beef stuffed with pickles and carrots, kielbasa (sausage) and pierogi (dumplings), stuffed peppers, and more. Entrées average less than $8. No alcohol is served.

✪ **St. Michel.** 7518 Third Avenue, between 75th and 76th streets, 748-4411. Tues.–Thurs., 5–9:30 P.M.; Fri.–Sat., 5:15–10:30 P.M.; closed Sun. and Mon. Reservations are recommended.

Something is right with this picture: romantic and French, but not stuffy. The owners—chef and maître d'—are two brothers from northeastern France, and they create a homey, relaxed atmosphere. Try the escargots, crab cakes, steak au poive, or fish dishes, but save room for desserts that shouldn't be missed. Service is casual, and classical music plays in the background. About $45 per person.

Sally's Place. 7809 3rd Avenue, near 78th Street, 680-4615. Tues.–Sun., lunch, noon–3 P.M.; and dinner, 5–11 P.M. Weekend reservations are recommended.

Sally's white-tableclothed ambience provides an alternative to the predominately Italian fare in the area. Try the tasty Middle Eastern dishes or the mini-soufflé omelet.

Salty Dog. 7509 Third Avenue, near 75th Street, 238-0030. Daily, 11:30–4 A.M.

The kids will love this sports bar started by a couple of New York's bravest. Besides the antique fire truck in the middle of the restaurant, there's plenty of firefighter memorabilia on the walls, large-screen televisions and monitors—there's almost always a game to watch while you munch on enormous salads, burgers, barbecue chicken and ribs, and brick-oven pizzas. The cost is about $15 for the average meal. Parental note: Serious drinking can go on at night.

✪ **Short Ribs.** 9101 3rd Avenue, corner of 91st Street, 745-0614. Mon.–Thurs., 11:30–2 A.M.; Fri.–Sat., 11:30–4 A.M.; Sun., noon–midnight.

Huge, tasty portions of barbecued ribs, chicken, seafood dishes, and gumbos are the highlights here. The combination dish—half a rack of ribs, barbecued shrimp, and chicken—is enough food for two. And, if you overdo it, they are happy to provide a doggie bag. Sunday brunch is popular, the place is open very late, and kids are welcome. Entrées range from $9 to $14.

T. J. Bentley. 7110 3rd Avenue, near 71st Street, 745-0748. Tues.–Thurs., 11:30 A.M.–10 P.M.; Wed.–Sat., 11:30 A.M.–11 P.M. (dancing till midnight); Sun., noon–10 P.M.; closed Mon. Call for a reservation.

Put on your dancing shoes. There's live music and lots of action nightly. The moderately priced meal averages about $15 per entrée, and you can wait until the music starts or have a drink at the bar, once part of the famous Luchow's restaurant in Manhattan. Casual attire is acceptable during weekdays, but dress up, please, for weekends. This is serious partying.

Tuscany Grill. 8620 Third Avenue, off 86th Street, 921-5633. Mon.–Wed., 5–10 P.M.; Thurs.–Sat., 5–11 P.M., Sun., 4–9 P.M. Reservations are recommended on weekends.

Since it opened in 1992, Tuscany Grill has garnered rave reviews for its satisfying, high-quality Tuscan-style Italian cuisine, with entreés running about $18 on average. Try the bruschetta, grilled vegetables, shrimp and garlic mashed potatoes. Traditionalists who are wed to red-saucy Italian food say this "ain't really Italian," perhaps a back-handed recommendation. Given a comforting ambience and good service (John, the owner, is usually there), this one is worth the trip from another neighborhood.

Cafés, Ice Cream Parlors, and Quick Meals

Anapoli. 6922 3rd Avenue, corner of 77th Street. Mon.–Sat., 8 A.M.–7 P.M.; closed Sun.

This little café used to be called Logue's, and its appeal is its old-fashioned setting. This is a nice place to come with the kids.

Caffè Café. 8401 Third Avenue, corner of 84th Street, 748-8700. Daily, 7–2 A.M.

Caffè Café serves espresso, flavored coffees, Japanese and Chinese green tea, smoothies, and Italian sodas. The place is clean and the vibes are good, maybe because psychic readings, *mehndi* painting sessions and other New Age entertainment is held here.

Hinsch's. 8518 5th Avenue, between 85th and 86th streets, 748-3412. Mon.–Sat., 8 A.M.–7 P.M.

For more than eighty-five years there has been an ice-cream parlor at this location, and Hinsch's makes a point of keeping tradition alive. As soon as you walk in the door, the old-fashioned soda fountain and booths will remind you of your childhood—no matter where you grew up. Hinsch's makes their own ice cream and candies and sells a line of candy cigarettes and solid chocolate crayons. This is a good place to come with the kids, as is the Logue family's other eatery in Bay Ridge, **Once Upon a Sundae** (see below).

Lento's. 7003 3rd Avenue, near Ovington Street, 745-9197. Daily, noon–11:30 P.M.

Thin crust lovers, this bar-cum-pizzeria is heaven! Just make sure you eat on the premises, or the thin crust gets hard. Lento's is near shopping and parks. There's a larger Lento's in Park Slope (399-8782).

Once Upon a Sundae. 7702 3rd Avenue, between 77th and 78th streets, 748-3412. Mon.–Fri., 8 A.M.–10 P.M.; Sat., 8 A.M.–11 P.M.; Sun., 9 A.M.–11 P.M.

The Logue family, which has been in the Bay Ridge ice-cream business for more than thirty-five years, transplanted the turn-of-the twentieth century furnishings of Brooklyn's oldest ice-cream parlor from Fulton Street in Bedford-Stuyvesant to these lodgings in Bay Ridge. The results are, well . . . go see for yourself!

SHOPPING

Specialty Food Shops

BAKERIES

Bay Ridge Bakery II Classic Patisserie. 7805 5th Avenue, near 78th Street, 238-0014. Daily, 9 A.M.–9 P.M. Cash only.

Movie star–handsome John Nikolopaulos and his family run this spic-and-span bakery, which turns out classic French pastries alongside Greek breads and snacks. John's savory olive-stuffed homemade "mama's bread" is so good it's habit-forming. Choose among beautiful chocolate cakes and fruit pies, cheese danish, mini pastries, baklava, and feta cheese turnovers. There are elegant wedding cakes, and "portrait" birthday cakes for kids which feature a portrait of the child right on the cake itself.

Börek Shoppe. 8420 5th Avenue, near 84th Street, 748-8645. Mon.–Fri., 8 A.M.– 8 P.M.; Sat.–Sun., 9 A.M.–8 P.M.

You may never have heard of börek (imagine a tiny lasagna filled with feta, covered with an apricot glaze) or, for that matter, Turkish pastry, but you'll probably want to take some home for dinner. There are a few small tables if you want to sit with a cup of coffee and munch a fabulously light breadstick.

Leske's Bakery. 7612 5th Avenue, between 76th and 77th streets, 680-2323. Tues.–Fri., 6 A.M.–6:30 P.M.; Sat., 6 A.M.–6 P.M.; Sun., 6 A.M.–3 P.M.; closed Mon.

A vestige of Bay Ridge's Norwegian population, Leske's sells a mouthwatering array of authentic Danish pastries, breads, cakes, and cookies, also known as *kringlers yulekarger, vorkarger,* limpia bread, and *kransekagge.*

✪ **Pierrot.** 7515 3rd Avenue, near 75th Street, 748-5840. Tues.–Fri., 9 A.M.–7 P.M.; Sat., 8 A.M.–7 P.M.; Sun., 8 A.M.–3 P.M.; closed Mon.

It's like a little taste of Paris. Nip into this tiny store for mouthwatering baked goodies that would blow the croissants out of any Rue de Rivoli pâtisserie. Try the fresh fruit tart, made of cookie shell and fruit in a bed of light cream, with a shiny apricot glaze. Or the Opera cake, which sports layers of nuts, mocha butter cream, and raspberry, all topped with chocolate.

ETHNIC DELIS

The Eastern European, Mexican, Greek, Turkish, Egyptian, and Italian delis in Bay Ridge give you a UN-worthy choice of authentic ethnic foods to sample. All are run by immigrants from their respective countries, who will be pleased to tell you how to prepare your food of choice. You could buy the same items in fancy-schmancy specialty store, of course, at twice the price.

Mediterranean:

A&S Greek American Meat Market. 798 5th Avenue, near 79th Street, 833-1307. Mon.–Sat., 9 A.M.–6 P.M.; Mon., 8 A.M.–9 P.M. Cash only.

Bay Ridge has a sizable Greek population, and alongside tuna and chicken salads, this Greek deli sells traditional large, crusty loaves of bread, imported feta cheese, olives, phyllo dough, squid salad, and packaged goods, including Greek incense and cake mixes.

Hellas American Food Market. 8704 4th Avenue, at 87th Street, 748-2554. Daily, 8 A.M.–8 P.M. Cash only.

Greek imported packaged goods, from soaps to cake mixes to sea salt to pastas and grains, are mixed in among the standard American products.

Middle Eastern:

Al-Amir Eastern and American Grocery. 7813 5th Avenue, near 78th Street, 748-7896. Daily, 10 A.M.–10 P.M. Cash only.

The huge hookah in the window is a giveaway to the distant roots of this little shop, which greets you with the scent of spices, and signs in swirling Arabic. The owners, Moroccan-born Fouizia and her Egyptian husband Abdou Gawad, sell necessities of life such as as *jalabas*, embroidered floor-length dresses, and tinted glasses for mint tea and Turkish coffee. A good place to stock up on Middle Eastern cheeses, breads, olives, lentils, cracked wheat—and tons of atmosphere.

A&T Turkish Halal Meat Market. 7919 5th Avenue, near 79th Street, 680-5057 Mon.–Sat., 9 A.M.–9 P.M.; Sun., 10 A.M.–9 P.M. Cash only.

It looks like a butcher shop from the outside, but venture in and you will find a small Middle Eastern oasis, with open bins of dried fruits, nuts, as well as inexpensive olive oil and Turkish Delight candy. The meats, by the way, are "halal," which is to orthodox Muslims what "kosher" is to orthodox Jews.

Family Store. 6905 3rd Avenue, corner of 69th Street, 748-0207. Mon.–Sat., 8 A.M.–8 P.M.; closed Sun.

One of the older Middle Eastern emporiums in this neighborhood, Family Store sells tasty hummus, cheeses, a variety of Middle Eastern breads and unusual packaged sweets. The owners are rightfully proud of their popular establishment.

Nordic:

✪ **Nordic Delicacies.** 6909 3rd Avenue, near 69th Street, 748-1874. Mon.–Sat., 9 A.M.–6 P.M.

Nordic Delicacies makes meatballs on Monday, fish pudding on Tuesday, *komper* (potato dumplings) on Wednesday, and so on throughout the week. Their potato cakes and traditional open-faced sandwiches are great. This and the old bakery Leske's are vestiges of the area's original Norwegian presence.

Mejlander and Mulgannon. 7615 5th Avenue at 76th Street, 238-6666. Daily, 8 A.M.–8 P.M.

Fill your pantry with hard-to-find Scandinavian staples, including delicious not-too-sweet lingonberry jam, a variety of flatbreads, canned fish balls, and candies.

Russian/Polish:

Astoria European Foods. 507 84th Street, off 5th Avenue, 745-5242. Daily, 8 A.M.–8 P.M.

If you had a Russian Grandma her pantry would probably have looked a lot like this stuffed-like-a-sausage shop. It's crammed with stuffed cabbage and peppers, army-sized loaves of thick-crusted breads, a wall of colorfully wrapped candies from Moscow and matzos from Israel, rows of jarred pickles, and a refrigerator case brimming with sausages and cold cuts. Ukrainian-born owners Alla and Irena recommend the soft cheeses combined with a pumpernickel bread.

Paradise. 7217 Third Avenue, near 72nd Street. Daily, 8 A.M.–8 P.M. No phone.

This hole-in-the-wall deli with the faint eau-de-smoked fish aroma captures a moment in immigrant time. Advertisements for phone cards with discounted rates to Russia and Israel are featured in the store window, along with handwritten signs in Russian. Basics such as sour cherries in syrup, herring, hearty loaves of bread, and a large selection of Russian videos are the mainstay.

Interesting Neighborhood Shops

A&J Police Equipment. 7115 Third Avenue, 833-5535. Mon.–Fri., 10 A.M.–7 P.M.; Sat., 10 A.M.–6 P.M.; closed Sunday.

Here's where the NYPD (yes, the NY Police Department)—and *you*—can buy police gear. Of course, you need a badge to get the official stuff, but the sign on the window says the general public is welcome. Venture inside to find T-shirts, sweatshirts, and hats with NYPD logos and sayings.

✪ **Brooklyn Gallery of Coins and Stamps.** 8725 4th Avenue, near 87th Street, 745-5701. Mon.–Fri., 9 A.M.–5:30 P.M.; Sat., 9 A.M.–4 P.M.

This small, thirty-year-old shop is a wonderful resource for beginners to experienced collectors of stamps, coins, antique toys, World's Fair items, trains, and baseball cards. They have some seven hundred reference books for every level and interest. People come from all over the tristate area to buy and sell.

Choc-Oh-Lot-Plus. 7911 5th Avenue, near 79th Street, 748-2100. Mon.–Wed. and Fri., 10 A.M.–6 P.M.; Thurs., 10 A.M.–8 P.M.; Sat., 10 A.M.–5 P.M.; Sun., noon–4 P.M.

Bay Ridge is a neighborhood that appreciates good old-fashioned family fun. This mom-and-pop specialty store sells more than five hundred plastic candy molds and several dozen Wilton cake molds in the form of Superman, Batman, Sesame Street characters, and other popular figures. There are bins of inexpensive cake toppings and over 250 varieties of Mylar balloons.

✪ **Dan Sacks Fabrics.** 8214 3rd Avenue, near 82nd Street, 748-0059. Mon.–Sat., 9 A.M.–4 P.M. Cash and checks only.

One of Brooklyn's best fabric shops, Dan Sacks sells bolts of just about everything short of lightening. You can purchase good-quality cotton goods, upholstery fabric, velvet and velveteen, lace, and more at prices that run about half of comparable goods elsewhere. The store is run by two elderly sisters who are very helpful.

✪ **Grassroots.** 8505 3rd Avenue, corner 85th Street, 745-9679. Daily, 11 A.M.–9 P.M.

Lovely, worn bits and folkloric pieces from a simpler era are sold in this rustic store, whose motto is "for the home and soul." Each piece speaks volumes—a rusty gate, antique tin canisters, an old red wooden bench, hand-painted French bowls, a blue-fleck enameled pot from the 1950s. The aesthetic here is not commonly found in Bay Ridge shops; it feels more like SoHo or Vermont. Prices are moderate. And, you can enjoy a glass of fresh-squeezed juice at the juice bar while you relax and browse. Worth the trip from another neighborhood.

Harry's P & G Furniture. 241 Bay Ridge Avenue, between 2nd and 3rd avenues, 745-0730. Daily, 8 A.M.–5:30 P.M., except Mon. and Thurs., open till 8:30 P.M. No credit cards.

Every ten days new merchandise arrives at this large warehouse which handles overstocks, including leather and contemporary styles. Most of the merchandise comes from large department stores or straight from the North Carolina manufacturers. Sofas, chairs, tables, and bedroom sets are 20 percent less than at retail outlets.

✪ **The Hutch.** 8211 5th Avenue, near 82nd Street, 748-4574 or (800) 303-9702. Tues.–Sat., 10 A.M.–6 P.M.

Catering to customers throughout the tristate area, the Hutch has carried a large selection of fine gift items, including crystal, silverware, place settings, imported ceramic bowls, glassware, and silver picture frames, for more than three decades. The store carries Herend hand-painted porcelain, Lalique, and Mdme. Alexander dolls as well.

✪ **John T. Johnston's Jukebox Classics and Vintage Slot Machines.** 6742 5th Avenue, near 67th Street, 833-8455. By appointment only, or Sat. 1–5 P.M.

You don't have to be a connoisseur to love John T. Johnston's colorful collection of antique gumball machines and jukeboxes—including a 1990s model that plays compact discs. Rock stars, Fortune 500 CEOs, and other deep-pocket types have all come to Johnston's for Wurlitzer jukeboxes dating from the 1930s and 1940s ($20,000 for the vintage models; reproductions starting at about $2,000). For those of you on a tighter budget, there are over 150 Betty Boop items (John claims to have the largest Boop selection in the country), as well as antique slot, vending, and arcade machines, cash registers, syrup dispensers, and neon signs and clocks. John used to be in the construction business but fell in love with jukeboxes in 1981 when he bought his first. He's been collecting ever since.

✪ **I. Kleinfeld and Son.** 8206 5th Avenue, between 82nd and 83rd streets, 833-1100. Tues. and Thurs., 11 A.M.–9 P.M.; Wed. and Fri., 11 A.M.–6 P.M.; Sat., 10 A.M.–6 P.M.

One of New York's most famous specialty stores, Kleinfeld's is a magnet for thousands of brides each year. They come from all over the U.S., Europe, and China for the enormous selection of gowns, accessories, and evening and dress wear for the bridal party. The main store has evening dresses, clothes for the mother of the bride or groom, formal wear, and more than a thousand wedding gown samples. The average gown costs between $1,500 and $3,000. An appointment is required. Allow six months for the gown to be measured, fitted, and sewn.

La Baronessa. 8418 3rd Avenue, between 84th and 85th streets, 921-4432. Mon.–Sat., 11 A.M.–6 P.M.; Closed Sun.

La Baronessa specializes in home and personal gifts appealing to the Bay Ridge market. You will find hand-painted ceramics and pottery, découpage items, and silver platters, in addition to evening bags and scarves. Gift baskets are a specialty and can be ordered by phone.

Little Lords and Little Ladies. 8217 5th Avenue, corner 82nd Street, 748-4366. Mon.–Fri., 10 A.M.–6 P.M.; Sat. until 6:30 P.M.

A doting grandmother's kind of store, here you will find baby and children's clothes that will remind you of picture-perfect Victorian children: starched bibs, lacy white dresses, divine dress-up outfits, some imported, for boys and girls ages five to ten.

Loretta's Antiques. 8614 7th Avenue, off 86th Street, 630-5620. Mon.–Fri. 10 A.M.–5 P.M.

Loretta buys and sells antique furniture. You can sometimes find her display of solid dressers, armoires, and chairs at the weekend flea market at Park Slope's P.S. 321. Her prices are good, as is the quality of the merchandise.

Mangos (A K A the "Z" Collection). 7115 3rd Avenue, near 71st Street, 748-5040. Mon.–Thurs., 11 A.M.–8 P.M.; Fri. and Sat., 11 A.M.–9 P.M.; Sun., noon–5 P.M.

Working gals who are young at heart (and reasonably slim of waist) will have a ball at this pocketbook-friendly boutique. There are suits (under $200), special-occasion dresses by brands such as XOXO, Bisou Bisou, and French Connection, trendy shoes and lots of gift items such as candles, picture frames, and "stuff."

Maternity Profile. 7311 3rd Avenue, near 73rd Street, 680-8399. Mon.–Sat., 10:30 A.M.–6 P.M.; Sun., noon–4 P.M.

Pregnant or nursing women will find a good selection of career and casual clothes at moderate prices here. This is one of the few maternity stores in Brooklyn outside of the orthodox Jewish neighborhoods. The service is friendly.

✪ **Novel Idea Bookstore.** 8415 Third Avenue, between 84th and 85th streets, 833 5115. Daily, 10 A.M.–8 P.M. Closed Sun. in summers.

Novels, children's books, Brooklyn history, poetry, cookbooks, and mysteries are on display at this welcoming bookstore. The carpet and comfortable chairs make you feel at home instantly, as do founders Mrs. Heaney and her three beautiful daughters, who, together, seem like characters out of *Little Women*.

✪ **Once Upon A Child.** 7206 3rd Avenue, near 72nd Street, 491-0300. Mon.–Wed., 10 A.M.–7 P.M.; Thurs.–Fri., 10 A.M.–8 P.M.; Sat., 10 A.M.–6 P.M.; Sun., 11 A.M.–5 P.M.

If secondhand stores make you nervous (Are these things clean? Did the previous wearer have head lice?), check out this appealing kiddie clothing store. It is part of a national chain and so the standards are high, but the two sisters who own the franchise make it feel like a family-owned business. They carry a large selection of brand-name children's apparel up to size 6x. The price can't be beat: OshKosh jeans that cost $20 new can be had for as little as $6. Car seats, cribs, and playpens meet current safety standards and are priced at less than half retail. Call for information on both selling and buying. For sheer size, a Brooklyn best bet.

✪ **Panda Sport.** 9213 Fifth Avenue, near 92nd Street, 238-4919. Mon.–Sat., 11 A.M.–7 P.M.; Thurs., 11 A.M.–9 P.M.; Sun., 11 A.M.–4 P.M.

In winter you'll find top-of-the-line ski equipment (including rentals), trained staff who know how to tune skis, and a schedule of ski trips that you can sign up for, whether you are single or traveling with the family. For beach bums they've got rafts, wet suits, kid-size vests, goggles, and surfboards. In-line skaters can find lots of gear, including a range of high-end and highly specialized stunt skates. Panda has whatever the latest sports craze is because owner Robert Ottofaro's mental wheels are always turning (which is probably why the store is a NYC service center for the Rollerblade company).

Royale Sporting Goods. 8102 Third Avenue, corner of 81st Street, 836-5601. Mon.–Sat., 9 A.M.–6 P.M.; Closed Sun.

This sprawling sporting goods store has an extensive inventory: hundreds of baseball mitts, football helmets, footwear, and clothing. Don't miss the display wall strutting replica professional jerseys, hats, and uniforms with coveted numbers, such as Michael Jordan's "23" and Wayne Gretzky's "99." The prices are very reasonable.

Shoe Factory. 6914 Third Avenue, near 69th Street, 680-4397. Daily, 10 A.M.–6 P.M.

While hoofing around Brooklyn, treat your feet. There's an unexpectedly large selection of quality shoes and boots by manufacturers such as Rockport and Timberland here, as well as attractively priced men's cowboy boots by leading manufacturers Dan Post, Justin and Durango, among others. Other brands include Doc Marten, Bostonian, Areosoles, and Skechers. The selection for men is somewhat bigger than for women; no children's shoes.

Swee' Peas. 8416 Third Avenue, corner 84th Street, 680–5766. Tues.–Sat., 11 A.M.–6 P.M.

Swee' Peas carries lovely, upscale special-occasion clothing for children up to age 8. Perfect for communions, bridal parties, and first birthday parties with the grandparents.

Threadz. 8503 Third Avenue, near 85th Street, 745-1500. Mon., noon–7 P.M.; Tues.–Wed., and Sat., 11 A.M.–7 P.M.; Thurs.–Fri., 11 A.M.–8 P.M.; Sun., noon–5 P.M.

Threadz keeps pace with trends in hot dressing for young women, and carries clothes by Diesel, Replay, Morgan, and Miss Sixty. You can walk out with a complete outfit for a dancing date on Saturday night, from lingerie to a sexy little top and skirt, to jewelry, and even shoes. Reasonable prices, personable service by the two young owners.

Lodging

Comfort Inn. 8315 Fourth Avenue, off 83rd Street, 238-3737.

The 70-room Comfort Inn (previously the Hotel Gregory) completed an extensive renovation in 1998. Centrally located to Bay Ridge shops and the subway, it's just a five-minute drive to the Verrazano Bridge and the BQE. Rates are around $160 per couple, per night.

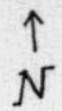
N

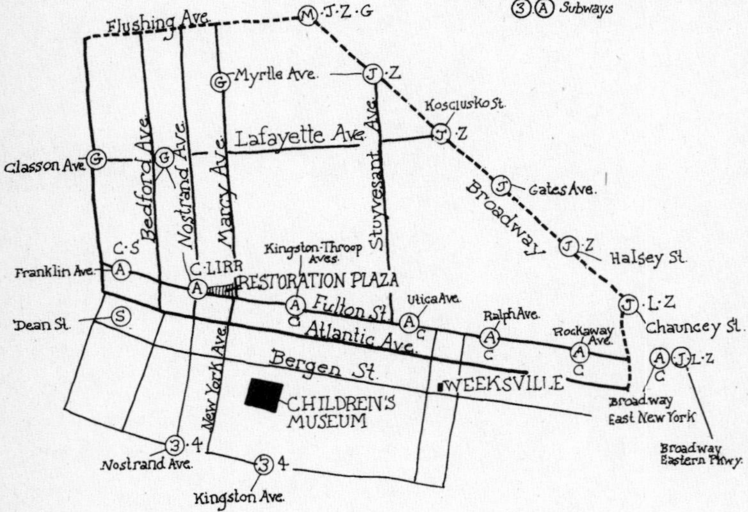
Neighborhood boundaries
Subways
Flushing Ave.
M·J·Z·G
Myrtle Ave.
J·Z
Kosciusko St.
J·Z
Lafayette Ave.
Classon Ave.
Bedford Ave.
Nostrand Ave.
Marcy Ave.
Stuyvesant Ave.
Gates Ave.
Broadway
Halsey St.
C·S
Franklin Ave.
C·LIRR
Kingston-Throop Aves.
RESTORATION PLAZA
Fulton St.
Utica Ave.
J·L·Z
Chauncey St.
Dean St.
Atlantic Ave.
Ralph Ave.
Rockaway Ave.
Bergen St.
New York Ave.
WEEKSVILLE
L·Z
Broadway East New York
CHILDREN'S MUSEUM
Broadway Eastern Pkwy.
3·4
Nostrand Ave.
3 4
Kingston Ave.

Bedford-Stuyvesant

Where it is: Bounded by Myrtle Avenue on the north, Eastern Parkway to the south (although some call Atlantic Avenue the southern boundary), Classon Avenue on the west, and Broadway on the east.

What's nearby: Crown Heights, Downtown Brooklyn, Fort Greene, Park Slope.

How to get there:

By car: Take Fulton Street from Flatbush Avenue through Fort Greene to Restoration Plaza. Turn left on Marcy, Throop, or Lewis streets to get to the brownstone district.

By subway: A train to Nostrand Avenue for Restoration Plaza, or to the Utica Avenue–Fulton Street stop for the Stuyvesant Heights brownstone area.

Cab services: White Top (774-6660) or Black Pearl (493-4959). Cost is about $13 to Brooklyn Heights, $23 to Grand Central Station.

Special events: Fulton Art Fair, three consecutive weekends at Fulton Park (June and July). International African Arts Festival at Boys' and Girls' High School, featuring one week of children's and evening entertainment and hundreds of vendors (July). Weeksville Family Festival (August). Fall house tour, organized by Brownstones of Bedford-Stuyvesant (October).

How it got its name: Bedford and Stuyvesant were two separate communities until the middle of the twentieth century. While they still retain some of their original differences, the combined name has been in use since the 1930s. Some experts say it gained prominence in 1931 when the *Brooklyn Eagle* reported on racial conflict between blacks in Bedford and whites in Stuyvesant; others suggest that it was coined by the Brooklyn Con Edison Company.

Historic District: Stuyvesant Heights, bounded by Macon and Decatur streets, Fulton Park and Stuyvesant Avenue.

Official Landmarks: Alhambra, Renaissance, and Imperial Apartments; Boys' High School; Girls' High School; Magnolia Grandiflora; 23rd Regiment Armory; and Weeksville, among others.

ABOUT THE NEIGHBORHOOD

Go take a look: you may be surprised at how lovely much of Bedford-Stuyvesant is. Indeed, the existence in Bedford-Stuyvesant of a sturdy middle class is one of Brooklyn's best-kept secrets. The well-maintained twelve-block **landmarked district of Stuyvesant Heights** is typical of any other tree-lined brownstone neighborhood of Brooklyn, with the important distinction that the caring, proud owners of these homes are African-American. The architectural variety of this area, with the largest stock of Gothic, Victorian, French, and other classic brownstones in New York City, is stunning. Equally impressive is the commitment of Bedford-Stuyvesant's middle class to improving the quality of life in the nation's second largest African-American community, which is second in size only to the South Side of Chicago. Homeowners here include lawyers, judges, businesspeople, teachers, and civil servants. One visit will show you that the blanket stereotype of Bedford-Stuyvesant as a model of inner-city decay simply does not hold true, especially in Stuyvesant Heights along such dignified streets as Chauncey, Macon, Decatur, Bainbridge, MacDonough, Hancock, Jefferson, and Stuyvesant.

Historic Bedford-Stuyvesant's brownstones and churches are an architectural feast. For a look at the history of African-Americans in Brooklyn, visit the reconstructed nineteenth-century houses and museum at **Weeksville**, a free black community well before emancipation. Contemporary cultural highlights include the **Billie Holiday Theater**, which produces shows written and performed by African-American playwrights, and the magnificent gospel choirs at Sunday church services. The weeklong **International African Arts Festival** in July is famous for the 300-plus vendors it attracts from around the world and the continuous entertainment by Africans and African-Americans that lasts for the whole week.

Both Bedford and Stuyvesant Heights have been undergoing a quiet renaissance for well over two decades. Many young black professionals have bought and renovated brownstones. Some grew up in Brooklyn; others hail from Manhattan, New Jersey, and the southern United States. Certainly one big attraction stimulating the rejuvenation of Stuyvesant Heights and nearby streets is the housing stock—brownstones of the same vintage as those in Fort Greene and Park Slope are a fraction of the price. Family also exerts a pull; many people live on the same block as their close relatives.

It would be hard to overestimate the importance of the many churches in Bedford-Stuyvesant. They provide a historical memory and continuity for the community, create social service programs to fill the vacuums left by inadequate government programs, and help knit together the area's social fabric. Among several outstanding institutions, the **Bridge Street African Wesleyan Methodist Episcopal Church** is the oldest African-American church in Brooklyn, dating from 1818. The pre–Civil War era **Siloam Presbyterian Church** was one of several stops in Brooklyn for slaves fleeing north via the Underground Railroad. The activist **Concord Baptist Church** has the largest black congregation in the United States, estimated at about twelve thousand.

First-time visitors may wish to get oriented by car or even take a guided tour, as the neighborhood's most interesting spots are far apart. (See the tour listings on page 335.) A pleasant time to visit is midday Sunday, when well-dressed families, with many woman sporting fabulous hats, are on their way to or from church. A trip to Bedford-Stuyvesant is not primarily for shopping (although there is a hub of West Indian shops at the intersection of Nostrand Avenue and Fulton Street, plus a smattering of national chains, banks, and small businesses around **Restoration Plaza**). Rather, a foray into Bedford-Stuyvesant gives visitors an appreciation for the historic and contemporary accomplishments of as well as the challenges faced by New York's African-Americans.

If you want to have a really special treat, stay at the spectacular **Akwaaba Mansion**, a beautifully restored bed-and-breakfast. However, book ahead; it is wildly popular among honeymooners.

Historical Notes

The two communities that comprise Bedford and Stuyvesant Heights today have very different histories. Bedford was originally a Dutch hamlet established in 1663. Even before the 1827 abolition of slavery in New York State, a free-black community thrived in the area. Bedford was also home to the Brooklyn Howard Colored Orphan Asylum (1866) and the Zion Home for the Colored Aged (1869).

To the east of Bedford, Stuyvesant was a fancier community built during the 1890s by the staunch upper middle class. F. W. Woolworth, the dime store titan, lived here at 209 Jefferson Avenue. The architecture is lavish, and many remaining structures recall Stuyvesant's high-rolling past: the **Masonic Lodge**, the fabulously decorative **Boys' High School**, the **Renaissance** and **Alhambra** apartments, and **Fulton Park**, designed to be reminiscent of London's Bloomsbury Square.

Through the 1930s Bedford, along with Harlem, was a major destination for rural southern blacks and West Indians. Many bought homes in the area. When the Brooklyn Navy Yard expanded during the 1940s, a huge influx of workers created intense housing pressure in both Bedford and Stuyvesant Heights. Many of the area's new residents were African-American or Caribbean islanders, and the now-familiar syndrome of fright and flight occurred. Racist scare tactics used by unscrupulous realtors in a blockbusting campaign led to the diminishing white population. In the wave of inner-city riots that occurred across the nation in the 1960s, Bedford-Stuyvesant "blew up" in riots twice, following the killing of a young boy by a policeman and following the assassination of the Reverend Martin Luther King, Jr. After a tour of the area, Robert Kennedy helped establish the Bedford-Stuyvesant Restoration Corporation, the nation's first community development corporation. Some New Yorkers who have never been to Bedford-Stuyvesant still may view it as a fearsome place, but its residents tell a different story thirty-five years after those riots—of a community determinedly on the mend, of neighbors working together toward common goals.

Kidstuff

The Brooklyn Children's Museum in nearby Crown Heights is one of the best places in all of New York City for preschool and grade school–age children. (See page 322 for a full description.) The **Magnolia Tree Earth Center** and **Weeksville** are naturals for an educational family visit. There are also several parks and playgrounds in the neighborhood. The **International African Arts Festival** in July is a huge attraction, with contests, performances, crafts, and other special entertainment for children. If your kids appreciate architecture, history, and soul food, there is plenty here for them to enjoy.

ENTERTAINMENT

Flamingo Lounge. 259A Kingston Avenue, between Saint John's and Lincoln Place, 493-7200. Thurs.–Sat., 10 P.M.–4 A.M.

One of Brooklyn's best but least-known jazz bars, the twenty-year-old Flamingo has attracted such artists as Eddie Stout, vocalist Irene Reid, Percy France, and trumpeter Walter Kelly. Many of these performers also play gigs at Manhattan hot spots. Some have jazz pedigrees, like veteran saxophonist Cecil Payne, who played with Dizzie Gillespie back in the 1940s. Given the hours and the club's location in a rundown residential section off Eastern Parkway, your best bet is to take a local cab service both to and from the club.

Sugarhill Supper Club. See page 36.

PARKS AND PLAYGROUNDS

Fulton Park. Fulton Street, between Stuyvesant and Lewis avenues.

Many cultural events are held in this renovated neighborhood park, including jazz concerts and the **Fulton Art Fair** during the summer. There is a play space for children here, too. While the kids are playing, take a long look at the lovely nineteenth-century houses along Chauncey Street. In the middle of this quiet park note the old statue of Robert Fulton holding a replica of his steamboat *Nassau*, the first to ferry between Brooklyn and Manhattan's Nassau Street.

POINTS OF CULTURAL INTEREST

Contemporary Bedford-Stuyvesant

Bedford-Stuyvesant Restoration Corporation at Restoration Plaza. 1368 Fulton Street, at New York Avenue, 636-6900 or 636-6906.

The enclosed mall and office complex called **Restoration Plaza**, which is located in the renovated Sheffield Farms milk bottling plant, is an important piece of recent Bedford-Stuyvesant history. The nation's first community development corporation, the Bedford-Stuyvesant Restoration Corporation was founded in 1967 with the bipartisan support of senators Robert F. Kennedy and Jacob K. Javits. Constructed with private and public capital and community resources, it has been a visible force in improving the neighborhood's business and residential communities. Among its achievements: restoration of the exteriors of thousands of homes, underwriting of home mortgages, creation of jobs and assisting local entrepreneurship, improving health services, and a range of cultural and recreational programs. Restoration Plaza is the unofficial "downtown" of the neighborhood, with its concentration of services such as utilities and post office. The Billie Holiday Theater and Restoration Dance Theater are located within the complex, as is the Skylight Art Gallery on the third floor and a commercial recording studio in the basement.

Billie Holiday Theater. 1368 Fulton Street at New York Avenue, 636-0918, Call for a schedule or to get on the mailing list.

Described as a "theater with a soul and a mission," the Billie Holiday Theater is home to one of New York's professional resident black theater companies. For nearly thirty years the "Billie" has been the artistic arm of the Bedford-Stuyvesant Restoration Corporation. There are three major productions a year, totaling about two hundred performances that usually play to capacity crowds. The shows, which are written by African-American playwrights and showcase Equity actors, get consistently good reviews from critics in the major New York dailies. The programs run the spectrum of comedies, dramas, and musicals. The theater is located in Restoration Plaza a block and a half down Fulton Street from the Nostrand Avenue stop on the A train.

✪ **Boys' and Girls' High School.** 1700 Fulton Street, near Utica Avenue, 467-1700. The interior may viewed by appointment.

Across from Fulton Park and near Atlantic Avenue, this 1974 building has a special significance to Bedford-Stuyvesant. It is the largest school in the neighborhood and the site of many important community events. In 1990 this was Nelson Mandela's first stop during his three-day visit to New York. The exterior artwork includes a powerful mural done by Ernest Crichlow depicting the struggles of African-Americans from slavery to present times. Inside, works by such African-American artists as Norman Lewis line the corridors. The original Boys' High School was in a fabulous building that still stands on Marcy and Putnam. The original Girls' High, now a New York City Board of Education building, was located at nearby 475 Nostrand Avenue.

Brownstoners of Bedford-Stuyvesant house tour, 574-1979.

On the third weekend in October the volunteers of Brownstoners of Bedford-Stuyvesant conduct a house tour of the interiors and gardens of several restored nineteenth-century brownstones in the area. These homes represent some of the most handsome in all New York City. The activist Brownstoners group includes a judge, an airline executive, a lawyer, and other professionals committed to the neighborhood. Their motto: "Come home to Bedford-Stuyvesant."

✪ **Gospel music, Sunday Services, International Revival Tabernacle.** 2260 Pacific Street, 346-8839.

If you want to experience gospel music in its home setting, come here on a Sunday morning. Reverend Timothy Wright, known for both his live concerts and recordings of gospel music, recently moved here from Washington Temple. Also see the listing for the Institutional Church of God in Christ in Fort Greene, and the Brooklyn Tabernacle in Park Slope. Call for times and directions. Car transportation is recommended.

✪ **The International African Arts Festival.** Boys' and Girls' High School, 636-6906. First weekend in July.

The largest Afro-centeric market in the United States, with 300 to 400 international vendors. Organizers estimate that it attracts about 15,000 to 20,000 people, many from out of town. Performers have included the likes of Hugh Masekela, Mighty Sparrow, Abbey Lincoln, John Luciene, Tanya Maria, and star Sela Kuti from Nigeria. Admission $7.

Medgar Evers College. 1650 Bedford Avenue, near Montgomery Street (Crown Heights), 270-4991.

The only black-oriented college in the City University of New York system is located on a campus in nearby Crown Heights. Call for information on services and activities.

Simmons African Arts Museum. 1063 Fulton Street, between Classon and Grand avenues, 230-0933. Weekends, noon–6 P.M. Call to check hours.

An unusual collection of contemporary African art and masks from twelve West African nations forms the nucleus of this neighborhood art gallery. The pieces are part of the private, nonfunded collection of the owner, who has traveled and collected in Africa for more than thirty years. He presents educational exhibits designed primarily for community residents, but all visitors are welcome.

Historic Bedford-Stuyvesant

The official New York City landmarks in this area are a varied lot: the incomparable remnants of a free-black community during the era of slavery, the **Weeksville Houses**; vast elegant apartment buildings designed by Montrose Morris, with grandiose names such as the **Alhambra, Renaissance**, and **Imperial Apartments**; institutions of higher education that played a role in the earliest history of public school in New York City such as **Boys' High School** and **Girls' High School**; churches such as **St. Bartholomew's** and **St. George's**; the ornate **23rd Regiment Armory**—and a tree, the **Magnolia Grandiflora**.

Alhambra Apartments. 500–518 Nostrand Avenue and 29–33 Macon Street.

An example of upper-middle-class Brooklyn apartment living, this landmarked building is "notable for its six towers, steep roof slopes, gables, loggias, arcades and lively terra-cotta detail," according to the *Guide to New York City Landmarks.* It was the first of three in the area designed by Montrose Morris and commissioned by prominent developer Louis F. Seitz around 1890. The building is scheduled for renovation.

Boys' High School. 832 Marcy Avenue, between Putnam Avenue and Madison Street.

Boy's High School was designed architecturally to reflect its important place in society as a highly recognized public educational institution of late nineteenth-century Brooklyn. This Romanesque Revival boasts an ornate building with a tower, campanile, and other architectural flourishes. The building has been restored.

Girls' High School. 475 Nostrand Avenue, between Halsey and Macon streets.

The oldest surviving high school building in New York City, this 1886 Victorian Gothic structure was built a mere ten years after the establishment, in 1878, of the old Central Grammar School, Brooklyn's first public high school. Brooklyn's population was expanding rapidly, and this single-sex institution was their answer to overcrowding.

Imperial Apartments. 1198 Pacific Street and 1327 Bedford Avenue, corner Bedford and Pacific avenues.

An ornate, upscale 1892 apartment building erected by the architect-developer team of Montrose Morris and Louis F. Seitz, the Imperial was occupied by the affluent middle class at the turn of the nineteenth century. Many people were building brownstones in the late 1800s; apartments represented a different concept in urban living.

✪ **Magnolia Grandiflora and Magnolia Tree Earth Center.** 679 Lafayette Avenue, opposite Herbert Van King Park, 387-2116. Call for hours.

This environmental education center, established in 1972, is famous for its lovely magnolia tree transplanted from North Carolina and now an official NYC landmark. With environmentalism on the rebound, the Earth Center continues to provide good programs on recycling and conservation to more than two thousand school children a year. The staff also can provide assistance to community groups on greening projects and care of street trees. The center is located on a well-kept block of brownstones facing a large park, Herbert Von King Park (previously known as Tompkins Park). While Magnolia is intensely committed to improving the quality of life in African-American communities, people come from all over to enjoy the various exhibits at the George Washington Carver Gallery. Call for an appointment first.

✪ **Renaissance Apartments.** 488 Nostrand Avenue, between Hancock and Halsey streets.

Renovated in 1995–96, the Renaissance was first built in 1892 by Louis F. Seitz, who again commissioned architect Montrose Morris for this third large apartment building in the area. Seitz, a prominent developer of his time, built a number of important apartment buildings in Brooklyn.

St. Bartholomew's Church. 1227 Pacific Street, corner of Rogers Avenue.

Set back from the street behind a garden, this irregularly shaped small church was built in the late 1880s by George Chappel, considered a "creative architect" of his time, who utilized some motifs of British Queen Anne–style architecture.

St. George's Episcopal Church. 800 Marcy Avenue, between Monroe Street and Gates Avenue.

Designed in the late 1880s by nationally acclaimed R. M. Upjohn, an architect who resided in Cobble Hill, this church displays striking high Victorian Gothic architecture as well as Tiffany windows.

✪ **The 23rd Regiment Armory.** 1322 Bedford Avenue, corner of Atlantic Avenue.

A 1890s architectural monument to the military, this vast, impressive armory was designed by local Brooklyn architects Fowler & Hough, with assistance from New York State architect Isaac Perry. It is considered the most outstanding of all Brooklyn armories. Today it serves as a social service center. It is within one block of two other landmarks, the Imperial Apartments and St. Bartholemew's Church.

✪ **Stuyvesant Heights Historic District.** This historic district within the larger Bedford-Stuyvesant neighborhood is roughly bounded by Stuyvesant Avenue to the east and Tomkins Avenue to the west along MacDonough. It also includes sections of Decatur and Bainbridge streets, between Lewis and Stuyvesant Avenues (not shown on our map).

✪ **Weeksville (Hunterfly Road) houses.** 1698–1708 Bergen Street, between Rochester and Buffalo roads, 756-5250. Call for hours.

Use your imagination when you make the pilgrimage here. These lonesome frame homes are remnants of nineteenth-century Weeksville, one of Brooklyn's most prominent free-black areas. The houses date from the period immediately before and after the American Civil War. To learn about Weeksville is to learn about the proud and difficult odyssey that American blacks made from slavery to freedom. The figures associated with Weeksville include Moses R. Cobb, a black policeman born into slavery in North Carolina who is said to have walked from North Carolina to New York City after emancipation; Major Martin Delaney, grandson of an enslaved West African prince, who became active in the Underground Railroad and wrote for the Weeksville newspaper, *Freedman's Torchlight*; and Dr. Susan Smith McKinney-Steward, the third black female physician in the nation, born in Weeksville in 1847.

The Weeksville houses were discovered in 1968 when historian James Hurley set out on an aerial exploration over an area that nineteenth-century documents indicated had been a thriving black community. He and pilot Joseph Haynes noted an oddly situated lane that did not coincide with the modern block layout. What they found were four frame houses, circa 1840 to 1883, located on the old Hunterfly Road. Since that exciting moment, the houses have been restored and declared landmarks, a small museum has been installed, and the Society for the Preservation of Weeksville and Bedford-Stuyvesant History has produced award-winning films, traveling exhibits, and educational materials dedicated to the rediscovery of black cultural roots in Brooklyn. Their excellent booklet on Weeksville is a must-read for people interested in historic Brooklyn.

Churches

Churches are an important part of everyday life and a community focal point in Bedford-Stuyvesant. And there are a lot of them. The **Bridge Street African Wesleyan Methodist Episcopal Church** at 273 Stuyvesant Avenue is Brooklyn's oldest African-American church, founded in 1818. A hundred years later, the first black church to move into Bedford-Stuyvesant during the great northward migration of rural blacks was **Bethany Baptist Church** at 460 Sumner Avenue. Among many other churches of architectural significance are **St. Mary's Church** at 230 Classon Avenue, built in 1858, and **St. George's Episcopal Church** at 800 Marcy Avenue, built by architect Richard Upjohn in 1887; both have original Tiffany windows.

✪ **Concord Baptist Church of Christ.** 833 Marcy Avenue, at Madison Avenue, 622-1818.

Concord Baptist Church boasts one of the nation's largest African-American congregations, numbering about twelve thousand and including many of Bedford-Stuyvesant's most prominent residents. A leader in community affairs, the church organizes scholarships, nursing home care, and other services. Founded in 1848, this is one of a handful of extant churches built by the early black residents of Brooklyn.

Our Lady of Victory Roman Catholic Church. 583 Throop Avenue, between Macon and MacDonough streets, 574-5772.

The bright red fences and window trim, well-tended shrubbery, and black stones give this stunning 1895 Gothic Revival church a striking appearance. Almost a half block in size, it is within walking distance of attractive brownstone blocks.

✪ **Washington Temple Church of God in Christ.** 1372 Bedford Avenue, between Bergen and Dean streets, 789-7545. Sun. services are from 11:30 A.M. to 1:30 P.M.; music, 11:30 A.M.–12:30 P.M.

Music lovers, take note! To hear a traditional gospel choir accompanied by keyboards and percussion instruments, come to Sunday services here. The music director is Brother M. Kinard, known for his live concerts. Washington Temple has not one, but several different choirs. Other churches with gospel choirs are the Institutional Church of God in Christ in Fort Greene and the Brooklyn Tabernacle in Park Slope (see pages 121 and 248, respectively).

Notable Restaurants

Auggie's Brownstone Inn. 1550 Fulton Street, between Albany and Kingston avenues, 773-8940. Mon.–Sun., 4–11 P.M.

We include this for the sake of history: it's the oldest black-owned bar in Bedford-Stuyvesant. Though its location is on a rundown block, there's a garden area for eating, TV, and music in the background.

✪ **Joloff.** 930 Fulton Street, between Washington Avenue and St. James Place, 636-4011. Mon.–Sat., noon–11 P.M.; Sun., noon–10 P.M.

This Senegalese restaurant gets high ranks marks for the filling food and cozy atmosphere. And you won't have to spend much for a couple of fish or veggie patties, or the vegetarian dishes cooked in a mélange of spicy sauces. By all means try the bean pie with cinnamon and a sip of sorrel, a beet-red drink not unlike cranberry juice.

McCafe. 327 Stuyvesant Avenue at Macon Street, 574-3728. Daily, 8 A.M.–10 P.M. Closed Sun.

A stop here is mandatory if you truly want to "see" Bedford-Stuyvesant. McDonald's Dining Room, which is what it used to be called, was established in 1948 and resembles many an old eatery in the Deep South: a simple, decent place with a counter, some booths, and a back room. This café-style eatery holds a special spot in the heart of many older residents, who remember parents scrimping and saving to be able to afford the dignity of a restaurant meal for Sunday dinner after church.

Under new ownership and with a new name (to avoid confusion with you-know-who), this old treasure has been given a facelift. It takes credit cards, and serves a more sophisticated menu. In addition to traditional southern breakfasts (Sunday grits and salmon cakes), for dinner there's Cajun-style shrimp, barbecued or blackened chicken, and a combo shrimp and steak plate. Dinner entrées range from $8 to $18. No liquor is served here.

✪ **North Carolina Country Kitchen.** 1991 Atlantic Avenue, corner of Saratoga Avenue, 498-8033. Restaurant: daily 7:30 A.M.–10 P.M. Store: 7:30 A.M.–8 P.M. Cash only.

Toss together a truck drivers' stop, a neighborhood store, and a pinch of Deep South, and you've got the North Carolina Country Kitchen. From Flatbush Avenue, go three miles east—it seems like forever—on gritty Atlantic Avenue to a most unlikely country-style building. This handsome pine-fronted restaurant was built on a gas station site by the woman who also owns the food store across the street. The kitchen serves up North Carolina specialities—grits, biscuits, bacon and eggs cafeteria-style for breakfast. The big lunch and dinner menu includes chicken, chitterlings, black-eyed peas, cornbread, and excellent sweet potato pie and cobblers. There are a few outdoor tables. The thirty-year-old food store sells hard-to-find items that spell home to traditional southern palates, including hams and sausages, fresh greens and canned goods such as King Syrup, old-fashioned molasses, grits, chow-chow condiment, pickled okra, hominy, boiled peanuts, chewing tobacco, and more.

Patty Palace Bakery. 918 Fulton Street, corner Washington Avenue, 789-1833. 11 A.M.–9 P.M. Cash only.

Jamaican and West Indian dishes are served up in this bright, clean environment. There's spicy jerk chicken, well-cooked stewed chicken, and the usual sorrel and other West Indian style juices.

Shala's Roti Shop and Bakery. 1285 Fulton Street, between Nostrand and Bedford, 783-2646. Daily, noon–9 P.M.; Sun. until 7 P.M. Cash only.

West Indian roti, with delicious goat, vegetable and fish fillings are served at this popular shop. The owners have a sense of humor, and if you are unfamiliar with the cuisine they will help you out.

Sugarhill Restaurant Supper Club. 609 DeKalb Avenue, at Nostrand Avenue, 797-1727. Call for hours and information on entertainment.

A large, popular restaurant located near Tomkins Park and east of Pratt Institute, Sugarhill serves great American country-style cooking. And, with live jazz and entertainment on the weekends, its a Bed-Sty hot spot which has dancing and offers a good time for all.

V's Caribbean Cuisine. 927 Fulton Street, between Clinton and Waverly avenues, 789-8067. Mon.–Sat., 11 A.M.–10 P.M.; closed Sun. Cash only.

Mildly spiced fillings and dynamite hot sauce aren't a bad combination for the excellent roti and chicken dishes you'll find at V's Caribbean. Try the jerk chicken (not overly spicy), the cod fish and fry bake, and make sure you ask for the peanut punch. There's only one small table; the food is mostly for take-out. A meal costs about $5.

Young Apache. 1501 Fulton Street at Kingston Avenue, 778-9341. Mon.–Sat., 8 A.M.–8 P.M.; closed Sun. Cash only.

Just a few blocks from Restoration Plaza, this bakery sells a range of Caribbean and Jamaican specialties, including roti and hardo bread.

Hotels

✪ **Akwaaba Mansion.** 347 McDonough Street. 455-5958

Since it opened recently, Akwaaba Mansion has received tremendous publicity. It is a beautifully restored villa, built in the 1860s, and its owners are as warm and welcoming as the place is elegant. As described, quite aptly, by the Brooklyn Tourist Council, and government-sponsored **BrookLynx** website: "an elegant, freestanding Italianate villa from the 1860s, complete with wraparound sun porch and 40-foot-long ballroom." (*Akwaaba* means "welcome" in the language of Ghana.) Choose from four guest rooms whose decor mixes Africana and Victoriana, including a romantic honeymoon suite or Jumping the Broom Room, named for the slave tradition of jumping over a broom on one's wedding day. Rooms cost $100–$125 per night. Book well in advance.

Bensonhurst

Where it is: Bounded by 14th Avenue to the northwest, 61st Street and MacDonald Avenue to the northeast, Avenue U and 26th Street to the southeast, and Gravesend Bay to the southwest.

What's nearby: Bay Ridge, Borough Park, Brighton Beach, Coney Island, Sheepshead Bay, Staten Island.

How to get there:

By car: Take the Belt Parkway to the 86th Street exit.

By subway: N train to the 18th Avenue Station.

Cab services: New York Car Service (745-0001) or YES Car Service (492-9300). Cost is about $10 to Brooklyn Heights, $18 to Grand Central Station.

Note: Check a map before you go. Bensonhurst's street grid is confusing. The streets called "Bay 6" or "Bay 7" exist only in Bensonhurst and are woven into a grid that includes plain numbered streets, as in "86th Street," and numbered avenues as well.

Special events: Procession of Saint Fortunata (July); Santa Rosalia Festival, celebrated by immigrants from Palermo, Sicily (September).

How it got its name: Bensonhurst was named after the Benson family, resident cabbage and potato farmers in the mid-1800s.

Official landmark: The New Utrecht Reformed Church.

ABOUT THE NEIGHBORHOOD

Bensonhurst is Brooklyn's Little Italy. You'll find some excellent Italian restaurants here plus several traditional Italian bakeries that rival the best of Manhattan's Mott Street. You'll find good local opera at the **Regina Opera Company** (see page 42) and plenty of outdoor activities as well. **Dyker Beach Golf Course, Nelly Bly Amusement Park**, and **Bensonhurst Park**, with its three-mile waterside promenade for jogging, biking, fishing, and kite flying, are all major attractions.

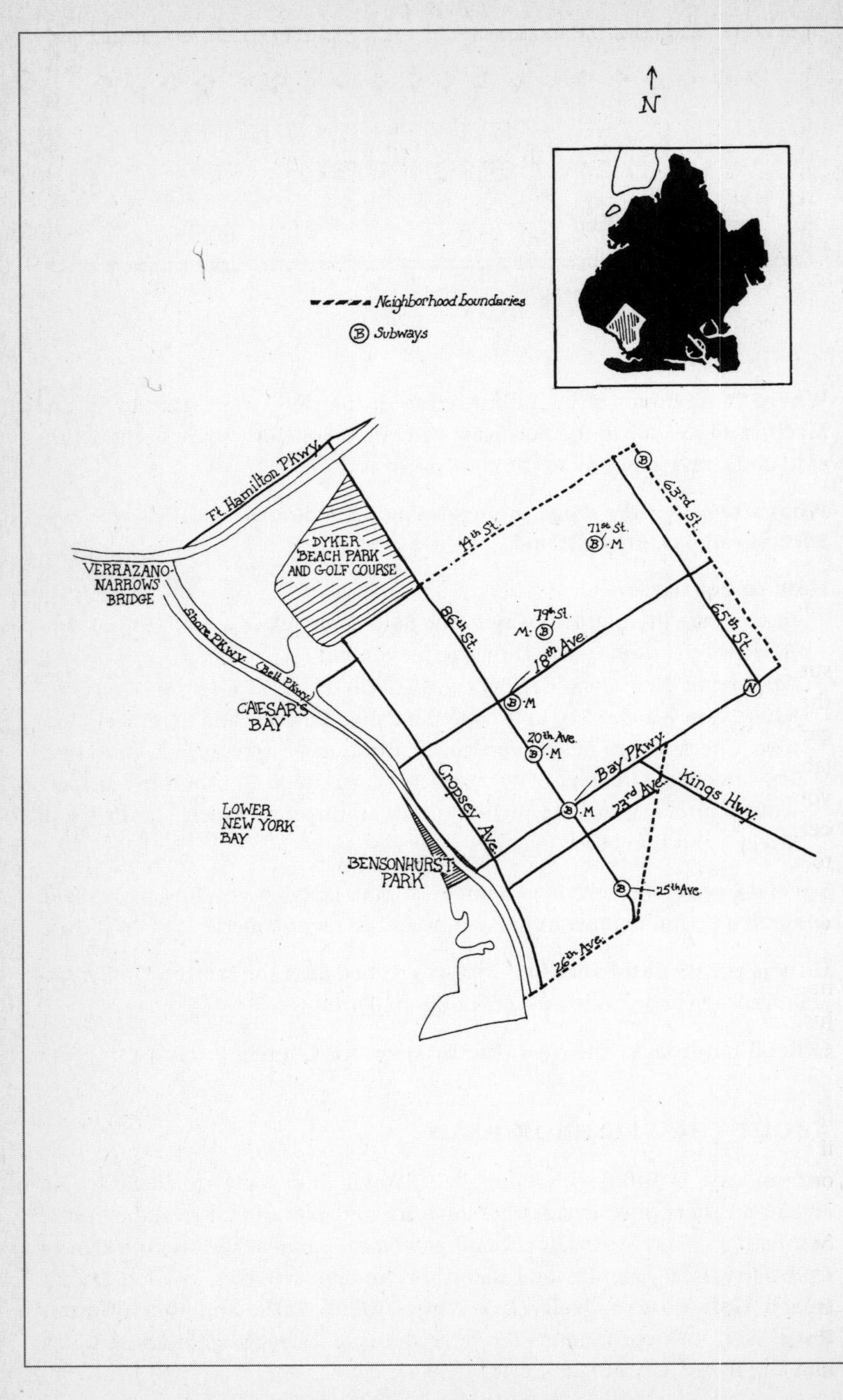
N
Neighborhood Boundaries
Subways
Ft. Hamilton PKwy.
DYKER BEACH PARK AND GOLF COURSE
14th St.
71st St.
63rd St.
VERRAZANO-NARROWS BRIDGE
Shore PKwy. (Bell PKwy.)
86th St.
79th St.
65th St.
18th Ave.
CAESAR'S BAY
20th Ave.
Bay PKwy.
Kings Hwy.
Cropsey Ave.
23rd Ave.
LOWER NEW YORK BAY
BENSONHURST PARK
25th Ave.
26th Ave.

The sense of humor born of workingclass Bensonhurst has helped some residents fulfill the American dream. Local-boys-made-good include Phil Silvers, Dom DeLuise, and Abe Burros. Bensonhurst was also the home of television's most beloved bus driver, "Honeymooner" Ralph Kramden.

Sex, soccer, family, and, of course, religion are big themes in Bensonhurst. Everywhere you look are clues to the local culture.

The names of clothing stores are suggestive, for instance, for women: "What Can I Do For U" and for men, "Male Ego." Hands down, Bensonhurst supports more nail salons than anywhere else in Brooklyn; you see one almost every other block. There are innumerable wedding shops selling bridal gowns, wedding gifts, photography, and honeymoon travel, and there are more big wedding halls here than in all of brownstone Brooklyn combined.

Residents follow Italian soccer matches religiously. In season, you will overhear passionate discussion of the latest soccer game in stores, in homes, at the pizzerias and in coffee bars such as **Caffè Italia** or **Caffè Mille Luci**, both styled as though straight out of a stage set for an Italian town or railway station.

Religious festivals are wonderful occasions to visit Bensonhurst. Most summer weekends you'll find a feast honoring a patron saint, culminating in the huge, ten-day **Santa Rosalia Festival** in September. And the extravagant, elaborate neighborhood **Christmas Lights in Dyker Heights** are a labor of love (and well worth a trip from another part of New York City). If you can come in the spring, try to attend the **Good Friday candlelight procession**, as thousands of people carry statues and banners through the streets to a late-night mass at Our Lady of Guadalupe Church.

Elderly gents sit on sidewalk chairs and watch the passing street scene while chatting in Italian. Looking somewhat mysterious from the outside are a half dozen or so private social clubs whose unadorned signs bearing the names of Italian towns punctuate the avenue; if you peek inside you'll see just tables and chairs. Mostly located on **18th Avenue**, they have names such as "Societa Figli di Ragusa," "Santa Rosalia Society," and the "Sciacci Social Club." Of all Brooklyn neighborhoods, Bensonhurst is most likely to be on the evening news in regard to a Mafia-related story. It's hard to know if locals are kidding or serious when they say things are quiet because "everyone's either locked up or dead."

And then there's food. Rivaling Little Italy in Manhattan, Bensonhurst could claim to be New York City's capital of Italian food. There are pork stores selling homemade sausages; *foccaceria* (selling pizza, riceballs, and other Italian fast foods); *fornio* (bread bakeries); *pasticieria* (pastry bakeries); and *latticini* (dairy shops). It is hometown to both the national **Sbarro** pizza empire, and the successful **Pastosa Ravioli** chain. If you like mozzarella, go to the decades-old **Lioni Latticini** or **Aiello Brothers**. For caponata and Italian imported goods, there's **Trunzo Brothers**, a wonderful Italian grocery. See the coffee roasting the old-fashioned way at **J & A Espresso Plus**. You can indulge in gorgeous, rich Italian cakes and pastries at **Alba's, Temptations**, or **Villabate**. Decide for yourself if reputations are deserved at acclaimed pizzeria **L&B Spumoni Gardens** (try the spumoni, too) and **Cristardi's Pizzeria**.

Woven into this profoundly Italian warp and woof of Bensonhurst life is a wariness about the newly arrived Asians and, to a greater extent, Russians. (Bensonhurst gained infamy in the early 1990s for the race-related murder of a black man, Yusuf Hawkins, by local youths.) As a Brooklyn tourist, you would barely notice this"diversity." Yet on 18th Avenue, stores have popped up that were not there a decade ago when this book was first written: a Chinese herbalist, complete with on-site acupuncturist, and a handful of Russian delis which sell blinis, smoked fish, and large rye breads. Just ask a local shopkeeper about this; he or she is likely to confide with a shake of the head and in a lowered voice that the Russians are "buying up" and "taking over" the neighborhood.

Where you go in Bensonhurst depends on what you want to do. There is excellent Italian food at a number of restaurants and you have your choice of environments, from the intimate grottolike **Il Grottino** to **Tomasso's**, where you can hear opera or Gershwin, to a garden setting at **Villa Vivolo**. You'll find bakeries like the **Alba** and **Angelo's. Bensonhurst Park** offers joggers, skaters, bikers, and romantics a great view of barges, sailboats, and the beautiful Verrazano-Narrows Bridge. Bargain hunters will revel in the display of everyday items, from cheap wristwatches to garbage pails, sold from outdoor stalls on two blocks along 86th Street.

To see how very distinct neighborhoods meld into one another—a true Brooklyn phenomenon—drive down 17th Avenue, a well-kept residential street, all the way from Bensonhurst to Borough Park. Italian pork stores give way to kosher butchers; teenagers in form-fitting clothing yield to demurely dressed girls and boys wearing yarmulkes.

Shopping Areas

13th Avenue: Take a walk up 13th Avenue from about 70th to 86th Street. You will see two-story brick buildings, a well-kept main street punctuated by new benches, potted plants and old-fashioned street lights. This avenue is a shopping strip serving Dyker Heights, a 1920s-era residential area of well-kept houses with ample lots on nicely kept streets. Culturally, it is a stable Italian community, rooted in old Italian family relationships. Many new homes are sold to relatives of current residents.

18th Avenue: The half-mile stretch from about 65th to 78th Street is lined with Italian food shops, along with shops specializing in imported Italian records, linens, and toiletries. Note here the several non-Italian shops, particularly the Chinese and Russian ones.

86th Street: An uninspired, if busy, main shopping drag, here you will find chain stores such as Lane Bryant, Rainbow Shops, Footlocker, Nine West outlet, and some mom-and-pops sprinkled throughout.

NOTE: There has been ongoing controversy over Brooklyn Junction, a large shopping center slated for the area between Bensonhurst and Borough Park, which local store owners oppose. Stay tuned.

Historical Notes

Little remains of Bensonhurst's early years as a rural farming area. One interesting remnant of the Revolutionary War is a "liberty pole" at the **New Utrecht Reformed Church**, which marks the site where colonial rebels taunted English soldiers by hoisting the American flag.

In the 1890s, when Coney Island was a world-famous seaside resort, a competitive complex called Bensonhurst-by-the-Sea was built. Although it tried to lure customers with new hotels, an amusement park, and racetracks, Bensonhurst-by-the-Sea never succeeded. Unfortunately, none of its grandeur remains.

The growth of Bensonhurst as a middle- and working-class community followed the extension of the subway lines in 1915. The 4th Avenue Subway (now the R and N trains) provided an escape for Italian and Jewish immigrants stuck in Manhattan's cramped and dirty Lower East Side. Many descendants of the neighborhood's original families still live here. Successive generations of Italian immigrants also have settled here, seeking out members of their extended families to help them adjust to a new country. Some have made their fortunes in America and returned to Italy; others have homes in both Italy and America. These multigenerational, bicultural ties contribute to the neighborhood's conservative, slightly Old World flavor.

Bensonhurst is not exclusively Italian. A long-standing Jewish community remains here, along with Irish, Polish, and most recently Asian and Russian residents. Typical of so much of Brooklyn, there are layers upon layers of different cultures even in this relatively concentrated Italian neighborhood.

Kidstuff

Families can easily spend the better part of a day in Bensonhurst, but to cover everything you'll need a car. Parents of young children will find in Bath

Beach Mall one of Brooklyn's two huge **Toys " Я " Us** department stores, and nearby, **Nellie Bly Amusement Park**, and a playground. It is easy to grab a bite at one of the numerous pizza parlors, and in warm weather, outdoor stands sell Italian ices. In the summer you may stumble upon a weekend street festival. For outdoor fun plan a picnic near the bike path and fly a kite in **Bensonhurst Park**.

ENTERTAINMENT

Maple Lanes. 570 60th Street, near 15th Avenue, 331-9000. Daily, 9–1 A.M.

For great people-watching, roll a ball or two down Maple Lanes. For outings with little kids call a day in advance so they can set up bumpers in the gutters. These almost guarantee that your tot will get a strike.

✪ **Nellie Bly Amusement Park.** 1824 Shore Parkway, near Toys " Я " Us, 996-4002. Open Easter to Halloween (weather permitting), from noon to dusk. Rides average $1; there is no admission or parking fee.

The petite, relatively clean amusement park is just a couple minutes' drive from Toys "Я" Us. Not only is it a little bit of heaven for toddlers and preteens, but it's also not too much of a headache for parents. The park features more than a dozen kiddie-sized rides, including a miniature roller coaster, Ferris wheel, carousel, and train, plus a petting farm, an eighteen-hole miniature golf course, and an arcade of games. This park is not nearly as hectic or as tacky as Coney Island, but note that aside from the small Ferris wheel, batting cages, and go-carts, Nellie Bly is strictly for young children. A family-owned business, it has operated for more than thirty years.

Regina Opera Company, Regina Hall. Corner of 12th Avenue, at 65th Street, 232-3555. Performances are at 7 P.M. on Saturdays and 4 P.M. on Sundays. Call for a schedule.

For opera buffs on a budget, this is one of the better small opera bargains in New York City. Performing for nearly thirty years, the company has helped launch the likes of Dolora Zajic, now with the Metropolitan Opera. Thrice yearly, operas with full orchestra are staged with elaborate scenery and costumes. The Regina also hosts concerts throughout the year. At $8 for adults and no charge for kids twelve and under, the price is right.

United Artists Marboro Quad. 6817 Bay Parkway, near 69th Street, 232-4000. Call for show times.

This four-screen theater in the heart of Bensonhurst shows the usual gamut of first-run movies. Although it has been overshadowed by the newer

United Artists complex at Sheepshead Bay, the lines may be shorter here. It is also near **Torre's Restaurant**, a definite plus (see page 45).

PARKS AND PLAYGROUNDS

Bensonhurst Park. Bay Parkway, at 21st Avenue.

The largest of Brooklyn's eighteen municipal neighborhood miniparks, this combination promenade and park stretches for over three miles along the Belt Parkway and is a favorite for jogging, roller-skating, and biking. You'll get views here of Staten Island's wooded shore from one end of the promenade and the Statue of Liberty from the other. Summer concerts are held at the Cropsey Avenue end. You can go kite flying and fishing at Bay 8th Street, just before exit 5 on the Belt Parkway.

Bensonhurst Park Playground. Cropsey Avenue, at Bay Parkway and 21st Avenue.

Do you and your little ones need a breather after Toys "Я" Us? Leave your car in the store lot and take a walk to this lovely playground. Just a few blocks away, it is right next to the entrance to the Belt Parkway westbound.

Bensonhurst Playground. 14th Avenue, at 86th Street.

This well-maintained, safe space is just a five-minute drive from the 86th Street shopping area. There is plenty of room for running around, plus modern wooden climbing equipment and swings.

Dyker Beach Park and Golf Course. From 86th Street to Shore Parkway, between 7th and 14th avenues, 836-9722.

Less than half the size of Prospect Park, Dyker nonetheless has 216 acres of grassy space that includes a soccer field, tennis courts, and the Dyker Beach Golf Course, a public course. It's located past the Verrazano-Narrows Bridge on the south side of Fort Hamilton. For golf information call 836-9722. The first tee is near 86th Street and 7th Avenue.

Garibaldi Playground. 18th Avenue, at 84th Street.

This small urban playground, across from the lovely **New Utrecht Reformed Church** (see page 44), is a place for the kids to let off some steam while you sneak a nibble of one of Bensonhurst's dreamy Italian pastries.

POINTS OF CULTURAL INTEREST

Beth Hatalmud Yeshiva. 2127 82nd Street, at 21st Avenue, 259-2525.

Jewish and Italian immigrants have lived side by side in Brooklyn for about a hundred years. This nationally known Orthodox boys' school is one of many local institutions, including nearly two dozen synagogues, that have been supported for decades by the small Jewish community that still lives in Bensonhurst.

✪ **Christmas Lights in Dyker Heights.** Christmas season only, evenings.

Around Christmas, an evening drive past the bright, elaborately decorated homes in this area, called Dyker Heights, would put a smile on any Scrooge's face. To see these extravaganzas head toward 84th Street between 11th and 12th avenues, and on 5th Avenue at 83rd Street. Many of these families have been lighting up the neighborhood for decades. A Brooklyn best bet.

New Utrecht Reformed Church. 1828 83rd Street, at 18th Avenue, 236-0678.

The oldest church in the area, this lovely, well-kept landmark was constructed in 1828. The stones come from a church built in 1700 that once stood in what is now the New Utrecht Cemetery, also a landmark, located nearby at 16th Avenue and 84th Street. The liberty pole in the front marks the site where the American flag was first raised at the end of the American Revolution.

Regina Pacis. 65th Street and 12th Avenue, 236-0909.

This is the largest church in Bensonhurst, with about four thousand congregants. During Easter, Christmas, and other festivals there are huge turnouts—on Good Friday, for example, about seven thousand people participate in a candlelit procession carrying large statues as far as a mile and a half. The **Regina Opera Company** (page 42) is a spinoff of this church.

Santa Rosalia Society. 18th Avenue, at 70th Street, no phone.

Social clubs like this one dot 18th Avenue in Bensonhurst. Named after a hometown in Italy by new immigrants from that town, these modest storefront clubs provide friendship and an opportunity to engage in what Americans now call "networking." People from (in this case) Santa Rosalia meet here to talk, to reminisce, and to get help in finding jobs and housing contacts. In the summer the social clubs celebrate the festival of their town's patron saint, and Italians from the town gather from all over New York City for the festival. The biggest of these is the Santa Rosalia Festival, organized by the Santa Rosalia Society.

NOTABLE RESTAURANTS

✪ **Il Grotino Ristorante.** 7123 18th Avenue, corner of 72nd Street, 837-7017. Mon.–Sun., 5 P.M.–midnight.

Nestled below ground under Caffè Mille Lucci, this intimate restaurant is a grottolike room with a small bar, visible kitchen, and about a dozen tables. Patrons come from New Jersey, Long Island, and all of New York City for the authentic Italian cuisine made of fresh ingredients. From the appetizers to pasta con fagioli to killer cream deserts like tiramisù, everything is impeccably done, including the service. Entrées average about $18 and pasta dishes are less. There's live music on weekends.

La Palina. 159 Avenue O, between West 4th and West 5th streets, 236-9764, Tue.–Fri., noon–10 P.M.; Sat., noon–12 P.M., Sun., noon–10 P.M.; closed Mon. Cash only.

La Palina, now run by the grandsons of founder Charles Vertolomo, knows how to cook Neapolitan. That means large portions, lots of garlic, and an enthusiastic clientele; that means you need to make reservations on the weekends.

Ponte Vecchio. 8810 4th Avenue, corner 88th Street, 238-6449. Sun.–Thurs. noon–10:30 P.M.; Fri.–Sat., noon–11:30 P.M.

We're embarrassed to say we didn't get to Ponte Vecchio. But, it's an old, established Italian restaurant in Brooklyn, so we feel safe suggesting that you try it out for yourself.

Rocco's. 6408 Fort Hamilton Parkway, near 64th Street, 833-2109. Tues.–Sat., 6:30 A.M.–8:00 P.M.; closed Sun.–Mon. Cash only.

Unpretentious, fresh, and lovingly made homestyle Italian food is the fare here. Try the clams, artichokes, and of course pasta dishes. It's a great place to bring the kids for lunch or an early dinner after an afternoon of sleuthing around Brooklyn. Entrées are inexpensive; a big plate of fried calimari is less than $8. Note the hours.

✪ **Tomasso's.** 1464 86th Street, between 14th and 15th avenues, 236-9883. Daily, lunch 11:30–4 P.M.; dinner 4–11 P.M.

The food is good, but the singing is why people travel here. Loud, exuberant opera with piano accompaniment is performed Wednesday through Saturday. Come before Lent for Carnevale.

Torre's Restaurant. 6808 Bay Parkway, near 68th Street, 256-1140. Mon.–Thurs., 11:30 A.M.–11:30 P.M.; Fri. and Sat., 11:30–12:30 A.M.; Sun., 11:30 A.M.–10 P.M. No credit cards.

Good Neapolitan cuisine at moderate prices make this a terrific local restaurant. The best dishes are the barbecued jumbo shrimps lathered with garlic, olive oil, and lemon juice for $13.50, lobster tail fra diavolo, and a heaping plateful of veal marsala for under $10.

Villa Fiorita. 7720 18th Avenue, between 77th and 78th streets, 837-7950. Daily, noon–midnight.

If ravioli is your thing, note that the daily homemade version here is worthy of Manhattan's best restaurants, but at very moderate prices. The restaurant's simple, intimate ambience and fresh Italian fare make this the kind of restaurant visitors wish they had in their own neighborhoods. A full meal comes to less than $22 a person. After dinner, visit one of several authentic Italian espresso bars a few blocks away.

Villa Ruggiero. 2274 86th Street, between 23rd Avenue and Bay 32nd Street, 373-2590. Tues.–Sun., noon–11:30 P.M.

If you want a good but inexpensive Italian meal near Shore Park, try this local favorite. Southern Italian cuisine is the specialty. Sample freshly prepared spaghetti, veal parmigiana, shrimp scampi, and other entrées for about $12.

Villa Vivolo. 8829 26th Avenue, near 88th Street, 372-9860. Mon.–Fri., noon–9 P.M.; Sat.–Sun., 12:30–10 P.M.

This sixty-year-old restaurant may be off the beaten track, but it serves wonderful homemade pasta and veal dishes, stuffed artichokes, and other Italian specialties at about $20 per dinner. Located in an attractive old home on a pleasant residential street, the patio garden will have appeal for claustrophobic New Yorkers. Rudolph Valentino (one of many Bensonhurst-based entertainers) is rumored to have worked here before he became a cinema heartthrob. Parking is available on the premises; call for directions. Weekend reservations are recommended.

Cafés, Ice Cream, and Pizzerias

Alba. See listing on page 49.

If anyone can make an aria out of a cake, Alba can. That's why you should visit this famous bakery's store next door, which sells tartuffo and ices, too.

Caffè Cesare. 7109 13th Avenue, 236-3342.

Your morning greeting at this mirror-and-chrome Milano-style cafe is not "hello" but "*bon giorno.*" As in European cafés, there are different prices for the freshly brewed cappuccino and espresso depending on whether you stand, sit at a table, or take it to go. The debate at the wood-paneled coffee bar is likely to be about last night's soccer game or about politics. Italian ice cream sold here in the summer, too.

Caffè Italia. 6917 18th Avenue, near 70th Street, no phone. Mon.–Sat., noon–11 P.M.; Sun., noon–9 P.M.

The scene here is straight out of Italy. On summer nights, local men in Italian-designed clothing and real shoes (no sneakers) hang around on the street and in the café, talking, gesticulating, laughing. The fare includes homemade gelati, spumoni, espresso, cappuccino, and Sambuca.

✪ **Caffè Mille Luci.** 7123 18th Avenue, near 72nd Street, 837-7017. Mon.–Fri., 7–2 A.M.; Sat.–Sun., opens 24 hours.

A trip to this Italian café is cheaper than a plane ticket to Italy, and it will transport you mentally to the same place. Try the outstanding coffee and choose from a wide assortment of Italian pastries and sweets. Just below is **Il Grottino** restaurant, owned by the same family.

✪ **Cristardi's Pizza.** 7001 13th Avenue, off 70th Street, 256-9100. Daily, 11:30 A.M.–11 P.M.

Cristardi's sticks with what it does best: pizza, calzone, and antipasti. The mozzarella, fresh of course, is made by famous Lioni Latticini, nearby. Toppings include fresh arugula, artichokes, and sun-dried tomatoes. If you're a pizza snob who only patronizes Brooklyn's favorites—**Totonno's, L&B Spumoni Gardens,** and **Patsy's**—add this one to your list. (Another branch is at 211 President in Carroll Gardens.)

✪ **L & B Spumoni Gardens.** 275 86th Street, near West 11th Avenue, 372-8400. Sun.–Thurs., 11:30 A.M.–midnight; Fri.–Sat., 11:30–2 A.M. Cash only.

People come here from the midtown Manhattan just for a slice of Sicilian. It's *that* good. L & B is an old pizzeria that serves a pie that is nothing less than splendid. The crust is light and crisp and the toppings are fresh. A large outdoor seating area makes the place as much fun as the food is tasty: you can eat in the sunshine and the kids can run around. Homemade spumoni ice cream is sold next door if you haven't filled up on the 'za. For "real food" try the restaurant inside. Pasta or seafood entrées cost less than $12.

SHOPPING

Specialty Food Shops

13TH AVENUE AND VICINITY

✪ **Aunt Butchie's.** 6903 13th Avenue, corner 69th Street, 256-2933. Mon.–Fri., 9 A.M.–6 P.M.; Sat., 9 A.M.–4 P.M.; closed Sun. Cash only.

If you're still dreaming about that chocolate mousse cake you enjoyed recently, it may well have come from Aunt Butchie's bakery. They sell hundreds every week to Barnes & Noble, fancy Manhattan restaurants, and retail customers like you.

B & A Pork Store. 7818 13th Avenue, corner 78th street, 833-9661. Mon.–Sat., 8 A.M.–6:30 P.M.; Sun., 8 A.M.–4 P.M.

When the local pizzeria owner and baker agree on the best pork store on the block, now *that's* a serious recommendation. B & A has sausages, homemade mozzarella and other cheeses that will make your meal.

Cangiano's Italian Deli. 6502 14th Avenue, corner of 65th Street. 236-3368 or 3363. Mon.–Thurs., 9 A.M.–7 P.M.; Fri., 8 A.M.–9 P.M.; Sat., 8 A.M.–7 P.M; Sun., 8A.M.–5 P.M.

Next door to the **Royal Crown Pastry Shop**, of crusty-loaf fame, you will find this family-run grocery store with inexpensive, authentic, imported and made-on-the-premises Italian foods. Cangaino's claims to be the largest Italian deli in Brooklyn and Staten Island. Their motto: "When you see Cangaino's on the label you have quality on your table."

Recommendations: Stock up on the little $2 bags of frozen pizza dough (so you can experiment at home), a few cans of delicious imported Italian tuna fish, a couple of huge jars of roasted red peppers and tomato sauces, and a gallon of quality olive oil. Or, take home some oven-fresh Italian cheesecake, prosciutto bread, or pizza rustica.

There's also a large fresh fruit and veggie stand across the street, so you can accomplish a lot of shopping on one small strip.

Goldstar Bakery. 7409 13th Avenue, corner 74th Street, 236-8560. Open daily, 7:30 A.M.–7 P.M.

The Sciandivasci family, originally from the Matera province of Italy, has a secret: they love breads. Try them stuffed with prosciuto and salami, topped with thinly sliced fried potato rounds, or filled with onion and rosemary. You can also pick up some fresh pasta here, along with Italian butter cookies and rolls.

J & A Espresso Plus. 6302 14th Avenue and 63rd Street, 232-7736. Mon.–Fri., 5:30 A.M.–6 P.M.; closed Sun.

Come see coffee roasted the old-fashioned way in this lovely old roaster. There are nice deli items here as well.

✪ **Lioni Latticini Mozzarella.** 7819 15th Avenue, off 78th Street, 232-7852. Mon.–Fri., 8 A.M.–4:30 P.M.; Sat., 8 A.M.–3 P.M.; closed Sun.

Lioni produces over a dozen different kinds of fresh mozzarella for both retail and wholesale customers. The owners, of the Salzarulo family, come from a long line of Italian cheese makers. Try the mozzarella while it is still a little warm; it's a primal experience that reminds you of the best of mama. (Even if mama wasn't Italian.)

✪ **Temptations.** 7406 13th Avenue, corner 74th Street, 680-5959. Tues.–Sun., 7:30 A.M.–8 P.M.; closed Mon.

Temptations specializes in high-end, artistic, calories-be-damned Italian pastries (and, by the way, they are kosher too, to appeal to residents of neighboring Borough Park, where the bakers are more subdued). You've probably never seen anything like the window display, a look-alike Madame Alexander doll in a wedding dress made of frosting and cake. The blueberry tart struts a lush pile of fresh unadorned blueberries, the apple turnover is sensuously overstuffed, and the opera cake is classy enough to debut at the Met.

18TH AVENUE AND VICINITY

✪ **Aiello Brothers Cheese Company.** 7609 18th Avenue. 256-1151. Open 5 A.M.–6 P.M. Close 11 A.M. on Sat. Closed Sun.

After twelve generations in the cheese business, the Aiellos have got the recipe down pat, and indeed this 40,000-pound-per-week cheese manufacturer is famous for their incredibly satisfying mozzarella (salted, unsalted, smoked, part skim, rolled with fillings such as proscuitto). Don't miss a stop here.

✪ **Alba.** 7001 18th Avenue, corner of 70th Street, 232-2122. Daily, 8:30 A.M.–8 P.M.

"Internationally famous for four generations" is what Alba's card says. With pastries this fabulous, it is easy to see why this bakery has been in business since 1932. The specialties are cream-filled confections. Everything is artfully done. One of the best products is a strawberry layer cake with whipped cream.

Angelo's Bakery. 2482 86th Street, near 25th Avenue, 372-3866. Tues.–Sun., 8 A.M.–7 P.M.; closed Mon.

Angelo's is a few minutes' drive away from the center of Bensonhurst, but customers have been taking the extra time to shop here for more than thirty-five years. The selection includes artful marzipan, cookies, and semolina bread, as well as Italian cheesecake, luscious strawberry shortcake, and banana cream pie. Along traditional lines, they make *pipatelle* (biscuits); tiramisù (made with mascarpone, Italian cream cheese); *sanguinaccio* (a folk dish with mysterious ingredients); and *gelati di campana* (which comes in the red, white, and green colors of the Italian flag).

Bari Pork Store. 7119 18th Avenue, near 71st Street, 266-9300. Mon.–Sat., 8 A.M.–7 P.M.; Sun., 8 A.M.–2 P.M.

In this era of lean cuisine, the words PORK STORE (and there are many such stores throughout Brooklyn) can evoke flashing red lights for health-conscious consumers. However, this store also sells low-cholesterol, low-sodium meats and cold cuts. The traditional southern Italian foods are fresh and truly tasty: fresh mozzarella and scamorza cheese, pizza rustica (which looks like apple pie but is filled with dried sausage and cheeses), homemade veal, pepper-onion, and broccoli-rabe sausages. Bari, by the way, is the name of a province in the Apulia region of Italy from which many of the local residents hailed. The place is especially crowded on Saturday.

18th Avenue Bakery. 6016 18th Avenue, at 60th Street, 256-2441. Daily, 8 A.M.–7 P.M.

Beautiful big loaves of raisin bread, semolina, lard bread, and more come out of the ovens here. Already fifty years old, this bakery is here for keeps.

✪ **18th Avenue Fruit and Vegetable Market,** corner 69th Street, 331-0766. Mon.–Sat., 8 A.M.–8 P.M.; closed Sun.

A cornucopia wouldn't be big enough to hold all the fresh fruits and vegetables you will want to buy at this overflowing Russian-style fruit stand. It stretches around the corner, and while the decor ain't nothing fancy, you can get hard-to-find petite artichokes, three different price levels of fresh apricots, several types of plump, purple eggplant, fistfuls of parsley, giant garlics, and a zillion other fresh ingredients essential to the discerning Italian cook.

Europa Bakery. 6423 20th Avenue, near 64th Street, 232-4845. Mon.–Sat., 7 A.M.–10 P.M.; Sun., 7 A.M.–9 P.M.

Europa has a broad variety of treats, including marzipan surprises, cakes, cookies, and pastries that look almost too good to eat. Or ask them to ship.

International Food. 7108 18th Avenue, near 71st Street, 259-6576. Mon.–Sat., 8 A.M.–6:30 P.M.; Sun., 8 A.M.–4 P.M.

We've included this store more for sociological than culinary reasons. As of mid-1998, this is the only Russian deli on Italian 18th Avenue. The foods are all labeled in Russian only, which suggests that the local Italian residents are not yet sold on *kasha varnishkes.* The underwhelmingly friendly staff sell big brochettes of beef, matzo balls, barley, bags of poppyseed, made-in-Brooklyn Russian breads, and other distinctly ethnic (but un-Italian) foods.

✪ **Pastosa Ravioli.** 7425 New Utrecht Avenue, near 75th Street, 236-9615. Mon.–Sat., 8:30 A.M.–6 P.M.; Sun., 8:30 A.M.–3 P.M.

Headquarters of a small pasta empire, Pastosa has four stores in Brooklyn alone and about a dozen in the tristate area. Each store makes pasta daily. With thirty-five years of experience, they've got their recipes right for home made ravioli, proscuitto balls, artichoke salad, stuffed mushrooms, meatballs, and sauces.

✪ **Prodotti Alimentari Italiani, Giordano and Sons.** 7614 17th Avenue, between 76th and 77th streets, 837-7200. Mon.–Sat., 8 A.M.–7 P.M.; Sun., 8 A.M.–2 P.M. No credit cards.

You could go to other specialty food stores and spend twice as much on Italian imported goods, but don't bother—the owner here prides himself on selling absolutely nothing American-made. This is a great source for imported Italian cheese, Italian salami, Italian olives, and lots of Italian-made pasta. For people who've just arrived from Italy, it's the closest thing they'll find to their hometown supermarket.

Queen Ann Ravioli. 7205 18th Avenue, near 72nd Street, 256-1061. Tues.–Sat., 9 A.M.–6 P.M.; Sun., 8 A.M.–2 P.M.; closed Mon.

The pasta sold here is made in the huge modern facility visible at the back of the store. Pasta doesn't come any fresher unless you make it yourself. Condiments and bottles of strained fresh tomatoes are also available to round out the menu.

✪ **Royal Crown Pastry Shop.** 6308 14th Avenue, near 63rd Street, 234-3208.

For Italian bread?

THE BEST.

One of Brooklyn's best bets.

Sbarro. 1705 65th Street, corner of 17th Avenue, 331-8808. Mon.–Fri., 8 A.M.–7 P.M.; Sat. and Sun., 8 A.M.–8 P.M.

Most folks know Sbarro as a pizza and pasta shop in their local mall, but this is Sbarro's original store, still in the same location since it opened in 1959. This excellent shop sells salads, pasta, gift packages, and a roster of prepared foods for catering. A display of photos and news clippings tells the proud family's story of success.

Tony's Focacceria. 2313 86th Street, near 23rd Avenue, 946-5700. Daily, 9 A.M.–9 P.M.

Locals swear by Tony's, an eat-in pizzeria and *tavola calda,* a kind of Italian deli. They have a large menu of delicious Italian foods—hot and cold hero sandwiches, baked clams and mussels marinara, broccoli rabe, spinach rolls, lasagna, and Sicilian ricotta rice balls. Cold buffets can be arranged for parties of ten or more. Delivery is also available.

✪ **Trunzo Brothers.** 6802 18th Avenue, corner of 68th Street, 331-2111. Mon.–Sat., 8 A.M.–7 P.M.; Sun., 8 A.M.–2 P.M.

This is a one-stop-shopping source for Italian foods. Imagine all of those little mom-and-pop Italian food shops rolled into one *latticina frescha*-grocery-dairy-deli-*salumeria*. The sandwiches are mouthwatering. Also try the mozzarella rolled with spinach, the *soppressa*, and the ready-to-bake homemade minipizzas.

✪ **Villabate.** 7117 18th Avenue, between 71st and 72nd streets, 331-8430. Daily, 7 A.M.–9 P.M.

A whiff of almond greets you when you walk in. Your eyes will spin from the swirls of vanilla, gobs of chocolate, and mounds of oversized strawberries in one display case, and spring-colored pistachio, lemon, and orange layer cakes. Just to recover from sensory overload, you'll have to replenish yourself with one of the all-time favorites: cannoli cream stuffed into shells, chocolate fudge rolls, or zabaglione.

✪ **Virabella Bakery.** 2278 86th Street, near 23rd Avenue, 449-3384. Daily, 7 A.M.–9 P.M.

An espresso bar in this bakery is a welcome sight, since you'll want some coffee or gelati to wash down the extraordinary cannoli, *bocconcini*, and other pastries. The beautifully shaped marzipan in the form of fruits and animals get high marks on both looks and taste.

Food for an Italian Pastry Tray

Where there's an Italian neighborhood, there are great bakeries. Try the following:
gelati di campana—rich ice cream
marzipan—almond paste molded in shapes of fruits
pipalette—cookies
zabaglione—a sweet froth made of eggs, sugar, and wine
tiramisù—light, sweet pudding of mascarpone, Italian cream cheese
zucotto—a soft cake made with cream
cannoli—rich cream-filled rolled pastry

Interesting Neighborhood Shops

✪ **Arcobaleno. 7306 18th Avenue, near 73rd Street, 259-7951. Daily, 10 A.M.–10 P.M.**

From compact discs to videotapes, this store stocks a full line of imported Italian music and movies. Many customers are locals and recent arrivals from Italy who like to keep in touch with Italian popular culture.

Berta 67. 6510 18th Avenue, near 65th Street, 232-4084. Mon.–Wed., 9:30 A.M.–7 P.M.; Thurs. and Sat., 9 A.M.–9 P.M.; Sun., 10 A.M.–6 P.M.

Prices at this department store are cheap, cheap, cheap. Shelves and racks are jammed with women's and children's wear, housewares, dishes, sheets, and luggage. Brand names include French Toast, Gitano, and Ocean Pacific. A few doors down, at 6708 18th Avenue, Berta's sells discount housewares, such as toasters, blenders, and microwave ovens by Hamilton Beach, Corning, and Wearever; discount bed and bath items by Fieldcrest, Springmaid, and Martex; plus gift items by Lenox, Murano, and Studio Nova. Berta 67 has stores throughout Brooklyn, at 2151 86th Street, 712 Brighton Beach Avenue, and 1120 Kings Highway.

Branna Bridal. 7518 18th Avenue, between 75th and 76th streets, 837-7223. Mon.–Sat., 10 A.M.–5 P.M.; Thurs., 10 A.M.–8 P.M.

Weddings are serious business here. The loveliest of several bridal specialty stores in the neighborhood, this small shop specializes in custom headpieces, dyeable shoes, and accessories for the bride and bridesmaid. An appointment is recommended.

Festival. 6412 18th Avenue, near 64th Street, 259-3811. Mon.–Wed. and Fri., 10 A.M.–7 P.M.; Thurs., 10 A.M.–8 P.M.; Sat., 10 A.M.–8 P.M.

Better children's wear for both boys and girls from layette to size 14 is sold here. Special items include boys' $200 white silk communion suits, $200 imported Italian christening gowns of organza and satin, and the Chico line, in addition to a good selection of everyday clothes.

✪ **Fiorentino.** 7102 18th Avenue, corner 71st Street, 234-2861 Mon.–Sat., 10 A.M.–6 P.M.; closed Sun.

It's worth a trip from brownstone Brooklyn to shop here for Italian-imported gold jewelry for men and women as well as classy silver gift items. The family business started in Palermo in the 1920s, and Fiorentino has been in business in Bensonhurst since the early 1990s.

Healing Treasure. 7618 18th Avenue at 76th Street, 621-0889. Mon.–Sat., 10 A.M.–7 P.M.; closed Sun.

It's hard to believe that there's a Chinese presence in Bensonhurst, but here it is: old Italian men buying herbal remedies for high blood pressure, and getting acupuncture treatment at this typical Chinese herbalist, with Chinese writing on the walls. The owner claims that the cultures are similar, with a strong emphasis on extended family life and family loyalty. There are a few Chinese markets on the street as well.

✪ **House of Costumes.** 7113-13th Avenue, near 71st Street, 833-7474. Mon.–Sat., 10 A.M.–6 P.M.

Angelo and Theresa Casale have been doing a year-round business in make-believe for more than thirty years. Their costume- and-balloon-filled store is a favorite at Halloween of course, but also at Christmas, birthdays, and, as they are close to Borough Park, Purim.

Among their hundred different costumes you'll recognize many mass-produced cartoon character outfits, but the best ones are the classics hanging from the ceiling rack: Nutcracker tin soldiers, Cleopatras, and circus ringmasters, designed and sewn by Theresa over the years. You can order a custom costume (allowing a couple of months' lead time) but Theresa will do free alterations of existing originals. This is an almost-dying art, so shut your eyes and make a wish, like Tinkerbell, that Theresa's carpal tunnel syndrome, a result of years of sewing, gets better.

Husband Angelo, an artistic retired model boat maker, does inventive balloon creations for parties. They are a team worthy of a children's tale: the Smithsonian Museum in Washington, D.C., displays a model boat for which he built the miniature rigging and she sewed the sails.

La Casa de la Bomboniera. 6915 18th Avenue, between Bay Ridge Avenue and 79th Street, 232-0230. Mon–Sat., 10 A.M.–6 P.M.; Thurs., 10 A.M.–8 P.M.

For that special wedding present, you will find gifts, china, crystal, and collectibles at this store. Many items are imported from Italy, including honeymoon lingerie, sold upstairs.

Maggio Music. 8403 18th Avenue, corner of 84th Street, 259-4468. Mon.–Fri., 1–9 P.M.; Sat., 10 A.M.–6 P.M.; closed Sun.

This father-son business has been in the Maggio family for forty-five years, but that doesn't mean it is old-fashioned. Electronic instruments are crammed into this small space, from electric guitars and beginner keyboards to top-of-the-line synthesizers. They also give lessons to kids ages six and up. Come with a sense of humor for amiable banter with the owners.

Male Attitude Clothing. 2084 86th Street, near 20th Avenue, 449-7518. Mon.–Fri., 10 A.M.–6 P.M.; Thurs.–Fri., 10 A.M.–8 P.M.; Sat., 10 A.M.–7 P.M.; closed Sun.

Tired of looking like a trout fisher, a tennis pro, or a buttoned-up Wall Street lawyer? The fashionable, high-quality men's sports clothes here are sharp, sexy, and Italian. These moderately priced to expensive items won't be found in most brownstone Brooklyn clothing stores, which tend more toward T-shirts, khaki, denim, and unisex clothes.

✪ **Mini Mansions.** 1710 86th Street, near 17th Avenue, 331-7992. Daily, 11 A.M.–6 P.M.

Brooklyn's largest independent dollhouse store, run by a husband-and-wife team, is a treasure trove of miniatures for both children and adult collectors. A range of large, unusual dollhouses, including mock Brooklyn brownstones, start at $350. Any accessory you can think of, from people to pool tables to chandeliers, is sold here starting at about $5. Carpeting, linoleum, electrical lighting, furniture of any period, and even landscaping, can be installed in your model house. Work is done on the premises, and the prices are lower than those in Manhattan.

S.A.S. Italian Records. 7113 18th Avenue, near 71st Street, 331-0539 or 331-0540. Mon.–Sat., 10 A.M.–9 P.M.; Sun., 10 A.M.–8 P.M.

If you want the sounds, sights, and smells of contemporary Italian life, pop in here to pick up Italian popular music, videotapes, soaps, and toiletries. Great for expatriates, and not a bad bargain for other New Yorkers who, for the price of a subway token and a tape, can imagine themselves on the Spanish Steps in Rome.

Something Else. 2051 86th Street, near 20th Avenue, 372-1900. Tues.–Sat., 10 A.M.–6 P.M.; Thurs., 10 A.M.–8 P.M.

Trendy casual clothing for women is the specialty here. The look is young, with lots of cotton shorts and slacks, appliquéd denim jumpsuits, and party dresses. Prices are moderate, ranging from $40 for pants to $130 and up for cocktail dresses.

Toys " Я " Us. 8793 Bay Parkway, at 87th Street and the waterfront, 372-4646. Mon.–Sat., 9:30 A.M.–9:30 P.M.; Sun., 10 A.M.–6 P.M.

Toys " Я " Us needs no introduction; Brooklyn has several. You can easily get lost in this chain store's warehouse of toys, clothing, games, layette equipment, and more. Many people come here to load up on heavily discounted essentials, such as disposable diapers and jars of baby food, and for big-ticket items, such as bikes.

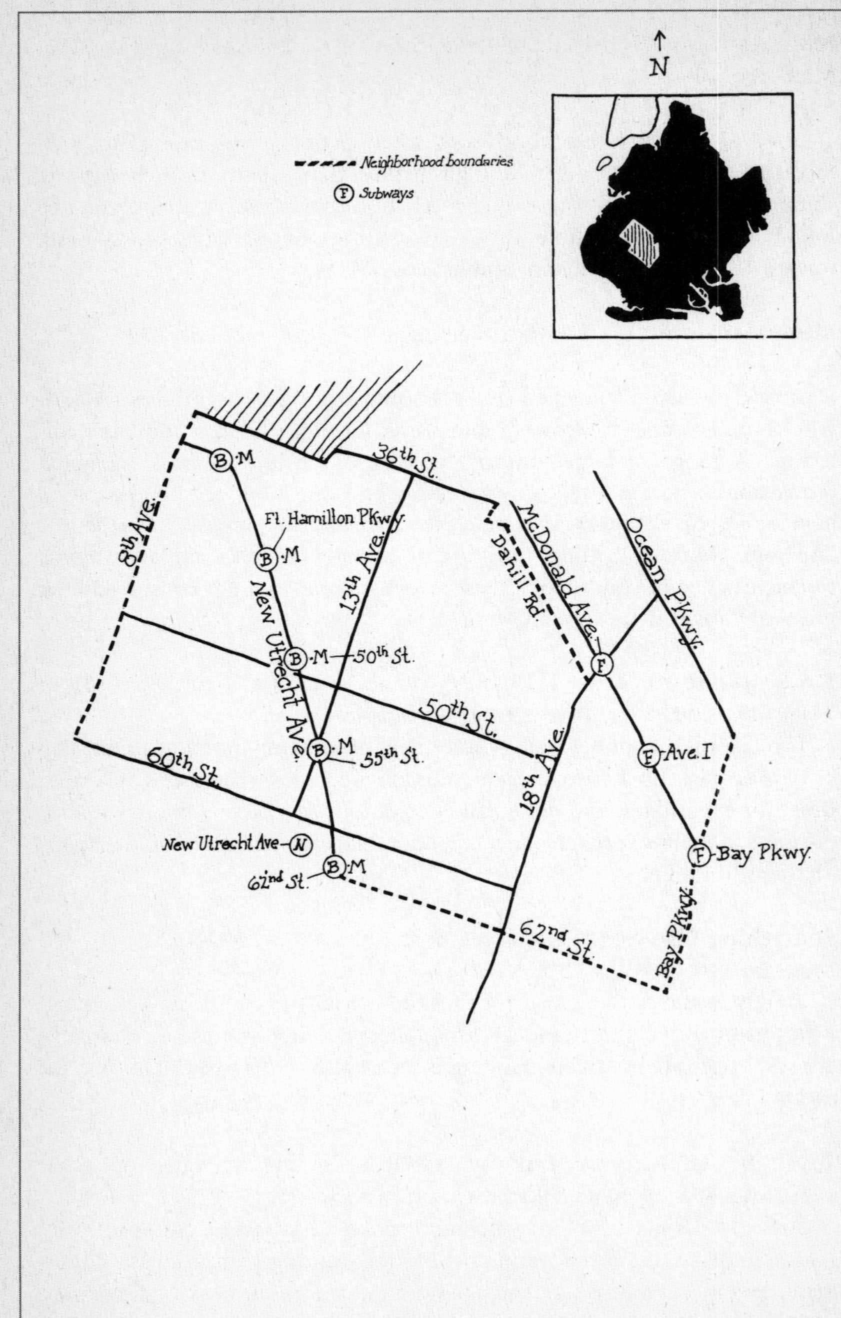
N
Neighborhood boundaries
F Subways
36th St.
8th Ave.
B·M
Ft. Hamilton PKwy.
B·M
New Utrecht Ave.
13th Ave.
B·M—50th St.
50th St.
B·M
55th St.
60th St.
New Utrecht Ave—N
B·M
62nd St.
McDonald Ave.
Dahill Rd.
Ocean PKwy.
F
18th Ave.
F-Ave. I
F-Bay Pkwy.
Bay Pkwy.
62nd St.

Borough Park

Where it is: Bounded by Fort Hamilton Parkway and 18th Avenue and by 38th Street and New Utrecht Avenue.

What's nearby: Bay Ridge, Bensonhurst, Flatbush, Midwood, Park Slope, Sunset Park.

How to get there:

By car: Take the BQE to the Prospect Expressway. Stay in the left lane (do *not* follow the signs to Staten Island) and exit at Fort Hamilton Parkway. Follow the cross streets (40th to 65th streets) to 13th, 16th, or 18th Avenue.

By subway: B or M train to Fort Hamilton Parkway.

Cab services: Natanya (436-2448) and Punctual (972-6100). Fares are about $17 to Grand Central Station, $10 to Brooklyn Heights.

Special events: The neighborhood is colorful during holidays. Stand on a busy street corner and watch the passing scene at the springtime holiday of Purim; the celebration is as close as Orthodox Jews get to a carnival. Locals dress in costume, perform clownish skits, and deliver baskets of food, called *schlachmonos*, to neighbors and friends. During the autumn holiday of Sukkoth, stroll past the many sukkahs, small thatched-roof huts in which meals are eaten. Prior to Passover, Borough Park stores sell all kinds of provisions, from handmade matzohs to silver seder plates.

How it got its name: This area was named after a large real estate development, Borough Park, east of New Utrecht Avenue.

ABOUT THE NEIGHBORHOOD

If we could use a single word to describe Borough Park's main attraction for most visitors, it would be *discount*. You can find just about anything, from housewares to top-of-the-line silver, linens, and fine china, at 10 to 50 percent below department store prices. From top-quality children's clothing at

Rachel's Boutique, to women's undergarments at **Underworld Plaza**, hats and accessories at **Gold's Trimmings**, suitcases at **A to Z Luggage**, and designer sheets at **D'Rose Linen's**, Borough Park is a discount shopper's heaven.

Those with an interest in things Jewish couldn't find a more authentic Orthodox community, replete with synagogues, yeshivas (religious schools), many Jewish bookstores and even the **Jewish Youth Library**. Kosher food stores aplenty offer the traditional chopped liver, chicken soup, eggplant salad, and baked goods. **Taam Eden** is a dairy restaurant straight out of Tel Aviv. Seafood lovers—kosher or not—will be thrilled with Brooklyn's widely acclaimed seafood restaurant, **Ossie's**, located here.

Borough Park is a formidable Jewish melting pot of immigrants from Israel, Russia, and Europe, plus members of more than twenty Hasidic sects, such as the Satmar, Bobov, and Belz. The air is filled with a babel of English, Yiddish, Hebrew, Russian, and various Eastern European languages. This is no accident—Borough Park is reputed to have the highest concentration of Orthodox Jews outside of Israel. The focus here, where four or more children per family is more the norm than the exception, is on family life. Numerous hat and wig shops reflect the Orthodox requirement that Jewish men and their wives cover their heads. In the weeks before Passover you can watch a centuries-old tradition being reiterated at the **Shmura Matzoh Factory**.

If you want a feel for the pace of the Orthodox Jewish life-style, visit Borough Park early on a Friday afternoon. During this pre-Sabbath rush hour (several hours before sundown), scholarly looking bearded men in black coats wait in line to buy foot-long challahs (traditional braided egg breads). Women with multiple children in tow rush to finish last-minute food shopping. Solemnly dressed schoolchildren, the boys in yarmulkes, play on the sidewalks. From the start of the Sabbath on Friday evening until its completion on Saturday evening, this community does not drive, turn on electricity, carry or use money, or conduct business. By late Friday afternoon the streets are completely devoid of activity, save groups of men and some women walking to synagogue.

Historical Notes

In the 1880s the Litchfield family, major landowners who also owned the vast area that became Prospect Park, developed a settlement in this area and called it Blythebourne. A nearby tract was called Borough Park. As the tale goes, a local realtor tried to convince Mrs. William B. Litchfield to sell Blythebourne, warning her that real estate values would plummet in rural Brooklyn as Jews fleeing pogroms in Eastern Europe invaded the area. She refused to sell. As it turned out, there was indeed an influx of refugee Jews into Borough Park. However, land values rose and Borough Park expanded, eventually overtaking Blythebourne. Today the only trace of Blythebourne is in the name of the Borough Park post office.

Borough Park has seen at least four waves of Jewish immigrants. The first group arrived at the turn of the century, marked by the construction of the synagogue that is now home of **Congregation Anshe Lubawitz**, at 4022 12th Avenue, and to **Temple Emanu-el**, at 1364 49th Street. The second wave arrived after World War I, as new train and trolley tracks made the area more accessible to Jewish residents of Williamsburg and Manhattan's Lower East Side. Another group fled Europe before and after World War II and the Holocaust. Since the 1970s, immigrants from Russia, Hungary, Poland, Romania, and Israel have come to Borough Park.

Shopping Areas

The majority of shops line 13th Avenue between 39th and 54th streets; others are scattered throughout the area. Some new stores have a spiffy, Madison Avenue look, but a few are overstuffed with a jumble of goods. Don't worry—there is a method to the madness and you'll get plenty of help if you ask for it.

Shopper's advisory: (1) Don't even *think* of setting out for a shopping expedition to Borough Park on Friday night or Saturday. Everything shuts down for the Sabbath. Most shops close early on Friday, are closed on Saturday, and are very busy on Sunday. If you can, shop during the week. (2) To feel comfortable in this neighborhood, it helps to "go native" a bit. Both women and men are advised to avoid short shorts and other scanty clothing, in keeping with the modest dress code of Borough Park residents. (3) In the kosher tradition, restaurants serving dairy meals such as pancakes or blintzes do not serve meat, and vice versa.

Kidstuff

It would be an understatement to say that this is a neighborhood geared toward children; there are children absolutely *everywhere*. If you have little ones, bring a supply of quarters for the mechanical rides on just about every block along 13th Avenue. There are many informal, inexpensive places to eat, such as (kosher) pizzerias. **Teacher's Pet** and **Scribbles** sell practical, fun, and inexpensive items. Nearby is **Train World**, which will be of interest to school-age kids. If the shopping doesn't tire the kids out, there is a playground nearby.

PARKS AND PLAYGROUNDS

Borough Park Playground. 18th Avenue, between 56th and 57th streets. The kids will enjoy the climbing equipment and basketball courts here.

Avid tennis players will be thrilled to discover nicely paved tennis courts that often sit empty.

Hockey rink, Joseph diGilio Park, corner of Ditmas, 18th and McDonald avenues.

There's a story behind this spanking-new renovated hockey rink, tucked under the elevated F train. It's about Joe Natoli, the handyman and fireman at local Brooklyn Public School 321. Joe has been the driving force behind the South Brooklyn Hockey League, which has grown over the decade from a bunch of roller hockey nuts to a dedicated 400-person league of 5-to-17-year-olds who play every weekend. Joe and a few buddies spent about seven years negotiating to get the city to allow them to renovate a beat-up rink, and finally, with several hundred thousand dollars of city money and zillions of hours of free labor, hammered and sawed and poured concrete at this site. He's proudest of the pro-level boards and bleachers. "It took us seven years to build it but I promised all these kids I'd build them a real rink and I did it." A Brooklyn hero.

POINTS OF CULTURAL INTEREST

Bobover Hassidic World Headquarters. 4909 15th Avenue, near 49th Street, 853-7900.

The Bobover sect is one of the largest Hasidic groups in Borough Park. Hasidism was born around 1800 in Eastern Europe as a populist revolt against a stringently intellectual Talmudic tradition. Religious but unlearned Jews led by charismatic leaders (*rebbes*) created an alternative approach, stressing joyous prayer over scholarship and illustrative moralistic tales (*midrash*) over legalisms. Most of Borough Park's Hasidic population arrived here after World War II. Today many Hasidic sects have themselves become insular, differing from one another in ways only the initiated might appreciate. Unlike most large synagogues, this one has no fixed pews, platform (*bimah*), or tables. Instead, the abundant floor space better accommodates the crowds of men praying, singing, and dancing when the revered Bobover Rebbe holds a gathering, which in these parts is called a *tish*.

Congregation Anshe Lubawitz. 4022 12th Avenue, at 40th Street, 436-2200.

This 1906 synagogue, originally known as Temple Beth El, was the first built in the area and became a haven for many Jews seeking to escape the overcrowding and slumlike conditions of Manhattan's Lower East Side. In 1916 the opening of the subway lines (B train) that connected Borough Park to Manhattan and Coney Island further increased the area's accessibility and created a housing boom. Today there are more than seventy-five active Orthodox congregations in Borough Park, including Russians, the most recent wave of Jewish immigrants to New York.

Jewish Youth Library. 1461 46th Street, between 14th and 15th avenues, 435-4711. Open afternoons; closed Sat. Call to check hours.

Jewish books for kids make this library unique. There are preschooler volumes in English that cover a wide range of Jewish topics. Visitors can use the comfortable reading room or borrow books with a $15 annual membership. Some volumes are also available in Hebrew and Yiddish.

✪ **Shmura Matzoh Factory.** 36th Street, end of 13th Avenue, 438-2006. Open in the pre-Passover season only. Call for hours.

There are a handful of Orthodox handmade matzo factories in Borough Park and Williamsburg, and it's worth a visit for those interested in T*R*A*D*I*T*I*O*N. Open only in the period before Passover, these hole-in-the-wall bakeries produce the most kosher of matzo, called *schmura. Schmura* means "watched," and there is a complement of rabbis on hand to watch the clock and the workers: Jewish law stipulates that to be kosher, matzo must be unleavened and cannot touch any leavened dough, and the entire process must not exceed eighteen minutes. Each time the dozens of workers complete a round, all utensils are changed, washed, and inspected, to avoid contact between batches. Don't expect to stay long; everyone is bustling about, and the place is not set up for tourists. No bare thighs or arms are permitted in this religious environment.

NOTABLE BOROUGH PARK RESTAURANTS

Two quite different restaurants in Borough Park stand out from the others:

✪ **Ossie's Table.** 1314 50th Street, near 13th Avenue, 435-0635. Sun.–Thurs., 11 A.M.–3 P.M. and 5–10:30 P.M.; Sat., 8:30 P.M.–midnight.

Unlike most kosher restaurants, Ossie's offers elegant, upscale dining. There is a wide selection of fish, all fresh. This is no surprise, given that the restaurant is owned by the same people who run the fish store next door, which has been in the neighborhood since 1966. The crowd is mixed: Hasidic, modern Orthodox, and everyone else. Homemade breads and desserts and outdoor seating in fine weather make this a great seafood dining option.

Red's Brick Oven Pizza. 3712 13th Avenue, between 37th and 38th streets, 436-1818. Tues.–Thurs. and Sun., noon–10 P.M.; Fri.–Sat., noon–11 P.M.

You'll never settle for ordinary pizza again. Red's, situated at the end of Borough Park's main shopping street, has a eighty-year-old brick oven that turns out light, crispy, absolutely scrumptious pies ($9.50), calzone ($3.50), and rolls. The "small" broccoli roll ($3.50), for example, is loaded with cheese and fresh broccoli and is easily a meal in itself. The pizza is fantastic—crispy with fresh crushed tomato sauce and little if any oil. The food and relaxing atmosphere (complete with a stuffed shark on the wall) make this a welcome retreat. This restaurant is not kosher.

Other restaurants include the following:

Cafe Shalva. 1305 53rd Street, near 13th Avenue, 851-1970. Mon.–Thurs. and Sun., 10 A.M.–6 P.M.; closes in midafternoon on Fri.; closed Sat.

For a pick-me-up while shopping, try the cappuccino and espresso at this unpretentious coffee shop. There's also a small lunch menu, and everything is kosher. Prices are low, low, low.

Taam Eden Kosher Dairy Restaurant. 5001 13th Avenue, near 50th Street, (800) 303-2522. Mon.–Thurs., 7 A.M–11 P.M.; Fri 7 A.M.–4 P.M.; Sun., 7 A.M.–6 P.M.; closed Sat.

If it is homestyle Jewish cooking you want, stop here. This tiny spot, with only five booths and a dozen seats at the counter, is where you'll taste the real thing: smoked whitefish salad, gefilte fish, stuffed cabbage, pea and dumpling soup, matzo ball soup, and, of course, knishes. Inexpensive and tasty, kids will love this place. Takeout is available. The name, by the way, means "Taste of Eden."

Food for a Traditional Jewish Feast

matzo ball soup
potato, kasha, and spinach knishes
chopped liver
challah or rye bread
dill pickles
baked salmon salad
babka cake
halvah

SHOPPING

Specialty Food Shops

A Touch of Spirit. 4720 16th Avenue, near 47th Street, 438-2409. Sun.–Thurs., 11 A.M.–6 P.M.; Fri., 10 A.M.–2 P.M. Closed Sat.

Manischewitz wine is not the only game in town. Owner Pinchus Wienberger has assembled over 170 kinds of kosher wine here, including Italian, French, and Californian varieties—and most *won't* remind you of the Passover seders of yesteryear. They will deliver in the neighborhood. (This is one of several such wine stores in Brooklyn.)

Fine-Ess Kosher Ice Cream. 4905 13th Avenue, near 49th Street, 436-1909. Mon.–Thurs. and Sun., 10 A.M.–8 P.M.; closes in midafternoon on Fri.; closed Sat.

Check out the tofu and nondairy ice cream, as well as standard fare. The novelty ice-cream cigars, parfait cups, and seashells are fun for a party. After an afternoon of shopping, this is a winner with the kids.

✪ **Korn's.** 5004 16th Avenue, near 50th Street, 851-0268 or 633-7466. Mon.–Thurs. and Sun., 6 A.M.–9 P.M.; closes Fri. in midafternoon; closed Sat.

Korn's has all of those Jewish baked goodies your bubba used to bring over, like great rye breads and huge challahs. For dessert try the rugalach, babka, and other freezable noshes. There are other branches on 12th Avenue near 49th Street, 15th Avenue near 43rd Street, and 18th Avenue near 41st Street.

Oneg Take Home Foods. 4911 12th Avenue, between 49th and 50th streets, 438-3388. Mon.–Thurs. and Sun., 9 A.M.–7 P.M.; closes Fri. in midafternoon; closed Sat.

Got a cold, or just a yen for traditional Jewish food? Of course, bubbie, there is chicken soup and schmaltz here. But eat, eat! Try the stuffed cabbage, corned beef, pastrami, potato knishes, or one of three dozen prepared salads. The store is conveniently located across from the 50th Street station, where you can catch the B and M trains. On Thursday and Friday, orders over $15 can be delivered to other Brooklyn neighborhoods. The food is kosher.

Ossie's. 1314 50th Street, near 13th Avenue, 436-4100. Mon.–Thurs., 7 A.M.–7 P.M.; closes Fri. in midafternoon; Sun., 8 A.M.–4 P.M.; closed Sat.

Some of the excellent take-home items made here are also sold at Zabar's in Manhattan and come highly recommended: whitefish with almonds and raisins, pastrami-cured carp, and, most particularly, baked brook trout filled with spinach and garlic—all kosher. Ossie's also has a very popular restaurant next door (see **Ossie's Table,** page 61).

✪ **Schwartz Appetizing.** 4824 16th Avenue, near 48th Street, 851-1011. Sun.–Thurs., 9 A.M.–6 P.M.; Fri., 9 A.M.–2 P.M.; closed Sat.

"Herring has been good to us, thank G-d." Schwartz Appetizing started with herring a generation ago, and today they still sell famously delicious herrings as well as over a dozen special homemade dips. Try the vegetarian pâté, spinach or tomato dip, and bring home some of the many fresh salads made daily. Great for a picnic or quick at-home meal. Kosher.

Scotto's Bakery and Pastry. 3807 13th Avenue, corner 38th Street, 438-0889. Daily, 7 A.M.–9 P.M. Cash only.

On the outskirts of Borough Park, here's a gorgeous, classical Italian bakery in its full splendor, with white creamy-icing cakes filled with chocolate crèmes, butter cookies, extraordinary pastries, and refreshing cappuccino. Nip in here when you experience shoppers' overload after bargain-hunting on 13th Avenue.

Strauss Bakery. 5115 and 5309 13th Avenue, near 51st and 53rd streets, 851-7728. Mon.–Thurs. and Sun., 6 A.M.–7 P.M.; closes early on Fri.; closed Sat.

Yum—cream cakes! Napoleons! Roll your eyes if you've tasted heaven. Everything here is kosher, to boot.

Tiferes Heimishe Bakery. 4016 13th Avenue near 40th Street, 972-6026. Sun.–Thurs., 8 A.M.– 6 P.M.; Fri., 8 A.M.–2 P.M.; closed Sat.

"Everything by the hand, like my own grandmother's recipe," is how the grandfatherly owner of this tiny bakery describes his irresistible pastries called "flakes," and "kokosh" (cocoa) cakes. Come in for a whiff of Old World Hungarian baking and a bag of freshly made baked goods. Cholesterol watchers note: the goods are "parve," so eggs may be used but butter is not.

Weiss Homemade Kosher Bakery. 5011 13th Avenue, near 50th Street, 438-0407. Mon.–Thurs. and Sun., 6 A.M.–8 P.M.; closes Fri. in midafternoon; closed Sat.

Judging from the number of customers and what they're buying, everything here must be tasty. The home-baked six-grain bread is particularly healthy and delicious. This is a good place to treat the kids after shopping.

Womens' Clothing and Accessories

All That Glitters. 4705 18th Ave, near 47th Street, 853-8789. Sun.–Thurs., 11 A.M.–6 P.M.; Fri., 10 A.M.–2 P.M.; closed Sat.

Gents, here's a good place to look for a special piece of jewelry for that gal in your life. Or, ladies, come and buy for yourself. Upscale, up-to-date, and expensive, these 14- and 18-karat gold necklaces, diamond pins, and pearl earrings are contemporary classics designed by the names such as Jose Jess, Penny Preville, and Doris Danos, whose jewelry is sometimes advertised in *Town and Country*–type magazines, or sold in leading department stores. You can count on getting a good price at this lovely shop.

A Touch of Class. 4921 16th Avenue, between 49th and 50th streets, 854-6814. Sun.–Thurs., 11:30 A.M.–6 P.M.; Fri., 11:30 A.M.–2 P.M.; closed Sat.

A Touch of Class sells top-of-the-line women's imported suits and sports clothes by designers such as Valentino, Ungaro, and Iceberg at prices that are high but not quite stratospheric. Suits start at $900, sportswear at $300. Founded almost twenty years ago by a trio of housewives named Bayla, Chedva, and Miri, this boutique's high style makes it one of Borough Park's more unusual "finds."

Beauty Fashion Wigs. 4517 13th Avenue, near 45th Street, 871-1366. Mon.–Thurs., 10 A.M.–6 P.M.; closes Fri. in midafternoon; closed Sat.

If you want or need a high-quality wig, this is a good place to go. Following Orthodox tradition, just about all of the women in this neighborhood wear hats, scarves, or wigs to cover their hair when in public. This store is reputed to be one of the best of its kind in the neighborhood.

Brenda's. 4518 18th Avenue between 45th and 46th streets, 435-1073. Mon.–Thurs., 10:30 A.M.–6 P.M.; Sun., 10 A.M.–5:30 P.M., and Fri., 10 A.M.–2:30 P.M.

This shop carries better clothing for women, ranging from blouses, skirts, dresses, and sportswear, with brand names including Calvin Klein and Donna Karan, with modest styles catering to the religious customer. The store is run by three siblings who lost both parents at an early age, and it is now named after their deceased mother, Brenda, who started the business nearly twenty years ago.

Coat Plaza. 4414 13th Avenue, between 44th and 45th streets, 972-2682. Mon.–Thurs. and Sun., 10 A.M.–6 P.M.; closes Fri. in midafternoon; closed Sat.

Coat Plaza has a good selection of classic raincoats and conservative wool coats at 25 percent or more below department store prices. The inventory changes frequently, so call ahead if you're looking for a particular designer.

Gold's Trimmings & Accessories. 4710 13th Avenue, near 47th Street, 633-3009. Mon.–Thurs., 10 A.M.–7 P.M.; closes Fri. in midafternoon; Sun., 10:30 A.M.–5 P.M.; closed Sat.

Hats are coming back in style, so don't be surprised at the high-fashion numbers sold here in Borough Park. This store appeals not just to the local Orthodox women for whom covering the hair is de rigueur—hat lovers come from all over to get simple $20 berets or exuberant, flashy styles costing well over $100. Gold's has belts and other accessories as well. Go downstairs for an excellent sewing and notions department.

Hindy's Maternity. 4902 New Utrecht Avenue, corner of 49th Street, 438-3840. Mon.–Thurs. and Sun., 11 A.M.–5:30 P.M.; closes Fri. in midafternoon; closed Sat.

Expecting a baby? Check out both of Hindy's stores. The New Utrecht Avenue location sells it all, from bathing suits and underwear to coats. They'll also sew fancy maternity clothes in fine fabrics to order. For maternity closeouts try the second store, at 4307 13th Avenue, near 43rd Street (438-2453).

✪ **Larisa Design Studio, Inc.** 4313 13th Avenue, near 43rd Street, 436-2022 or (212) 695-8989. Sun.–Thurs., 11 A.M.–6 P.M.; Fri., 11 A.M.–2 P.M.; closed Sat.

Romantic hats, practical hats, mannish hats, quirky hats, colorful hats, hats with veils, brims, flowers, polka dots, wraps. Hats off to one of the best designer hat boutiques in New York City. If you don't fall in love with one of these creations, the author will eat her you-know-what.

M and H Cosmetics. 4911 13th Avenue, near 49th Street, 871-6600. Mon.–Thurs. and Sun., 10 A.M.–6:30 P.M.; closes Fri. in midafternoon; closed Sat.

Enormous, modern, and very popular, the entire store resembles a cosmetics department at Macy's or Bloomingdale's complete with a facial salon. However, many prices are pure Brooklyn—meaning discounted. This is one of several cosmetics stores in the area that sell Chanel, Dior, Borghese, and other top-of-the-line fragrances and cosmetics.

✪ **M & M Shoe Center.** 4526 13th Avenue near 45th Street, 972-2737. Sun.–Thurs., 10 A.M.–6 P.M.; Fri., 10 A.M.–2 P.M.; closed Sat.

Shoe lovers will enjoy the shoe stores along 45th and 47th streets on 13th Avenue, and especially M & M (also on the Lower East Side), which has high-quality shoes for women, men, and children. The styles tend toward classic, with a practical emphasis on fit, comfort, and durability. Brand names include Charles Jordan, Adrienne Vittadini, Bostonian, Bruno Magli, and Mephisto as well as Bally and Munroe, among many others. The prices are lower than most Manhattan stores, and there's a special balcony section for designer shoes on clearance sale. Be prepared for delays; the store may be a little understaffed.

Marcy Clothing, Boys Club. 4409 13th Avenue, near 44th Street, 854-3977. Sun.–Thurs., 10:30 A.M.–6 P.M.; Fri., 10:30 A.M.–2 P.M.; closed Sat.

A cheery green façade greets you at this serious, old-fashioned men's clothing store. On the main floor there are hundreds of high-quality suits, with tailoring on the premises. Upstairs, second-generation owner Gary Stern oversees a Ralph Lauren lookalike shop, featuring size 8–20 boys clothes. You'll find Italian up-to-date fashions for young men, as well as reasonably priced sportswear.

S and W. 4217 13th Avenue, between 42nd and 43rd streets, 438-9679. Sun.–Thurs., 10 A.M.–6 P.M.; closes early on Fri.; closed Sat.

In the tradition of Loehmann's, the great Brooklyn-born discount store, this women's clothing store is a big discounter of both American and European fashions. Even the separates tend to be dressy rather than sporty, and all items have long sleeves and high necklines.

Simpson Jewelers. 4922 13th Avenue between 49th and 50th streets, 872-0120. Sun.–Thurs., 10:30 A.M.–6 P.M.; Fri., 10:30 A.M.–2 P.M.; closed Sat.

"Forty years in the business," Simpson's carries lots of pretty, valuable jewelry and a wide assortment of high-quality watches. There is a tremendous selection of gold bracelets, necklaces, earrings, and brooches, as well as pearl and diamond pieces. The service is knowledgeable and patient. And, of course, the prices are low.

Sylvia's. 5101 13th Avenue, corner of 51st Street, 436-4771. Sun.–Thurs., 10:30 A.M.–6 P.M.; Fri., 10:30 A.M.–2 P.M.; closed Sat.

Elegant shoes, elegant clothes, and an elegant setting describe the newly revamped Sylvia's. You will find both stylish and practical shoes.

✪ **Underworld Plaza.** 1421 62nd Street, near 14th Avenue, 232-6804. Mon.–Thurs. and Sun., 10 A.M.–5 P.M.; closes Fri. in midafternoon; closed Sat.

What **Train World** (page 69) is to model trains, Underworld is to those little unmentionables. This is one store to visit at least semiannually. Whether you're rejuvenating a worn collection of underwear or looking for a romantic teddy that won't break the bank, come here. The selection of name-brand negligees, bathrobes, slips, bras, panties, and so on at wholesale prices is vast. Parking is free.

Clothing, Equipment, and Supplies for Kids

Berkowitz. 5216 13th Avenue, between 52nd and 53rd streets, 436-3333. Sun.–Thurs., 10 A.M.–8 P.M.; closes early on Fri.; closed Sat. No credit cards.

This is one of several discount juvenile furniture shops on 13th Avenue that stock cribs, dressers, rocking chairs, and other items.

Judy's Nook. 4608 16th Street, near 46th Street, 633-4340. Mon.–Thurs. and Sun., 11 A.M.–5:30 P.M.; closes Fri. in midafternoon; closed Sat.

Shop here for a tasteful selection of upper-end children's clothing, from infant to preteen. Prices generally are discounted at least 10 percent. Still, snowsuits are in the $120-and-up range, and complete outfits for boys and girls run $50 and up. Weary customers can relax on the pastel sofa and armchairs.

✪ **Le Petit.** 4619 18th Avenue, between 46th and 47th streets, 851-2921. Mon.–Thurs. and Sun., 10:30 A.M.–6:30 P.M.; closes Fri. in midafternoon; closed Sat.

You would have to go to the Champs-Elyseé to find some of these designs. The owners travel to Italy and France to select these top-of-the-line clothes for infants through juniors. For special occasions there are black velvet dresses, satin jumpsuits, and fur-collared wool coats. Little boys aren't left out—there is plenty of tailored, classic clothing for boys, plus dressy items, such as tuxedo shirts. Coats are $250 and up; dresses start at $150. Even the play clothes are elegant. Ask to be put on their mailing list for seasonal sales.

Little King and Queen. 4415 13th Avenue, between 44th and 45th streets, 438-2007. Mon.–Thurs. and Sun., 10 A.M.–7 P.M.; closes Fri. in midafternoon; closed Sat.

Just start with the baby carriages—MacLaren, Inglesina, Chico, Silver Cross—and you'll know you've found a huge selection of furniture and equipment for your little "royals." The prices are discounted 10 percent or more and the salespeople couldn't be nicer. Imported cribs are $190 to more than $500; carriages start at $200.

✪ **Rachel's Boutique.** 4218-22 13th Avenue, between 42nd and 43rd streets, 435-6875. Mon.–Thurs. and Sun., 10 A.M.–6 P.M.; closes Fri. in midafternoon; closed Sat.

Rachel's has a truly huge inventory of tops and mid-tier children's clothing, all heavily discounted. The sheer volume—for instance, floor-to-ceiling racks of boys' shirts—is unusual for a children's store. Pick a size and you'll find about 150 outfits available for your toddler (we know, we counted). And that doesn't include the nighties, raincoats, jackets, suspenders, socks, and other incidentals for newborns to size 14 boys and junior girls.

✪ **Scribbles.** 4403 13th Avenue, 438-8711 Sun.–Thurs., 10:30 A.M.–6 P.M.; Fri., 10:30 A.M.–2 P.M.; closed Sat.

Eureka! This well-stocked educational arts and crafts store also carries something that almost every elementary school child eventually needs: equipment for science projects. When the kids need petri dishes, droppers, pulleys, and components for electricity experiments, and science kits, Scribbles probably has it. Also worth noting is the rack of literally a hundred different kinds of inexpensive party favors.

Stern's Fashions. 5501 16th Avenue, corner of 55th Street, 972-7931. Mon.–Thurs. and Sun., 10 A.M.–7 P.M.; Fri., 10 A.M.–2 P.M.; closed Sat.

Stern's is straight out of an old-fashioned retail mold. Like many other children's clothing stores in Borough Park, the accent is on classic styles, durable quality, and discounted prices. OshKosh, Healthtex, and other popular brands for infants through size 14 are crammed into racks and racks here. There is also a good collection of bathrobes, 1950s-style crinoline slips, and Carter's underwear.

✪ **Teacher's Pet.** 4809 16th Avenue, between 48th and 49th streets, 436-6600. Mon.–Thurs. and Sun., 10 A.M.–7 P.M.; Fri., closes in midafternoon; closed Sat.

Teacher's Pet sells inexpensive, practical arts and crafts and school supplies. Giant money-saving sizes on everything from glitter and glue to maps and toys are typical. You can phone your order in for shipment by UPS, but visiting is half the fun.

Train World. 751 McDonald Avenue, near Ditmas Avenue, 436-7072. Mon.–Sat., 10 A.M.–6 P.M.

Even if you're not a train buff when you enter, you will be before leaving this store. Loaded with hundreds of trains, pieces of scenery, miniature figures, and lots of track, you'll think you've landed in Penn Station. One of the biggest train stores in New York City, Train World carries Lionel, American Flyer, and LGB, among others. Prices range from under $10 to $300. This is a terrific place to bring children, but expect to go home with something on wheels.

Whispers 'N' Whimsies. 4919 16th Avenue, between 49th and 50th streets, 633-3174. Mon.–Thurs. and Sun., 10:30 A.M.–6 P.M.; Fri., 10:30 A.M.–2 P.M.; closed Sat.

The housekeeping may be a bit helter-skelter here, but don't be discouraged. Unusual toys, books, funny pencils, and well-designed backpacks, lunchboxes, and other practical gear are sold here at reasonable prices. There's even a collection of Pauline dolls downstairs.

Wonderland. 5309 13th Avenue, near 53rd Street, 435-4040. Sun.–Thurs., 10 A.M.–6 P.M.; closes early on Friday; closed Sat.

Like **Rachel's** but in more modern facilities, this huge, busy, and very popular clothing store has better-quality merchandise for children at a hefty discount. Sizes range from layette to preteen.

Yeedl's. 4301 13th Avenue, corner of 43rd Street, 435-5900. Mon.–Thurs. and Sun., 11 A.M.–6 P.M.; Fri., 11 A.M.–3 P.M.; closed Sat.

For great prices on imported, top-drawer strollers, cribs, and other juvenile furniture, check out Yeedl's. Beware of stroller gridlock, however; this place gets busy!

Interesting Neighborhood Shops

A to Z Luggage. 4627 New Utrecht Avenue, near 47th Street, 435-6330 or 435-6331. Mon.–Thurs., 9 A.M.–5:45 P.M.; Fri. and Sun., 9:30 A.M.–5 P.M.; closed Sat.

Some people won't buy luggage anywhere but this Brooklyn shop under the "El." You'll find unbelievable discounts on more than a dozen well-known brands of handbags, suitcases, garment bags, and sample cases. Orders can be placed by phone.

Better Health. 5302 New Utrecht Avenue, 436-4801. Mon.–Wed., 10 A.M.–6 P.M.; Thurs., 10 A.M.–8 P.M.; Sun., noon–5 P.M.; closed Fri. and Sat.

Fitness buffs and even a few couch potatoes will go crazy over the top-of-the-line exercise equipment at 10 to 50 percent discounts. The store provides free consultation on setting up a home gym and sometimes will swap equipment with you. Rowers, bikes, treadmills, stair climbers, ski machines, weights, mats, benches, and pool tables—they've got it all.

✪ **Continental Tablesettings.** 4622 16th Avenue, near 46th Street, 435-1451 or 438-2522. Mon.–Thurs., 11 A.M.–6 P.M.; Fri., closes in midafternoon; closed Sat.

You wouldn't travel all this way for one fork, but you'll save a bundle if you're looking for a set of new crystal, china, or silver. Top brands include Lenox, Limoges, Royal Dalton, Villeroy & Boch, Wedgwood, Rosenthal, and Orreförs. Some are discounted 25 percent below department store prices.

D'Rose Linens. 1315 47th Street, off 13th Avenue, 633-0863. Sun.–Thurs., 10:30 A.M.–6 P.M.; closes early on Fri.; closed Sat.

After one visit to this discount shop, you'll never consider buying sheets at full retail price again. Better-quality sheets, towels, tablecloths, bedspreads, and comforters are all sold at 30 percent off department store prices. Name brands include Luxor, Springmaid, Martex, and Dan River. Got a pear-shaped or half-oval table? Want custom made curtains or bedspreads in designer fabrics? If they don't have it here, they can order it for you.

✪ **Eagle Electronics.** 5005 13th Avenue, corner 50th Street, 438-4401. Sun.–Thurs., 10 A.M.–6 P.M.; Fri., 10 A.M.–2 P.M.; closed Sat.

Eagle is house-electronics heaven, selling everything you might need from cellular phones to Cuisinarts to refrigerators and air conditioners. It's also an interesting place to shop for a gift, such as an electric dog hair clipper, projection TV, or keyboard. An unusual specialty is a large range of 220-volt appliances, popular among locals who travel frequently to Europe and Israel. The prices are good and, after thirty years in business, service is reliable.

✪ **East Side China.** 5002 12th Avenue, at 50th Street, 633-8672. Mon.–Thurs., 10:30 A.M.–6 P.M.; Fri., closes in midafternoon; Sun., 10 A.M.–5 P.M.; closed Sat.

For more than two decades this store has made its reputation on discounted giftware, china, and dinnerware with names such as Wedgwood, Lenox, and Mikaasa. You can choose from the variety of items on display or order a specific pattern. Discounts are substantial, starting at about 25 percent.

✪ **Elegant Linens.** 5719 New Utrecht Ave.; another at 13th Avenue between 48th and 49th streets, 871-3535. Sun.–Thurs., 10 A.M.–6 P.M., Fri., 10 A.M.–2 P.M.; closed Sat.

If you spend one-third of your life in bed, why not do it with style? Elegant Linens sells major brands from Canon to Springmaid, priced at one-half to one-third of comparable items in Manhattan. But what really sets them apart is their custom manufacture of bed linens, dust ruffles, and pillow shams. They supply custom linens for most of New York's fanciest stores and major department stores and will design some 'specially for you, too. "We can make whatever you want" is what they say, and they mean it.

Flohr's. 4603 13th Avenue, at 46th Street, 854-0865. Mon.–Thurs. and Sun., 10 A.M.–6 P.M.; Fri., closes in midafternoon; closed Sat.

Hand in glove, Orthodox Jewish communities and bookstores go together. There are at least eight bookstores in this neighborhood—many more than in Brooklyn's gentrified brownstone communities. Although you won't be able to read most of these tomes, called *sphorim,* unless you are fluent in Hebrew or Aramaic, the sheer volume is impressive. In addition to books, Flohr's sells gift items and Judaica.

✪ **Grand Sterling.** 4921 13th Avenue, near 49th Street, 854-0623. Sun.–Thurs., 10:30 A.M.–6 P.M.; Fri., 10:30 A.M.–2 P.M.; closed Sat.

One of the largest silver stores in the nation, Grand Sterling sells top-of-the-line brand names at discounts that can run as deep as 50 percent off regular retail. The elegant new showroom displays hundreds of silver items, including candelabra, bowls, knickknacks, coffee sets, and, of course, flatware. You can find antiques and reproductions as well as new designs, some made exclusively for the store. This is a three-generation business with a store on the Lower East Side, and they pride themselves on reliability and service.

Lamp Warehouse. 1073 39th Street, corner of Fort Hamilton Parkway, 436-2207. Mon.–Tues. and Fri.–Sun., 10 A.M.–5 P.M.; Thurs., 10 A.M.–8 P.M.; closed Wed.

Here's a bright idea: reduced prices on all major names in lamps. This is purported to be New York's largest discount lamp store, so it is well worth the trip if you're buying to light up an apartment or a house.

Loeffler. 5127 New Utrecht Avenue, between 51st and 52nd streets, 436-8989. Mon.–Thurs., 10 A.M.–7 P.M.; Sun., 10 A.M.–6 P.M.; closed Fri. and Sat.

Toeffler is one of Brooklyn's largest discount decorator furniture stores. The high-fashion merchandise is from top designers—sofas, bedroom sets, dining room sets, and accessories—and sold at a discount.

London Silver Vaults. 4922 16th Avenue, between 49th and 50th streets, 436-2800. Mon.–Thurs., 9:30 A.M.–8:30 P.M.; Fri., closes in midafternoon; Sun., 10 A.M.–7 P.M.; closed Sat.

Have you always wanted silver just like grandma's? The proprietor buys his flatware from estates, polishes it, and sells it for between $100 and $250 for a five-piece setting. The store also sells candelabra, tea sets, serving trays, and an extensive collection of Judaica, ranging in price from $200 to $2,000. There is a silversmith on the premises.

Mandel. 4215 13th Avenue, between 42nd and 43rd streets, 435-6695. Mon.–Thurs. and Sun., 8 A.M.–7 P.M.; Fri., closes in midafternoon; closed Sat.

This fifty-year-old family business sells a wide range of men's everyday and dress suits from mainstream designers at a 20 to 40 percent discount. A typical two-piece suit averages $250, including alterations. High-end suits sell for about $450. The salespeople are friendly and helpful.

Mildred's for Fine Linen. 4612 13th Avenue, near 46th Street, 435-2323. Mon.–Thurs. and Sun., 10 A.M.–6 P.M.; Fri., closes in midafternoon; closed Sat.

If you want your bedroom to look like that luscious magazine picture, with just a phone call Mildred's can ship the goods to you—at up to a 25 percent discount. There are half a dozen curtain and linen shops in Borough Park, but Mildred's claim to fame is a big phone-and-mail business on duvets, sheets, bath accessories, shower curtains, and other linens. The store itself has two floors crammed with attractive name-brand items and includes an extensive bath shop.

Royalty Tableware. 1845 50th Street, between 18th and 19th avenues, 854-6689. Hours are by appointment.

You'll have to put up with the limited hours here if you want to find stainless-steel and silver-plated tableware at 25 to 60 percent discounts. But at $150 for twelve-place settings, it's worth the hassle.

Travel Depot. 5015 18th Avenue, near 50th Street, 633-6622.
Sun.–Thurs. 10 A.M.–7 P.M.; Fri. 10 A.M.–2 P.M.; closed Sat.

Travelers: You can get almost everything you'll need for your next trip here except maybe your airplane ticket. Owner David Schischa has a keen eye for handsome name-brand luggage and accessories such as traveling alarm clocks, matching handbags, and briefcases, Swiss Army watches, and even buckwheat-filled travel pillows. Brands represented include Hartman, French, Delsey, and Samsonite, among others. The prices are lower than at most department stores.

✪ Underground Stores

Only the UPS delivery man knows for sure how many underground businesses exist in Borough Park. We found at least a dozen home-based stores run by women, literally in the basements of their homes. These are not fly-by-night operations, but well-run outfits that have, in some cases, been in operation for decades. They pay taxes, take credit cards and phone orders, and are open regular, if truncated, hours (usually 11 A.M.–5 P.M.). Career women on Wall Street aren't the only ones juggling jobs and kids; for these Orthodox women whose first priority is family life, basement stores are a sensible solution—you can boil the chicken soup and tend a sick baby upstairs, and run the business below.

It's hard to find out about who sells what, except by word of mouth. The best strategy is to talk with some of the store owners who sell women's clothing, and can usually recommend someone who has a basement shop specializing in lingerie, children's clothes, linens, kitchenware, and even jewelry. Then you can say someone sent you—and that's helpful in this usually close-knit community.

Please remember, these stores are all closed Friday afternoons, Saturdays, and on Jewish holidays.

Shoes and Handbags: For over two decades, Channi and her family have sold handbags from home, as well as shoes. There are over 100 different styles of bags, including exquisite evening bags and everyday soft leather satchels. Shoes include well-known European names such as Sesto Meucci and Vaneli. Prices run at least 20 percent less than prices in "regular" stores. **Sol's Dolls**, 1624 48th Street off 16th Avenue, 435-9444. Repeat: Closed Friday afternoons and all day Saturday.

Lingerie: Mrs. Saposh sells bathing suits, undergarments, and nightgowns, both imports and top-quality made-in-America brands, at a fraction of the price in boutiques and department stores. The little basement-turned-store itself seems made of Spandex, there's so much merchandise jammed into a small space. It can get very busy, so leave yourself some time. **Sara Saposh Corset Shoppe,** 1730 46th Street, between 17th and 18th avenues, 438-9497. Repeat: Closed Friday afternoons and all day Saturday.

Evening Wear: Walk up the driveway past the redbrick house in this residential block and down a few dim steps to a boutique of expensive gowns and party dresses of satin, brocade, lace, and silk. Heavy, expensive fabrics are the ticket here. "**Goldie**," at 1436 46th Street, 436-5781. Repeat: Closed Friday afternoons and all day Saturday.

Tablecloths: Reflecting the needs of a community that enjoys many celebrations—and has big families—all sizes of tablecloths are sold here, including some for king-sized sixteen-foot tables! Some are imported, some are American, and both the price and quality can't be beat. There's a small selection of towels sold here, too. **Gitta Steinmetz Tablecloths** is located at 1729-46th St., across the street from the basement lingerie shop (see above), 871-6964. Repeat: Closed Friday afternoons and all day Saturday.

HOTELS

Avenue Plaza Hotel. 47th Street and 13th Avenue. (As of this writing, no phone number was available.)

A new hotel with luxury accommodations geared for Orthodox Jewish customers opened in April 1999. Rates are about $170 per night. The food is vegetarian and kosher, and there are special facilities for the Sabbath observant, such as a continuously running elevator.

Park House Hotel. 1206 48th Street, at 12th Avenue, 871-8100.

One of the few hotels in Brooklyn, this small one caters to the kosher crowd. It is only one block from the nearest synagogues for visitors observant of the Sabbath. Rates start at $90 per night for a double room.

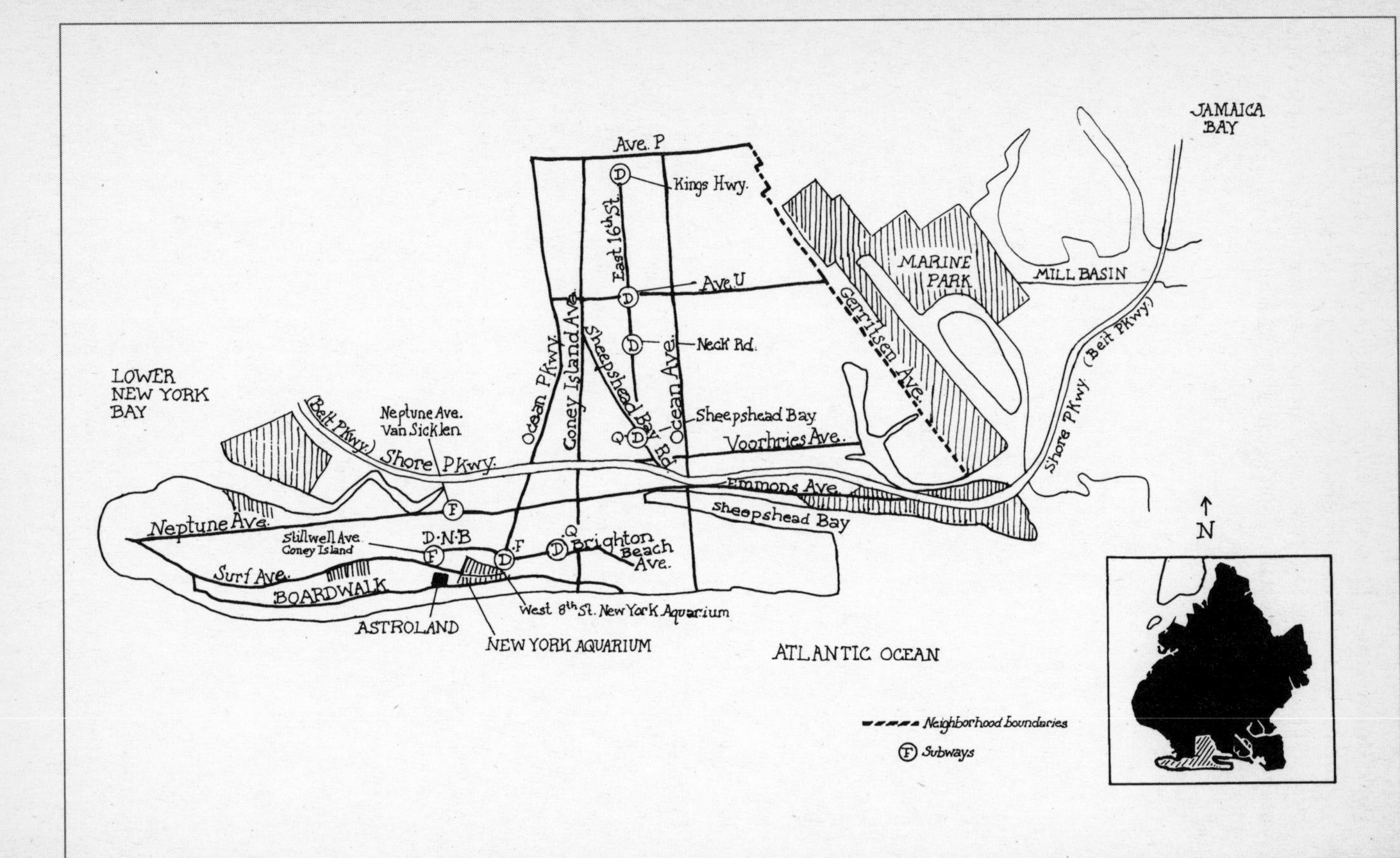
JAMAICA BAY
Ave. P
Kings Hwy.
East 16th St.
Ave. U
MARINE PARK
MILL BASIN
Gerritsen Ave.
Neck Rd.
Ocean Pkwy.
Coney Island Ave.
Sheepshead Bay Rd.
Ocean Ave.
Sheepshead Bay
Voorhries Ave.
Shore Pkwy. (Belt Pkwy.)
LOWER NEW YORK BAY
Neptune Ave. Van Sicklen
(Belt Pkwy.) Shore Pkwy.
Emmons Ave.
Sheepshead Bay
Neptune Ave.
Stillwell Ave. Coney Island
D·N·B
Brighton Beach Ave.
Surf Ave.
BOARDWALK
West 8th St. New York Aquarium
ASTROLAND
NEW YORK AQUARIUM
ATLANTIC OCEAN
N
Neighborhood boundaries
Subways

Brighton Beach, Coney Island, and Sheepshead Bay

Snug against the Atlantic Ocean at Brooklyn's southern end, Brighton Beach, Coney Island, and Sheepshead Bay offer an unparalleled combination of fun, food, and fashion. Because you can spend a full day here, combining a walk on Brighton's boardwalk with a roller coaster ride in Coney Island and dinner in Sheepshead Bay, we've included all three neighborhoods in this single chapter.

Where they are: Along the Atlantic Ocean. From west to east: Coney Island, Brighton Beach, and then Sheepshead Bay.

How to get there:

By car: Take the Belt Parkway to exit 7, head south along Ocean Parkway toward the ocean, then west on Surf Avenue (Coney Island) or east on Brighton Beach Avenue (Brighton Beach). Exits 8 and 9 drop you at either end of Sheepshead Bay's Emmons Avenue.

By subway: D or Q train to Brighton Beach Avenue (Brighton Beach), or Sheepshead Bay Road (Sheepshead Bay). The D or F train to West 8th Street (Coney Island).

Cab services: Best Way Car Service (252-6363), Avenue J Airport Service (251-3200), Sheepshead Car Service (769-2700), Plaza Car Service (615-2000). Fares are about $15 to $20 to Brooklyn Heights, $25 to Grand Central Station.

Kidstuff

Plan to spend at least half a day with kids in this section of Brooklyn. The **New York Aquarium** at Coney Island is educational, fun, and parent-friendly. Weather permitting, more vigorous play can be found at nearby **Astroland** amusement park or the indoor ice-skating rink at **Abe Stark**.

Sheepshead Bay's **Emmons Avenue fishing pier** is entertaining for all ages, and when combined with dinner nearby, it makes for a refreshing family outing. Very young children will happily walk across the **Ocean Avenue Bridge**, a long footbridge to **Manhattan Beach**, and then back again. The huge **UA Cinema Complex** at Sheepshead Bay is always inviting. Older kids may want to blow their accumulated savings on learning to sail, or on some fishing gear and a day hanging a line off the pier. You also can take the whole family out on a fishing boat.

Of course, people of all ages enjoy playing in the sand and surf at **Coney Island, Brighton Beach**, or **Manhattan Beach Park**, and strolling or biking along the boardwalk.

Brighton Beach

Special events: Brighton Jubilee, street fair, and concert, the last Sunday in August. Call 891-0800 for information.

How it got its name:
Named after England's most distinguished seaside resort, Brighton Beach was developed in the 1880s as a posh competitor with nearby Coney Island.

ABOUT THE NEIGHBORHOOD

At Brooklyn's southernmost end is a seaside neighborhood you won't want to miss. Commonly referred to as "Little Odessa," Brighton Beach is a Russian enclave in New York. Since 1989, nearly 100,000 Russians have settled in New York City, and many of them started here. If fifty years of the Cold War didn't rouse your curiosity about the former Soviet Union, a trip to Brighton Beach will.

The main thoroughfare, Brighton Beach Avenue, is peppered with Russian delis and restaurants, Russian-run clothing shops, and Russian-language (Cyrillic) newspaper stores and shop signs. During the winter months an amazing number of both men and women do their daily errands dressed in heavy fur or leather coats. Residents of Brooklyn, surrounding suburbs, and even Manhattan trek here to "ooh" and "aah" over the delicious authentic Russian foods and wild tabletop dancing at such well-known nightclubs as the **National Restaurant, the Odessa**, and **Primorski's**.

Food mavens should not miss three specialty stores in the area. **M & I International** is the largest of several Russian stores; the array of sausages, cheeses, and breads is boggling. Snackers will delight in nearby **Mrs. Stahl's Knishes**, in business for more than sixty years, and **EFE International**, where exotic dried fruits and flavored bonbons can be had by the handful. Visitors may be surprised by the number of vegetable stands—there are at least two on every block. As one local Russian summed it up: "They are hungry from Russia still. One vegetable stand would be for a whole town there."

The shops along Brighton Beach Avenue are packed tightly under the elevated subway tracks. In this darkish, noisy atmosphere, with the sound of spoken Russian all around you, you can almost imagine yourself in Kiev or Moscow.

The Russian-Americans of Brighton Beach are cultural packrats, incorporating anything bright and (perhaps) beautiful into their concept of what looks, feels, or sounds "cool." Window shopping here will bring you face to face with the gaudiest printed silks, as well as more traditional Russian furs and leathers. Local music stores are brimming with sounds from all over the globe. Big American luxury cars line the streets, while corner bookstalls offer the best of Cyrillic science fiction. Russian delis and bakeries vie for space with sushi bars and taco joints, and Russian teens dance to creative interpretations of American hip-hop tunes in the local nightclubs.

So, while a visit to Brighton Beach may feel at first like a visit to Russia, it is more like a country of its own, where the weight and depth of Russian culture has met and mixed with fervent American capitalism in pleasant disharmony.

Historical Notes

Like the Cyclone in nearby Coney Island, Brighton Beach has had its ups and downs. In the 1880s it was an affluent seaside resort complete with casino, racetrack, and a major hotel. It remained that way for decades; in 1907 the new Brighton Beach Baths (now the proposed site of a major residential development) boasted several swimming pools, a beach, and nightly entertainment by the country's top performers. By the 1930s Brighton Beach had become a densely populated year-round residential area with a sizable Jewish community, but after World War II the area went into decline along with Brooklyn's economy and an aging local population.

In the mid-1970s, the neighborhood was, as one local leader puts it, "like a dried-up sponge." That sponge has since absorbed nearly 100,000 immigrants, most of them Russian. In the seventies and eighties, these Russians were mostly workingclass Jews, many of them from Odessa (hence the neighborhood's nickname).

In the early nineties, the collapse and fall of the Soviet Union opened the doors of Russian emigration, and a second wave of immigrants—mostly white-collar professionals from Moscow, Leningrad, and Kiev—began to arrive.

These days, though a strong Jewish community persists, the neighborhood exhibits influences from all over the former Soviet Union.

ENTERTAINMENT

Forget the movies, and plan a weekend night out with a dozen friends at a Russian nightclub. We list several below.

The Russian Nightclub Experience

You start off the night with a platter of smoked fish the size of an aircraft carrier, a little caviar here, a lot of citrus-infused vodka there, and a tremendous dollop of sour cream. At about nine o'clock, the band takes the stage—real Russian rock'n'rollers sporting black leather jackets and distant, world-weary stares. They power up the synthesizers and slide into the "Macarena," followed by "Jailhouse Rock." Russians from all walks of life storm the dance floor—matrons in furs, elderly gentlemen in corduroy suits; young hipsters in white dinner jackets and gold plastic sunglasses. Onstage, things start to get weird: a young Harlemite emerges in a shimmering zootsuit, microphone in hand, and dives into a soulful version of "I Just Called To Say I Love You." Russian girls from all over the hall scream in unison and rush the new singer, forming a circle around him and jumping up and down. In the middle of the song, he points to one of the girls and croons, "I just called to say I love you, Maftuna!" The adolescent beauty squeals and giggles. It's her birthday. The song will be requested five more times that night. Unbelievable? Yes. Utter confusion? Only on your part. But are we serious when we tell you there's no better place to try out your latest moves? Absolutely. Brighton Beach's restaurant/dance halls are beyond doubt the best place to experience the strange and joyful mishmash that is Russian-American immigrant culture.

✪ **National Restaurant.** 273 Brighton Beach Avenue, between Brighton 2nd and 3rd streets, 646-1225. Fri. and Sat., 9 P.M.–3 A.M.; Sun., 7 P.M.–1 A.M.

When you walk into the National—the largest and some say tamest of Brighton Beach's nightclub/restaurants—the banquet-style tables are already set with about twenty cold appetizers, including eggplant salad, cold duckling, pickled vegetables, pâté, big plain boiled potatoes, and, of course, a cold bottle of vodka. That's just for starters—wait until the hot foods arrive. The live entertainment is more "floor show" than "cover band," but the dance floor is still packed. A wonderful night that starts no earlier than 8:30 and can go on until 3 A.M. costs about $45 per person on Fridays, $55 on Saturdays. The building is huge; it used to be a movie theater, and accommodates more than 350 people. The National gained some fame in the eighties as Robin Williams's haunt in *Moscow on the Hudson*. Be sure to make reservations.

✪**Odessa.** 1113 Brighton Beach Avenue, between Brighton 13th and 14th streets, 332-3223. Tues.–Thurs., 10 A.M.–midnight; Fri.–Sat., 9 P.M.–3 A.M.; Sun., 8 P.M.–2 A.M.

Odessa has atmosphere, lively dancing, terrific food, and keeps the vodka flowing. While more family-style than the National, Odessa is still huge; one flight above street level, it occupies the space taken up by a half-dozen shops, and seats more than 300 people. The Odessa is a favorite of Russian locals, who congregate here at lunchtime. Try the chicken Kiev, meat loaf, and potato salad with meat. Dinner and entertainment run about $60 per person on the weekend; during the week the Russian foods are à la carte and cost about $30 for dinner, sans music. This restaurant is about ten blocks away from the heart of Russian Brighton Beach Avenue.

✪**Primorski.** 282 Brighton Beach Avenue, near Brighton 3rd Street, 891-3111. Weekdays, 11 A.M.–midnight; Fri. and Sat., 11–3 A.M.; Sun., 11–2 A.M.

With capacity for about 80 people, Primorski is one of the more intimate Russian restaurants, but still is a spot for a boisterous evening reminiscent of a wild bar mitzvah. The eclectic mix of covered tunes tends towards fabulously schmaltzy renditions—go ahead and sing along, no one will mind. Entrées here are very tasty, and dinner is less than $30 per person. During the day, you can get an enormous lunch for under $6. Reservations are recommended.

(See also the Sheepshead Bay Russian nightclubs, **Rasputin** and **Paradise**, page 96.)

PARKS AND PLAYGROUNDS

✪**Brighton Beach and Boardwalk.** One block from Brighton Beach Avenue is the boardwalk, the sand, the surf, and good people-watching. The beach is somewhat cleaner than at adjacent Coney Island, and the human geography is considerably different. The boardwalk is lined with old Russian gentlemen in deck chairs and traversed by a meandering pageant of Eastern Europeans in various stages of assimilation.

✪**Brighton Beach Playground.** Between the Boardwalk and Brightwater Court, near Brighton 2nd Street.

If the beach is too windy or too tranquil for your kids, here's a large urban playground (no grass), with colorful new equipment, a water fountain for hot days, and a padded rubber "floor," to keep them happy.

POINTS OF CULTURAL INTEREST

Black Sea Bookstore. 3175 Coney Island Avenue, near Brighton Beach Avenue, 769-2878. Daily, 11 A.M.–7 P.M.

Two doors down from **Mrs. Stahl's Knishes** (page 84) is this one large room, stuffed with CDs, videos, audio tapes, and rows and columns of Russian tomes. Black Sea is different than most American bookstores: low on knickknacks and flashy promotional displays, high on cover drawings of Boris Yeltsin, nude. Twenty minutes spent scanning the book jackets here will give you invaluable insight into the Russian sense of humor, adventure, and sexuality. If this puts you in the mood to learn more, you can also purchase tickets to occasional cultural events, such as poetry readings in Russian.

✪ **Vegetable stands.** Along Brighton Beach Avenue. Daily, 8 A.M.–8 P.M.

Maybe these folks are making up for lost time—and food shortages—in the old country. Fresh produce is everywhere in Brighton Beach. It seems as if there are a hundred Korean-owned vegetable stands in the neighborhood, ranging in style from the elegant and inexpensive **Fruits and Vegetables** (241 Brighton Beach Avenue), to the basic and unbelievably cheap **Golden Farm** (611 Brighton Beach Avenue). The prices are among the lowest in Brooklyn: if kiwis are two for a dollar in your neighborhood, you'll find the same quality here at five for a dollar. People stand around the fruit stands looking, selecting, discussing—from a distance, you'd think the stores were giving the stuff away.

NOTABLE BRIGHTON BEACH RESTAURANTS

For Russian nightclubs, see Entertainment, page 80.

These Russian immigrants have extravagant taste, so local cafés may tout their lobster and foie gras. Our advice: skip the haute cuisine, and stick to the vareniki, borscht and blini. Pedestrian as they may seem to the average Russian-American, these are the dishes local chefs know best, and are almost certain to provide an exotic treat for the visitor.

A tip: Water service is not automatic in Brighton Beach, and Russian waiters will do their best to sell you bottled water. If all you want is a glass from the tap, your only hope is to stick to your guns, even if it means sending back a bottle you didn't ask for. Remember, most of the nightclubs listed in the Entertainment section (pages 80–1) also serve lunch and dinner.

Café Pearl, also known as the Best Pearl Café. 303 Brighton Beach Avenue, near Brighton Beach 3rd, 891-4544. Open 24 hours.

For $30 bucks a head you can get Georgian cooking at this Brighton Beach newcomer. There are lamb dumplings that some reviewers rave about, cheesy roles, and herring with potatoes, eggplant, fish, and more Russian delicacies.

✪ **Caffe Cappuccino.** 290 Brighton Beach Avenue, near Brighton 3rd Street, 646-6297. Mon.–Fri., Sun., 11 A.M.–10 P.M.; Sat., 11 A.M.–11 P.M.

Highly recommended for lunch, this small European-style café offers light Russian food—you won't need a three-hour nap after eating here. There are vareniki (Russian-style ravioli), pickled vegetables, Ukrainian borscht, steamed cabbage, schnitzel, cheesecake, baba-rum pastries, and excellent coffee. The decor is casual—white tablecloths under glass and flowers on every table, with mounted TVs playing low-volume Russian MTV. It's the custom to share a table with other customers if the place is full, so you might meet local Russians. Lunch costs less that $10. High chairs are available.

Gambrinus. 3100 Ocean Parkway, corner of Ocean Parkway and Brighton Beach Avenue, 265-1009. Daily, noon–midnight.

This popular lunch and dinner spot is decorated like a sunken ship, with rigging and buoys and mizzen masts strewn about. Try the salty-sweet pickled herring, which comes with sugary onions and a heaping plate of roasted potatoes, and the generous seafood salad (order the dressing on the side). The Seafood Gambrinus ($20) is overflowing with lobster, snow crab, blue crab, mussels, shrimp, calamari, clams, and scallops. If you stick to appetizers—more than enough food for the average North American—dinner will run you about $15. Otherwise, expect to spend around $30 per person. The waitstaff is pleasant and helpful, and the spacious porch is great for a relaxed summer meal.

SHOPPING

Specialty Food Shops

EFE International. 243 Brighton Beach Avenue, 891-8933; and 1117 Brighton Beach Avenue, 332-3312. Daily, 8 A.M.–9 P.M.

These twin dry goods stores, one on each end of the neighborhood, specialize in dried fruits, nuts, and chocolates of wonderful quality and variety. Unusual dried fruits like cherry apples, yellow prunes, and blackcurrants are delicious and reasonably priced, as are chocolate cordials of cognac, plum brandy, and other liqueurs, and dark chocolate bonbons with apricot and pineapple centers (among many others). You can also find milk- and dark-chocolate–covered nuts, coffees and teas, and colorfully wrapped Russian fruit candies.

✪ **M & I International.** 249 Brighton Beach Avenue, between Brighton 2nd and 3rd streets, 615-1011 or 615-1012. Daily, 8 A.M.–10 P.M.

The labels on M & I's store brand of sausages feature old-fashioned black-and-white photos of smiling babies, as if to say, "We'd feed our child this two-foot bologna, wouldn't you?" A homey feel permeates this, the best and largest of a dozen local Russian food stores. In addition to cured meats of all kinds, you'll find a dizzying array of farmer, feta, and other cheeses; smoked fish and herring; prepared salads; and, of course, caviar, borscht, and sour cream. Prepared foods include kebabs, stuffed cabbage, chicken Kiev, and eggplant in garlic sauce. Don't miss the bakery upstairs. The local color is so compelling it's hard to know what to check out first, the people or the food. For takeout, try a potato or cheese pierogi. Though the main floor is sometimes an obstacle course of half-unpacked crates of food, this is a very clean, very European store.

Mrs. Stahl's Knishes. 1001 Brighton Beach Avenue, corner of Coney Island Avenue, 648-0210. Daily, 8 A.M.–7 P.M.

Mrs. Stahl's has used the same recipe for these famous low-cholesterol knishes for over fifty years, and current owner Les Green (proprietor since 1985) has expanded the menu to include a rainbow of more than twenty fillings, including spinach, cabbage, cherry-cheese, kasha, mushroom-potato, and chili. Though the landmark eatery is rather rundown, a knish from Mrs. Stahl's is still a treat. *A warning thought*: Do not allow the clerk to warm your knish in the microwave—a process that gives the pastries a soggy, leaden quality. If you're going to be in the neighborhood for awhile, find out when a fresh batch is due out of the oven, and grab one while it's still hot. Cocktail-size knishes are also available. Long-distance shipping to knish-starved friends can also be arranged: the minimum order is one dozen, shipped overnight express for $59. There's a small space for eating on the premises, but you're better off enjoying your knishes on the boardwalk or at home.

✪ **#1 Fish Market.** 421 Brighton Beach Avenue, corner of Brighton 5th Street and Brighton Beach Avenue, 743-3763. Daily, 8 A.M.–8 P.M.

This clean, bright little store is decorated with gargantuan and beautiful sea creatures. Early in the afternoon, the market fills with Russian women who order one leviathan apiece and lug them home whole and unfilleted in straining plastic sacks. All the signs are in Russian, but it doesn't take a marine biologist to recognize the heavily armored sturgeon, nor does it take an economist to realize that the fish here is a tremendous value, if you can figure out what to do with it.

Food for a Russian Feast

pickled mushrooms
lobio satsivi—string beans in white sauce
chicken Kiev
pilmeni—dumplings
bureka—phyllo dough filled with cheese
seltzer with strawberry juice

Gifts

Classic Fur. 221 Brighton Beach Avenue, near Brighton 2nd Street, 332-5138. Daily, 10 A.M.–7 P.M. except Sun., 10 A.M.–6 P.M.

Visitors usually remark on the number of fur coats worn in Brighton Beach. Here, second-generation Kiev furrier Anatoly Alter and his wife Raya have assembled a beautiful collection of mink, fox, lamb, lynx, suede, raccoon, and other furs with a European flair at good prices, starting at $800 and going up to several thousand. Tailoring is done on the premises, along with monogramming, cleaning, and storage. Lay-away plans are available.

RCB Video. 269 Brighton Beach Avenue, 769-8605. Daily, 10 A.M.–9 P.M.

Most Russian teens will only sheepishly admit to liking Russian pop music, but someone must be buying it, as RCB is just one of scores of shops hawking thousands of Russian, European, and American CDs. Want a free sample? The travel agency over Magic Corsets (two blocks down at 231 Brighton Beach Avenue) pipes high-energy Russian rock out onto the sidewalk. If you're really feeling adventurous, pick up a Russian video. (*Tip*: check out the work of the formerly underground auteur André Tarkovsky, whose image-heavy, Bergmanesque films entertain even across the language barrier.)

Contributed by Andy Gerstig.

Coney Island

Where it is: Bounded by the Belt Parkway to the north, Ocean Parkway to the east, Nortons Point to the west.

What's nearby: Brighton Beach, Sheepshead Bay.

How to get there:

By car: Belt Parkway, exit 75, or Ocean Parkway South to Surf Avenue. Parking on the street or for a fee at the New York Aquarium.

By subway: B, N, or D, F, M trains to Stillwell Avenue station.

Special events: January 1: Polar Bear Club Atlantic Ocean swim; Mermaid Parade (June); Nathan's Hot Dog Eating Contest (July 4); Irish Fair (September).

How it got its name: However ridiculous it may sound, the story goes that when the Dutch first discovered this area, it was overrun with rabbits. They called it "Rabbit Island"—in Dutch, *Konjin* (Coney) *Eiland*.

Official landmarks: Parachute Jump, Wonder Wheel, Cyclone.

ABOUT THE NEIGHBORHOOD

Step right up, ladies and gentlemen!

Coney Island is as well known as Times Square, but unlike Times Square it hasn't yet seen revitalization. So don't expect to find a sanitized, corporate-owned amusement park. Coney is a dreamland of fun and the press of human flesh, one of those magical places where a vivid past—known from movies, books, some collective American memory—crowds out today's lesser reality. When you go to Coney Island, you see the boardwalk, the distant beach, four blocks of amusement park anchored by the Cyclone, Parachute, and Wonder Wheel rides, now official New York City landmarks. And your imagination adds what your eyes miss—the raw immigrant energy, amusement arcades as far as the eye can see, the kaleidoscopic images of an old New York, and the cacophony of barkers announcing their attractions, laughter, lovers' kisses, children crying, couples screaming, "Cumm'on over *here*." Just standing here stirs up a thick soup of memories, even among people too young ever to have come to Coney in its heyday.

Snap back to today. There's enough to do here to spend an afternoon or a day. Coney Island attracts a mishmash of tourists, locals, working people, artists, eccentrics, and parents with children; that it is a little tacky and very mixed appeals to bohemians. It is one of New York's safest spots, with an extremely low crime rate due to a beefed-up police presence.

The dizzying, wooden **Cyclone** roller coaster ride (yes, it still works, a tribute to its original handcraftmanship) and **Dino's Amusement Park** entertain thousands of families, every spring, summer, and autumn. **Astroland** has arcade games and adult rides. **The New York Aquarium**, right next door, houses a world-class facility with year-round exhibits, shows, and programs. You can include a walk on the recently renovated **boardwalk and beach**, a visit to the funky **flea market** across the street, and even a twenty-minute stroll down the boardwalk to **Russian Brighton Beach**. There are two annual events. **Nathan's July 4 hot-dog-eating contest** is an acrobatic exercise in mouth-stuffing. The fabulous, funky annual June **Mermaid Parade** is an entertaining caper that's not to be missed. And on January 1, the Polar Bear Club takes a dip in the icy Atlantic Ocean just for the fun of it.

And you won't starve. The original **Nathan's Famous Restaurant** makes hot dogs and fries that some New Yorkers swear taste better than any others in New York City. Otherwise sane and sober men have been heard to compare eating **Totonno's** pizza with having a religious experience. Two nearby old-style Italian restaurants, **Gargiulo's** and **Carolina**, still serve up heaping plates of pasta and seafood. Restored and reopened **Lundy's of Sheepshead Bay** is within a ten minutes' drive, offering fresh lobster and other seafood specialties.

You don't have to look far to learn more about Coney Island. Dozens of books have been written about it, dating as far back as the 1880s, including some wonderful photo essays.

Historical Notes

Coney Island's sensational era as a seaside resort lasted for more than a hundred years. As early as the 1830s the rich and famous played here—from writer Herman Melville and poet Walt Whitman to actress Lillian Russell. When the subway gave millions of workingclass New Yorkers access to Coney Island in the 1920s, the crowd changed, the entertainment cheapened, and it became the "playground of the people." On summer weekends, thousands of people of all ages, sizes, shapes, and nationalities poured through the subway turnstiles for entertainment and relief from the city's crushing heat. Among the most famous restaurants of the time was the German-owned Feltman's, whose founder reputedly conceived the notion of serving a sausage in an elongated roll, thereby inventing the hot dog.

Coney Island declined after World War II, and Steeplechase Park finally closed in 1965. Much of the bungalow housing around Coney Island was bulldozed and replaced with large public high-rises that remain today.

The old feisty Coney Island of Steeplechase and Luna Park fame, the rides like the Thunderbolt and the Mile Sky Chaser, the racetracks, huge beach pavilions, flashy hotels, dozens of honky-tonk restaurants, and championship prizefights between muscle men in striped trousers exist mostly in memory and the movies.

Coney Island on the brink of a new millennium may be at a turning point. In true spirit, Coney may be coming back up. There's been talk of the possible construction of an amateur sportsplex stadium here, which would be Brooklyn's biggest gym. Powerful real estate interests have proposed a large retail center, a multiplex cinema, and a virtual-reality amusement park.

Meanwhile, Coney Island is more Brooklyn than Brooklyn itself. Don't miss it, ladies and gentlemen.

ENTERTAINMENT

Abe Stark Ice-Skating Rink. Surf Avenue and the boardwalk, at West 19th Street, 946-6536. Open Oct.–March; call for hours. Rentals are $4.00.

Part of a huge New York City Parks and Recreation Department sports complex, this indoor ice-skating rink is next to Astroland Amusement Park. When warm weather melts the ice at outdoor rinks, or when it rains, Abe Stark is the winter solution. The property is owned by the city, but operation of the facility is subcontracted, so double-check the hours before you go. There is parking on the premises. Trivia question: Who was Abe Stark? Answer: One of Brooklyn's former borough presidents.

Astroland Amusement Park, "Home of the Cyclone." West 12th Street and the Boardwalk, at Surf Avenue, 372–0275. Opens weekends in April, and daily mid-June to September, noon–midnight.

Astroland is the bigger of the two amusement parks here, with about 30 rides and games for adults and older kids. The wood-framed Cyclone Roller coaster, considered one of the best by roller coaster aficionados, and featured in Woody Allen's classic movie, *Annie Hall,* is a screamer's delight. One price for all rides, $13 at selected times. Ten kiddie rides cost $15. Call for information.

Boardwalk and Atlantic Ocean Beach (see listing on page 90).

✪ **Deno's Wonder Wheel Amusement Park.** West 12th Street and the Boardwalk, at Surf Avenue, 372-2592. June to Labor Day, 10 A.M.–midnight; open till 1 A.M. weekends. Weekends in April, May, September, October, weather permitting.

Right next door to Astroland is a family attraction: an amusement park featuring the stomach-churning Wonder Wheel, an official New York City landmark, which since 1920 has towered 150 feet over the Boardwalk, giving thrill-riders a tremendous view of the ocean and Brooklyn's rooftops and streets. The Wonder Wheel, constructed of Bethlehem steel, claims to have maintained a perfect safety record.

You can also take younger kids on about two dozen juvenile rides here, hop on an antique carousel, visit the spookhouse, play video games, grab a hotdog, and go on to visit the **New York Aquarium** nearby or the beach and boardwalk, or **Brighton Beach**, also nearby.

Deno's is named after the Deno Vourderis, a Greek immigrant who jumped ship, swam to Coney Island, sold hot dogs, and bought the Wonder Wheel years ago. His sons run the amusement park today, and they're always there; look for the guys who act like they're in charge.

There's no admission charge to the park; pay as you ride. Ten rides go for $15.

✪ **New York Aquarium for Wildlife Conservation.** Surf Avenue, at 8th Street West, 265-3474 (265-FISH). Daily, 10 A.M.–5 P.M., until 7 P.M. on summer weekends and holidays. Admission is $8.75 for adults and $4.50 for children under 12. Parking is additional. Call for directions. (One hour from Long Island.)

Located at the foot of the boardwalk in Coney Island, the New York Aquarium is home to giant sea turtles, tiger sharks, sea otters, beluga whales, and 10,000 other species. Rated one of the best aquariums in the nation, it is a year-round, indoor-outdoor facility that draws three-quarters of a million visitors annually. Expanded facilities include: *Conservation Hall,* which focuses on worldwide conservation concerns; *Discovery Cove,* a sophisticated display of coastal ecosystems, complete with miniature crashing wave which dumps 400 gallons of water every 30 seconds in a simulated wave motion; *Touch A Ray,* a shark and ray tank; the popular *Aquatheater,* an open-air amphitheater with a narrated dolphin and sea lion show, and *Sea Cliffs,* a re-creation of a rocky Pacific coastal habitat in which sea otters, an adult walrus and her children, and penguins and seals frolic.

Snacks are available at an indoor-outdoor cafeteria. Or, bring your own lunch and have a boardwalk picnic.

Check out the seasonal programs for Halloween, winter holidays, and, of course, summer family camp. You can have birthday parties here, and get lots of information on shipwreck snorkeling off Long Island Sound, setting up home aquariums, and other terrific family activities.

Tip: It is economical to get a Wildlife Conservation Society membership if you plan to visit repeatedly, or visit other NYC area zoos.

Sideshows by the Seashore, 3006 West 12th Street and Surf Avenue, 372-5159. Open summer weekends, Fri., 7 P.M.–midnight; Sat. and Sun., 2 P.M.–midnight. Run by Coney Island, USA, http://www.coneyislandusa.com.

Part nostalgia, part freak-show, part fun, this is a 1990s version of an old-time Ten-in-One Sideshow—that is, ten acts in one show. There are sword swallowers, a "bearded lady with an attitude," snake charmers, and more.

Some of the acts are really fascinating. Sometimes the show folks seem depressed, though; perhaps Coney Island in its glory days is just a hard act to follow.

PARKS AND PLAYGROUNDS

Coney Island Boardwalk. Along the Atlantic Ocean, between Coney Island and Brighton Beach, 946-1350.

Coney Island's massive wooden boardwalk is as much a symbol of this section of Brooklyn as the Brooklyn Bridge is an icon for Brooklyn Heights. This big, beautiful boardwalk extends all the way from Brighton Beach through Coney Island. The natural scenery is as you would expect: the crashing Atlantic, a somewhat littered broad beach—and the people-watching is good too. Old-timers and retirees stroll and converse on the myriad benches along the route, as parents push carriages and joggers speed past. In the winter, the Polar Bear Club has been known to take an icy dive here. This is a well-patrolled and safe stroll during the day, which makes it perfect for a walk after eating in either Brighton Beach or Coney Island. By order of the Parks Department it's also a "quiet zone," which means that loud radios are prohibited. Biking is allowed from 5 to 10 A.M. only.

Seaside–Asser Levy Park. Next to the New York Aquarium, between Surf and Sea Breeze avenues, 946-1364.

This little twenty-two-acre park is a good place to let kids run off some steam after an afternoon at the **New York Aquarium** (see page 89), and it's also notable for summer performances in its bandshell. These shows are arranged in cooperation with BACA, the Brooklyn Arts Council (call 783-3077 to get a schedule).

POINTS OF CULTURAL INTEREST

✪ **Amusement Park Landmarks.** Coney Island.

The Parachute Jump, Cyclone, and Wonder Wheel are all official New York City landmarks dating from the 1920s; the latter two are still in operation. The Cyclone, engineered in 1927, is a rare wooden roller coaster. Cars are pulled up by a chain pulley to the top, and gravity to pulls them down nine spectacular drops and around six curves, reaching a speed of up to 68 miles per hour. The Parachute Jump was built for the New York World's Fair of 1930–40, and then transported to Steeplechase Park. It is closed but the original steel tower is still visible from the Belt Parkway, Verrazano-Narrows Bridge, and many other vantage points. The Wonder Wheel was built in

1918–20 by the Eccentric Ferris Wheel Amusement Company. It is unusual in that eight of the cars are stable, while 16 of them swing on tracks, enhancing the thrill of this 150-foot Ferris wheel.

Coney Island, USA, since 1982 has made its mark by resurrecting fading Coney traditions: freak shows, vaudeville, and other forms of old-fashioned, hard-biting, sometimes corny workingclass entertainment. This unusual nonprofit arts organization has created the **Sideshows by the Seashore** and the **Mermaid Parade**, amassed a collection of Coney memorabilia, mounted art exhibits with a Coney theme, and hosted cutting-edge theater and music. Who makes all this honky-tonk? It is powered by a polyglot mix—people with academic credentials (the founder, Dick Zigun, has a degree from Yale in theater), Coney credentials (grandparents and parents who worked at Coney Island), artists, enthusiasts of the bizarre, and a multicultural mix of local residents who, after all, live there. Coney Island, USA, *is* what they say they want to do: use Coney Island as a way to "champion the honor of American popular art forms through innovative exhibitions and performances." It sounds complicated, but it ain't. Come see for yourself.

✪ **Mermaid Parade.** Surf Avenue and West 12th Street (June).

Combine raucous theater with good clean fun and what you get is a Brooklyn original, the Mermaid Parade. A good-natured, somewhat disorganized affair, the midafternoon parade gets bigger and better every year. Dozens of gorgeous vintage cars lead the procession, followed by mermaids, mermen, and merkids in sometimes freaky, always fishy costumes and floats. Many of the wildest costumes are designed by theater people and artists. It is a photographer's delight of sequins, scant costumes, and corny humor. There's a celebrity King Neptune and Queen Mermaid, and trophies. Everybody has a good time.

✪ **Ocean Parkway Scenic Landmark.** From Seabreeze Avenue to just south of Coney Island.

Brooklyn's premier park architects, Frederick Law Olmsted and Calvert Vaux, envisioned Ocean Parkway as the link between green Prospect Park and the Atlantic Ocean waterfront. The tree-lined parkway has a bike path (once a bridle path), walkways, and wide drives.

Ocean Parkway Viaduct Murals. Intersection of Ocean Parkway and Brighton Beach Avenue.

Sometime after the year 2000, you will see huge murals erected under the Ocean Parkway Viaduct. Commissioned by the MTA, Williamsburg-based artist Deborah Masters has created 128 giant reliefs depicting the parade of humankind on Coney Island—fat and skinny, young and old, ugly and beautiful. The murals have been completed, but can't be installed until after the viaduct's leaks are fixed.

NOTABLE CONEY ISLAND RESTAURANTS

Carolina. 1409 Mermaid Avenue, between West 15th Street and Stillwell Avenue, 714-1294. Mon.–Sat., noon–10 P.M., Sun., 1–10 P.M.

Carolina was founded in 1928, just seven years after the boardwalk opened. In those days the Luna and Steeplechase amusement parks were flourishing and masses of workingclass people of many nationalities—Italian, Jewish, Greek, Polish, German, African-American, Irish—came by subway from Manhattan every summer weekend for relief from the heat. Along with Gargiulo's, Carolina is one of the few surviving eateries from that era, which included the now-defunct Childs and Feltman's, Coney Island's largest restaurant at the time. There is a lot of colorful history here and the food is good, with big portions of old-fashioned Neapolitan home cooking. The interior sports lots of mirrors, a glass wall, and seats for 300 people. Prices are moderate (entrées range from $10 to $18), and you're just a few blocks from the ocean. Valet parking is available.

✪ **Gargiulo's.** 2911 West 15th Street, between Surf and Mermaid avenues, 266-4891. Wed.–Mon., 11 A.M.–10:30 P.M.; closed Tues.

When people speak of dining in Brooklyn, they often mention Gargiulo's. This large family-run Italian restaurant is so popular that regular customers come from as far as New Jersey and Long Island—just check the license plates in the restaurant's huge parking lot. The menu is extensive and many half-portions are available. Don't be shy about asking for something you don't see on the menu or hear about—they'll prepare almost any dish you can think of. One final note: you can eat here for free if you're lucky. At the meal's end, your waiter will ask you for a number from one to ninety. He'll then produce a bucket of small chips, shake it up, and pull one from inside. If the numbers match, the meal is on the house (only applies to groups of ten or fewer). Reservations are necessary almost anytime.

Nathan's Famous Restaurant. Surf Avenue, near Stillwell Avenue, 946-2202. Sun.–Thurs., 8–4 A.M.; Fri.–Sat., 8–5 A.M.

This is the *original* Nathan's. The experts contend that the fries, hot dogs, and corn on the cob here are still better than those at the franchised Nathan's. You can just stand here munching while imagining the days when shrieking riders enjoyed the Thunderbolt, the Mile Sky Chaser, the Loop-o-

Plane, the Whip, the Flying Turns, the Chute-the-Chutes, and the Comet. Or come on the Fourth of July for the twelve-minute Annual Hot-Dog-Eating Contest.

✪ **Totonno's.** 1524 Neptune Avenue, between West 15th and 16th streets, 372-8606. Fri.–Sun., until they run out of dough. No credit cards.

You probably wouldn't stop here in a million years unless you knew what was inside. This Brooklyn institution serves what many consider to be the best brick-oven pizza in the entire Big Apple (except for their new Upper East Side location—maybe). There can be a long wait, but the crowd is jovial. What you've heard is true: they are open only as long as the dough lasts, which means that often they're through before 8 P.M.

And Then There's . . .

Phillips Candy Store. 1237 Surf Avenue, corner of Stillwell Avenue, 372-8783. Daily, 11 A.M.–3 A.M.

It sounds nuts, but this candy store is open until 3 A.M. every night. Why? Because some folks just can't do without their hand-dipped chocolates filled with raisins, cashews, almonds, and more. For the past forty years, Phillips has stayed open late, and he's not about to change things. Located across the street from the original Nathan's, it's a Brooklyn institution.

Sheepshead Bay (including Manhattan Beach and Mill Basin)

Special events: Art shows along Emmons Avenue (May and September). Commemoration of Holocaust Memorial Mall (June).

How it got its name: Sheepshead Bay is named for the sheepshead, a once-common fish in nearby waters, now long gone due to urban pollution.

ABOUT THE NEIGHBORHOOD

The pressure of New York's urban hustle fades quickly amid piers and fishing boats, dressed-down seafood restaurants, and the lovely beach breezes of Sheepshead Bay. Maybe it's the ocean air, but the waterfront at Sheepshead Bay feels as if it belongs in Rhode Island. You can go out with a half-day fishing boat from the **Emmons Avenue piers** in the morning, or come around 4 P.M. to purchase the day's catch. There's a wonderful lobster and fish shop called **Jordan's Lobster Dock** and a completely suburban **ten-screen**

movie theater in Sheepshead Bay. **Lundy's** restaurant—famous in its heydey for accommodating up to 3,000 guests—has reopened, and **Pips on the Bay** is still in business. This pioneer comedy club gave the young Joan Rivers, David Brenner, and Rodney Dangerfield their early breaks. For dinner there is excellent Italian fare at **Maria's** and **Nino's**, among others; and hearty, inexpensive roast beef dinners at **Brennan & Carr**.

Inland, don't be fooled by the modest presence of some of the stores along Sheepshead Bay Road or Avenue U. Like so much of Brooklyn, the plain façades at stores like **Jamar** mask behind-the-scenes bargains on top-of-the-line merchandise. Shoppers can find elegant women's bathing suits year-round at **Seahorse** and discounted designer clothes at **Loehmann's** new store.

Across the inlet from Sheepshead Bay is **Manhattan Beach**, an exclusive residential area. The homes here are luxurious; many have views of the ocean or inlet. Residents now include a growing number of Russians spilled over from nearby Brighton Beach. At its eastern end, **Kingsborough Community College** occupies a stunning piece of real estate, bounded on three sides by the water. The view alone is reason enough to attend one of the free outdoor concerts held here in the summer.

East of Sheepshead Bay in the Mill Basin are a number of attractions, including **Marine Park**, the **Jamaica Bay Riding Academy**, the **Kings Plaza Shopping Mall**, and **Gateway National Park**.

Historical Notes

A bit of colorful history graces Sheepshead Bay. In the late 1800s a horse-racing track ran along Ocean Avenue between Jerome Avenue and Neck Road. During this era wealthy Manhattanites frequented the many fancy Manhattan Beach hotels and resort homes. After racetrack betting was outlawed, the racetrack tried unsuccessfully to shift from horses to cars. The Sheepshead Speedway lasted a brief four years, giving way in 1919 to residential development.

The area benefited greatly from two municipal building programs. In the 1930s the piers along Emmons Avenue were built as part of a Works Progress Administration project. In the 1950s the new Belt Parkway vastly improved access to Sheepshead Bay, which stimulated the growth of the solidly middle-class Jewish and Italian community.

Driver's advisory: Have patience; you'll need it to find a parking spot in the Emmons Avenue area.

ENTERTAINMENT

Century Theater—Cineplex Odeon Kings Plaza. 5201 Kings Plaza, at Flatbush Avenue and Avenue U, 253-1110 or 253-1140. Call for show times.

There are four screens here, on the upper level of the mall. You can send the kids here while you shop; ample parking space is available.

Fun Time, USA. 2461 Knapp Street, between Avenues X and Y. Open daily, year-round including holidays. In winter, Mon.–Thurs., noon–10 P.M.; Friday until 1 A.M. Sat., 10–1 A.M.; Sun, 10 A.M.–10 P.M.; check summer hours. Entrance package goes for $16 or less.

This large indoor amusement park offers over 50,000 square feet of rides, including a maze, tornado ride, bumper cars, batting cages, video arcade, and an arts and crafts center. It will keep the kids entertained for a couple of hours on rainy days. You pay an additional fee to play laser tag.

Adults may find it a little, umm, tacky, but the kids don't mind. There is heavy security at the door. Fun Time is located on an industrial stretch of road just a half mile past the movie theater.

Gambling Boats. Emmons Avenue. Parking available.

Why trek to Atlantic City when you can spend the night on a gambling cruiser right out of Brooklyn? **Manhattan Cruises** (332-1100) advertises "7,000 square feet of casino excitement," for about $20 per person. Gamblers of all types and nationalities come on board and sail past the 12-mile offshore limit to play the slot machines, and games of crap, roulette, blackjack, and poker. Watch newspaper listings for other boats.

Kingsborough Community College. 2001 Oriental Boulevard, off Quentin Avenue, 368-5000. Call for a concert schedule.

For a romantic oceanside Saturday evening, check out the summer concerts here at the far eastern end of Brighton Beach. Bounded on three sides by the Atlantic Ocean, this modern fifty-three-acre campus with its own private beach is one of New York City's loveliest and most secluded spots.

Pips on the Bay. 2005 Emmons Avenue, corner of Ocean Avenue, 646-9433. Wed.–Sun. Call for hours and show details.

Joan Rivers, David Brenner, Rodney Dangerfield, and Andy Kaufman all tried out their early comic routines at Pips. You never know what up-and-comer you may hear first at Pips, or what star may pop in to test a new bunch of jokes. If you're given to making people laugh, you may want to come here, too; talent agents have been known to haunt the place. Food is pretty basic—mozzarella sticks, burgers, chicken—but that's not the main attraction.

Shows are at 9:15 P.M., 11:15 P.M., and sometimes 12:45 A.M. on weekend nights. There is a cover and two-drink minimum. Reservations are recommended.

UA Movies at Sheepshead Bay. 3907 Shore Parkway, between Knapp Street and Harkness Avenue, 615–1700. Call for show times.

It seems like the suburbs here at Brooklyn's largest movie complex, a ten-screen theater easily reached from the Belt Parkway's Knapp Street exit. It's only twenty minutes from Brooklyn Heights in moderate traffic, so you may wait longer to get into the movie than to get to it. The picturesque harbor and **Jordan's Lobster Dock** (see page 105) across the street both contribute to a sense that you've left the city behind.

Russian Nightclubs. See page 80 for a general description of Russian nightclubs. The Russians have arrived in Sheepshead Bay, as is evident by the two following nightclubs.

Paradise Restaurant. 22814 Emmons Avenue, between Nostrand and Bedford avenues, 934-2283. Fri.–Sun., 9 P.M.–3 A.M.; Sun., 7 P.M.–1 A.M.

The scene at Paradise is hard to match, at least this side of the Volga. At this Russian nightclub, you can plan on a late night of dancing, eating, and general fun. It is open only on weekends, when the band playing "international" music is the big attraction. The food is plentiful, good, and heavy; the cost is about $50 per person.

Rasputin. 670 Coney Island Avenue at Avenue X, 332-8111. Mon.–Thurs., noon–10 P.M.; Fri.–Sun., noon–4 A.M.

Ach! The good life! If you haven't guessed, it's a Russian restaurant/nightclub (named after a famous Russian mystic with political clout). Since 1992, Rasputin has made a name for itself by treating customers to a French-Russian version of a Las Vegas dinner, dancing, and floor show. It's larger (and louder) than life: the Russian clientele is outrageously flashy, the food is overwhelming, the cultural innuendo flows thick, and the icy cold Absolut, well, just flows. It's an experience. About $55 per person.

PARKS, PLAYGROUNDS, AND BEACHES

Bill Brown Park Playground. Bedford Avenue, at East 24th Street between Avenues X and Y.

Set among well-kept redbrick row houses but at some distance from the commercial hub of Sheepshead Bay is this pleasant three-acre playground. There's another at Avenue V and East 24th Street.

Fishing Boats. Emmons Avenue, between Ocean and Bedford avenues.

For a wonderfully picturesque Brooklyn activity, walk along this pier at around 4 P.M. any afternoon and watch the fishing boats unload their daily haul of bluefish, flounder, and mackerel. You can buy fresh fish at rock-bottom prices or, if you are in the mood, you can book onto any one of about a dozen party fishing boats that dock here. Both half-day bay fishing boats and full-day ocean fishing boats are available. Half-day boats, more appropriate for families and casual fishermen, leave hourly from 7 A.M.–1 P.M. for four-hour trips and cost $17–$30 for adults, with discounts for kids under twelve. Try the *Pastime* (252-4398) or the *Dorothy B.* (646-4057). It's a good idea to chat with the captains to get full details. Find out where they will be fishing, whether they supply bait and rods, if the crew can help out, and if they provide snacks, restrooms, and, just in case, motion-sickness medication on board.

✪ **Manhattan Beach Park.** Oriental Boulevard, between Ocean and Mackenzie streets.

A favorite among families, Manhattan Beach is a forty-acre public park and beach area, complete with ball fields, surf and sand, concession stands, and room for parking. Located at the southernmost tip of Brooklyn, the beach is most easily accessible by car. After a few hours at the beach, head over to Emmons Avenue for a stroll past the fishing fleet, or inland to Sheepshead Bay Road to do a little shopping. If you're lucky, you may catch an outdoor concert at nearby **Kingsborough College** (see page 95).

Plum Beach. Along BQE, near Floyd Bennett Field. 338-3799.

Stop for a beach walk along a mile and a half of protected shoreline along Dead Horse Bay and Sheepshead Bay. This is an environmentally protected salt marsh area, under the joint jurisdiction of the New York City parks department and the federal park system. School groups often come to explore the salt marsh, which is an estuary for fish and mollusks.

Adults looking for a getaway can bring a picnic or take a mental health break just by strolling along the water. Although not allowed officially, some people go wind surfing here. Fishing is allowed, without a permit.

By car: exit off BQE to right between the Flatbush and Knapp Avenue. By bus, take the 235 from Flatbush Avenue to Floyd Bennett Field, and walk the greenway.

Sheepshead Bay Sailing School. 377-5140. Mid-May through Oct.

You can learn to handle sails and moorings and maneuver a sailboat right here in Brooklyn. Since 1966 Irving Shapiro has given private lessons to aspiring sailors ranging in age from thirteen to sixty. There are beginner, intermediate, and advanced sessions aboard his *Ensign* sloop, which leaves from one of the yacht clubs in Sheepshead Bay on Emmons Avenue. For $50 an hour you can hire out a thirty-five-foot C and C sailboat.

The following parks are in nearby Mill Basin:

✪ **Floyd Bennett Field.** Flatbush Avenue, past Avenue X and Belt Parkway.

For some reason, Brooklynites seem to forget about Floyd Bennett Field. But this old, unused airfield that takes up more than 1,500 acres still rates as one of the city's scruffy rural treasures. There are rarely crowds here. You can zoom around on a bike, try out your homemade recumbent vehicle, or bring a bunch of kids for a birthday party with remote-controlled cars or, better, airplanes. In the summer, hundreds of people come to garden in a designated three-acre area comprised of over 500 individual plots, under the city's Green Thumb project.

And, there's a lot to do nearby. You are just across the street from **Gateway Sports Center**, near the **Sebago Kayak and Canoe Club**, and the wildlife refuge of Jamaica Bay, and across the bridge, Jacob Riis Beach on the Atlantic Ocean.

Who was Floyd Bennett anyway? The pilot who made the virgin flight over the North Pole with Adm. Richard Byrd in 1926. This airfield was built four years later as New York City's first municipal airport, but it was bypassed in favor of the more centrally located LaGuardia as the site for an expanded commercial airport. Floyd Bennett Field was used for several decades by the U.S. military, but since 1972 it has been part of the National Park Service.

Gateway National Park. Floyd Bennett Field, below Shore Parkway, 338-3799.

Go on an adventure stargazing or bird watching or take a self-guided nature walk at America's largest national urban park. The entire expanse of Gateway stretches over 26,000 acres of coastline, marsh, and parks that include Floyd Bennett Field in Brooklyn, Jamaica Bay Wildlife Refuge in Long Island, Breezy Point in Queens, and Sandy Hook in New Jersey.

✪ **Gateway Sports Center.** 3200 Flatbush Avenue, across from Floyd Bennett Field, 253-6816. Daily, 9 A.M.–11 P.M.

At Gateway you can brush up your golf skills, hit a few tennis balls, or take a swing or two at some fastballs. Open year-round, this facility has a driving range, tennis courts, and batting cages plus an eighteen-hole miniature golf facility. It isn't far from **Toys "Я" Us**, the huge **Kings Plaza** shopping mall (page 108), or **Marine Parkway Bridge** which leads to **Jacob Riis Park Beach**.

✪ **Jamaica Bay Riding Academy.** 7000 Shore Parkway, between exits 11 and 12, 531-8949. Daily, 10 A.M.–7:30 P.M.

It isn't exactly a dude ranch, but your child can learn to ride a horse in Brooklyn. There are wonderful trails through 300 acres of bird-watching country, including three miles along the beaches of Jamaica Bay. Kids as young as four can take lessons, and teenagers can ride with a guide for nearly an hour for only $25. The under-four set gets a 20-minute pony ride—with mom or dad holding the horse—for $10. The exit for the riding academy is marked by a large horse. Call for directions.

✪ **Marine Park.** Between Flatbush and Gerritsen avenues, exit 11 off Shore Parkway, 965-6551 or 965-8973.

At 798 acres, Marine Park is Brooklyn's largest outdoor recreation area, and it's worth a visit. There are about a dozen tennis courts on Fillmore Avenue and Stuart Street (call 965-8993 for permit information), playgrounds at East 38th and East 33rd streets, and a running track at East 33rd street. The Urban Park Rangers lead a "haunted" twilight walk at Halloween that some youngsters call "intense"—flashlights are provided. This walk is so popular that the line starting at the ball field has been known to run three blocks. You also can enjoy kite flying, bird-watching, biking, and the usual park related activities, as well as summertime concerts. Marine Park also is home to Brooklyn's largest golf course (call 338-7113 for information).

Marine Parkway Bridge. Southern end of Flatbush Avenue. The one-way car toll is $1.75.

Most kids love bridges, and this is a pleasant one, connecting Brooklyn to the public beach at **Jacob Riis Park** and more secluded beaches off residential streets in Rockaway, Queens. Between the bridge and **Kings Plaza Shopping Center** (see page 108) you will pass a **lobster shop, Toys "Я" Us, Gateway Golf and Tennis Range, Dead Horse Inlet**, and the old **Floyd Bennett Field**. Once over the bridge, bear left and follow the signs to the public beach areas. The bridge also has a bike path.

✪ **Sebago Canoe Club.** Avenue N and Paerdegat Avenue North, 241-3683.

For an annual fee of about $100 members here store their kayaks and canoes for trips out into Jamaica Bay. Call for information on classes, membership, and a bimonthly newsletter.

POINTS OF CULTURAL INTEREST

F.W.I.L. Lundy Brothers Restaurant. Emmons Avenue, corner of Ocean Avenue.

A New York City landmark, Lundy's of Sheepshead Bay was considered America's largest restaurant when it was built in 1934. It is said that the restaurant could serve as many as 5,000 meals a day, and 15,000 on a major holiday. Closed in 1979, it remained an empty shell for many years, but a smaller, renovated Lundy's has now reopened and is back in business (see below). F.W.I.L., by the way, is not a clever acronym, but the initials of the founder, Frederick William Irving Lundy. The building is unusual for the area: a two-story stucco Spanish Mission style.

Wyckoff-Bennett Residence. 1669 East 22nd Street, corner of Kings Highway.

Admire this homestead, a national historic landmark, from the outside only; it is still privately owned. Built in the Dutch style, it was used by Hessian troops during the Revolutionary War. The date of its construction is discreetly carved into one of the wooden beams: 1766.

NOTABLE SHEEPSHEAD BAY RESTAURANTS

Emmons Avenue

Along Emmons Avenue or within walking distance of the piers you'll find the following:

Castle Harbour. 3149 Emmons Avenue, corner of Coyle Street, 332-0046. Daily, 11 A.M.–11 P.M.

Tasty continental cuisine and seafood are the main attractions at Castle Harbour, but so is the decor. Come inside and you'll be met by a grizzly bear and a lion, courtesy of the big game hunter-owner. Entrées average about $14 and include fresh fish, veal marsala, and chicken dishes. Sheepshead Bay denizens give Castle Harbour a big thumbs-up.

Jordan's Lobster Dock. 3165 Harkness Avenue, 934-6300. Tues.–Thurs, Sun., 11:30 A.M.–8 P.M.; Fri–Sat., until 11 P.M.

A Cape Cod–style restaurant, Jordan's serves lobster dinners in three price ranges, starting with a $15 special for a one-pounder, as well as fried clams, flounder, soft-shell crabs, bay and sea scallops, homemade fish cakes, and a huge fisherman's platter combo. It's all as fresh as can be; Jordan's runs the fish store next door, by the same name.

Lundy Brothers. 1901–1929 Emmons Avenue, corner of Ocean Avenue, 743-0022. Mon.–Thurs., 5–10 P.M.; Fri.–Sat., 5 P.M.–midnight; Sun., 3–9 P.M.

There's nothing fishy about this legend revisited. The newly renovated

Lundy's opened its doors in 1996, launching a second chapter in the 62-year history of Brooklyn's most famous and popular seafood restaurant. Just about anybody who was anybody in old Brooklyn ate at Lundy's, located on the Emmons Avenue waterfront across from the fishing boats, and a relic of the once-thriving fishing industry here.

Certain things have changed: the airy, bright renovation seats fewer people, and surly waiters are no longer likely to insult you. But tradition is kept alive in its specialties of seafood, especially shellfish (you can't miss the big tank stocked with dozens of lobsters ranging from one to eight pounds) big portions, great desserts, and an informally elegant ambience. From the pictures of old Coney Island hanging on the walls, to the annotations on the menu describing some favorite dishes of the original Mr. Lundy, or the corner gift shop selling memorabilia, you can't forget that you are eating not in a restaurant, but a tradition.

You'll feel comfortable here with your 82-year-old grandfather or your 10-year-old child. Lundy's service is professional and the food is reliably excellent. For a quick or solo meal, check out the raw bar up front; special events are held upstairs.

✪ **Maria's Restaurant.** 3073 Emmons Avenue, near Brown Street, 646-6665. Daily, noon–11 P.M.; closed Tues.

For more than sixty years Maria has won the hearts of locals. The food is fresh, the service is friendly, and it is as good a restaurant for the entire family as you're likely to find. There are many seafood specials, along with traditional veal Milanese, chicken rollatini, and pasta dishes. Most entrées are about $10. And since the restaurant is just a few blocks from the fishing piers, you can take a stroll before or after you eat.

Randazzo's Clam Bar. 2017-23 Emmons Avenue, between Ocean and Bedford avenues, 769-1000. Daily, noon–midnight.

Unpretentious, noisy, and fun, Randazzo's has been serving up fresh fish for more than 25 years. If specializes in fried calamari, scungilli, and baked clams.

Scoop Du Jour Cafe. 1738 Sheepshead Bay Road, at Shore Parkway, 646-4923.

This quiet little café is a great place to stop for coffee, sweets, ice cream, and hand-dipped chocolates. It's just a few blocks away from Emmons Avenue if you want a break from the fishing pier ambience.

Other Restaurants

"Inland" restaurants worth checking out include the following:

Abbracciamento on the Pier. 2200 Rockaway Parkway, off exit 13 from the Belt Parkway, 251-5517. Sun.–Thurs., noon–11 P.M.; Fri.–Sat., noon–midnight.

As you dine on Italian specialties and seafood, enjoy great views of Jamaica Bay. The peripherals here are a real attraction: the panorama, piano music in the evenings, outdoor balcony dining, and yes, courtesy docking for those who arrive by boat. Located near Kennedy Airport (not exactly in Sheepshead Bay!), it is off the beaten track but certainly offers an elegant way to reenter reality after jetting—or boating—home from a vacation. Dinner entrées range from $18 up. There is a champagne brunch on Sunday for about $17.

✪ **Brennan and Carr.** 3432 Nostrand Avenue, at Avenue U, 769-1254. Mon.–Thurs., 10–1 A.M.; Fri.–Sat., 11–2 A.M.; Sun., 11 A.M.–1 P.M.

The aroma of roast beef positively wafts out of this unassuming redbrick building. Brennan and Carr has been around for about sixty years, and this is still one of the best places in Brooklyn for roast beef. A good-size sandwich is about $4.50; a full plate that includes french fries and vegetables is under $8. You can take out or eat in the small, pleasant back room. A small parking lot is on the premises.

✪ **Fiorentino.** 311 Avenue U, near McDonald Avenue, 372-1445. Daily, noon–midnight.

This large, noisy, busy two-hundred-person restaurant gets rave reviews. The reason is clear: excellent Italian fare at moderate prices in a very convenient location on one of Sheepshead Bay's neighborhood shopping strips. Weekend reservations are recommended. A branch of the family that owns Fiorentino started **Carolina's Restaurant** in Coney Island (see page 92).

Michael's Restaurant. 2929 Avenue R, near Nostrand Avenue, 998-7851. Daily, noon–11 P.M.

The setting couldn't be nicer at this family-owned, 150-seat restaurant. Live music, moderately priced excellent food—the menu runs seven pages—and a steady clientele have contributed to its success for thirty-five years. It is located in Marine Park between Sheepshead Bay and Midwood. Reservations are needed on weekends.

Nino's Restaurant. 1971 Coney Island Avenue, between Avenue P and Quentin Road, 336-7872. Daily, noon–11 P.M.

Brooklynites who wander the borough in search of good Italian fare say that moderately priced Nino's ranks high for tasty northern and southern cuisine. Pasta dishes run about $10–$12, and seafood entrées are a few dollars more. Reservations are recommended on weekends.

Original Captain's Quarters. 2990 Avenue U, between Brown and Batchelder streets, 368-1097. Weekdays, noon–10 P.M., Sat.–Sun., noon–11 P.M.

A Marine Park landmark, the white building with the greenhouse is overflowing with the nautical motifs inside—nets, stuffed fish, you name it. We don't need to tell you what to order since the seafood here is fresh, and cooked the way you want it. If you can, leave room for some key lime pie for dessert. Not far from the **Kings Plaza Movies**, or nearby beaches.

Pizzarini Natural. 2812 Ocean Avenue, near Avenue X, 648-4248. Daily, 11 A.M.–11 P.M.

Health-conscious types will love the eat-in–take-out menu here: whole wheat batter-dipped zucchini, stir-fried vegetables, lots of salads, and interesting stuffings for pita bread sandwiches. But not all is straight from the garden: the menu also includes such old favorites as chicken florentine, beef and broccoli, and shrimp marinara. Good quality, a broad range of entrées under $10, and a commitment to fresh ingredients make this a good choice. It is close to Sheepshead Bay shopping.

Roll 'N' Roaster. 2901 Avenue U, at Nostrand Avenue, 769-5831. Daily, 11–1 A.M.

The owners call this "a grownup fast-food restaurant" serving roast beef, burgers, and fries. In business for more than thirty years, Roll 'N' Roaster is a little more expensive than fast-food chains, but it sells good food in a clean environment.

✪ **Sahara Mediterranean Restaurant, King of Shish Kebab and Gyro.** 2337 Coney Island Avenue, between Avenues T and U, 376-8594. Daily, 11 A.M.–2 P.M.

When a NYPD car is parked outside a restaurant at night, it's either trouble or a recommendation for low-cost, high-quality food. In this case, it's a recommendation.

You will find knock-out homemade kebabas and gyros made of finely chopped lamb, wonderful lentil soup, crunchy-fresh salads with lemon and parsley, stuffed borekas and eggplant done three ways, and an array of honey-rich sweets. Appetizers average about $3 and a kebab with rice is $9. Take out or eat in the unadorned back room and patio.

Avenue U: Another Brooklyn Chinatown

Melting pot indeed! Second only to **Sunset Park**, this is a burgeoning Chinatown, with Chinese trading stores, Chinese fish stores, Chinese travel agents—and, of course, Chinese restaurants. Here are several:

✪ **Hop Sing Seafood Restaurant.** 1241 Avenue U at East 12th Street, 375-3388. Daily, 10:30 A.M.–11 P.M. Cash only.

A highly rated Chinese restaurant, Hop Sing has wonderful duck and noodle dishes, soups and tasty fish dishes. Daring customers might ask the waiter to bring some *ja g guy, seeaw ong, yow ja tofu*, or *chow fun naachoy* . . . (and nope, we're not telling what they are!).

Ocean Palace Seafood Restaurant. As good as the original; you can't go wrong here. See listing in Sunset Park, page 288.

Pho Hoai Vietnamese Restaurant. 1906 Avenue U, between East 19th and 20th streets, 616-1233. Daily, 10:30 A.M.–10:30 P.M.

You know it's good when there are more South Asians in the restaurant than Americans, and that's often the case in this large, friendly Vietnamese restaurant. And, it's gotten rave reviews in local papers.

The portions are almost as big as the names of the dishes (a spicy shrimp dish is called *tom ram man ot zanh*) and the food is simply delicious. A specialty of the house are the "rice noodle beef" soup dishes; there are eighteen varieties. It's not a Chinese restaurant, so don't expect fortune cookies or those pre-dinner fried noodle sticks. *Tip*: Skip the wine and have beer instead if you want an alcoholic drink.

✪ **Win Sing Sea Food Restaurant.** 1321 Avenue U, at East 13th Street, 998-0360. Daily, 8 A.M.–10 P.M. Cash only.

The most popular restaurant on the strip, Win Sing is filled with local Chinese customers. There are some unusual dishes such as Singapore fried rice stick noodles, as well as the usual General Tso's shrimp, roast duck on rice, and many seafood dishes. Dim sum are served daily from 8 A.M. to 4 P.M.

SHOPPING

Specialty Food Shops

Bagels: There are no fewer than 21 listings in the Brooklyn White Pages under "bagel" (and more in the Yellow!). Here are two in this neighborhood:

Bagel Station. 1425 Sheepshead Bay Road, corner of East 15th Street, 769-8200. Mon.–Sat., 6 A.M.–11 P.M.; Sun., 6:30 A.M.–7 P.M.

Coney Island Bialy. 2359 Coney Island Avenue, at Avenue U, 339-9281. Mon.–Thurs., 5 A.M.–midnight; Fri.–Sun., open 24 hours.

✪ **Jordan's Lobster Dock.** 3165 Harkness Avenue, off Belt Parkway, 934-6300. Sun.–Thurs., 9 A.M.–6 P.M.; Fri. and Sat., 9 A.M.–7 P.M.

You may feel as if you're in Seattle or Cape Cod at this appealing shop that overlooks a harbor full of cabin cruisers. This is no average fish store—you can actually walk out with a complete meal. Jordan's sells delicious take-out Manhattan and New England clam chowder; lobsters steamed to order while you wait; fresh-cooked shrimp; and a full clam bar from which to select your evening appetizers. There's also plenty of fresh raw fish, baskets of clams, and frozen shrimp, octopus, Alaskan king crab claws, and squid, along with plenty of condiments. Kids will enjoy watching the staff clean and chop the fresh fish and catch live lobsters from a three-tiered holding pen. A little out of the way, Jordan's is behind the cinema complex known as **UA Movies at Sheepshead Bay** (see page 96). You'll know it by the huge statue of a fisherman in foul weather gear out front. They've got a restaurant, too (see page 100).

Interesting Neighborhood Shops

A Little Jazz. 20–27 Emmons Avenue, at Loehmann's Seaport Plaza, 934-9100. Mon.–Fri., 11 A.M.–7 P.M.; Sat.–Sun., 11 A.M.–9 P.M.

A terrific store for girls and boys, Little Jazz sells a large array of Speedo swimgear, practical daily wear, dress-up clothes, lots of froufrou for little girls, and a sensible selection for boys as well.

Field Brothers. 1665 Sheepshead Bay Road, between Emmons and Voorhies avenues, 615-3030. Mon.–Wed. and Fri.–Sat. 11 A.M.–6:45 P.M.; Thurs., 11 A.M.–8:30 P.M.; Sun., noon–5 P.M.

This men's department store is part of a national chain now, but it started out as a local store on Kings Highway. The ambience is reminiscent of the men's department in an old department store, like the now-defunct Altman's: carpeted, calm, and classic. Field Brothers sells moderate to better brand-name suits, including Dior, Mani, Valentino, Louis Roth, and LeBaron, plus sportcoats, slacks, and accessories. Alterations are free.

Here's A Bookstore. 1989 Coney Island Avenue, between Quentin and Avenue P, 645-6675. Mon.–Fri., 11 A.M.–6 P.M.; Sat., 11 A.M.–4 P.M.; Sun., noon–4 P.M.

It's hard to maintain a mom-and-pop bookstore, but if you come in here and peruse the wide variety of kids' books, fiction, and nonfiction, you'll see what a labor of love means. It's one of the few remaining independent bookstores in Brooklyn—and it's enormous! It's just a few blocks from **Lester's.**

Jamar. 1714 Sheepshead Bay Road, between Shore Parkway and Voorhies Avenue, 615-2222. Mon.–Sat., 11 A.M.–5:30 P.M.; Thurs., 11 A.M.–7:30 P.M.; closed Sun.

Specializing in fine jewelry and giftware with brand names such as Movado, Lenox, and Waterford, this little store sells many of the better-quality items you'd expect to find only in larger Manhattan department stores. Some lines are discounted from 10 to 40 percent. The friendly sales staff will work with you on special orders.

Jazz. 432 Coney Island Avenue, 627-0100. Mon.–Sat., 10 A.M.–6 P.M.

Youthful styles for "sharp" dressers, with American and French designer sportswear. Sweaters are in the $100 range, shirt or pant sets about $140.

✪ **Learning Wheel.** 1514 Avenue Z, between East 15th and East 16th streets, 934-5540. Mon.–Fri., 11 A.M.–6 P.M.; Sat., 11 A.M.–5:30 P.M.; closed Sun.

You could call this the toy equivalent to a health food store—a large store dedicated to educational supplies. The target market is schoolteachers, but kids and parents will find plenty of games, art supplies, books, flash cards, workbooks, math and language games, puzzles, stickers, posters, and other gizmos here. The shop is a few blocks from Sheepshead Bay Road, but it's within walking distance. Ask to see the mail-order catalog. Phone orders are accepted.

✪ **Lester's.** 2411 Coney Island Avenue, near Avenue U, 336-3560. Fri.–Mon. and Wed., 10 A.M.–6 P.M.; Tues. and Thurs., 10 A.M.–9 P.M.; Sun., 11 A.M.–5 P.M.

Lester's is a famous discount family clothing empire. Started in 1940 by Lester and Lil, the seven separate stores feature trendy styles for girls, boys, and preteen juniors. Other shops feature activewear; men's clothing and shoes; women's and kids' shoes, clothing for toddlers, and an extensive layette department. This is a great place to divide and conquer—each family member to his or her own shop. Prices on name brands are about 20 percent below department store prices.

✪ **Loehmann's at Loehmann's Seaport Plaza.** 2103-2127 Emmons Avenue, on the waterfront, 368-1256. Mon.–Sat., 10 A.M.–9 P.M., Sun., 11 A.M.– 6 P.M.

They call themselves an "upscale, off-price specialty retailer." At prices that are 30 to 65 percent less than at department stores, Loehmann's has about 9,000 pairs of shoes, an extensive collection of women's suits, sportswear, and intimate apparel. Its famous Backroom is stuffed with 6,000 pieces of designer clothing and expensive evening wear and dress suits.

As always, there's the thoughtful comfort of the hubby lounge—overstuffed chairs for the guys to slouch in while the wives get busy shopping and spending.

Loehmann's, the store that gave birth to the word "discount," was itself born in Brooklyn in 1921. The old Duryea Place store is gone, and in its stead there's this spiffy two-story shop, opened in 1996 and one of largest in the now publicly held Loehmann's national empire. If shopping whets your appetite, check out **Randazo's Clam Bar** nearby.

MB Discount Furniture. 2311 Avenue U, between East 23rd and 24th streets, 332-1500. Mon., Tues., Thurs., and Fri., 10 A.M.–9 P.M.; Wed. and Sat., 10 A.M.–6 P.M.; closed Sun.

The huge showroom here is packed with lovely, high-quality American and imported gear for the youngest generation; cribs, high chairs, and rocking chairs. The layette selection is equally attractive. Sales staff are service-oriented and friendly, and prices are heavily discounted. They'll help you design the color scheme and theme of your child's room for free. Delivery is available for a modest fee.

Natural Herb Shop Co., 210 East 14th Street, between avenues U and V, 998-9359. Daily, 10 A.M.– 8:30 P.M.

This clean, well-organized Chinese herbalist shop sells ginseng and teas that are widely accepted as cures. There is also a New York State–licensed acupuncturist available, and a masseuse who uses natural herbs and lotions in body and foot massage.

PJS Cosmetics. 2516 Avenue U, between East 25th and 26th streets, 646-1151. Mon.–Sat., 10 A.M.–6 P.M.; Thurs.–Fri., 10 A.M.–7 P.M., Sun., 11 A.M–5 P.M.

Better brands of cosmetics and perfumes are sold at a discount here, from Borghese, Orlane, and Elizabeth Arden skin products to Chanel, Guerlain, and Christian Dior perfumes. There's also a good selection of jewelry and other accessories.

✪**Sam Ash.** 2600 Flatbush Avenue, 951-3888. Mon.–Fri., 11 A.M.–8 P.M., Sat. 11 A.M.–7 P.M., Sun. noon–5 P.M.

Sam Ash is famous nationwide among musicians as a discounter of top-quality musical instruments. You will find plenty of top electric guitars, synthesizers, and high-tech equipment to choose from as well as more traditional instruments. A Brooklyn legend, it was founded by Sam and Rose Ashkenase (she reputedly pawned her diamond engagement ring to start the business) and their descendants now oversee an empire in six states that has served the likes of Stevie Wonder and Garth Brooks. The shop on East 13th Street has been closed.

✪ **Seahorse.** 1716 Sheepshead Bay Road, between Shore Parkway and Voorhies Avenue, 646-9133. Mon.–Wed., Fri., and Sat., 10 A.M.–7 P.M.; Thurs., 10 A.M.–8 P.M.; Sun., 11 A.M.– 5 P.M.

You won't find a more sophisticated and attractive collection of swimwear for the entire family north of Rio. Husband-and-wife team Marcel and Nancy Goldfarb have assembled an exciting range of imported Israeli, Italian, and Spanish swimwear for women, men, boys, and girls that includes such brand names as Gottex, Diva, and Gideon Oberon. They also sell beach shoes, bags, and other paraphernalia. Women's suits start at $65; top-of-the-line Le Perla suits cost about $200.

In nearby Mill Basin you'll find the following:

Kings Plaza Shopping Center. Corner of Flatbush Avenue and Avenue U, 253–6842. Mon.–Sat., 10 A.M.–9:30 P.M.; Sun, noon–5 P.M. Parking is $1.

Anchored by Macy's at one end and Alexander's at the other, this mall has more than 135 different retailers under one roof. Clothing and shoes make up about one-quarter of all the merchandise sold here, but food, sporting goods, and jewelry are also heavily represented with national chains (the Gap and Radio Shack) and many smaller outfits. Little kids can ride the indoor carousel on the lower level, and older kids can wander at will or watch one of four movies at the mall's RKO Century Theater while the adults shop (or maybe it's the other way around). Within walking distance on Flatbush Avenue are other major chains.

✪ **Toys "Я" Us.** 2875 Flatbush Avenue, between Belt Parkway and Kings Plaza Shopping Center, across from Marine Park Golf Course, 258-2061. Mon.–Sat., 9:30 A.M.–9:30 P.M.; Sun., 10 A.M.–6 P.M.

Brooklyn has three Toys "Я" Us stores. This Mill Basin branch of the national chain has just about anything a kid could want–at low, discounted prices. As at all Toys "Я" Us stores, disposable diapers and baby food are about as cheap as you'll ever find them.

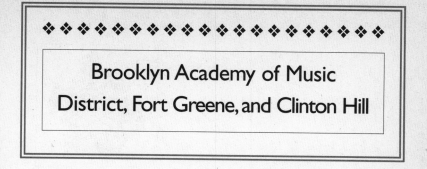

Brooklyn Academy of Music District, Fort Greene, and Clinton Hill

Where it is: An area in northwestern Brooklyn, halfway between the Manhattan Bridge and Park Slope. Specifically:

BAM district is loosely defined as located in the triangle created by Atlantic Avenue, Fulton Avenue, and Hanson Place.

Clinton Hill is centered at Pratt Institute, and is bounded by the BQE to the north, Classon Avenue to the east, Atlantic Avenue to the south, and Vanderbilt Avenue to the west.

Fort Greene is bounded by the Brooklyn Navy Yard on the north, Classon Avenue to the east, Atlantic Avenue on the south, and Flatbush Avenue to the west. The boundary between Fort Greene and Clinton Hill is Vanderbilt Avenue.

What's nearby: Atlantic Center and the LIRR, Bedford-Stuyvesant, Brooklyn Heights, Carroll Gardens, Cobble Hill, Park Slope and Prospect Heights, Downtown Brooklyn, and the waterfront.

How to get there:

By car: Coming from Manhattan along Flatbush Avenue, turn left onto Myrtle Avenue or Fulton Street.

By subway: Numbers 2, 3, 4, 5, D, or Q train to Atlantic Avenue; B, M, N, or R train to Pacific Street; C train (A on weekends) to Lafayette Avenue.

By cab: Atlantic Avenue Car Service (797 5666). Fares are about $7 to Brooklyn Heights, $18 to Grand Central Station.

By BAMbus: For most events a BAMBUS leaves for BAM one hour before curtain time from 120 East 42nd Street in Manhattan, across from Grand Central Terminal.

How each got its name:

BAM area is of course named for the prestigious Brooklyn Academy of Music (BAM).

Clinton Hill, literally just up the hill from Fort Greene Park, was a fashionable nineteenth-century residential area named for New York governor DeWitt Clinton.

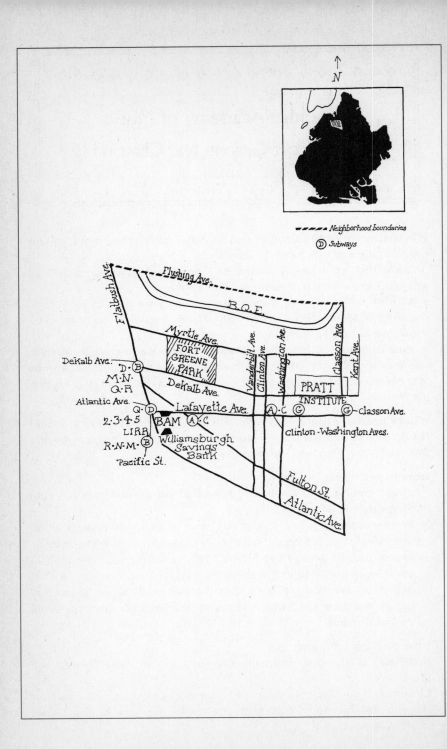

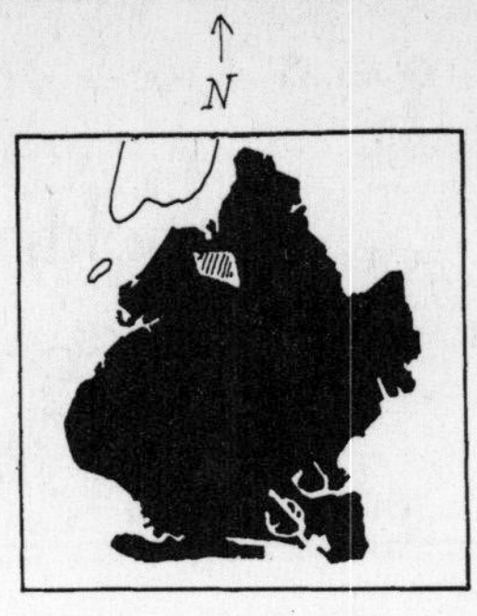
N
Neighborhood Boundaries
D Subways

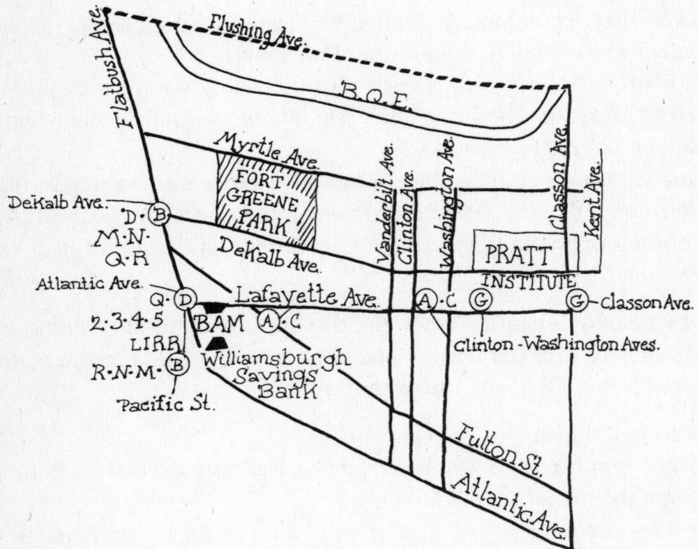
Flatbush Ave.
Flushing Ave.
B.Q.E.
Myrtle Ave.
FORT GREENE PARK
DeKalb Ave.
D · B
M · N ·
Q · R
DeKalb Ave.
Atlantic Ave.
Q · D
2·3·4·5
LIRR
R·N·M· B
Pacific St.
Lafayette Ave.
BAM
A · C
Williamsburgh Savings Bank
Vanderbilt Ave.
Clinton Ave.
Washington Ave.
Classon Ave.
Kent Ave.
PRATT INSTITUTE
A · C
G
G
Classon Ave.
Clinton-Washington Aves.
Fulton St.
Atlantic Ave.

Fort Greene is named for Gen. Nathaniel Greene, who served in the Battle of Long Island during the Revolutionary War.

Special events: Fort Greene historic home tour (May every other year); Cultural Crossroads Fair (May); Garden tour (June); Dance Africa at BAM (June).

Historic Districts: All three areas are historic districts: the Brooklyn Academy of Music district, Clinton Hill, and Fort Greene.

ABOUT THE NEIGHBORHOODS

BAM Area

The immediate area around the Brooklyn Academy of Music is a New York City landmarked district. Some of the old buildings you'll see here are architectural remnants from the nineteenth century, when this section of Brooklyn was first a thriving cultural and business center, which it is again becoming.

If you've been to BAM before, and are queasy about the neighborhood, *come again*. Things are changing rapidly. (This refers mostly to Manhattanites; both Brooklyn residents and foreign tourists seem more adventurous.) The area is much busier since the 1998 opening of BAM's four-screen **Rose Cinemas**, and the long-anticipated relocation of the **Mark Morris Dance Company**. There are now nearby places to eat—the on-site **BamCafé** and **New City Café** across the street. By car, Park Slope and Brooklyn Heights restaurants such as **Cucina, Max & Moritz, La Bouillabaisse**, and **Henry's End** aren't far away. And the nearby mall, the **Atlantic Center** and offshoot businesses surrounding it, are almost, well, suburban.

If you are going to the Majestic, which is one block from the BAM Opera House, try to stop in at **UrbanGlass**, a major glass-making studio with an interesting shop and occasional curated shows (see listing for hours). For dinner, you can go to the above-mentioned, have deli at **Junior**'s, or walk a few blocks to two very good and casual neighborhood restaurants: **Cambodian Cuisine** and **Keur N'Deye**, a Senegalese restaurant.

For beginning collectors of art, the **Clinton Hill Simply Art Gallery** offers a low-key introduction to emerging African-American artists.

And a final honest word about safety: According to NYC Police Department information, the area around BAM and the Majestic is as safe as most places in Manhattan.

Shopkeepers and restaurateurs will welcome visitors and BAM patrons. Fort Greene is mostly middle class—brownstones here sell for $300,000 and up. It is a very cool place: a predominantly African-American but interracial community, and many residents are trend-setting designers, writers, entrepreneurs, and professionals.

Fort Greene and Clinton Hill

Many visitors have actually been to Fort Greene without even knowing it. Just five minutes from the Manhattan Bridge, you can't visit the **Brooklyn Academy of Music** without coming to Fort Greene. But BAM is *not* the only reason to visit Fort Greene.

Here's why: With its rows of renovated nineteenth-century brownstones and sycamore-lined streets, Fort Greene is one of Brooklyn's loveliest landmark brownstone areas. Neighboring **Clinton Hill**, once a silk-stocking, mansion-filled retreat for wealthy industrialists, is home to **Pratt Institute**—and throughout, the architecture is superb.

Something about Fort Greene attracts talent: residents have included poet Walt Whitman, who penned "Leaves of Grass"; author Richard Wright, who wrote "Native Son"; poet Marianne Moore, who rhymed that "Writing is exciting, and baseball is like writing." Octogenarian and accomplished artist Ernie Chrichlow lived in Fort Greene for many years, not to mention jazz saxophonists Steve Coleman and Branford Marsalis, film director Spike Lee, jazz vocalist Betty Carter, and trumpet master Lester Bowie.

From passersby, you'll see that contemporary Fort Greene is one of New York's refreshingly integrated neighborhoods. The population is about two-thirds black, one-quarter white, and a tenth Latin American, according to the *Encyclopedia of New York City*. It is home to many artists, designers, filmmakers, and musicians who, along with foreigners and yuppies, have been drawn to Fort Greene by its proximity to Manhattan, its historic charm and its affordable housing stock. Among residents in the late 1990s are playwright Michael Weller, author Nelson George, and actress Rosie Perez. Artist Richard Artschwager has his studio here.

Fort Greene has an eclectic group of restaurants and shops worth a visit, including **Keur N'Deye**, a Senegalese restaurant, and **Cambodian Cuisine**, and the **E-Shop** for women's clothing. Sundays are particularly good for hearing gospel music during services at the **Institutional Church of God in Christ**.

After years of relative quiet, Fort Greene has undergone many changes recently, with the opening of the **Atlantic Center**, expansions of **BAM**'s activities, a large new endowment for the prestigious public **Brooklyn Technical High School** in the area, and an increasingly well-heeled population.

Historical Notes

After the Dutch sailed into New York harbor in 1624, a few of them created farms in "Breuckelen," stretching uphill from the East River to about Greene Avenue today. The initiation of Fulton Ferry transportation from Manhattan to Brooklyn sparked the suburbanization of nearby farmlands.

Shipbuilding at the **Brooklyn Navy Yard** was the main occupation here for over a century, as it was through much of coastal Brooklyn. The Navy Yard remained an important source of jobs until the yard finally closed in 1966.

From its earliest beginnings, there was an independent black community in this area. In the 1940s a free-black community of shipbuilders lived here—that was before the Civil War brought widespread emancipation. Indeed, the **Hanson Place Baptist Church**, now known as the **Hanson Place Seventh Day Adventist Church**, was an important stop for slaves fleeing the South via the Underground Railroad. More than half of the black population in Brooklyn lived in Fort Greene by 1870.

European immigrants arrived, too. Upper-class street names such as Portland and Oxford, reminiscent of London, were given to the newly created nineteenth-century developments to attract new residents. Irish, German, and English settlers occupied some of the row houses still seen today. In 1848, Fort Greene Park was created as part of the grand scheme to create urban oases of green throughout New York City.

Lower Fort Greene was settled by the middle and working class. But the neighborhood's most desirable residential location—up the hill on Clinton and Washington avenues—was the site of sumptuous villas with great lawns, backed by elegant carriage houses like those that still line Waverly Avenue. Clinton Hill became known as a fashionable district of great mansions designed by famous architects of the era. Charles Pratt of the Standard Oil Company catalyzed the neighborhood by building a home at 252 Clinton Avenue in 1874. Each of Pratt's sons also was presented with a fine home along the avenue as a wedding present. Number 229 recalls a Tuscan villa; 241 is a brick Queen Anne, with a glistening green tile roof and a porte-cochère, now the home of the Roman Catholic Bishop of Brooklyn; 245 is a neo-Georgian owned today by St. Joseph's College. Other merchants and industrialists who followed Pratt's lead included Cuban coffee magnate John Arbuckle, members of the Underwood family of typewriter fame, lace manufacturer A. G. Jennings, and D. R. Hoagland, a baking soda merchant.

At the turn of the century the area down the hill was developed further. Fulton Street thrived, and the **Brooklyn Academy of Music** (BAM) was built in 1907 along with the Martyrs Memorial in Fort Greene Park (1907) and the Masonic Temple (1907). In her essay "Brooklyn from Clinton Hill," Pulitzer Prize–winning poet Marianne Moore captured the elegance of the era from her home at 260 Cumberland Street. By the 1920s, with the surge of the film industry, great movie palaces such as the Paramount (now **Long Island University**) brought in crowds to see the likes of Al Jolson. The Williamsburgh Savings Bank went up in 1929.

In the Depression years much of the era fell into disrepair, and during World War II many brownstones were subdivided into rooming houses to accommodate the seventy thousand workers laboring at the nearby Brooklyn Navy Yard. Many mansions in nearby Clinton Hill were razed; a precious few were incorporated into Pratt Institute and St. Joseph's College. Gentrification began in the late 1960s and 1970s, leading to renovation and rising real estate values. The area bounded by Willoughby and Vanderbilt avenues and South Elliot Place, Fulton Street, and Fort Greene Park is now a landmark district.

Fort Greene has survived and thrived for years as a racially and economically mixed area—a record of which the community is justifiably proud.

On the brink of the twenty-first-century, Fort Greene and the BAM area are poised for a new phase of development. The recent opening of the **Atlantic Center**, **Marriott Hotel**, and expansion of BAM's facilities and the district all bode well for the ongoing renaissance here.

Kidstuff

Fort Greene Park's rolling hills and playgrounds, plus the special events run by the Urban Park Rangers, are a child's treat. **BAM** has many programs geared toward the young, and at the **Williamsburg Savings Bank** you can open an interest-bearing savings account for your child with only a $2 deposit.

PARKS AND PLAYGROUNDS

✪ **Fort Greene Park.** Bounded by Washington Park, DeKalb and Myrtle avenues.

Thought to have the world's only all-marble bathrooms, this lovely park designed by Olmsted and Vaux of **Prospect Park** and Central Park fame is topped by a 148-foot Doric column, built in 1908 as a monument to the Prison Ship Martyrs. The park also contains six beautiful tennis courts. (For tennis permits, contact Brooklyn Parks Dept., 95 Prospect Park West, Mon.–Fri., 9 A.M.–4 P.M., 965-8914.)

✪ **Underwood Playground.** Washington Avenue at Lafayette Avenue.

This big, lovely playground is one of the nicest in the area. The land used to be the site of a mansion belonging to typewriter baron John T. Underwood. As the story goes, his widow had it demolished so that her precious home would not fall into the "wrong hands" when she thought the neighborhood was deteriorating. As is apparent from surrounding homes in the area, the original mansion would have fit in just fine.

POINTS OF CONTEMPORARY CULTURAL INTEREST

✪ **Brooklyn Academy of Music.** 30 Lafayette Avenue at Ashland Place, 636-4100. Phone to be put on the mailing list.

BAM, the jaunty nickname for the Brooklyn Academy of Music, is one of New York City's premier cultural institutions. Less than one mile from either the Brooklyn or Manhattan bridges, it is near to brownstone neighborhoods, fine eateries, and extensive public transportation. BAM is creating a minicultural space here, akin to London's National Theater complex, combining movies and live performances, bookshop and café—a cultural destination with amenities, a good place to meet friends.

The BAM Next Wave Festival, begun in 1983, is an internationally acclaimed showcase for leading avant-garde performance art. BAM presents leading performers from the equestrian Zingaro to composer Philip Glass, dancers Twyla Tharp to Mark Morris, as well as Britain's Peter Brooke and Royal Shakespeare Company and other international troupes as well as works by playwrights such as Caryl Churchill. Opera and the **Brooklyn Philharmonic** appear through June. **DanceAfrica**, the largest festival of African-American dance in the U.S., featuring American as well as African troupes, is staged in the spring.

Excellent children's shows are staged during the school year through the BAM Performing Arts for Young People program. There's also a Family Fun Series on weekend afternoons.

The creative director of BAM from 1967 to 1998, Harvey Lichtenstein, was the powerhouse behind these innovative programs and also spurred revitalization of the sixteen-block area surrounding the Academy.

BAM, the oldest performing arts center in America, opened in 1859 in Brooklyn Heights. BAM moved to its present quarters after the original theater burned down. The present neo-Renaissance building dates from 1908, and was designed by theater architects Herts & Tallent. In its early years, BAM hosted Enrico Caruso, Isadora Duncan, Mary Pickford, Gustav Mahler, Martha Graham, even Gertrude Stein.

There's a lovely **BAMCafé** on the premises (page 116), a new **Rose Cinema** movie theater (page 116), and the **BAMShop** (page 117).

✪ **BAM Majestic Theater.** 651 Fulton Street, corner of Ashland Place, 636-4100. Call for a schedule.

Back in 1904 when the Majestic Theater opened, there were twenty large theaters in Brooklyn, with resonant names like the Star, Billy Watson's Pearl, the Novelty, the Gaiety, the Unique, and the Folly. (Very few of them are still standing; most have been razed, some are churches, and the Prospect Theater on 9th Street between 5th and 6th avenues in Park Slope became a supermarket.) In its early years the 1,800-seat Majestic was considered an important "tryout" house for Broadway-bound theatrical productions. Subsequently it hosted everything from Shakespearean plays to opera, vaudeville, and movies. Then it lay dormant for two decades. A cooperative effort by the city and the Brooklyn Academy of Music led to the theater's restoration. The façade has been preserved but the interior has been remodeled after Peter Brook's Parisian theater, Les Bouffes du Nord. Watch BAM listings for a schedule of programs.

✪ **BAM Rose Cinemas.** Brooklyn Academy of Music, 30 Lafayette Avenue, 623-2770.

Wow! The Angelika comes to Brooklyn!

The Brooklyn Academy of Music recently launched a new state-of-the-art multiplex cinema for select independent and foreign films. The four theaters, opened in 1998, have a combined seating of 800, and are open seven days a week. The theaters will also be used to screen films as part of BAM's music and dance programs. They were built as part of an $18-million renovation project (also creating the BAMCafé, BAMShop, and renovation of the lobby) and named in honor of a major donor.

✪ **BAMCafé.** Brooklyn Academy of Music (2nd floor), 636-4148. Opens two hours prior to any performance at the Opera House. Hours may be expanded; call for information about hours and reservations.

BAMCafé is a scene not to be missed: the international, eclectic crowd that gathers here before any BAM performance, both live theater and foreign flicks, makes for great people-watching. The oversized armchairs and potted trees are inviting, there's pre-concert live jazz, and the architecture is notable, too; this used to be the Opera House's grand ballroom, the Lepercq Space.

Whether you are coming from Park Slope, or Park Avenue, you'll enjoy a delicious meal here; BAM hired chef and restaurateur Michael Ayoub, whose restaurant smash hits include **Cucina**. A two-course dinner without drinks but with tip, runs about $30. Come early if you want a seat.

(And, in case you are wondering, that enormous TV tower you see out the window here has nothing to do with BAM; it belongs to nearby **Brooklyn Technical High School**.)

BamShop. Brooklyn Academy of Music.

A retail shop selling books, CDs, and BAM souvenirs is part of the new BAM complex. See listing on page 115.

651, an Arts Center, at the BAM Majestic Theater. 651 Fulton Street corner Ashland Place, 636-4181.

651 is a community-based arts center which, in its own words, "develops, produces, and presents art programming grounded in the African Diaspora." It was born in 1988 under the auspices of a New York City financing arrangement for the renovation of BAM's Majestic Theater, to enhance the local community. This energetic organization has brought Betty Carter, Tito Puente, Abbey Lincoln, Anna Deavere Smith, and many others to the Brooklyn stage.

Brooklyn Community Access Television (BCAT). 647 Fulton Street, two blocks from Flatbush Avenue, around the corner from BAM's Majestic Theater, enter on Rockwell, 935-0275.

BCAT operates four public-access cable television channels in Brooklyn; check Cablevision channel 57 and Time-Warner channel 70. Also, here you can find Internet classes and check in on the electronic BCAT Bulletin Board (via www.brooklynx.org/neighborhoods) on which hundreds of community-based organizations post announcements.

Brooklyn Philharmonic. 1 Hanson Place, corner Flatbush Avenue. 622-5555 or 636-4100 for concert and ticket information.

The Brooklyn Philharmonic is a freelance ensemble with a national reputation which, under musical direction of Robert Spano, has gained increasing recognition in the past several years. Don't miss the opportunity to hear them play; watch for listings in New York area newspapers. Note that the Brooklyn Philharmonic has a relationship with the Brooklyn Academy of Music, but is not part of BAM.

✪ **Mark Morris Dance Group.** New location and phone to be announced in 1999.

The world-famous Mark Morris Dance Company will establish its home base in Brooklyn, across from the Brooklyn Academy of Music. There will be offices and studios—and a lot of hardworking, talented dancers. Stay tuned for more developments.

✪ **UrbanGlass—New York Center for Contemporary Glass.** 647 Fulton Street, two blocks from Flatbush Avenue, around the corner from BAM's

Majestic Theater, enter on Rockwell, 625-3685. Mon.–Wed., 10 A.M.–7 P.M.; Thurs., 10 A.M.–8 P.M.; Sat., 10 A.M.–6 P.M.; Sun., 11 A.M.–5 P.M.

UrbanGlass is a nationally recognized center for the creation and appreciation of new art made from glass. It was founded in 1977 as the New York Experimental Glass Workshop, moved to Brooklyn in 1991, and is now the largest artist-accessible glassmaking center in the world. Hundreds of trained artists (and well-heeled beginners, too) rent time at the extraordinary glass working facilities at this 17,000-square-foot production studio.

An exciting schedule of classes in glassblowing and a neon shop (and easier techniques as well) are open to the public, including high school students. Other activities include quarterly curated exhibits in the UrbanGlass Gallery, a fashionable benefit auction called the Glassblowers Ball, a quarterly magazine dedicated to art glass making, and a new on-premises **Store at UrbanGlass**. There will be a huge June 2000 event when UrbanGlass hosts the international Olympics of Glass, expected to attract thousands of glass artists from around the world.

UrbanGlass revives a long Brooklyn tradition of glassblowing.

✪ **Williamsburgh Savings Bank.** 1 Hanson Place, across from the Long Island Railroad at Atlantic Center, 722-5300. Mon.–Fri., 9 A.M.–5 P.M.; closed weekends and bank holidays.

Brooklyn's tallest building offers breathtaking views of much of Brooklyn and beyond. And, it can be seen from as far away as Sutton Place.

This New York City landmarked building, designed as a "skyscraper" by the firm of Halsey, McCormick, and Helmer just a few years before the Depression, resembles the grand Bowery Savings Bank opposite Grand Central Station. It is 512 feet high, with setbacks at the thirteenth and twenty-sixth stories. If you go inside you will see a wonderful mosaic mural on the ground floor, a gilded dome, arches, stained-glass, and marble rails. The Williamsburg Savings Bank company left their architectural mark; their 175 Broadway building in Williamsburg is also a New York City landmark.

Williamsburgh Savings Bank Clock. Williamsburgh Savings Bank, 1 Hanson Place, across from the Long Island Railroad at Atlantic Center.

Yes, you can set your watch by it. Taller than London's Big Ben, and visible from many parts of Brooklyn—as far away as 25 miles!—the four-faced Williamsburgh Savings Bank Clock sits more than 400 feet above sidewalk level, and measures 27 feet in diameter. The 1929 clock still has all its original mechanisms and equipment except for the north-facing hour hand, replaced after damage incurred in a winter storm.

NOTABLE BAM AREA RESTAURANTS

New City Bar and Grill. 25 Lafayette Avenue, across from Brooklyn Academy of Music building. 622-5607. Open daily for lunch and dinner. Call for reservations and hours.

This Brooklyn success story has moved to spiffy new quarters, complete with a 65-person restaurant and bar, conveniently located directly across from the world-famous Brooklyn Academy of Music. The New City Bar and Grill serves creative American cuisine which pays extraordinary attention to your tastebuds, and pampers the rest of your senses as well. The new, expanded menu will include light meals as well as the long, leisurely romantic dinners for which New City is known. Call for hours, as the restaurant was, literally, in transition at time of publication.

BAMCafé. See page 116.

BAM AREA SHOPPING

Atlantic Center. Intersection of Flatbush and Atlantic avenues. Open daily.

Opened in 1988, this large, airy new mall has 380,000 square feet of large chain stores, including Circuit City, House and Home, Marshall's, Old Navy Clothing, Office Depot, Pathmark, and others. Across the street is PC Richards Electronics. There's a large, inexpensive underground parking area. Atlantic Center, a mixed-use residential and commercial project, is a major force in the redevelopment of **Downtown Brooklyn**.

BamStore. See page 117.

Fort Greene and Clinton Hill

POINTS OF CULTURAL INTEREST

Brooklyn Masonic Temple. 317 Clermont Avenue at Lafayette Avenue, 638-1256.

One of Fort Greene's few twentieth-century buildings, this neoclassical structure was designed by McKim, Mead & White. Note the broad Ionic pilasters and decorative symbols in terra cotta.

Brooklyn Music School & Playhouse. 126 St. Felix Street, between Hanson Place and Lafayette Avenue, 638-5660.

This school began in 1912. Faculty members often present their own recitals and concerts and invite the public. Phone for a schedule.

Brooklyn Technical High School. 29 Fort Greene Place to South Elliott, off DeKalb Avenue.

Brooklyn Technical High School is one of New York City's leading specialized public high schools. To be admitted, students must take the same demanding competitive examination as for the better-known stars of the New York City system, Stuyvesant and Bronx High School of Science. Brooklyn Tech was founded in 1922 and moved to this site in the 1930s. About 5,000 students representing a wide variety of races and nationalities attend, studying an advanced curriculum in science, math, computer science, premedical education, as well as liberal arts. In 1998, Brooklyn Tech received a large private endowment. Brooklyn Tech counts two Nobel Prize winners among its alumni.

Church of St. Luke and St. Matthew. 520 Clinton Avenue, between Atlantic Avenue and Fulton Street, 638-0686. Phone for hours.

Described as a "voluptuous Victorian valentine," the church of St. Luke and St. Matthew is distinguished by a long porch, sculpted teak columns, and Tiffany windows. Built by Episcopalian industrial barons, the hundred-year-old church today is still a landmark. It is located not far from **Pratt Institute** and the mansions along Clinton Avenue, where some of the church's original congregants lived in splendor.

Clinton Hill Hasidim. In response to acute housing shortages in **Williamsburg**, there is a burgeoning presence of Satmar Hasidim in Clinton Hill. Walk around the northeastern corner of the neighborhood, which abuts Williamsburg, and you'll see people outfitted in the unmistakable dress of Hasidim.

Emmanuel Baptist Church. 279 Lafayette Avenue at St. James Place, Clinton Hill, 622-1107. Phone for hours.

This large French Gothic church, with its twin towers and triple entrance, is reminiscent of a medieval cathedral. Completed in 1887, it is a notable landmark contributing to the nineteenth-century ambience of the neighborhood. The church was built with financial support from Charles Pratt, industrialist and founder of Pratt Institute.

House Tours of Fort Greene (237-9031) and of Clinton Hill (624-1712).

The tour of Fort Greene homes occurs in even-numbered years, while the garden tour is held annually. Tickets cost about $12 to $15.

Even if you miss the tours, a walk along South Oxford Street and South Portland Avenue in Fort Greene, and Clinton Avenue in Clinton Hill, helps explain why dyed-in-the-wool Manhattanites fall in love with Brooklyn.

Fort Greene has a full spectacle of wooden homes, Italianate-style brownstones, as well as British designer Charles Eastlake's geometric influence from the 1870s and 1880s. Clinton Avenue's Pratt mansions are equally captivating.

Hanson Place Central Methodist Church. 1 Hanson Place, at St. Felix Street, 783-0908. Phone for hours.

This 1929 "Art Deco–Gothic" wonder, located in the BAM historic district and designed by the same firm as designed BAM itself, has been called the Cathedral of Methodism. Nearby are streets of row houses with cast-iron railings and wooden doors, reminiscent of the time when Fulton Street was a major commercial center.

Hanson Place Seventh Day Adventist Church. 88 Hanson Place, at South Portland Avenue, 789-3030. Phone for hours.

Monumental in scale, this Greek Revival and Italianate church is of the same 1850s–1860s architectural generation as **Borough Hall** and the landmark **State Street Houses** (pages 231 and 217, respectively). Once a Baptist congregation, this church welcomed southern slaves traveling the Underground Railway to Fort Greene's community of free blacks, many of whom were employed in the nearby **Brooklyn Navy Yard**.

✪ **Institutional Church of God in Christ.** 170 Adelphi Street, between Willoughby and Myrtle avenues, 625-9175. Phone for hours.

Here is celebrated gospel music, joyously sung by the nationally known Institutional Choir that has also performed on Broadway and in Europe.

✪ **Lafayette Avenue Presbyterian Church.** 102 Lafayette Avenue, at South Oxford Street, 625-7515.

Depending on your bent, this church offers spiritual uplift, social action—and joyful gospel from the choir and four-keyboard organ. Pulitzer Prize–winning poet Marianne Moore called this her church. A leader in progressive social causes for over a century, this church was an abolitionist headquarters, and more recently was an instigator of the public education campaign about abusive labor practices in textile factories in El Salvador. It was also the birthplace of noted publishing company Kitchen Table: Women of Color Press, founded in 1981 by Audre Lorde and Barbara Smith with the mission of publishing the writings of lesbians and women of color. They have published—with some notable success—where commercial houses dared not tread; for instance, the successful *This Bridge Called My Back: Writings by Radical Women of Color* and *Home Girls: A Black Feminist Anthology.*

And, it's a New York City architectural landmark. Glorious, pastoral windows in the Underwood Chapel of this 1864 Romanesque building are among the last completed by the Tiffany Studio about 1920.

Paul Robeson Theatre. 40 Greene Avenue, between Carlton Avenue and Adelphi Street, 783-9794.

The Paul Robeson Theatre produces a range of entertainment, including ethnically oriented theater, dance, and movies; works of Athol Fugard and Angus Wilson are part of the repertory. It is housed in a building that used to be a Polish Catholic church and is now a community cultural center.

✪ **Pratt Institute.** 200 Willoughby Avenue, gateway at DeKalb Avenue and Hall Street, 636-3600. Call for events and information.

More than a century old, the pioneering educational institution Pratt was founded in the 1880s by oil baron Charles Pratt, a pragmatist who recognized the growing need for trained industrial workers in a changing economy. Pratt encouraged students in the study of mechanical drawing, engineering, sewing, and typing. The school was progressive for its day, admitting both men and women of all races. Pratt's Free Library was the first free library in Brooklyn. Today, Pratt grants degrees in schools of architecture, art and design, information and library science, liberal arts and professional studies. The Institute's nearly 4,000 multinational students appreciate their gated, green oasis in downtown Brooklyn, where neighbors also come to read, or attend lively performances at the restored Memorial Hall.

Queen of All Saints Roman Catholic Church. 300 Vanderbilt Avenue, at Lafayette Avenue, 638-7625. Call for hours.

A flamboyant Gothic nave in this 1913 church, heightened by lavish windows, takes its inspiration from the Sainte Chapelle in Paris.

Steele House. 200 Lafayette Avenue, diagonally across from Queen of All Saints Church at Vanderbilt Avenue.

As though plucked from a Massachusetts seacoast town, this nineteenth-century frame house, with its small widow's walk, stands out from the surrounding brownstones and churches in the area. It is a landmark of architectural interest, since successive owners combined Federal, Greek Revival, and Italianate elements, and the small east side wing may date to 1812. Originally built for Joseph Steele, it was later owned by the first president of Brooklyn Union Gas Company.

NOTABLE FORT GREENE RESTAURANTS

Brooklyn Mod. 271 Adelphi Street, corner of DeKalb Avenue, 522-1669. Daily, 6 P.M.–4 A.M.

Brooklyn Mod is a "scene" to be seen in, in Fort Greene—just take a look at their hours. This self-styled champagne bistro in a beautiful old brownstone is a good place to have a drink and engage in some heavy-duty socializing and people-watching. The food, however, is of uneven quality.

✪ **Cambodian Cuisine.** 87 South Elliot Place, at the intersections of Lafayette Avenue and Fulton Street, 858-3262. Daily, 11 A.M.–10:30 P.M.; some credit cards.

You can't miss the huge green sign marking Cambodian Cuisine and Southeast Asian Cooking (its full name), and you shouldn't miss its tasty and prodigious menu featuring both mild and spicy Asian fare. Lovers of tingling-hot chicken, veggies, or seafood will be in heaven. And if your palate is more reserved, don't fear—the menu's more than 140 different items guarantees there's something here for everyone. While the restaurant offers take-out, you'll want to eat in for fresh-from-the-kitchen taste. Cambodian Cuisine's motto, seen all over its menus and signage is, "no pork, less fat, better than Chinese food." They've got that right.

Cino's. 243 DeKalb Avenue, between Claremont and Vanderbilt avenues, 622-9249. Mon.–Sat.; 11:30 A.M.–2:30 P.M. and 4–10:30 P.M.; closed Sun.

You won't find too many restaurants in Fort Greene that have survived since the 1950s, but Cino's Italian food is so homey the locals keep coming back for more. Of course, nouvelle cuisine and all the other cooking styles du jour have bypassed this kitchen, so stick to the tried-and-true—like spaghetti with garlic, stuffed mushrooms and, yes, clams casino.

✪ **Keur N' Deye.** 737 Fulton Street, between South Elliot and South Portland streets, 875-4937. Tues.–Sun., noon–10:30 P.M.

Proprietor Salif Cisse' has transported the dishes of his native Senegal to Fort Greene, and the lines outside the door of this small, handsome restaurant are testimony to the wondrous tastes and reasonable prices. *Tiebou dieun* is the national dish of fish and rice and takes center stage. But don't miss the peanut chicken, *mafe guinaar*, or the curried vegetables. The spicy ginger drink is refreshing, as is the sorrel, which is sweeter and will please the kids. Keur N' Deye is light, airy, clean, and filled with Senegalese art and music. To avoid the crowds, try a weeknight. The restaurant also delivers locally.

✪ **Kum Kau Kitchen.** 465 Myrtle Avenue, corner Washington Avenue, 638-1850. Daily, 11–1 A.M., later on weekends.

Terrific and cheap, cheap, cheap, this eat-in, take-out, no-frills Chinese restaurant has an extensive menu. It offers entrées such as BBQ boneless spare ribs, fantail shrimps, over fifty different kinds of Hunan Szechuan dishes, and combination platters of a main dish, egg roll, and pork fried rice, all for about $7.

CAFÉS, ICE CREAM PARLORS, AND QUICK MEALS

Brooklyn Moon. 745 Fulton Street, between South Elliot and South Portland streets, 243-0424. Cash only.

You may think you've wandered into a private party in this small, clean living-room–like café and arts salon. Some nights poetry is read while on others a guitarist may be performing. The menu is simple sandwiches and the like—but fresh and good. Relax on the sofa, pull up a chair, put up your feet, have a bite, and enjoy the evening. With the lights turned low for the performers' benefit you may think Brooklyn Moon is closed. It isn't.

Pork Knockers. 956 Atlantic Avenue, between Washington and Grand avenues, 638-0727. Tues.–Thurs., 4 P.M.–1 A.M.; Fri. and Sat., 4 P.M.–4 A.M.; Sun., noon–1 A.M.

After only nine weeks in business, certain circles in Brooklyn have been abuzz about the Caribbean, or more specifically, Jamaican, food here. You can get vegetarian, seafood, spicy chicken, and curry goat, and either take it out or sit here in a lovely garden and enjoy. There's a large bar in the front, and the vibes are great. We don't like to list such newcomers but we hope this one lasts.

✪ **Richlene Caribbean American Café.** 83 Lafayette Avenue, off Fulton Street, 243-2040. Mon.–Sat., noon–9:45 P.M.; Sun., 1–8:45 P.M. Cash only.

"It's just like being in Negril," is what the satisfied customers say, and so they come back regularly for fried plantains, roti, oxtail, brown stew chicken, and other island specialties. There are just a few tables here, but lots of takeout.

Sapodilla Café. 412 Myrtle Avenue, between Vanderbilt Avenue and Clinton Avenue, 797-1213. Tues.–Thurs., Sun. noon–10 P.M.; Fri–Sat. until 11 P.M.

The setting's unpretentious, but you can fill your belly just fine at this friendly establishment with comforting, tasty, well-spiced Caribbean and Southern dishes. Try the BBQ or jerk chicken, blackened catfish, or Creole seafood, with a side of collard greens or candied yams.

Sprinkles Restaurant and Bakery. 466 Myrtle Avenue, between Washington and Hall streets, 399-3085. Daily, 11 A.M.–11 P.M.; open to midnight on weekends.

Sprinkles serves West Indian dishes and curries, oxtail stew, jerk chicken, roti, and patties, as well as homemade breads and pastries. Eat here or take some home.

Sunshine Juice Bar. Fulton Street, 222-1705. Mon.–Fri, 8:30 A.M.–7:30 P.M.; weekends, 9:30 A.M.–9:30 P.M. Cash only.

Another new spot, this little health food corner store specializes in crunchy fresh salads, freshly juiced vegetable and fruit drinks, and good vibes for the neighborhood artists and entrepreneurs.

SHOPPING

✪ **Clinton Hill Simply Art Gallery.** 583 Myrtle Avenue, near Classon Avenue, 857-0074. Tues.–Sun., noon-7 P.M.

If you are a beginning art collector, and want a friendly, down-to-earth place to learn about and buy ethnic art, drop by Lurita Brown's successful gallery, located one block from Pratt Institute. Since 1991, Lurita has pioneered a full-service art gallery focusing on what she describes as the "beginning collector of ethnic art." Her gallery includes original artwork by selected African-American, Caribbean, and Native American artists. The clientele are upscale businesspeople and professionals, who are interested in developing their eye—and who are willing to pay from $250 to $5,000 for a sound investment in up-and-coming artists. Several Brooklynites are among the emerging artists shown here.

There's also a collection of fine art reproductions and posters, ranging up to $65.

✪ **E Shop.** 771 Fulton Street, 246-0321. Tues.–Sat., 1–8 P.M.; closed Sun.

You'll recognize this clothing boutique by its hip, spare, artistically designed display window. Inside, shoppers will find a small collection of unique gear for New York women. The designers, two delightful guys by the names of Epperson and Berry, describe their style as "edgy" (that's a *good* thing), and a rave review in *The New York Times* called it "whimsical," "mind-stretching," and "artful." In plainer English, these are clothes you can *wear*—linen tops, layered tops, patchwork shirts—when you want to stand out from the crowd. Prices run about $25 for a shirt and up to $150 for a dress. Special-occasion wear, including wedding gowns, can be made to order.

4W Circle of Art & Enterprise. 704 Fulton Street, near South Oxford Street, 875-6500. Tues.–Sat., 11 A.M.–9 P.M.; Sun. 1–7 P.M.

You'll find cool fashions and interesting gifts and cards, many with African themes, here.

Moshood Creations. 698 Fulton Street, near South Oxford Street, 243-9433. Mon.–Sat., 10 A.M.–10 P.M.; Sun., noon–8 P.M.

Well-crafted ethnic fashion designs are the ticket at Moshood. Look again at the store window: did that statuesque mannequin wink? The mannequins are actually young models from the neighborhood. Bring your friend or kids and watch their surprise when the mannequins move.

✪ **South Portland Antiques.** 753 Fulton Street, corner of South Portland Avenue, 596-556. Mon.–Fri., 9 A.M.–7 P.M.; Sat., 11 A.M.–7:30 P.M.; Sun., noon–6:30 P.M.

You can find Victoriana and other furniture to befit a brownstone here. There are dressers, chairs, and chests, all tastefully displayed, along with paintings, china, and other European and American items. This is a lovely store with helpful staff, and they've been here for almost twenty years—that's a lot of brownstone renovations' worth.

The Store at UrbanGlass. 647 Fulton Street, corner Rockwell, enter on Rockwell, 625-3685. Mon.–Fri., 9 A.M.–5 P.M.

Opened in 1998, this store on the premises of **UrbanGlass Studio** sells handmade glass objects ranging in price from $5 to $500, perfect for holiday and home gifts. For those with deeper pockets, there's an Annex Gallery that shows the work of established glass artists and UrbanGlass faculty, with pieces ranging in price from $1,000 to $5,000.

Tribal Truths Collection. 704 Fulton Street, between South Oxford and South Portland streets, 875-6500. Mon.–Fri., 11 A.M.–9 P.M.; Sat., 10 A.M.–9 P.M.; Sun., 1–7 P.M.

The work of several African-American artists is shown here, so there's a nice range of different styles of exuberant, colorful clothing (men's, women's, and children's), jewelry and hair ornaments, brilliantly dyed scarves, and stylish, unusual hats. The main designer is Brenda Brunson-Bey. This is a fun store, with lots of possibilities for gift items and one-of-a-kind clothes to bring home.

Contributed in part by Howard Pritsch.

Cobble Hill, Carroll Gardens, and Red Hook

Where it is: Taken together, these three neighborhoods are bounded by Atlantic Avenue and the water (Erie Basin) on the north and south, and Hoyt Street and the water (Buttermilk Channel and Atlantic Basin) on the east and west.

What's nearby: Atlantic Avenue, Brooklyn Heights, Park Slope, New York Harbor, Manhattan.

How to get there:

By car: Follow the first exit off the Brooklyn Bridge. Staying to the left off the exit, turn left onto Court Street. Stay on Court until you cross Atlantic Avenue.

By subway: Take the F or G train to Bergen Street for Cobble Hill, to Carroll Street for Carroll Gardens, or to Smith and 9th Street for Red Hook. Other subway stops are about six blocks the other side of Atlantic Avenue: take the 2, 3, 4, or 5 train to Borough Hall, the M, N, or R to Court Street, or the A or C to Jay Street.

Car services: Cobble Hill Car Service (643-1113), Atlantic (797-5666), or Bergen (855-1400). Cost is about $15 to Grand Central Station, $15 to Sheepshead Bay.

For Brooklynophiles Only

We know that for some of you it's almost a crime to violate neighborhood boundaries by lumping them together. But the irregular lines of demarcation between areas can make sticking with the official boundaries confusing for visitors. So, restaurants and shops in Cobble Hill, Carroll Gardens, and Red Hook are combined here. Restaurants and shops on Atlantic Avenue are included in the Atlantic Avenue chapter, pages 214–222.

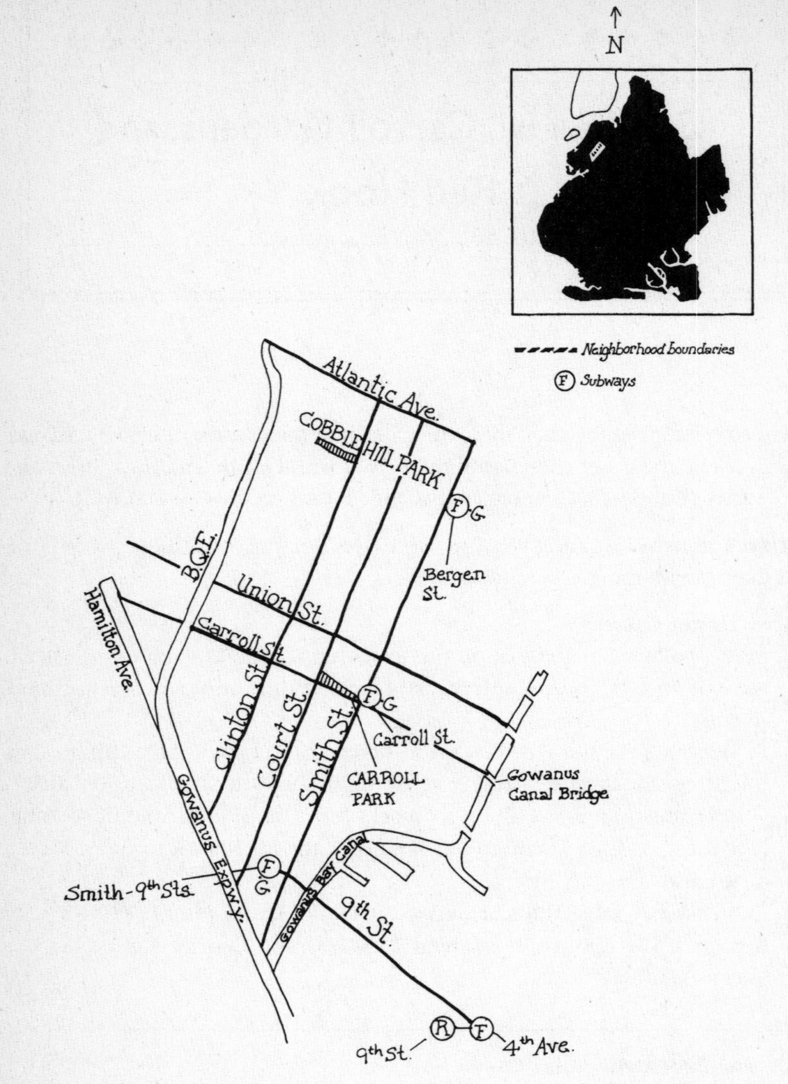
N
Neighborhood boundaries
Subways
Atlantic Ave.
COBBLE HILL PARK
F G
Bergen St.
B.Q.E.
Union St.
Hamilton Ave.
Carroll St.
Clinton St.
Court St.
Smith St.
F G
Carroll St.
CARROLL PARK
Gowanus Canal Bridge
Gowanus Expwy.
Gowanus Bay Canal
F G
Smith-9th Sts.
9th St.
R F
9th St.
4th Ave.

Historical Notes About All Three Neighborhoods

These three neighborhoods—Cobble Hill, Carroll Gardens, and Red Hook—differ, but they were linked historically by the fact that all were established to meet the voracious needs of the old, now defunct, port industry.

The first Europeans to settle here were seventeenth-century Dutch farmers and middle-class English who moved in through the early 1800s. But it was the immigrant sailors and longshoremen—initially Irish, but overwhelmingly Italian by 1900—who labored on the nearby docks that gave the neighborhood its flavor. In those days the entire area was simply called "Red Hook," and it covered present-day Red Hook, Carroll Gardens, and parts of nearby Boerum Hill (but not the more rarefied Cobble Hill).

The ports of the Atlantic and Erie Basins, the busy State Barge Canal Terminal, and the connecting railways made this one of the nation's busiest shipping centers for more than a century. It is no accident that the headquarters of the Longshoreman's Union is right here on Court Street. The passions and raw energy of Red Hook were captured in Arthur Miller's *A View From the Bridge* and Elia Kazan's *On the Waterfront*; its worst aspects were epitomized by Al Capone, who plied his trade as petty thief here before moving to Chicago.

After World War II the entire area declined as Brooklynites raced to the suburbs. The newly built Brooklyn-Queens and Gowanus expressways and Brooklyn Battery Tunnel amputated the industrial waterfront from the residential areas farther inland. Shipping and related businesses moved out to more modern facilities in New Jersey when containers revolutionized the industry in the 1960s.

Old Red Hook was ruined by the highway construction and loss of jobs. The row houses were razed, with isolated low-income projects erected in their place. Cobble Hill and Carroll Gardens also declined, but retained their core Italian community, and then began to revive in the 1960s, fueled by activist residents and an influx of younger newcomers. (Indicative of the most recent changes are the churches-turned-condos at 360 Court Street and 450 Clinton Street.) Commercial growth in the nearby downtown area has also helped the area. In the 1990s, as real estate prices in Cobble Hill and Carroll Gardens themselves have begun squeezing people out, the gentrification frontier has pushed farther south along Smith Street, across to the waterfront side of the BQE in Carroll Gardens, and even south along Van Brunt Street into Red Hook.

Food Shopping and Eating:

In Carroll Gardens and Cobble Hill, shopping is straight out of the Old World. You buy bread at the bakery, pastries at the pastry shop, sausage at the pork store, meat at the butcher, fruit and vegetables at the greengrocer, and fresh pasta at the pasta shop. Walk down Court Street or the small commercial strip on Henry Street and you'll find more than a dozen small, family-owned food stores—**Caputo's Bake Shop, D'Amico Foods, G. Esposito Pork Store**, and **Pastosa Ravioli**, among them—that have been riding Brooklyn's ups and downs since World War II. **Staubitz Market** butcher and the less venerable (at only thirty years in business) **Jim & Andy Fruit and Produce Market** are also on Court Street.

You have your choice of nearly a dozen reliable Italian restaurants that serve tasty, family-style food at moderate prices, including the modern, renovated **Nino's**, old-fashioned **Monte's Italian Restaurant**, the huge **Marco Polo**, and the wildly popular newcomer, **Rosina's**. A number of upscale new restaurants have opened in the past several years, including **Harvest's** southern home cooking, **Patois'** eclectic French, and **Kalio's** new American.

Kidstuff:

There's not much out of the ordinary here for kids, but there are plenty of playgrounds, bookstores, and pizza places to satisfy little stomachs. There is a bike lane down Union Street all the way to Prospect Park, and a few local parks (see below) with playground equipment and basketball courts. Check out the paint-it-yourself pottery at **The Painted Pot**. There's also a small multiscreen movie theater on Court Street, the **Cobble Hill Cinemas**. Kids who like to fish or who are interested in the waterfront will be fascinated by **Red Hook**, whose colorful maritime history echoes in nineteenth-century street names like Seabring, Pioneer, and Creamer streets, and the cleanup of the Gowanus Canal. (Call **Brooklyn Center on Urban Environment** for a Gowanus tour schedule.)

Cobble Hill

How it got its name: The name was revived in the 1950s by brownstone enthusiasts who discovered that the area had been designated "Cobbleshill" on a 1766 map of New York. The map referred to a long-gone hill near the modern intersection of Court Street and Atlantic Avenue.

Historic district: Cobble Hill historic district is bounded by Atlantic Avenue, and Court, DeGraw, and Hicks streets.

ABOUT THE NEIGHBORHOOD

Historically, Cobble Hill shares more with patrician Brooklyn Heights than with workingclass Carroll Gardens. Defined by a twenty-block officially designated New York City landmark district north of DeGraw Street, its elegant town houses were mostly built between 1840 and 1880 by members of the upper middle class, including distinguished architect (and resident) Richard Upjohn, of Trinity Church fame. A significant Middle Eastern immigration began in the early twentieth century; many of their descendants remain, as is obvious from the variety of food shops and restaurants along **Atlantic Avenue** and Court Street. After a period of economic decline, Cobble Hill has gone through an upswing, largely due to an influx of affluent young professionals, an activist community, and the brownstone revival movement. Residents managed to secure landmark status and block public housing, and real estate values have risen sharply since the 1970s.

In Cobble Hill, visitors can wander lovely tree-lined streets past pre–Civil War architecture; walk by the nineteenth-century "socially enlightened" low-income housing at **Workingmen's Cottages** (also known as Warren Place and Cobble Hill Tower) built by philanthropist Alfred Tredway White; or rest in lovely **Cobble Hill Park**. Those looking for the footsteps of the famous can see Thomas Wolfe's Verandah Mews row house, and the childhood home of Churchill's mother at 154 Amity Street.

ENTERTAINMENT, PARKS, AND PLAYGROUNDS

Cobble Hill Cinemas. 265 Court Street, corner of Butler Street, 596-9113. Call for show times.

This multiscreen theater shows blockbusters as well as independent films, and there is always at least one kids' movie playing. A ticket to the first show every day costs $5. The theater is right in the middle of everything: an easy walk to upscale Cobble Hill eateries and cafés, Carroll Gardens Italian restaurants, and Middle Eastern fare on Atlantic Avenue.

Note: As of this writing, there are plans to build a twelve-screen movie theater and Barnes & Noble bookstore on Court Street between State and Schermerhorn Streets.

✪ **Cobble Hill Park.** Enter on Clinton and Henry streets, between Congress Street and Verandah Place.

One of the first "vest-pocket" parks in the city, this park was created by community activists who wanted to prevent construction of a supermarket in this residential section. One of the loveliest parks in Brooklyn, it has antique-style benches and tables and marble columns at the entrances. It is near Thomas Wolfe's Verandah Place home. If you are hungry, walk over to **Court Street** or stop at the nearby **Delicatessen at Verandah Place.**

POINTS OF CULTURAL INTEREST

✪ **Brooklyn Youth Chorus.** 138A Court Street, near Atlantic Avenue, 243 9447. By appointment.

Like the melting-pot dream come true, the ten-year-old Brooklyn Youth Chorus has melded the voices of some of Brooklyn's multiracial, ethnically diverse youth into an extraordinary, harmonious chorus. Founded by Diane Berkun, who first launched it at **Brooklyn Friends School**, this excellent chorus has traveled to Europe, sung in front of presidents, and emerged as a world-class youth ensemble.

✪ **Cobble Hill Historic District:** Along Clinton Street, near Henry Street.

Take a walk along Clinton Street to get a taste of the history of this neighborhood:

Number 296 Clinton was the residence of Richard Upjohn and his son, both famed turn-of-the-century architects who built **Grace Church** in Brooklyn Heights (see page 209).

Numbers 301 through 311 Clinton Street are Italianate-style houses built about 1850 by lawyer and developer Gerard Morris.

Number 334 was built in 1850 by established Brooklyn architect James Naughton, who also built the architecturally acclaimed **Boys' and Girls' High School** in Bedford Stuyvesant (see page 29).

Number 340 is the widest house in the area, built for Dr. Joseph Clark in 1860.

Verandah Place, between Clinton and Henry streets, is a lovely mews full of carriage houses, one of which was inhabited for a time by writer Thomas Wolfe.

Kane Street Synagogue. 236 Kane Street, between Court and Clinton Streets, 975-1550.

The congregation housed here, Beth Israel, founded in 1856, claims to be the oldest Jewish congregation in Brooklyn. Its fate followed that of the neighborhood, prospering through the 1920s, languishing until the 1960s, and coming to life again as the brownstone gentrification movement brought in younger members. The original synagogue was located on the site now occupied by the Brooklyn House of Detention; the current synagogue building was erected in 1855 as a Dutch Reformed church.

✪ **Model Tenements: Home and Tower Buildings.** Warren Place, between Hicks and Henry streets.

Make a short detour off the main Court Street commercial strip and visit two of the nation's first low-rent housing units. Philanthropist Alfred Tredway White built these units in 1877 as an innovation to provide decent, affordable housing for workers. The design was inspired by London's Victorian apartment buildings, and incorporated modern concepts of ventilation, plumbing, and natural light, which were then uncommon in workingclass housing. They are considered unique and important architectural innovations of the nineteenth century.

The tiny workingmen's cottages—less than twelve feet wide—line a lovely mews, Warren Place, which runs one block from Warren to Baltic Street, between Henry and Hicks streets. They face a common garden.

The Home and Tower apartment buildings are now restored as "Cobble Hill Towers." The original "Towers" apartments are located at 417–435 Hicks Street, 136-142 Warren Street, and 129–135 Baltic Street. The original "Home Buildings" apartments are located at 439–445 Hicks Street and 134–140 Baltic Street.

See also the **Astral Apartments** in Greenpoint, page 191.

Notable Restaurants and Shopping

For the sake of convenience, all restaurant and shop listings for Cobble Hill, Carroll Gardens, and Red Hook are combined on page 138.

Carroll Gardens

How it got its name: Carroll Gardens was originally a section of **Red Hook**, and was given its current moniker by real-estate brokers in the 1960s, after the neighborhood was cut off from the waterfront by the construction of the BQE.

"Carroll" refers to Maryland's Charles Carroll, an Irishman and the only Roman Catholic signer of the Declaration of Independence, in honor of the Maryland regiment that defended the **Old Stone House at Gowanus**, a local landmark, against the British in the Revolutionary War. And "Gardens" refers to the many deep front-yard gardens in the neighborhood.

Special events: Court Street Summerfest (summer), Court Street Crawl (September); call 858-0557 for dates. Smith Street Fun-Day Sunday (second or third Sunday in June; call 825-0328).

Official landmarks: Carroll Gardens Historic District; Carroll Street Bridge; the Gowanus Canal Bridge.

ABOUT THE NEIGHBORHOOD

Carroll Gardens used to be a mixed Italian neighborhood, known as much for its rough-and-tumble as its rows of nicely kept homes. It was a tight-knit community where the little old ladies in black leaned out the brownstone windows and knew everything that went on down the street. Fathers and sons worked hard at the nearby docks. The strikes, the graft, the ups and downs of the longshoremen, whose union is still located here on Court Street, wasn't just a story in the newspaper—it was often a very personal matter, sometimes of life or death.

That's why, for those who know Brooklyn, a trip to this small area about a third of a square mile is usually motivated by a craving for that New York sense of "real Italian." Freshly made Italian food—the taste of fresh pasta sauce and soft, warm mozzarella, the aroma of coffee newly roasted in an old cast-iron roaster is an allure. So is watching a game of boccie, or chatting with the old greengrocer. Statues of the Virgin populate many front yards, there is a colorful parade on Good Friday, and epic displays of Christmas lights dazzle passersby every winter. Although locals swear that the best Italian cooking still comes from mama's kitchen, there are a half-dozen good family-style restaurants here to fill the belly and satisfy the soul. What brings people back to this part of **Court Street** time and time again is ethnic authenticity.

Carroll Gardens is not the most populous Italian neighborhood in Brooklyn; Bensonhurst, with its nonstop influx of new Italian immigrants, is the true Little Italy of New York City. Yet Carroll Gardens retains a palpable sense of ethnic community. Many descendants of Carroll Gardens' original Italian families have stayed in the neighborhood—children, parents, and grandparents often live on the same street, if not under the same roof. Their homes are row upon row of neat brownstones with flowering, well-tended front gardens.

In the 1980s and 1990s an influx of entrepreneurs, professionals, artists, writers, and others attracted to the brownstone housing and sunny openness of this residential area have brought new restaurants, cafés, and boutiques to the shopping areas. About 13,000 people live in Carroll Gardens, according to the 1990 census.

Smith Street is the most recent frontier, where the past few years have seen the openings of a handful of antiques stores, galleries, and upscale restaurants. The residential area near to the **Gowanus Canal** is looking up.

Smith Street: A Happening Place

Most of these shops are new arrivals, transforming Smith Street into a trendy new pocket of boutiques and eateries.

Antique Shops:
Astro Turf
Main Street Ephemera
Baseball Card Dugout
Montgomery Antiques
Treasures I

Clothing Shops:
Frida's Closet
Hoyt & Bond
Refinery
Stacia

Restaurants:
Patois
Rosina's Bistro
Sur

Follow Union Street west across the BQE/Gowanus Expressway overpass until you hit the intersection with **Columbia Street** to see a transitional area which has been adopted by many artists and artisans. Visit **Ferdinando's Focacceria**, an old-style Sicilian luncheonette, and **Latticini-Barese**, which makes incredible homemade mozzarella. A stretch of Columbia Street between Union and 9th streets also has a smattering of stores, including **Defonte Sandwich Shop** (379 Columbia), where many a good, cheap sandwich awaits.

And, watch as the cleanup of the **Gowanus Canal** (below) opens up new waterside land for residential and park use.

Official landmarks include the **Carroll Gardens Historic District**, the 1889 **Carroll Street Bridge**, the **Gowanus Canal Bridge**; unofficial landmarks include **Carroll Park, Jim & Andy**'s produce store, and **Staubitz** butchers.

PARKS AND PLAYGROUNDS

Carroll Park. Carroll Street, corner of Court Street.

The main park in Carroll Gardens has swings and seesaws as well as a boccie game on a nice afternoon. It's a very safe, neighborhood environment, and while there's not much shade in hot weather, the sprinkler keeps the kids cool.

Once a private garden, this park was built in the 1870s, and rapidly became a centerpiece of the neighborhood. The park was renovated in 1998.

Gowanus Canal. The redevelopment of the Gowanus is in the planning stages as this book is being written. But it could accelerate rapidly.

The odiferous (Brooklynese translation: "stinking") industrial waterway that has divided brownstone Carroll Gardens from brownstone Park Slope is the post–Civil War era Gowanus Canal. A twenty-five-year cleanup campaign may pay off around the year 2000. In 1998, a $450-million sewage treatment plant was installed to clean up the Canal, and a tunnel to circulate the water is expected to be opened soon.

Visionaries imagine a multiplex theater, tree-lined walkways, parks, and waterside housing on both sides of a clean-water canal. Fish in the canal would be a sure sign of an ecological success. If the Gowanus is cleaned up, it will benefit an estimated quarter of a million residents who live within walking distance. The first possibly viable development plan was announced by New York City Mayor Rudolph Giuliani in 1998. See **Brooklyn Common**, page 243.

POINTS OF CULTURAL INTEREST

Carroll Gardens Homes. 1st Place through 4th Place, between Henry and Smith streets.

It is no accident that Carroll Gardens has the word "garden" in its name. The homes on these blocks have unusually large front yards, thanks to an innovative surveyor, Richard Butts, who mapped out this area for development in 1846.

✪ **Carroll Gardens Historic District.** President and Carroll streets between Hoyt and Smith streets.

This small residential area of nineteenth-century brownstone homes is a lovely remnant of local architecture from the period 1870–1885. The front yards are particularly deep, and the street design minimizes traffic. These homes were built by local builders.

Carroll Street Bridge. Between Hoyt and Nevins streets.

Declared a landmark and renovated, this historic bridge spans the Gowanus Canal, built in 1889 as part of Brooklyn's network of industrial waterways. The waters of the canal are still polluted and no longer carry heavy industrial barge cargo, but the bridge is unusual: it opens by sliding along the tracks on the shore. It is the oldest of four such bridges in the country. Within walking distance is **Monte's Italian Ristorante**, whose Venetian gondola logo reflects wishful thinking, and a variety of more contemporary eateries on **Smith Street** (see page 135). See **Gowanus Canal** (page 135) for an update on what this area might become.

Community Arts Organizations. There are several outstanding community arts organizations that create community theater, music, and technology-art programs. For information, contact **PAWI** (Promote Art Works, Inc.) at 797-3116 and **Flying Bridge Community Arts, Inc.**, at 852-3926.

440 Clinton Street House. 440 Clinton Street, off Court Street.

F. G. Guido Funeral Home occupies this 1840s New York City landmark building, which was one of the biggest of its time in Brooklyn. Note the fine old granite entrance.

International Longshoremen's Union, Local 1814. 343 Court Street, at Union Street, 875-3865.

This innocuous, official-looking building is the headquarters of what remains of the longshoremen's union, once a powerful force on the Brooklyn waterfront and in local and national politics. The tumultuous, sometimes violent history of the union reflected the brutal physical demands on the longshoremen, whose back-breaking work required loading and unloading shipments of sugar, coffee, and other goods. Sometimes colorful, sometimes corrupt, always noisy, the longshoremen were a tremendous influence on Carroll Gardens and the neighboring waterfront community of Red Hook, which was built primarily by and for the people who worked at the Brooklyn ports. The introduction of containerization in the 1960s began a rapid decline of the longshoremen industry.

Jerard Studio. 131 Union Street, off Columbia, 852-4128. By appointment only.

So you've driven up Union Street and seen the venerable old bank building with an attractive modern sign. What *is* Jerard Studio? Inside is a large, airy private art studio, where artists and local residents John Jerard and Mary Crede create puppets, mechanical costumes, and stage sets (their credits include scenes from Broadway blockbuster *Beauty and the Beast*, and the Chicago Lyric Opera company), design furniture, and, in their words, "solve visual problems." Their brochure offers "illustration, design, fabrication, alchemy."

South Congregational Church. 358–366 Court Street, corner of President Street.

Built in stages from 1851 to 1893, this Romanesque Revival church, a New York City landmark, once had an active congregation of South Brooklynites, including longshoremen, merchants, and tradespeople. It housed a church, ladies parlor, and rectory. The original church and chapel have been renovated into residential apartments.

NOTABLE RESTAURANTS (INCLUDES COBBLE HILL, CARROLL GARDENS, AND RED HOOK)

✪ **Café on Clinton.** 268 Clinton Street, between Warren and Congress streets, 625-5908. Mon.–Thurs., 5–11 P.M.; Fri.–Sun., 11 A.M.–3:30 P.M. and 5–11 P.M.

Warmth pours forth from this intimate little restaurant, with its oak-and-exposed-brick walls, and beautifully restored pressed-tin ceilings. The menu features fresh-from-the-market grilled fish plus Mexican, Oriental, and Italian dishes, with entrées priced from $8 to $14. A real treat is the Tuesday night $12.95 lobster special. Don't miss the hand-wrought iron brain-teaser puzzles hanging near the bar. They'll keep you busy for hours.

Caffè Carciofo. 248 Court Street, corner Kane Street, 624-7551. Daily, 5:30–10:30 P.M. ; brunch Sun., 11 A.M.–3 P.M. No credit cards.

Despite the name, artichokes are *not* a theme of the menu. The eclectic Northern Italian fare is good and reasonably priced (entrées from $10 to $16), and the menu changes daily, but the real star here is the restaurant itself, with its bright tile floor, exposed-brick walls, and muted dark wood accents. When the weather permits, the restaurant opens onto the sidewalk, offering a not-to-be missed dining experience.

Casa Rosa. 384 Court Street, between Carroll and President streets, 625-8874. Daily, 11:30 A.M.–11 P.M.

Good, solid Italian fare in a simple, old-fashioned setting. The sort of place where you can still get a full (and filling) dinner—including antipasto and coffee—for less than $20.

✪ **Harvest.** 218 Court Street, between Warren and Baltic streets, 624-9267. Tues.–Thurs. 11:30 A.M.–3 P.M.; 5:30–11 P.M.; Fri. and Sat., 6 P.M.–midnight.

Harvest's hearty comfort food, outrageously large portions, and reasonable prices (entrées from $9 to $15) can't be beat. The Southern and Louisiana cuisine includes fried catfish, meat loaf, and jambalaya; daily specials feature seared duck breast, chicken fried steak, and chicken livers with caramelized onions; and the menu also offers sweet mashed potatoes, shredded pork, and four kinds of greens. Child-friendly butcher's paper tablecloths come complete with crayons.

Harvest East. 242 Court Street between Baltic and Kane streets, 254-9375. Tues.-Thurs., 11:30 A.M..–11 P.M.; Fri., 11:30 A.M.–midnight; Sat., 10 A.M.–midnight; Sun., 10 A.M.–11 P.M.

The owners of the wildly successful Harvest restaurant opened this restaurant in late 1998, with a hipster Asian theme. For appetizers try the Shanghai-style dumpling, a crabmeat potsticker that's crunchy on the bottom, or the crispy Peking duck-and-chive pancake. Entrées include a pad thai served with chicken and shrimp, and braised short rib with crispy tempura long beans, served over coconut rice. There's a large sake list, too. Appetizers are about $6, and entrées $9–13.

✪ **Kalio.** 254 Court Street, between Kane and DeGraw streets, 625-1295. Mon.–Thurs., 5:30–10:30 P.M.; Fri.–Sat., 5:30–11 P.M.; Sun., 4–10 P.M.

On the pricey side (appetizers up to $10.50, entrées up to $21) but well worth it, Kalio's new American cuisine is prepared by George Sayegh, formerly of Park Slope's **Cucina** restaurant. The menu is overhauled five times a year, and fare concentrates on grilled and roasted meats, poultry, fish, and vegetables, with influences ranging from Japan to Morocco to Louisiana. There is a gourmet cheese menu and full bar with an extensive tequila selection.

Marco Polo Restaurant. 345 Court Street, corner of Union Street, 852-5015. Mon.–Thurs., 11:30 A.M.–11 P.M.; Fri., 11:30 A.M.–midnight; Sat., 3 P.M.–midnight; Sun., 1–10 P.M.

A local favorite, Marco Polo's extensive menu includes about fifteen seafood and fifteen meat entrées, with specialties like porcini mushroom pasta and black pasta with scallops and shrimp. Entrées cost from $13 to $20. The pasta is made in-house, and the bread is from **Caputo**'s, a local bakery. There's live piano every night, an enclosed sidewalk café, valet parking, and a fireplace in the winter. Make reservations for weekend dinners.

✪ **Monte's Italian Ristaurante.** 459 Carroll Street, between Nevins Street and 3rd Avenue, 625-9656 or 624-8984. Mon–Fri., noon–10 P.M.; Sat., 4–11 P.M.; Sun., 2–10 P.M.

Tucked away on a nondescript residential street, Monte's lays claim to being the oldest Italian restaurant in Brooklyn, having opened in 1906. The hand-painted Venetian scenes on the walls of the single small dining room lend romance along with familial ambience. The local joke is that it's best to sit facing the door; if you have to ask why, don't.

Nino's. 215 Union Street, between Clinton and Henry streets, 858-5370. Mon–Fri., noon–10 P.M.; Sat., 4–10 P.M.; Sun., 2–10 P.M.

A few blocks off Court Street lies Nino's, a spiffy Sicilian place known for its ample use of fresh vegetables. Dinner entrées range from $8 to $15 and are served with excellent homemade sauces. The decor is attractive, with blond wood, green-and-white tablecloths, and a working fireplace. A large private room upstairs is used for parties.

Osaka. 272 Court Street between Kane and DeGraw Streets. 643-0044. Mon.–Thurs., 11:30 A.M.–10 P.M.; Fri., 11:30 A.M.–11 P.M.; Sat., 5 P.M.–11 P.M., Sun., noon–10 P.M.

Here's a welcome newcomer to the small world of sushi in Brooklyn, and although new, it is getting early rave reviews. There's a sake bar, and a Japanese garden out back.

✪ **Patois.** 255 Smith Street, between DeGraw and Douglass streets, 855-1535. Tues.–Thurs., 6–10:30 P.M.; Fri.–Sat., 5:30–11:30 P.M.; Sun., 5–10 P.M.; weekend brunch, 11 A.M.–3 P.M. Reservations are recommended.

Patois got a huge welcome from Brooklynites when it opened in 1998. This little bistro is moderately priced (entrées from $10 to $15) but offers a fantastically tasty French and American menu that changes seasonally. The eccentric chef (he wears a beret *inside* the kitchen) produces excellent fare, including grilled meats and fish, flavorful sauces and sides. There's a decent wine list. The interior is cosy, with tin ceilings, exposed-brick walls, and the 30-person capacity expands somewhat in the summer with garden seating. Watch for a new Vietnamese restaurant—complete with lichee margaritas—to open in 1999, next door, same owners.

Red Rose. 315 Smith Street, between President and Union streets, 625-0963. Mon., Wed., and Thurs., 4:30–10:30 P.M.; Fri.–Sat., 4:30–11 P.M.; Sun., 2–10:30 P.M.

This old-fashioned restaurant with hearty food and good prices caters primarily to locals. You can have a bowl of soup and pasta for less than $10, and the food is well prepared and fresh. Come early on Sundays and you'll dine among Carroll Gardens' older Italian crowd.

✪ **Rosina's Bistro.** 288 Smith Street, between Union and Sackett streets, 855-0681. Sun.–Thurs., 5:30–10 P.M.; Fri. and Sat., 5:30–11 P.M. Reservations are recommended.

Rosina's was an instant hit when it was opened in 1998 by long-standing Carroll Gardens resident Roseann Natale and her husband. The hearty cuisine includes grilled fish and meats, zestily complemented with mint, lemon, cumin, fruit glacés, and any number of other flavors that remind you less of traditional Northern Mediterranean than of Moroccan and the Middle Eastern spicing. The small, 32-seat space is bright, colorful, and inviting. Entrées range from $14 to $22.

Siam Garden. 172 Court Street, between Amity and Congress streets, 596-3300. Sun.–Thurs., 5–10 P.M.; Fri.–Sat., 5–11 P.M.

Siam Garden rates a "pretty good" from locals for its Thai food and relatively elegant setting. Entrées cost about $10.

Sur. 232 Smith Street, between Butler and Douglass streets, 875-1716. Tues.–Fri., 6–11:30 P.M.; Sat.–Sun., 11 A.M.–4 P.M.; closed Mon.

This Euro-Argentinean restaurant serves Argentinean imported beef, along with special chimichurri sauce, and a variety of tasty empañadas, pasta dishes, and other entrées. Try the sirloin steak or the *parrillada*, a huge mixed grill dish made for two. Things get busy around eight P.M., and there's sometimes live music in the bar area. The weekend brunch can be a long, lingering affair. The owners, local residents, also run the restaurant Novecento in Manhattan.

Quick and Casual Meals

Bagel Point. 31 Court Street, between Baltic and Warren streets, 522-2220. Mon.–Fri., 7 A.M.–midnight; Sat.–Sun, 8–1 A.M. Cash only.

It's not just bagels. Bagel Point serves very good lunches and dinners, the latter Middle Eastern–influenced. It's a good place for a vegetarian, and has about the nicest garden on Court Street. The bagels are good too, with everything you'd expect, great for a weekend brunch.

Buddy's Burrito and Taco Bar. 260 Court, between Baltic and Kane streets, 488-8695. Mon.–Sat., 11:30 A.M.–11 P.M.; Sun., 11:30 A.M.–10 P.M.

Buddy's is informal as can be, but you can't beat it for basic good Mexican food and a quick bite before the movies (the theater is right across the street).

California Taqueria. 187 Court Street, corner of Bergen Street, 624-7498. Sun.–Thurs., noon–10 P.M.; Fri.–Sat., noon–11 P.M. No credit cards.

"New York's First" East L.A.–style burrito place (everyone else makes them Mission style) recently moved into this larger space, and opened two Park Slope branches. The food is filling and not overwhelmingly spicy. Standard Mexican fare is made with your choice of stewed or grilled meats (don't miss the tangy chile colorado). Six bucks buys you a burrito the size of your head, or a huge platter with a taco, enchilada, or chile relleno (sort of a cheese-and-pepper omelette here) plus rice and beans, guacamole, nacho chips, and pico de gallo.

✪ **Ferdinando's Focacceria.** 151 Union Street, between Hicks and Columbia streets, 855-1545. Mon.–Thurs., 10 A.M.–6 P.M.; Fri.–Sun., 10 A.M.–9 P.M. No credit cards.

Nine decades old and a little out of the way on the waterfront side of the BQE, this tiny Sicilian diner will give you some feel for the workingclass Italian Red Hook of yesteryear. There's a certain romance in the old tiled floors and pressed-tin ceiling. But what keeps this focacceria busiest are its lunch specialties, such as rice balls with ricotta and panelli, a stuffed Sicilian bread, as well as the high-voltage Manhattan Special, a Brooklyn-made coffee-flavored soda.

Joe's. 349 Court Street, between Union and President streets, 625-3223. Daily, "five or six-ish" A.M.–7:30 P.M. No credit cards.

Joe's old luncheonette attracts the locals for breakfast and lunch. The prices are low, the food is hearty, and the owners and clientele are as down-to-earth as you can get. Joe's also serves a mean cup of espresso.

✪ **Leonardo's Brick Oven Pizza.** 383 Court Street, corner of 1st Place, 624-9620. Daily, 3–11 P.M. No credit cards.

You can't throw a rock in Carroll Gardens without hitting a pizzeria, and Leonardo's is one of the best one in the neighborhood. The crust is thin, comes with lots of different toppings, and is cooked in an old-style brick oven. There is outdoor seating in good weather, and children are welcome.

Nino's Pizzeria. See Nino's, page 139.

It's not fair to list a place twice, but Nino's pizzeria is the heart of the Henry Street end of the neighborhood. If you want to have a good slice and also hear the local gossip among shopkeepers, Columbia Street artists, and urban soccer moms, come here.

Sam's Restaurant. 238 Court Street, between Kane and Baltic streets, 596-3458. Wed.–Mon., noon–10:30 P.M. No credit cards.

For seventy years Sam's cozy local spot has been turning out Italian food, so no wonder the rollatini, spaghetti, and brick-oven pizzas are excellent. You can't get more authentic or informal than this. Prices are low.

Souperb. 140 Smith Street, between Dean and Bergen streets, 624-7710. Mon.–Sat., 7 A.M.–10 P.M.; Sun., 11 A.M.–10 P.M.

A newcomer serving (it was bound to happen sooner or later) creative multiethnic wraps, smoothies, soups, and salads.

Bars and Cafés

✪ **Brooklyn Inn.** 148 Hoyt Street, corner of Bergen Street, no phone. Daily, "whenever someone walks in lookin' for a drink" until 4 A.M. No credit cards.

A no-nonsense neighborhood bar, the Brooklyn Inn has no TVs and no food, but it doesn't need them; it has a pool table, a great jukebox full of country, old R&B, and jazz, and an eclectic clientele of local writers, artists, and other creative types. Featured in the movie *Smoke*, the bar itself is turn-of-the-century, made all the more dramatic by a huge mirror and beautifully carved wood detailing. Brooklyn Inn is usually packed.

Cousins II. 160 Court Street, corner of Amity Street, 596-3514. Mon.–Tues., 4 P.M.–2 A.M.; Wed.–Thurs., noon–2 A.M.; Fri.–Sat., noon–4 A.M.; Sun., 11:30–
2 A.M.

This recently renovated corner bar is enclosed by huge plateglass windows (excellent for people-watching). Cousins serves inexpensive sandwiches, burgers, and other pub fare, as well as steaks and veal dishes that run up to $17. You can catch brunch on weekends and a game on one of the bar's TVs anytime.

✪ **Fall Café.** 307 Smith Street, between Union and President streets, 403-0230. Mon.–Fri., 7:30 A.M.–9 P.M.; Sat., 8 A.M.–9 P.M. Sun., 9 A.M.–8 P.M. No credit cards.

Furnished in Salvation Army–style armchairs, this coffee bar has become a center of life in Carroll Gardens for generation Xers, writers, and moms of preschoolers desperate for a good caffè latte and adult conversation. It is mainly a coffee bar, with a few munchies, including hot oatmeal in the morning, chilis and vegetarian soups, and sandwiches. They display locals' artwork and feature music on many weekend evenings, from jazz to baroque, as well as poetry readings.

Mazzola. 295 Court Street, between Bergen and Wyckoff streets, 797-2385. Mon.–Fri., 7 A.M.–8 P.M.; Sat.–Sun., 8 A.M.–7 P.M. No credit cards.

Owned by Mazzola's Bakery in Carroll Gardens, this little café offers tea and coffee (of the drinkable and by-the-pound varieties), as well as a variety of Italian cakes, cookies, and pastries. Of course, they also have scones, croissants, muffins, and other de rigueur café munchies.

✪ **Roberto Cappuccino Caffè and Tea Room.** 221 Court Street, between Wyckoff and Warren streets, 858-7693. Daily except Wed., 7:30 A.M.–6 P.M. No credit cards.

Roberto serves up rich egg dishes, Italian panino sandwiches, specialty crêpes, crisp waffles, and oatmeal that will keep winter chills away for a week. Antique furnishings (including church pews) and cornucopia-like displays of imported foods and drinks add to the atmosphere. The price of success? You'll be lucky to find a seat on a weekend morning.

P. J. Hanley's Tavern. 449 Court Street, near Nelson Street, 834-8223. Mon.–Wed., 5–11 P.M.; Thurs.–Sun., noon–11 P.M. Cash only.

Hanley's Tavern claims to be the oldest bar in Brooklyn, dating from 1874. Today it's a low-key sports bar, with a fireplace that lends a nice atmosphere on winter nights.

Sinatra's Museum Caffe Nostalgia and Coo Coo Nest. 371 Court Street, between First Place and Carroll Street, 2nd flr, 855-0587. Mon.–Sat., 11 A.M.–11 P.M.

Elvis has his shrines, and so do the Beatles. This quirky upstairs café serves coffee and "just a little alcohol, not much," but you can't get away from loving Frankie memorabilia plastered here, there, and everywhere. It's a folksy, Carroll-Gardens version of a Disney theme restaurant. Without the Disney, of course.

Sparky's Ale House. 481 Court Street, corner of Nelson Street, 624-5516. Sun.–Thurs., 4 P.M.–2 A.M.; Fri.–Sat., 4 P.M.–4 A.M. Cash only.

It's located in Carroll Gardens, but Red Hook aficionados love it. One of a half-dozen Irish pubs in Carroll Gardens (which may or may not testify to the one-time Irish population of the area), Sparky's is the least slick and pretentious of the bunch. Just good people and lots of good brews (Irish, English, and American) in a small, friendly corner bar. You can also play darts or the jukebox here—and Broadway wannabes will appreciate the monthly open-mike evening.

SHOPPING (INCLUDES COBBLE HILL, CARROLL GARDENS, AND RED HOOK)

Specialty Food Shops

Biscotti Ilene Bakery. 251 Smith Street, between DeGraw and Douglass Streets, 852-0256 Mon., Wed-Sat.; 10–6, closed Tues. and Sun. Cash only.

Who can resist fresh biscotti and brownies? You don't have to go as far as Dean & Deluca to indulge in Ilene's creations, because this wholesale outfit has now opened a tiny retail shop next to the bakery kitchen and workroom. You can get coffee and pastries to go. Brownies are 85 cents apiece. Two dozen small biscotti cost $6.50 a pound, jumbo chocolate cookies $7.20 a dozen. For a $60 minimum they will ship next-day by UPS–call before 3 P.M. for next-day delivery.

Caputo's Bake Shop. 329 Court Street, between Union and Sackett streets, 875-6871. Mon.–Sat., 6 A.M.–7 P.M.; Sun., 6 A.M.–5 P.M. No credit cards.

Caputo's fourth-generation family bakery is a great place for bread. About ten different kinds are baked on the premises, and you can make a meal out of a special bread filled with salami and provolone.

College Bakery. 239 Court Street, between Warren and Baltic streets, 624-5534. Tues.–Sun., 7 A.M.–8 P.M. No credit cards.

Not much of the original German population is left in this neighborhood, but one survivor is this sixty-six-year-old, family-run German bakery, which makes old-fashioned whipped cream birthday cakes, chocolate layer cakes, and rye and sourdough rye breads, as well as snack-sized tarts, strudels, hamantashen, and other delicacies. Their prices, like the decor, remain in the 1950s.

Court Pastry Shop. 298 Court Street, between DeGraw and Douglass streets, 875-5403. Daily, 8 A.M.–8:30 P.M.

Wonderful traditional Italian sweets are the treat here, from cannoli to sfogliatella (huge lobster-tail pastries filled with cream) and sfinge, also known as "Saint Joseph's pastries." Seasonal holiday treats like strufoli and cassata are also available.

D'Amico Foods. 309 Court Street, between DeGraw and Sackett streets, 875-5403. Mon–Sat., 9 A.M.–7 P.M.; closed Sun.

What could be more authentic and scene-setting than a huge old-fashioned cast-iron coffee roaster and grinder smack-dab in the middle of a food shop? More than sixty different kinds of coffee are roasted on the premises. You'll also find large jars of olives, pimientos, spices, cheeses, and biscotti.

✪ **Defonte's Sandwich Shop.** 379 Columbia Street at Luquer Street, 625-8052. Mon–Sat., 6 A.M.–4 P.M.

You could easily miss this unassuming storefront (indeed, we did in our first book), but it has been thriving since 1922 because the sandwiches are so darned good. Try a multilayered hero with fresh vegetables, grilled vegetables, and several kinds of cured meats. Close to the Columbia Street "renaissance."

Delicatessen at Verandah Place. 264 Clinton Street, corner of Verandah Place, 852-1991. Mon.–Fri., 7 A.M.–8 P.M.; Sat.–Sun., 8 A.M.–5 P.M. No credit cards.

Heading to Cobble Hill Park? Well, this is the perfect place to grab provisions for lunch. The new owner-and-chef counts the Prime Minister of France and the Paris Hotel Ritz as previous employers.

Fish Tales. 191A Court Street, between Bergen and Wyckoff streets, 246-1346. Mon.–Fri., 9 A.M.–8 P.M.; Sat., 9 A.M.–6 P.M.

Fish Tales, which opened in 1996, specializes in gourmet, sushi-quality fish and live shellfish, brought in daily. Fish Tales also sells prepared take-out dishes (including crab-stuffed sole and grilled salmon and swordfish) and soups, and is planning a sit-down raw bar. The staff is extremely friendly and knowledgeable and more than willing to offer serving suggestions (or cautions).

Frazier Morris. 102 President Street, between Columbia and Hicks streets, 643-3507. Daily, 10 A.M.–6 P.M.. Stay tuned for a possible move to another location.

Frazier Morris was a well-known Upper East Side shop for about fifty years, and in 1998, under new management, moved its mostly mail-order business to Brooklyn. You can order expensive gift baskets or drop into this retail shop for smoked salmon, caviar, foie gras, imported chocolate, nuts, teas, preserves, and more.

G. Esposito Pork Store. 357 Court Street, near President Street, 875-6863. Mon.–Sat., 8 A.M.–6:15 P.M.; Sun., 9 A.M.–2 P.M. No credit cards.

Esposito's family-owned shop has been selling homemade sausages since 1922. Among the seven varieties are sausages flavored with fennel, pepper and onion, and cheese and parsley. You can pick up all of the ingredients for a feast here—three kinds of mozzarella; eggplant, olive, or mushroom salad; delicious milk-fed veal; rice and prosciutto balls; and, if you're in the mood, pigs' feet.

✪ **Jim and Andy Fruit and Produce Market.** 208 Court Street, between Wyckoff and Warren streets, 522-6034. Mon.–Sat., 9 A.M.–6 P.M.; closed Tues. during July and August. No credit cards.

Welcome to THE classic Brooklyn vegetable stand. In the heart of Cobble Hill for three decades now, Jim and Andy's small, selective store sells hand-picked fresh fruits and vegetables, from apples to zucchini. It's an unassuming old place, the proprietors are not chatty, and the prices are on the high side, but the folks at Jim and Andy's are true food professionals and their produce is of the highest quality (which is why the local restaurateurs depend on them, too).

✪ **Latticini-Barese.** 178 Union Street, between Columbia and Hicks streets, 625-8694. Mon.–Sat., 8 A.M.–8 P.M.; closed Sun. Cash only.

Get the fresh, still-warmed homemade mozzarella cheese and you will think you died and went to heaven. People have traveled back from Manhattan at lunchtime just for the caponata at this unpretentious store that's been in business since 1927. Enough said.

✪ **Margaret Palca Bakes.** 193 Columbia Street, between Sackett and DeGraw streets, 802-9711. Daily, 7 A.M.–6. P.M. Sun., until 2 P.M. only. Cash only.

If it's good enough for Balducci and Dean & DeLuca, it's good enough for Brooklyn. Or maybe that's the other way around. Anyway, Margaret has been baking in Brooklyn for fifteen years, and turns out great rugalach, muffins, brownies, fruit tarts, chocolate chip cookies—and birthday cakes, too.

Mazzola's Bakery. 192 Union Street, corner of Henry Street, 643-1719. Mon.–Fri., 6 A.M.–8:30 P.M.; Sat., 7 A.M.–8 P.M.; Sun., 7 A.M.–6 P.M. No credit cards.

For more than sixty years in the same location, Mazzola's has specialized in bread. The loaves stuffed with pepperoni and provolone (sold under the unfortunate name "lard bread") are delectable, as are the extra-fluffy torrese bread and magnificent raisin bread.

✪ **Pastosa Ravioli.** 347 Court Street, near Union Street, 625-9482. Mon.–Fri., 9 A.M.–7 P.M.; Sat., 9 A.M.–6 P.M.; Sun., 9 A.M.–2 P.M.

The original Pastosa opened more than thirty years ago, and another dozen or so have since been launched by members of the Ajello family throughout New York City (one is Fratelli Ravioli at 200 Court Street). They sell a great variety of classic (four-cheese, spinach) and eclectic (pumpkin, sun-dried tomato, and lobster in squid's ink dough) ravioli and tasty homemade sauces (tomato, vodka, pesto, marinara, etc.), along with gourmet pastas, olives, and other delicacies.

✪ **Staubitz Market.** 222 Court Street, between Baltic and Warren Street, 624-0014. Mon.–Fri., 9 A.M.–7 P.M.; Sat., 8 A.M.–6 P.M. Delivery available.

An institution for more than eighty years, Brooklyn's most upscale butcher shop carries a wide selection of "health food meats"—no-nitrate turkey and hot dogs; mousses, pâtés, and sausages by Les Trois Petits Cochons; hormone-free chicken and veal; organic beef; and a good selection of standard meats. The store also sells top-quality gourmet foods, such as imported cheese, pasta, chutney, barbecue sauce, fresh-ground coffee beans, and bread. Call in your freezer orders and they'll pack it for instant storage.

✪ **Sweet Melissa Pâtisserie.** 276 Court Street, between Kane and DeGraw streets, 855-3410. Tue.–Thurs. 7 A.M.–10 P.M.; Fri.–Sat., 7 A.M.–midnight; Sun., 8 A.M.–10 P.M. No credit cards.

Ah! Peace and quiet! For a cup of tea, a back garden reverie, and great pastries, try this little French-style café. The goodies are made by a pastry chef who used to work for a well-known Manhattan restaurant (there are several such entrepreneurs in this neighborhood!), and you'll enjoy the lemon tart and croissants, among other treats.

Galleries, Antiques, and Collectibles

See Red Hook listings, too, page 152.

Astro-Turf. 290 Smith Street, between Union and Sackett streets, 522-6182. Tues.–Fri., 1:30–8 P.M.; Sat., 9:30 A.M.–8 P.M.; Sun., 10 A.M.–7 P.M.

They call it "twentieth-century furniture and objects," and if you're into fifties and sixties haute kitsch, this antiques store is a little slice of heaven. Plastic and Formica dominate, and any of the rocket-age glasses, containers, wall decorations, and other knickknacks would be at home in the Cleaver household. Is it for you? Well, the millennium is around the corner, and, like seafront property, they ain't making any more of it.

Brooklyn Artisans Gallery. 221A Court Street, corner of Warren Street, 330-0343. Wed.–Fri., noon–8 P.M.; Sat., 11 A.M.–7 P.M.; Sun., 11 A.M.–6 P.M.

Cooperatively owned by ten local artists and craftspeople, this tiny shop shows handmade glassware, ceramics, candles, textiles, books, picture frames, and other objets d'art. The owners also handle consignment sales and show rotating exhibitions of work by local and national artists.

Claireware Studio. 543 Union Street, corner of Nevins Street, 875-3977. Call for an appointment.

New York–born potter Claire Weissberg calls her work "urban folk pottery." Her porcelain cups and saucers, plates, serving bowls, and other items have been carried by gift shops at the Guggenheim and other leading museums. You can buy them directly from her studio. Seconds run $5 to $50, top-quality products start at about $20. There's a terrific annual Christmas sale; call to get on Claire's mailing list.

Flickinger Glass Studio. 204–207 Van Dyke Street, Pier 41, Red Hook, 875-1531. Call for information.

Once a year this art-glass studio opens for a big sale of things that they make: lamps and bowls and platters and serving dishes, all out of glass. Most of their work, however, is custom designed for architects and designers. They use over 6,000 steel molds, some of them created in the 1800s for antique lighting fixtures and other purposes. Charles Flickinger became involved in the art of bent glass while working on the restoration of the Statue of Liberty's torch.

Granny's Attic. 305 Smith Street, corner of Union Street, 624-0175. Tues.–Fri., 3–8 P.M.; Sat., 10 A.M.–8 P.M.; Sun., 11 A.M.–7 P.M.

At the ripe old age of six years, this shop is the oldest of the handful of antiques shops on Smith. It carries a fantastic variety of just about anything that's old: from furniture, light fixtures, and wall hangings to typewriters, golf clubs, and stethoscopes. It is uncharacteristically well organized and tidy for an antiques store. The same owners also opened **The Attic** (220 Court Street).

The Kasbah. 194 Court Street, between Bergen and Wyckoff streets, 222-4261. Daily, 11 A.M.–9 P.M. No credit cards.

A tiny but richly varied new gallery of Moroccan crafts, including rugs, wall hangings, furniture, glass and dishware, and clothing. The owner also does henna tatooing.

Main Street Ephemera. 272 Smith Street, between Sackett and DeGraw streets, 858-6541. Wed.–Fri., 3–7 P.M.; Sat., 11 A.M.–7 P.M. No credit cards.

If you're looking for twentieth-century movie posters, ads, postcards, magazines, or other paper collectibles, you'll be thrilled at this selection. Also available: Gowanus Canal Yacht Club T-shirts. For cards-and-comics-type collectibles, try the nearby **Baseball Card Dugout** (276 Smith Street).

Refinery. 254 Smith Street, corner of DeGraw Street, 643-7861. Tues.–Sat., noon–8 P.M.; Sun., noon–6 P.M. Closed Mon.

This small gallery is owned by Suzanne Bagdade and Andrew Raible. She—a fashion-industry refugee—creates handmade bags and purses, and he—a Pratt-trained industrial designer—crafts custom-made furniture.

G. H. Restoration Company. 277 Smith Street, between Sackett and DeGraw streets, 237-4233. Mon.–Sat., 10 A.M.–6 P.M. No credit cards.
Montgomery Antiques. 261 Smith Street, between DeGraw and Douglass streets, 834-1998. Daily, 10 A.M.–6 P.M. No credit cards.

These small, cramped stores are heaped with jumbles of old stuff, where great finds lurk among garage sale rejects. Effective display and ease of access are not strong suits, but if the search is as important as the find, then dig in. G. H.'s inventory leans more towards restored furniture and lighting fixtures. If you're small-item antiquing, also check out the nearby **Treasures** (249 Smith Street) and **Treasures II** (187 Smith Street) thrift shops. (See also the **Treasures** listing in the Park Slope section, page 263.)

OTHER SHOPPING

Books and Music

Bookcourt. 163 Court Street, between Pacific and Dean streets, 875-3677. Mon.–Sat., 10 A.M.–10 P.M.; Sun., 11 A.M.–8 P.M.

Comfortable and filled with a good selection of contemporary paperbacks, new hardcovers, and local-interest books, this pleasant and recently expanded bookstore also has an attractive children's room in the back with cute seats for the little browser.

The Community Bookstore. 212 Court Street, corner of Warren Street, 834-9494. Mon.–Thurs., 11 A.M.–10:30 P.M.; Fri.–Sat., 11 A.M.–midnight; Sun., 11 A.M.–10 P.M.

Don't let the messy housekeeping deter you from exploring this Court Street veteran. This is one very full store, with discounted hardcover best-sellers, both new and many used books, and a good selection of kids' books and even toys. Good prices.

Don's Music. 192 Amity Street, between Court and Clinton streets, 246-0458. Mon.–Fri., 11 A.M.–8 P.M.; Sat., noon–8 P.M.; Sun., noon–7 P.M. No credit cards.

Don sells used LPs (a great selection of which cost only $1), CDs, and cassettes from a cramped store that spills onto the sidewalk when it's not raining. There are also a couple of used guitars, and (why not?) children's bicycles.

Kane/Miller Book Publishers. 310 Court Street, between Sackett and DeGraw streets, 624-5120. Mon.–Fri., 10 A.M.–5 P.M. No credit cards.

Kane/Miller publishes English translations of illustrated foreign children's books—and the product is first-rate. Some titles come from Europe, but others come from places as varied as Ghana, Venezuela, and Sri Lanka. These are the folks who brought our kids those useful favorites entitled *Everyone Poops* and *The Gas We Pass*, translated from Japanese. Retail customers can purchase seconds at half-price.

For the Kids

✪ **Hoyt & Bond.** 248 Smith Street, between Degraw and Douglass streets, 488-8283. Tues.–Sun., 11 A.M.–7 P.M. Closed Mon.

Delicious, boutiquey children's clothing (sizes 2–7) is sold here, along with a line of casual wear for women, such as T-shirts, pants, and shirts. All feature the "Hoyt & Bond" label of owner-designer Elizabeth Beer, a local resident who counts some of Manhattan's toniest department stores among her customers. In the winter you can pick up a child's fleece sweatshirt for $38; a velvet smocked top for $50, disarmingly sweet handknit sweaters in a range of prices, and women's angora mittens, hats, and scarves for $80.

Doesn't the store's name sound frightfully British? It's actually named after two nearby Brooklyn streets.

✪ **Johnnie's Bootery.** 208 Smith Street, between Baltic and Butler streets, 625-5334. Mon.–Sat., 10 A.M.–6:30 P.M.

A second-generation family business, Johnnie's hallmark for sixty years has been experienced service and careful attention to fitting children's shoes, something woefully lacking in this big-box retail era. Most of the shoes are moderately priced Stride Rites.

Laughing Giraffe at Monkey's Wedding. 324 Court Street, corner of Baltic Street, 852-3625. Mon.–Sat., 10 A.M.–6 P.M.

Chock–full of children's toys, including "educational" toys mixed in with more pedestrian offerings like crayons, paper, and other basics. You won't find a cozier environment or a more helpful sales staff.

The Painted Pot. 333 Smith Street, between Carroll and President streets, 222-0334. Mon.–Wed., 11 A.M.–8 P.M.; Thurs.–Fri., 11 A.M.–10 P.M.; Sat.–Sun., 11 A.M.–6 P.M.

Paint-your-own-ceramic is the latest kiddie craze but adults will appreciate this too. You buy the plate or candlestick or mug or figurine and, well, paint your purchase. (Then they fire it for you.) The resulting masterpieces are oven, microwave, and dishwasher safe. Owner Lisa Mendoza, who quit her day job to make her fourteen-year ceramics hobby a career, also gives lessons on wheel and hand-built pottery in the downstairs classroom, hosts children's parties, and sells local artists' work.

Women's Clothing

Frida's Closet. 296 Smith Street, off Union Street. 855-0311. Tues.–Fri., 11 A.M.; Sun. 11 A.M.-6 P.M. Closed Mon.

The window display is likely to feature a coy black skirt, sassy knitted hat, and a sweet, fragile necklace. Cute, unusual clothes designed by Sandra Paez for the hip single gal or young mom are sold here, ranging in sizes from 2 to 12. Tops are in the $40 range, skirts closer to $65.

Stacia. 267 Smith Street, corner of Degraw Street, 237-0078. Tues.–Sat., 11:30–8 P.M.; Sun., 11:30 A.M.–6:30 P.M.

While you are waiting for a table at Patois, check out this little boutique selling hip, sexy, one-of-a-kind women's clothing, designed by a Brooklyn resident who until recently worked for fashion whiz Cynthia Rowley. Who's the market, according to Stacia's owner? "Women in their twenties and thirties who are used to shopping in Manhattan, and paying Manhattan prices—just because they've moved to Brooklyn from the East Village doesn't mean they want to start going to the mall." Prices for dresses run from $170–250, skirts around $160, and tops from $90–115.

Red Hook

Where it is: A peninsula bounded by the Gowanus Expressway and entrance to the Brooklyn-Battery Tunnel to the northeast, by Gowanus Bay to the south, by Buttermilk Channel to the northwest.

How to get there:

By car: (1) Battery Tunnel from Manhattan: Take first exit, Hamilton Avenue, stay in left lane, make U turn under BQE to Hamilton Avenue West. Continue past tunnel entrance to Van Brunt Street.

(2) Traveling East on BQE from Belt Parkway/Verrazano Bridge: Take Hamilton Avenue exit, go past Battery Tunnel entrance to Van Brunt.

(3) Traveling West on BQE from Long Island/Queens: Take Atlantic Avenue exit, turn left on Columbia Street, right onto Sackett, left on to Van Brunt, and continue almost to the end of Van Brunt Street.

By subway: Take the A, C, or F train to Jay Street–Borough Hall, exit at Jay Street and transfer to the B-61 Bus at the corner of Smith and Livingston. Get off at Van Dyke Street. Be prepared to wait for the bus.

How it got its name: Red Hook: Called *Roode Hoek* by the Dutch, Red Hook's name is straightforward: "Roode" because the soil was red, "Hoek" because of the peninsula at its south end that hooks out into New York Bay. You can see the hook on a map.

ABOUT THE NEIGHBORHOOD

It's gritty. It's a fringe neighborhood. Don't expect amenities such as cafés or shops. Look instead for magic and imagination, vision and eccentricity.

Take artists and put them in the industrial, grunge-romantic waterfront setting of old Red Hook: alchemy happens. You will see the magic in the **Hudson Waterfront Museum and Showboat Barge** and the **Kentler International Drawing Space.** You'll see imagination at the **Spring Festival and Pier Show**, usually held in a Civil War–era warehouse, and the

Open Studio and Garden Tours, which draw thousands of visitors to the area.

The surprising, wonderful **Coffey Street Pier**, renovated in the late 1990s, has incredible views of the Statue of Liberty and Governors Island, especially at sunset.

And, in good weather, there is always a weekend fiesta going on at the vast **Red Hook Recreational Area** on Columbia Street, as crowds of immigrants Dominicans, Mexicans, and other Latino immigrants enjoy picnics, intense soccer games, and makeshift taco stands.

Tip: Transportation is a problem. Red Hook is hard to reach by subway or bus. It's best to travel by car—or bike here—as the distances can be long. Consult a detailed map. Stick to Van Brunt Street, which enables you to avoid getting lost in the low-income residential area.

Historical Notes

Water and transportation have been defining factors in the development of Red Hook. A marshy area unsuitable for farming, it was transformed by the development of New York Harbor, quickly becoming one of the nation's premier shipping centers. Boats from all over the world docked, loaded, and unloaded here. Typical nineteenth-century industrial harbor life grew up around the port: bars, boisterous eateries with inexpensive, hearty food; shops for ship repair and maintenance; flophouses for the workmen, and expensive homes for the mercantile class (Red Hook was the second only after Brooklyn Heights in the development of row houses). Rough, colorful, and sometimes violent, this waterfront was dominated for decades by Italian dock workers and their **Longshoremen's Union**. An enclave of Lebanese tradesmen who settled on Atlantic Avenue and whose ancestors still run shops there also worked in port trades.

After World War II, the once-thriving industrial, residential, and maritime life of Red Hook died under the combined impact of a decline of New York Harbor and Robert Moses' construction of the highway system to ease middle-class access in and out of New York. Cut off from Carroll Gardens' shops, churches, and social life, and now on the wrong side of the BQE, Red Hook went into rapid, steep decline. Most of the area was gutted to clear way for low-income housing projects, leaving only the extreme eastern blocks of old row houses intact. From the 1960s through the 1980s, "Red Hook" was synonymous with a crime-plagued, inner-city neighborhood. In the mid-1990s, the daytime murder of a dedicated and beloved school principal was headline news, a reminder of the social ills of the area.

However, by the late 1990s Red Hook's dirt-cheap rents and waterfront possibilities began to attract some artists and musicians, dreamers and developers. Behind the industrial façades, they now are creating museums, molding architectural glass, making music—and renovating buildings. Substantial properties have been purchased by ex-policeman-turned developer Greg O'Connell, and warehouses on Van Brunt and Van Dyke have been renovated for use by small businesses. Crime in Red Hook declined in the 1990s (as it did in the rest of New York City). Still, the majority of Red Hook's estimated 15,000 residents are poor and live in housing projects.

A political fight is brewing with City Hall over the city's tentative plan to use Red Hook as a garbage dump after the closure of Staten Island Fresh Kills Landfill. It remains to be seen whether the small community of artists and activists will catapult Red Hook—desolate, but with spectacular waterfront views and interesting industrial spaces—into a revival. If so, there will be a bitter political struggle for the soul of the area, between those who want gentrification and fancy condos, and those who want basic jobs and affordable homes.

Food Shopping and Eating

Go to Carroll Gardens. Or, bring a picnic.

Kidstuff

Use your imagination: There's nothing formal for kids in Red Hook. If you don't mind the desolation, there are wide-open spaces for biking, a big soccer and baseball field and pool, and lots of places to go fishing. But bring your street smarts.

PARKS AND PLAYGROUNDS

✪ **Coffey Street Pier.** Daily, closes at 9 P.M.

James Dean would have loved it here. Coffey Street Pier is one of New York City's unknown peaceful destinations, at the end of nowhere in this mostly abandoned industrial section of Brooklyn. The pier was newly renovated in 1998 and, as piers go, it is gorgeously done, providing the average Tom, Dick, and José with access to a billion-dollar view (In keeping with this democratic sentiment, the pier is dedicated not to a politician but to "hero firefighter Louis Valentino, Jr.") You can see Staten Island, the Statue of Liberty, Manhattan's skyline, and the Brooklyn and Manhattan bridges. You can see where the Hudson and East rivers meet, Governor's Island, and more.

Bring your kids, your paints, your fishing rod, or come alone for the solace of a beautiful view. If you are unfamiliar with Red Hook, bring a map, too. You won't be alone, of course; there are picnickers and lots of men fishing.

You can launch your own kayak (there are no rentals or facilities whatsoever here) from the **Coffey Street Pier** and paddle to the South Street Seaport or Jamaica Wildlife Refuge.

Red Hook Pier Promenade. There are 600 square feet of public-access space along the pier.

Red Hook Recreation Area/Red Hook Pool. Between Clinton, Bay, and Henry Streets. 722-3211.

Come to this vast recreational area to experience a weekend fiesta or see some serious soccer games. It's nothing formal, but huge numbers of Dominicans and other Latino families gather on good-weather weekends to cook, eat, and play. Locals set up small cooking stands to feed the crowd. Everybody's welcome, and of course it helps to speak Spanish.

The facilities here include many sports fields, an excellent 400-meter composite track, and the larger-than-Olympic–sized **Red Hook Pool**, with a separate wading pool and an indoor fitness center. It gets crowded on weekends and used to be somewhat rough, so the wise come early.

Note: Bike or car transportation is recommended. The nearest subway is a hike away, at the corner of Smith and 9th streets; from there you can pick up the number 77 bus, and get off at Clinton and Bay streets.

POINTS OF CULTURAL INTEREST

✪ **Art Shows.** For further information call the artist-run group, **BWAC—Brooklyn Waterfront Artists Coalition** (596 2507), which organizes these and other events.

Beard Street Pier. The well-known arts group called Dancing in the Streets has held The Young People's Performance Festival at the **Beard Street Pier**.

✪ **Hudson Waterfront Museum and Showboat Barge (also known as Lehigh Valley Railroad Barge #79).** Pier 45, 290 Conover Street on the industrial waterfront, 624-4719. Weekend events in the summer or by appointment; best to call. Free shuttle bus is available from Brooklyn Heights, Park Slope, Carroll Gardens, and Red Hook. Take Van Brunt, make a right on Reed, left on Conover.

What a wonderful adventure! The peace and quiet is overwhelming at this museum boat. It's poetry-in-motion, a character-filled historic wooden barge built in 1914, rescued and restored, and now permanently docked at a renovated pier of the once bustling Red Hook waterfront. (And if that doesn't impress you, it's also listed on the National Register of Historic Places.) Come in the summertime for sunset jazz and folk concerts, art exhibits, wonderful small circuses, weddings, parties, a small quiet garden, and environmental education classes. In the winter there are school group tours and lessons on how cargo came to New York before the bridges and tunnels.

It is all the brainstorm of museum director and barge captain David Sharps, a young man with a romantic vision of the Brooklyn waterfront. Speaking of views, there are spectacular ones of the Statue of Liberty and New York Harbor. This effort has garnered support from the New York City Department of Cultural Affairs, Chase Manhattan, and Citibank and many other donors. Nearby are other pioneering efforts to transform the waterfront, including the idea of a trolley museum and trolley train.

Tip: Call for detailed directions, or you will surely get lost!

Garden Pier in Red Hook. Pier 45, 290 Conover Street, on the industrial waterfront, 624-4719. Open year-round.This is also where the **Hudson Waterfront Museum and Showboat Barge** is docked.

A New York gem, this beautiful little waterside garden, isolated at the end of a long, unused dock in Red Hook, is open to the public 24 hours a day. Its peaceful views of New York Harbor and the extraordinary quiet here are hard to match. The place is small—there's only one bench. But the idea behind it—that New Yorkers should have public access to the waterfront—has vast implications.

Come in the summer and enjoy a country-style patch of garden with thriving black-eyed Susans and other beautiful, tough flowers appropriate to the setting.

✪ **Kentler International Drawing Space.** 353 Van Brunt Street, off Wolcott Street, 875-2098. Open for shows or call for an appointment.

The Kentler is a nonprofit gallery that runs monthly and bimonthly exhibitions of local, American, and international artists. Paper is the theme here. That is, the gallery is dedicated to bringing to the public contemporary drawings and works on paper. Opened in 1990 by local artist Florence Neal (who designed the maps for this guidebook, incidentally), the Kentler and the nearby **Hudson Waterfront Museum** are the only open-to-the-public gallery spaces in the neighborhood.

You'll find the Kentler in the heart of old industrial Red Hook, located in the storefront space of a studio-residence building, one of several in the area that were renovated under New York City's Artist Housing Program begun in 1984. The gallery is named after the building's original nineteenth-century owners, a local men's haberdashers for the dockworkers of Red Hook by the name of "Kentler," which you can see chiseled just below the roof.

✪ **Open Studio and Garden Tours.** 596-2507.

Artists from Brooklyn Heights to Red Hook open their working studios to visitors for two afternoons on a given weekend. There are lots of opportunities for first-time collectors, with paintings, sculpture, and other works of art ranging in price from $50 to $5,000. This is part of the **Spring Festival and Pier Show.**

✪ **Spring Festival and Pier Show.** May–June, weekends. 596-2507. Call or watch listings for time and place.

Ten thousand visitors came to view the work of 250 artists, dancers, and performers in the 1998 show. Organized by the **BWAC**, the **Brooklyn Waterfront Artists Coalition**, the Spring Festival and Pier Show has been called the "the world's most democratic art show," and a "wildly eclectic mix of art." There are also performaces, films, photography, and outdoor sculpture.

This annual artist-run show began in 1979, and for the past six years has taken place in the dramatic setting of the Red Hook piers, in an 1840s-era stone and wood warehouse, loaned for the occasion by waterfront developer Greg O'Connell.

Notable Restaurants and Shopping

For the sake of convenience, all restaurant and shop listings for Cobble Hill, Carroll Gardens, and Red Hook are combined starting on page 138.

Contributed in part by Hal Cohn.

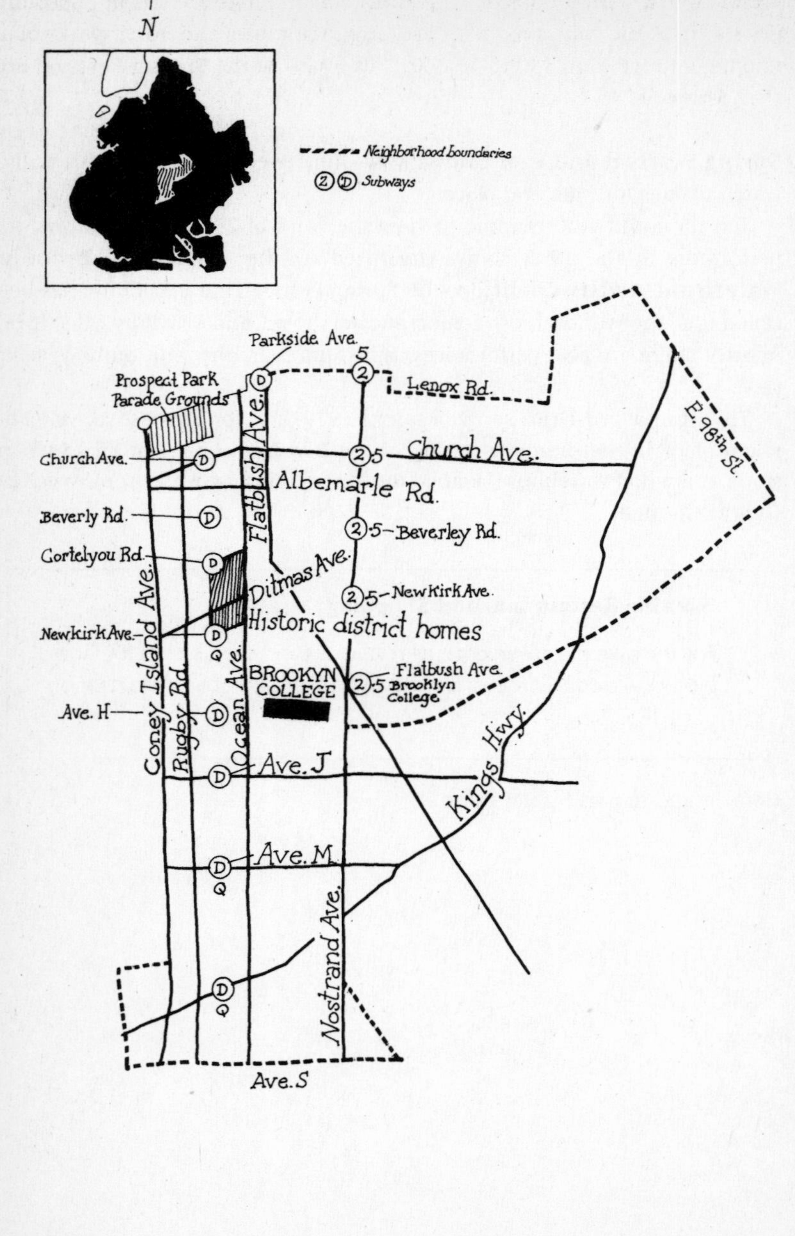
N
Neighborhood boundaries
2 D Subways
Parkside Ave.
Prospect Park
Parade Grounds
Lenox Rd.
E. 98th St.
Church Ave.
Church Ave.
Albemarle Rd.
Flatbush Ave.
Beverly Rd.
2 5 Beverley Rd.
Cortelyou Rd.
Ditmas Ave.
2 5 New Kirk Ave.
New Kirk Ave.
Historic district homes
Coney Island Ave.
Rugby Rd.
Ocean Ave.
BROOKYN COLLEGE
Flatbush Ave. 2 5 Brooklyn College
Ave. H
Kings Hwy.
Ave. J
Ave. M
Nostrand Ave.
Ave. S

Flatbush

This chapter provides a bird's-eye view of several strikingly different areas in the heart of Brooklyn: Flatbush.

Starting from the areas closest to Prospect Park and moving south, it encompasses the large district that lies between Prospect Park and the Brighton Beach strip of the Atlantic Ocean, including: (1) the residential areas near Prospect Park, such as Ditmas Park, Prospect Park South, Prospect-Lefferts Gardens, and Albemarle-Kenmore; (2) East Flatbush; (3) Midwood, covering avenues J and M near Coney Island; and (4) the Kings Highway retail center. It's a fascinating pastiche of cultures, food, shopping, and history.

Born-and-bred Brooklynites will split hairs over whether something is in Gravesend or Kings Highway, and residents of Ditmas Park may not like being lumped with Avenue M. Because our guide is written with the casual tourist and Brooklyn novice in mind, the following is an unconventional stew of what we have dubbed "Flatbush—more or less."

Where it is: "Flatbush" proper—the relatively small neighborhood which, confusingly, has lent its name to this much larger area—is bounded by Parkside Avenue on the north, Nostrand Avenue on the east, Avenue H on the south, and Coney Island Avenue on the west. It is the *heart* of Brooklyn.

"Kings Highway" is bounded by Avenue M to the north, Nostrand Avenue to the east, Avenue T to the south, and Ocean Parkway to the west. It covers most of the area once known as Gravesend.

"Midwood" is bounded by Avenue H to the north, Flatbush Avenue to the east, Kings Highway to the south, and Coney Island Avenue to the west.

The Prospect Park suburbs: "Prospect Park South," "Ditmas Park," "Albemarle-Kenmore," and "Prospect-Lefferts Gardens" are all defined by their proximity to the south or west of the park; see page 168 for precise boundaries.

What's nearby: Most of Brooklyn. Nearest are: Prospect Park, Borough Park, Sheepshead Bay, Brighton Beach.

How to get there:

As you might expect from its central location, there are many ways to get to Flatbush neighborhoods. Certain locations are easily reached by public transportation; for others, a car would be helpful unless you have plenty of time to wait for buses and subways. Consult *both* a subway and road map.

By car: One easy, if not elegant way to explore Flatbush, is to follow Flatbush Avenue itself, which runs through the middle of this large urban area. Scenic Ocean Parkway is the fastest north–south artery, runs through a residential area, and allows cars only. Other main arteries are Coney Island Avenue and Ocean Avenue, which allow commercial traffic and have shops and apartment buildings along the roadside.

The following directions assume you are traveling south from Manhattan, Brooklyn Heights, or Park Slope.

Brooklyn College: Go south on Flatbush, turn right on Bedford Avenue and follow it to Avenue H, or take Coney Island Avenue south. (You can call for detailed directions.)

Prospect Park South, Albemarle-Kenmore, Ditmas Park, and Little Pakistan : The best route is south on Coney Island Avenue, turn left onto Albemarle Road, Beverley Road, Cortelyou Road, or Ditmas Avenue.

Prospect-Lefferts Gardens: Take Flatbush Avenue from Grand Army Plaza. Immediately past the intersection of Washington and Flatbush avenues, turn left into Midwood or Rutland streets.

Midwood: Go via Ocean Parkway, or Coney Island Avenue.

By subway: Take the D, Q, or M train to Church Avenue (Prospect Park South), Newkirk Avenue (Ditmas Park), or to Avenue J, Avenue M, or Kings Highway (Midwood and Kings Highway). Or, take the 2 or 5 train to Sterling Street (Prospect-Lefferts Gardens) or to Flatbush Avenue (Brooklyn College), or the 2 or 5 train to Church Avenue (East Flatbush).

By cab: Best Way Car Service (252-6363), Avenue J Airport Service (251-3200), Prompt Car Service (284-2288), Shalom Car Service (236-5777). Fares are about $14 to $19 to Brooklyn Heights, $22 to $24.50 to Grand Central Station.

How it got its name: Reflecting Brooklyn's early Dutch settlers, Flatbush derives from the Dutch word for wooded area, *Vlackebos*.

Special events: Mardi Gras (Avenue M, June), historic house tours of Victorian Flatbush (spring, call 859-3800).

Offical Landmarks: Erasmus Hall Academy, Flatbush Town Hall, Flatbush Reformed Dutch Church, Johannes Van Nuyse House, Joost and Elizabeth Van Nuyse House, Flatlands Dutch Reformed Church, and Wyckoff-Bennett Homestead, among others.

ABOUT FLATBUSH

The string of neighborhoods known collectively as Flatbush is one of Brooklyn's most famous regions. It is no longer the mostly Jewish area it was in the first half of the twentieth century, and some old-timers bemoan the fact that "the neighborhood has changed." In fact, Flatbush remains largely middle- and working-class but now encompasses a varied and truly international population distributed among many sub-neighborhoods.

There is a wonderfully urbane incongruity in contemporary Flatbush. Hungering for Caribbean flavors and sounds? Take Flatbush Avenue to the Caribbean community in East Flatbush. West Indians from more than thirty Caribbean nations reside here. Sample Guyanese codfish cakes and ginger beer at **Sybil's Bakery & Restaurant**, or indulge in Jamaican fruit turnovers at **Hammond's Finger Lickin' Bakery**. If music is your interest, check out the latest in African and Caribbean music trends at the **African Record Center**. If you're shopping for top-notch jewelry, handbags, and home decorations, you'll love the prices in Midwood at such boutiques as the **Yellow Door** and **Carole Block** on Avenue M, and famous **Jimmy's** and **Chuckies** on Kings Highway. The largest community of non-European Jews outside of Israel lives in Midwood, too; try the food at **Mansoura's Oriental Pastry** or **Negev Caterers**. Speaking of nourishment, you'll find some for the mind at lectures, concerts, and kids programs at **Brooklyn College**, and Judaica at places like **Hecht's Hebrew Book Store**. After all this culture shock, you may need a respite—a half dozen blocks down Coney Island Avenue from Prospect Park is the peaceful residential area of **Prospect Park South**, and a bit farther, **Ditmas Park**. Even Brooklynites are surprised to find block after block of turn-of-the-century urban mansions here.

Historical Notes

With thousands of single-family homes and well over 30,000 apartment buildings in Flatbush today, it is hard to imagine this as farmland, but that's what it was just 150 years ago. The area was first settled in 1652 by Dutch farmers, remaining a sleepy backwater until the opening of the Flatbush and Coney Island Railroad in 1878. Access to transportation "suburbanized" the northern parts of Flatbush, drawing middle- and upper-middle-class New Yorkers from Manhattan and brownstone Brooklyn to what, literally, were greener pastures. (The legacy of the early developers has survived into the twenty-first century as names of areas such as Ditmas Park and Albemarle-Kenmore Terrace.) The opening of a subway line in 1920 to the Atlantic Ocean beaches and nearby amusement park attractions sped the development of residential areas deeper into Brooklyn. Large apartment buildings, many of which still line Ocean Parkway, were erected. Their early occupants were mainly Jewish, lending the area its mid-twentieth-century association with Jewish mores, New York Jewish humor, and Jewish delis.

In the decades after World War II many Jewish residents of Brooklyn relocated to the suburbs. A large immigration of Caribbean islanders moved in, along with other immigrant groups from Asia, Central America, and Russia, transforming Flatbush. Today, Flatbush is a fascinating pastiche of immigrant and old New York cultures, ethnic foods, discount shopping, and New York City history.

What *Is* That Tree That Grows in Brooklyn?

Everyone has heard of the famous book-turned-movie, *A Tree Grows in Brooklyn*, by Betty Smith. And, indeed, there are lots of leafy friends throughout Brooklyn.

The tree in question is called the *Ailanthus altissima*, dubbed the "tree of heaven." It is a tough survivor, able to establish roots under difficult circumstances, regardless of concrete pavement above and rocks and rusty nails below. Not a bad metaphor for Brooklyn itself.

Shopping Areas

We've listed shops in the following retail "strips" for easy convenience. But don't hesitate to explore on your own!

Kings Highway: A popular street filled with small clothing and shoe stores of widely varying tastes that sell a wide price range of clothing, shoes, and basic foodstuffs; there are some chain stores here as well.

Avenues J and M: Two Midwood commercial streets filled with mom-and-pop stores. Many offer discounted prices on high-quality housewares, jewelry, and clothing, with an emphasis on serving the needs of the local orthodox Jewish population. Some of the best buys can be found in stores that look like a wreck from outside.

Church Avenue: A busy retail thoroughfare through East Flatbush, lined with a combination of low-end chain stores, and small businesses selling cheap basic housewares, clothing, kids toys, and necessities of life, sprinkled throughout with West Indian, Pakistani, and Bangladeshi restaurants, bakeries, food shops.

Coney Island Avenue, between Cortelyou Road and Avenue H: A Little Pakistan, a growing community of Pakistani immigrants and the retail stores that serve them.

Kidstuff

There are terrific shows for kids at **Brooklyn College**. You're in the heart of the city here, so of course there are urban playgrounds and basketball courts as well as hockey rinks. The huge wholesale **Terminal Market** nearby may also be of interest. But unless you (or Grandma) happen to live here, Flatbush is not kiddie heaven. See the Parks and Playgrounds section below.

ENTERTAINMENT

Brooklyn Center Cinema. Whitman Hall, Brooklyn College, intersection of Hillel Place and Campus Road, 951-4610 or 4600. Call for show times. Tickets are only $5; free for sneak previews.

Film buffs! In an era when many Manhattan revival theaters are closing down, Brooklyn's Walt Whitman Hall is going strong. This is Brooklyn's first and only retrospective movie house, complete with seating for thousands and a forty-foot-wide by two-story-high CinemaScope screen. Here's the hitch: showings are less frequent than at commercial houses. Call to get on the mailing list, or watch local listings—especially for sneak previews of "big" movies. The B41 or B44 bus stops at Avenue H, a stone's throw away from here.

✪ **Brooklyn Center for the Performing Arts at Brooklyn College (BCBC).** Intersection of Hillel Place and Campus Road, Call for a schedule of performances, 951-4500. Tickets available through Ticketmaster: (212) 307-7171.

More than eighty excellent musical, dance, and theater performances make their way here each year. Well-known names include Alvin Ailey, José Limon, the Shanghai String Quartet, and the King Singers. Even Mel Tormé comes to Brooklyn College! Theater productions range from Rodgers and Hammerstein's *Oklahoma!* to a Yiddish version of Gilbert and Sullivan's *HMS Pinafore*, to reggae and calypso shows. You can buy a BCBC subscription series or get single tickets for Saturday evening and Sunday afternoon performances. Get a calendar and directions by writing to the Conservatory Concert Office, c/o BCBC, Box 163, Brooklyn, NY 11210. For information on the "Family Time" series call 951-4500. Tickets under $10.

Kent Triplex Movie Theater. 1168 Coney Island Avenue, near Avenue H, 338-3371. Call for show times.

This local triplex is close to both the Ditmas Park and Midwood areas and not far from Prospect Park. Ticket prices are reduced substantially for matinees.

Kingsway RKO Cinema. 946 Kings Highway, corner of Coney Island Avenue, 645-8588. Call for show times.

Smack in the middle of Kings Highway you'll find this large movie theater—a good stop for a midafternoon break from shopping.

PARKS AND PLAYGROUNDS

✪ **Bike Path:** A bike lane runs down a special sidewalk path along Ocean Parkway all the way from Prospect Park to the Atlantic Ocean Boardwalk, accessible at the corner of at Brighton Beach Avenue and Ocean Parkway. It's a wonderful, if slow ride (due to many traffic lights) and safe for accompanied kids, or teens riding alone.

Bike riding on the Atlantic Ocean Boardwalk is not allowed after 10 A.M. Once you arrive at the boardwalk it is only another few minutes' ride to the **New York Aquarium**, **Coney Island amusement park**, and **Nathan's** to the right (see pages 86–93), or to the left along Brighton Beach Avenue to the Russian emporium, **M & I International Foods**, and **Mrs. Stahl's Knishes** (see page 84).

Colonel David Marcus Park. Avenue B, between East 3rd Street and Ocean Parkway.

This spacious and recently renovated playground is a wonderful find. Worthy on its own of a visit, this lovely kiddie spot also happens to be a short drive from several interesting shopping areas, such as Avenue M and Kings Highway. It is also on the way to the **New York Aquarium, Coney Island**, and **Brighton Beach**.

Kolbert Playground. Avenues L and M, between East 17th and East 18th streets.

Here's a microcosm of the neighborhood: Russians playing checkers and chess, mothers with baby strollers, and elderly women chatting on the benches. There's a big renovated playground for the kids and a large basketball area for teenagers. Located within walking distance of most of Avenue M shopping in a pleasant middle-class neighborhood behind Edward R. Murrow High School, this is a fine place for a picnic lunch—and people-watching.

Ocean Parkway Mall. Ocean Parkway, from Prospect Park to the Atlantic Ocean.

Ocean Parkway is one of the finest boulevards for riding or strolling in New York City. It was designed by Frederick Law Olmsted and Calvert Vaux, creators of Central Park and Prospect Park. Along the way you'll pass through a middle- and upper-middle-class, largely Orthodox Jewish area (many people will be strolling to and from synagogue on Friday evening and Saturday).

Prospect Park, Brooklyn's biggest playground and one of New York City's finest parks, is easily accessible from Flatbush.

POINTS OF CULTURAL INTEREST

Brooklyn College. Intersection of Hillel Place and Campus Road, 434-1900.

Old flicks, theater, dance, lectures—all are available at Brooklyn College. For generations of Brooklyn kids the American Dream started on this site, which was once used to host the Barnum & Bailey Circus. Since its inception in 1930 Brooklyn College has been one of New York City's great educational resources. Students reflect Brooklyn's wide spectrum of ethnic groups.

Brooklyn Dodgers and Ebbets Field. Empire Boulevard.

The Dodgers are long gone. The Jackie Robinson Apartment complex, so-called after America's first, and legendary, black major league baseball player (he was of course a Brooklyn Dodger), covers over most of what was the home ballpark for the Brooklyn Dodgers. Ebbets Field, opened in 1913 in Flatbush, remained home to "dem Bums" until they moved to Los Angeles in 1957. Both the ballpark and the team are Brooklyn cultural icons.

As for the mythology of the Brooklyn Dodgers—and their enthusiastic, eccentric fans—entire books have been devoted to the subject. With all their foibles and antics, they were the most human of competitors, they were beloved—and they are sorely missed.

Brooklyn Terminal Market. Main gate is on Foster Avenue, near East 85th Street, 968-8434 or 444-5700. (Take exit 13 off the Belt Parkway, go north on Rockaway Parkway, then left on Foster Avenue to the main gate.) Daily, 7 A.M.–6 P.M.

This market actually is in Canarsie, close to Flatbush. This big, bustling wholesale food and plant market, in operation since 1945, is a great place for showing kids where the store owners go shopping—call it Economics 101 or Introduction to Wholesaling. Many of the establishments here are open to the public. Lots of people like the pickles and ambience here better than what they find on Manhattan's Lower East Side. Of particular interest to gardeners are the fruit vines (watermelons, wine grapes) sold by **Watermelon Plus**, at stall 62 (968-7400), Christmas firs at Anthony Visconti and Sons, stall 14 (241-7776), and Lapides' (763-3665) low-cost spring shrubs and plants.

✪ **Erasmus High Academy/Erasmus High School Museum of Education.** 911 Flatbush Avenue, between Church and Snyder avenues, 282-7804. By appointment.

Once called "the Eton of High Schools," Erasmus is one of New York's most famous high schools. Opened by the **Flatbush Reformed Dutch Church** in 1786, it became a public school one hundred years later, as part of the nation's emphasis on providing education for all children. Thousands of ambitious, upwardly mobile, sometimes brilliant children of European immigrants were educated and Americanized here. Its alumni include a Who's Who list of achievement, from Alexander Hamilton to Barbara Streisand, Beverly Sills, Neil Diamond, and basketball player Billy Cunningham, among many others.

Inside the original Georgian-Federal building with a columned porch, visitors can view old yearbooks, desks, and framed photos of famous alumni.

✪ **Flatbush Reformed Dutch Church.** 890 Flatbush Avenue, corner of Church Avenue.

A New York City landmark, the Flatbush Reformed Dutch Church was built in the 1790s. It has the unique distinction of occupying the site of the longest continuous religious congregation in the City of New York. It is a Federal-style brick and stone building. In the adjacent cemetery are the graves of prominent citizens of the day, whose family names are familiar to twentieth-century residents as Brooklyn street names: Cortelyou, Lefferts, and Bergen.

Flatbush Town Hall. 35 Snyder Avenue, near Flatbush Avenue.

Flatbush Town Hall is a remnant of the days when Flatbush was an independent community, two decades before Brooklyn made the fateful decision to become part of New York City (which some Brooklynites now regret). A New York City landmark, this restored 1870s brick and stone building is within a short walk to **Erasmus Hall High School**. Today it is used by the New York City Department of Education.

Flatlands Dutch Reformed Church. 890 Flatbush Avenue, at Church Avenue, 284-5140.

The original church was built in 1654 on this site by the order of Dutch Colonial Governor Peter Stuyvesant, and the existing structure was built in 1796. Note the wonderful stained-glass windows, including many Tiffany originals. This New York City landmark church has held a Sunday service every week for the last 345 years!

✪ **Johannes Van Nuyse House.** 1041 East 22nd Street, between Avenues I and J.

Take a trip in time away from the cars and commerce to this typical Dutch colonial farmhouse, a New York City landmark that was erected in 1800. It was built by the son of Joost and Elizabeth Van Nuyse, whose house, remarkably, is also still standing in this area.

Joost and Elizabeth Van Nuyse House (Coe House). 1128 East 34th Street, near the intersection of Kings Highway and Flatbush Avenue.

Built before 1792, the Dutch Colonial–style Joost and Elizabeth Van Nuyse House is the sole remnant of what was the Joost's 85-acre farm in this area. It is a New York City landmark.

Loew's King. Flatbush Avenue, corner of Beverly Road.

Anyone who grew up in Jewish Flatbush will remember Loew's. It was a fabulous, ornate, enormous movie house built with all the panache of the roaring twenties.

✪ **NBC Studios.** East 14th Street, off Avenue M, 780-6400.

Some of the earliest silent films were made in this building, the old Vitagraph Studios. Mary Pickford had a house built on the corner of nearby Ditmas Avenue and Rugby Road so she could live it up in style while filming here. The original *Peter Pan* was filmed here during the 1950s. Sammy Davis, Jr., recorded shows here in the 1960s, and this also was the base of operations for *The Cosby Show* during its heyday in the mid-1980s. The soap opera *Another World* has been videotaped and edited here for over thirty-five years, and periodically the two state-of-the-art studios broadcast *Saturday Night Live*. Tours are limited to school groups and last only fifteen minutes; call NBC public relations in Manhattan, (212) 664-4444, for information.

Singer and Singer Hardware. 1266 Flatbush Avenue, 859-7700. Mon.–Sat., 8 A.M.–4:45 P.M.; closed Sun.

This hardware store is, reputedly, where the great escape artist of all time, Houdini, bought his locks, chains, and other props of the bizarre.

✪ **Watt Samakki Dhammikarm.** 26 Rugby Road, off Caton Avenue.

A Cambodian temple and related school, indicative of the diversity of the neighborhood, sits on this residential street one block away from the Prospect Park soccer fields in one direction and free-standing historic nineteenth-century homes of industrial barons in the other direction.

Wyckoff House Museum. Clarendon Road and Ralph Avenue, at East 59th Street, 629-5400. Weekdays, by appointment. Call for schedule of events.

One of the oldest buildings in New York City, and restored to reflect the lifestyles of wealthy Dutch settlers of the 1650s, this historic oasis is worth visiting. Today there are lectures, weekend craft sessions, children's story hours, and outdoor programs held on a large lawn area. Standing here all those years, the Wyckoff House is a remainder of all the social configurations Brooklyn has witnessed: from a rural Dutch colonial farming settlement to a retreat for wealthy nineteenth-century industrialists, to a haven for Jewish, Italian, and other immigrants in search of the American dream, to today's urbanized hodgepodge of yentas, yuppies, Caribbean islanders, African-Americans, and Eastern European refugees. Cultural events are held here, including summer concerts.

Prospect Park South, Ditmas Park, Prospect-Lefferts Gardens, and Albemarle-Kenmore Terraces

Special events: House Tours of the landmarked districts are run in the spring. Call Flatbush Development Corporation, 469-8990.

Historic districts

✪ **Albemarle-Kenmore Terraces Historic District:** A tiny historic district, Albemarle-Kenmore Terraces Historic District is bounded by Dorchester Road to the north, Ocean Avenue to the east, Newkirk Avenue to the south, and East 16th Street to the west.

✪ **Ditmas Park Historic District:** This residential area is bounded by Dorchester Road to the north, Ocean Avenue to the east, Newkirk Avenue to the south, and Marlboro Avenue to the west.

✪ **Prospect-Lefferts Gardens Historic District:** This historic district is defined by Flatbush Avenue to the west, Fenimore Street to the south, Rogers Avenue to the east, and a jagged line going from Lincoln Road up to Sterling Street to the north. A small two-block area bounded by Rogers Avenue, Sterling Street, Lincoln and Nostrand avenues is included.

✪ **Prospect Park South Historic District:** Prospect Park South is a residential area bounded by Church Avenue to the north, Buckingham Road to the east, Beverley Road to the south, and Stratford Road to the west.

ABOUT THE NEIGHBORHOOD

If you have the idea that Brooklyn is all old brownstones, a trip to Prospect Park South, Ditmas Park, and the other nearby historical areas will turn that notion on its head. You'll think you're dreaming when you first spot elegant Victorian mansions with spacious porches, decorative turrets, bay windows, stained glass, and well-kept lawns throughout the area. Busy two-career couples of the 1990s can only imagine the pampered life-style once lived here. The architecture says it all: sweeping mahogany-banister staircases lead to sumptuous bedroom suites; steep backstairs ascend from the kitchen to third-floor servants' rooms.

Take your pick from among many delicious fantasies: the so-called Japanese house (131 Buckingham Road); the lovely home where the movie *Sophie's Choice* was filmed (101 Rugby Road); the "Honeymoon Cottage" (305 Rugby Road), built for one of the Guggenheim daughters; and for gardeners, the private botanic gardens at the rear of 145 Argyle Road. Or walk down Albemarle Road, off Stratford Road, to see former homes of the industrial elite. Number 1519 Argyle Road was built by the president of the American Can Company in 1905; down the street at 1505 is a Queen Anne–style home built by Elmer Sperry, of Sperry-Rand fame, back in 1990. The architect of Manhattan's famous Chrysler Building designed the Spanish-style home at number 1215 for the Fruit of the Loom family.

For an excellent series of self-directed walking tours contact the **Flatbush Development Corporation** (859-3800) and ask for their "Flatbush Tour" brochure. In April, this organization sponsors a four-hour shuttle-bus tour of a dozen private homes that are restored and original mansions dating from the turn of the century.

NOTABLE LOCAL RESTAURANTS

Los Mariachi's. 805 Coney Island Avenue, near Cortelyou Road. 826-3388. Sun.–Thurs., 10:30 A.M.–11:30 P.M.; Fri.–Sat., 10:30–1 A.M.

The zest of Mexico City, with all its energy, noise, and life, is almost palpable at Los Mariachi's. Gringos love the big portions of authentic Mexican food and live mariachi music (weekends only; call ahead to make sure), which make for a festive ambience. Entrées run from a low $5 to $15.

Mike's International. 552 Flatbush Avenue, between Lincoln and Maple streets, 856-7034. Mon.–Wed., 8 A.M.–11 P.M.; Thurs.–Sat., 8 A.M.–midnight; Sun., 8 A.M.–9 P.M.

Anyone who knows anything about Jamaica knows about spicy jerk chicken and pork. Mike's serves a full menu of specialties, such as oxtail stew, curries, fish cakes, fried plantains, and powerful-tasting juices of sorrel and soursop. West Indian food, live music on summer weekends, an informal elegant island atmosphere—you'll feel like you are on vacation.

Punjab. 691 Coney Island Avenue, near Albemarle Road, 856-6207. Daily, 10 A.M.–10 P.M.

Catering to the local immigrants from the Indian subcontinent, Punjab serves Pakistani curries and kebabs. It's a bare-bones joint, but what do you expect for about $5 per entrée? If you would prefer to cook at home, there's a twenty-four-hour grocery by the same name a few blocks down Coney Island Avenue, which sells Indian spices, rice, and other ethnic ingredients (434-9310).

SHOPPING

Most residents shop in Park Slope or Windsor Terrace. Here are a few standouts. (For Indian and Pakistani listings, see page 350.)

Bania. 602 Coney Island Avenue, near Beverley Road, 853-2525. Mon.–Thurs., 10 A.M.–midnight, Fri.–Sun., 8 A.M.–midnight.

Steam your heart out in an old-fashioned Russian-style *schvitzer,* located closer to Prospect Park than Brighton Beach. The clientele is about 75 percent European and Russian at this new bath house, which offers you a full day of Russian- and Turkish-style steam rooms and dunk baths for less than $20. The steam rooms are coed, so bring a bathing suit or a cover-up. Locker rooms are separate. For extra you can get a massage or chow down on borscht, herring, and shish kebab. It's run by Craig (from Brooklyn) and Alona (from Russia).

✪ **Bicycle Land.** 424 Coney Island Avenue, between Church and Caton avenues, 633-0820. Mon.–Fri., 11 A.M.–7 P.M.; Sat., 11 A.M.–6 P.M.; Sun., 11 A.M.–4 P.M.

BMXers will go crazy at Bicycle Land and its great selection of two-wheelers for hotdoggers. This family-owned and -run shop is chockablock with gear that will have you spinning out the door and around Prospect Park, which is just a few blocks away. In fact, if you're in the park and need a fix, take the Coney Island exit, go partway around the circle, and ride down two blocks. Owner Carlos Cortes, his son Carlos Jr., or any of the rest of the family will be happy to get you up and on your way in a jiffy. By the way, while BMX bikes dominate, Carlos, a former Colombian bike racer, also sells several high-end road bikes as well as kiddie bikes for your little ones.

✪ **Hollywood Car Wash.** 488 Coney Island Avenue, 854-3200. Daily, 7 A.M.–8 P.M.

A car wash in a travel guide? Well, Brooklyn is a practical place—and no, you can't watch movies, get a manicure, or do your laundry here. And the only glamorous thing about Hollywood is that it was voted "best car wash" by readers of *Brooklyn Bridge Magazine* by a three-to-one margin, which makes it a local institution. Don't go on a Friday afternoon unless you are prepared to wait.

Uncle Luigi's. 363 Coney Island Avenue, ½ block from Park Circle, 435-9378. Mon.–Thurs., and Sun., 11 A.M.–10 P.M., Fri.–Sat., 11 A.M.–midnight.

Through the small sidewalk window counter Luigi's passes out a cornucopia of delicious homemade ice cream and gourmet Italian ices. If you haven't had a *creamolata* ice, try it, or dive into the apple pie à la mode ice cream (yes, it's an ice cream flavor, and darned tasty). With more than fifty flavors, everyone will be satisfied, and at $1.50 for a big scoop, it's a bargain as well.

East Flatbush

Special events: The colorful annual **West Indian American Day Parade,** New York's largest Caribbean celebration, takes place not in East Flatbush but along Eastern Parkway in Crown Heights (Brooklyn's other big Caribbean population center) on Labor Day.

ABOUT THE NEIGHBORHOOD

Many Americans know something of the Caribbean: since the advent of discount airfares, vacationers by the millions have fallen in love with it. Music born of the islands seems almost as American as apple pie, from Harry Belafonte's calypso "Day-O" in the "Banana Boat Song" to the reggae and salsa beats that influence modern jazz and permeate rock-and-roll. This cultural and human traffic travels a two-way street; today Brooklyn is home to hundreds of thousands of pizza-eating, subway-riding islanders from more than thirty different nations.

The biggest attraction for visitors to Caribbean East Flatbush is unquestionably culinary. The enticing fruit and vegetable markets are exotic, with piles of mangos and coconuts, huge plantains, and innumerable mysterious-looking roots. A quick trip along Church Avenue will bring you to small, informal, and inexpensive eating establishments bubbling over with the true flavors of the Caribbean. The food and ambience bear the stamp of authenticity.

Some of the ingredients of this West Indian cuisine deserve a note because they reflect so clearly the combined African and Indian origins of West Indian culture as it is today. *Bammy* is a flatbread made of the cassava root (also the basis of tapioca), which is indigenous to the West Indies; Columbus reportedly feasted on cassava bread given to him by the local Indians. On the other hand, a spinach lookalike called *callaloo* is an indigenous African vegetable said to have been introduced to the Caribbean islands by enterprising African slaves. An okra dish with the wonderful name *coo-coo* also has African origins. And exactly what goes into the soft drinks with erotic names such as "Agony: Peanut Punch Plus" and "Front End Lifter and Magnum Explosion Combo," which are sold at some of the bakeries, is anybody's guess.

Historical Notes

For decades Caribbean islanders have come to Brooklyn seeking a better life. Of 300,000 West Indian immigrants who arrived in the United States between 1900 and the 1930s, tens of thousands ended up in Brooklyn. Many had a strong work ethic, and they scrimped and saved and eventually bought homes in neighborhoods such as Bedford-Stuyvesant, East Flatbush, and Crown Heights. Following World War II the flow of immigrants picked up again. Since 1960 more than 600,000 Caribbean immigrants have sought their fortunes in New York City. The largest group is Haitian—an estimated one in every three Haitians in New York lives in Brooklyn. In addition to Caribbean immigrants, there are sizable pockets of Muslims from Pakistan and Afghanistan, as well as Cambodians, Koreans, Central Americans, and, since the demise of the Soviet Union, increasing numbers of Russians. For the most part, these many different nationalities coexist in reasonable harmony. However, this area was the site in the 1990s of an angry boycott by African-Americans of a Korean grocery, spotlighting tensions between these two communities.

Which is not to say that every ethnic group is internally cohesive. West Indians are considered the second-largest immigrant group in New York City (after Italians), but they are hardly one united community. Rivalries and tensions are said to run strong, which is not surprising given the diversity of their backgrounds and native tongues: English in Trinidad, Jamaica, Grenada, and Barbados; Dutch in Aruba and Curaçao; Spanish in Puerto Rico and the Dominican Republic; and French and Creole dialects in Martinique, Guadeloupe, and Haiti.

Note: This isn't a Caribbean resort, so don't wear your latest fur-lined leather coat; sneakers and jeans are fine.

ENTERTAINMENT, RESTAURANTS, AND SPECIALTY FOOD SHOPS IN EAST FLATBUSH

Food for a Caribbean Feast

jerk chicken, curried goat, or shrimp
steamed red snapper
johnny cakes (fried yeast balls)
fried *bammy*
carrot juice with nutmeg
vanilla mango ice cream

B and H Fruit and Vegetable. 5012 Church Avenue, corner of Utica Avenue, 345-7839. Daily, 8 A.M.–8 P.M.

To get the flavor of the neighborhood, check out the wonderful Korean-run multiethnic grocer next to **Hammond's Bakery** (p. 174). It sells not only the standard array of grapes, carrots, and kiwis one finds everywhere in New York, but also breadfruit, a boggling array of yams with such foreign names as dasheen and edo, plus salted beef, plantain flour, and an international assortment of packaged goods.

Badoo's International Restaurant. 5422 Church Avenue, between E. 54th and E. 55th streets, 345-7654. Daily, 7 A.M.–8 P.M.; Sat., 7 A.M.–9:30 P.M. Cash only.

About two miles away from Flatbush, and a few long blocks from Kings County Hospital, Badoo's serves spicy, authentic Caribbean food in a big, popular eatery. It's a favorite for breakfast, lunch, and dinner among the large Caribbean population who reside in this easternmost part of Flatbush.

Buzz-a-rama. 69 Church Avenue, between MacDonald Avenue and Dahill Road, 853-1800. Erratic hours; call ahead.

Never heard of slot cars? Imagine little electric cars zooming around a curvy miniature track so fast they'd fly into orbit if they weren't running in grooves (or "slots") in the track. Slot car racing was a 1950s craze, and there aren't many of these joints left, but guys pushing forty and kids celebrating their eighth birthday party both just love Buzz-a-rama. It's noisy, fast, and, in its own way, thrilling. Call Frank Perri to discuss hours or children's parties.

Cheffy's Jamaican. 707 Nostrand Avenue, corner of Park Place, 363-9515. Mon.–Sat., 10 A.M.–10 P.M.

If you're in the mood for authentic Jamaican food, the locals say you should try Cheffy's. This hole-in-the-wall restaurant is one of several in the area serving fried dumplings, oxtail stew, fish cakes, cow's feet or goat curry, and more. A full meal runs less than $10 per person.

✪ **Edna's Glatt Kosher Delicatessen.** 125 Church Avenue, between East 2nd and MacDonald avenues, 438-8207. Sun.–Thurs., 11 A.M.–10 P.M.; Fri., 8 A.M.–2 hours before sunset; closed Sat.

Edna's is a popular kosher deli that makes the usual Eastern European specialties: corned beef, potato pancakes, pickles, coleslaw, and more. It's a local establishment and has a good old-fashioned environment. So, come, eat!

✪ **Flatbush Food Cooperative.** 1318 Cortelyou Road, between Argyle and Rugby roads, 284-9717. Daily, 7 A.M.–9 P.M.

This health food cooperative specializes in organic foods. There is a big selection of organic produce and specialty natural and kosher foods. The coop is owned and operated by members (who get discounts off shelf prices), but you don't have to be a member to shop here.

Hammond's Finger Lickin' Bakery. 5014 Church Avenue, near Utica Avenue, 342-5770. Mon.–Sat., 8 A.M.–7:30 P.M.; Sun., 8:30 A.M.–5 P.M.

While cruising Church Avenue in search of a Caribbean taste or two, stop here for Jamaican treats: cinnamon buns, tropical fruit turnovers, beef patties, and more. All goodies are under $1. The food made at this small bakery is traditional and very tasty. There's another Hammond's at 1436 Nostrand Avenue.

✪ **Sybil's Bakery and Restaurant.** 2210 Church Avenue, near Flatbush Avenue, 469–9049. Daily, 9 A.M.–11 P.M.

This clean, friendly West Indian (Guyanese) restaurant and bakery is centrally located if you happen to be driving down Flatbush to the beach or **Kings Plaza Shopping Center** (page 108) or are setting out to explore Caribbean Brooklyn. The bakery section is filled with an exotic array of pastries, such as coconut sweet bread, doughy cheese rolls, glazed jelly-filled triangles, and *salaras,* red coconut cookies. Sit at the counter, or at one of the green and white tables for a meal of baked chicken, stewed fish, codfish cakes, and goat roti curry. Try a few drinks: cane juice, sorrel, ginger beer, mauby (from a bark akin to cinnamon). There are Guyanese newspapers, too, for a change of perspective.

Interesting Neighborhood Shops

✪ **African Record Center Makossa Distribution.** 1194 Nostrand Avenue, between Hawthorne and Fenimore streets, 493–4500. Daily, 9 A.M.–8 P.M.

New York City's largest importer and producer of pan-African sounds for thirty-five years, this shop is a central resource for many musicians. You'll find a wealth of compact discs, music videos, records, and tapes here from Nigeria, Ghana, Zaire, Cameroon, Ethiopia, and South Africa by such prominent third-world artists as Fela Kuti, Franco, and OK Jazz group, whom Makossa Distribution Company helped launch. There's also an extensive collection of popular Haitian music. If you're interested but unfamiliar with the music, come in and chat with the knowledgeable staff, who will play demonstration tapes for you.

Discmart Black Mind. 610 New York Avenue, corner of Rutland Road, 774–5800. Mon.–Sat., 11 A.M.–7 P.M.; Closed Sun.

Afro-centric books and records are sold at Discmart, one of Brooklyn's premier black book shops. In tune with cultural trends in the intellectual and spiritual life of African-Americans, the store has a large collection of books on the Nigerian-based Yoruba religion and its manifestations in the New World, including Cuba and Brazil. As slaves adapted to meet the harsh living conditions and degradation of slavery, their religion changed and, in many ways that are just now being documented, went "underground," disguised as casual folkways and idiosyncratic habits. The store receives inquiries from major museums, scholars, and Europeans who are interested in the syncretism of this religion. (A similar social phenomenon occurred to the Jews under the Spanish Inquisition whose now-Catholic ancestors in Mexico cling to curious folkways strongly resembling Jewish religious tradition.)

There is also a good selection of African writers and sounds, some produced by Makossa Distributing Company, in addition to Caribbean and Haitian imports.

Dorsey's Picture Frame and Art Gallery. 553 Rogers Avenue, between Hawthorne and Fenimore streets, 771–3803. Daily, 1–8 P.M.

Framing is the business at hand at Dorsey's, but there's also a small display of artwork by Caribbean and Afro-American artists. Check it out if you're in the area. The owner is charming.

Midwood

Special events: Believe it or not, a Mardi Gras along Avenue M (June).

How it got its name: From the Dutch *Midwout* or "Middle Woods." In fact, many streets are still tree-lined.

ABOUT THE NEIGHBORHOOD

Drive along Ocean Parkway on a Friday or Saturday evening and you'll see a constant flow of well-dressed Jewish families going to one of Midwood's many synagogues. Dubbed "kosher yuppie land" by one New York daily, Midwood recently has undergone a youthful gentrification. Demand for housing within walking distance of the Sephardic synagogues is so strong that the price of some homes has shot past the million-dollar mark.

For those so inclined, there is a great deal of Jewish cultural life here. There is also good shopping. And, yes, this is where actor-director Woody Allen went to high school.

Midwood is home to both Sephardic (Middle Eastern and South European) and Ashkenazi (Northern European) Jews. The Ashkenazi presence is visible in Midwood's old German bakeries and the world-famous Flatbush and Mirrer yeshivas (religious schools). Members of the wealthy Jewish community that have settled around Ocean Parkway are mainly Syrians from Aleppo and Damascus. Their style and affluence is apparent in the stunning $7-million Sephardic Community Center and Sha'are Zion Synagogue on Ocean Parkway.

The Orthodox Jewish Syrian community is tight-knit, and to outsiders the "SY," as they call themselves, may appear clannish. Arabic and French are spoken along with English, young people marry within the community, and many people work in family businesses. Their year is punctuated by highly formal holidays and customs; many of the fancy local clothing stores are fueled by the Syrian demand for orthodox elegance.

On the other hand, **Avenue J** reflects old Jewish Flatbush. In its past Avenue J served a thriving German and Eastern European Jewish community; it still helps to know a little Yiddish here. In the clothing shops you are likely to hear talk of *hassanas* (weddings) and *shidduchs* (arranged marriages) as well as bar mitzvahs. Typical of Brooklyn, where Jews and Italians have lived side by side for decades, the neighborhood used to be partly Italian.

Avenue M is a thriving shopping street with a mix of local stores and expensive boutiques catering to both the affluent Syrian community and escaped-to-the-suburbs ex-Brooklynites—many of whom still make shopping expeditions back to Brooklyn in search of good prices and storekeepers who know them on a first-name basis. Incongruously located near a kosher fast-food joint called **Chapanosh** (which in Hebrew translates to "Grab-a-Bite") is the old Vitagraph movie studio, now used by NBC. Silent-movie stars Mary Pickford and Laurel and Hardy were filmed at the Vitagraph; later, Perry Como, Steve Allen, and recently *The Cosby Show* were all produced here. The nearby Edward R. Murrow High School specializes in communications.

Nearby, **Coney Island Avenue** between Avenues J and M is chockablock with no-frills discount shops ranging from interior design and silver shops to the one-of-a-kind **Miss Pauline's Bras and Girdles**. Many of these stores have such minimal window displays that they hardly look like retail shops at all. But the merchandise is good, the service is great, and of course many prices are discounted—not to mention that the experience of shopping here is different from what you'll get at any bland suburban mall.

Kings Highway, which intersects Ocean Parkway, has been a major shopping thoroughfare for decades. The decorative two-story buildings that line the avenue date from the 1930s, when the strip was first built; note the decorative Alexandria at 809 Kings Highway. The section of Kings Highway from about East 2nd Street to East 9th Street is part of the Syrian Jewish enclave; among expensive clothing shops, Middle Eastern grocery stores carry the names of Israeli and Lebanese cities: Bat Yam, Holon, and Beirut. On Saturday most stores in this area are closed for the Sabbath. From East 9th Street farther along Kings Highway, the numerous clothing and shoe stores serve the general public and are open on Saturday.

PARKS AND PLAYGROUNDS

See page 164.

POINTS OF CULTURAL INTEREST

There's a ton of local color in this old Jewish neighborhood. And, you will find New York City historic landmarks **Johannes Van Nuyse House; Joosts and Elizabeth Van Nuyse House**, and the old **Flatlands Dutch Reformed Church**, all remnants of Brooklyn's earliest days. More contemporary sites include the **NBC Television Studios** (see page 000) and Midwood High School, at Bedford Avenue and Glenwood Road, which is one of New York City's premier public high schools, known for producing winners of the prestigious Westinghouse Science Research awards.

NOTABLE MIDWOOD RESTAURANTS

Avenues J and M

✪ **Bernie's Place.** 217 Avenue J between East 12th and 13th streets, 677–1515. Mon.–Thurs., 11:30 A.M. 11 P.M., reopens Sat. one hour after sundown.

Bernie's, an upscale kosher Italian–French dairy restaurant, serves tasty fish, pasta, and salad entrées (no meat). The carpeting and classical music create a genteel atmosphere.

✪ **Caraville.** 1910 Avenue M, near East 19th Street, 339–2540. Daily, 6 A.M.–midnight.

Caraville serves good kosher-*style* food and a wide range of other dishes, ranging from Italian veal dishes to crab meat salad and pancakes. Caraville's is a dead ringer for a Greek diner in terms of low price and vast menu, but the ambience is more comfortable. Caraville is popular with an older set.

✪ **Essex on Coney Deli.** 1359 Coney Island Avenue, corner of Avenue J, 253–1002. Mon.–Thurs., 10 A.M.–6 P.M.; Fri., 10 A.M.–2:30 P.M.; Sun., noon–5 P.M.; closed Sat.

Wonder of wonders, the corned beef is lean, the pickles are just right, and the service is peppered with friendly wisecracks. You can get heroes by the foot, 1950s-style Jewish chicken chow mein, fresh chicken soup, of course, and a dozen overstuffed combo sandwiches named after Coney Island rides, such as "Cyclone," "Whip," "Funhouse," and more. New York has just a fraction of the number of kosher delis it did thirty years ago, so come, *fress* and enjoy Essex on Coney.

Kings Highway

✪ **Adelman's Family Restaurant.** 1906 Kings Highway, between East 19th Street and Ocean Avenue, 336–4915. Mon.–Thurs., 7 A.M.–10 P.M.; Fri., 7 A.M.–4 P.M.; Sun., 7 A.M.–10 P.M.

Don't beat around the bush: Adelman's menu says, "All Deli Mavens agree that Adelman's is one of the finest Kosher Delis in the New York area." And it probably is. The extensive menu starts with chopped liver, Hungarian goulash and fried kreplach, moves onto matzo ball soup, and then presents you with the misery-making choice of a hot tongue sandwich, corned beef, salami, and rolled beef "overstuffed combo sandwich" and, for variety, hot Oriental beef on garlic bread. If all this eating gives you *agita,* you can always stop into the Chinese acupuncturist whose office incongruously is located next door.

✪ **Mabat.** 1809 East 7th Street, off Kings Highway, 339–3300. Daily, noon–midnight; closed midday Fri. and Sat.; reopens one hour after sundown on Sat. nights

Not only kosher, but glatt kosher, this Moroccan-Jewish-Sephardic restaurant caters to the religious crowd. They serve authentic dishes familiar to North African Jewish communities, such as okra and rice, turkey with onions, lamb soup, tahini, and various grilled meats. If you've ever eaten in the Middle East, this will bring back fond memories of your favorite hole-in-wall, good-food joint, but at about $20 per person for a full meal, it will cost you more than a few lira.

✪ **Nick's Restaurant.** 2777 Flatbush Avenue, between Kings Plaza and Toys "Я" Us, 253–7117. Daily, 11 A.M.– 11 P.M.

The only thing missing from Nick's Cape Cod–like seafood restaurant is sand on the floor and sunburned kids in wet bathing suits. Everything else is straight out of an oceanfront fish shack, including the plastic cups and nearly frozen bottles of beer. The seafood is superfresh (you walk through the retail fish store to make your reservation) and kids will love the multiple televisions running old John Travolta films like *Grease* nonstop. Try the fish or crab cakes—fantastic.

Sal's Pizza. 1800 Kings Highway, corner East 18th Street Mon.–Sat., 10 A.M.– 10 P.M.

Brooklynites tend to be inordinately loyal to their local pizzerias (does the man make the pizza, or the pizza make the man?) but Sal's is one local residents *swear* by. If you want a whole pie, ask Sal to make special toppings with fresh vegetables and his personal touch.

SHOPPING

Avenues J and M

SPECIALTY FOOD SHOPPING

Chiffon's Bake Shop. 1373 Coney Island Avenue, between Avenues J and K, 258-8822. Mon.–Thurs., 6 A.M.–8 P.M., Fri., closes early; closed Sat.

Your Jewish grandmother would be at home here. Chiffon's has been turning out baked goodies—rye breads, challahs, and cheesecakes—for years, using the same time-tested recipes.

✪ **Gus' Pickle Look-Alike.** Avenue M., off East 19th Street, 375-6899. Mon.–Fri., 10 A.M.–6 P.M. Call for special orders.

Hey! It's pickle man!

Joe and John Davide, once worked with Gus' Pickles on the Lower East Side (the elder Davide will gladly show you photos). This bargain-barrel sidewalk stand is brimming with a dozen varieties of kosher sweet, dill, three-quarter-sour pickles, plus pickled celery, mushrooms, *giardiniera,* pickled tomatoes, hot peppers, and more. We don't know if there are enough pickle-eaters in Midwood to keep them afloat, but we hope so; the good-natured vendor is a jagged-toothed, beret-wearing Dickensian character who ruefully confides that although he is Italian, his pickles have 101 percent rabbinical approval.

If you stick your nose in for a whiff, its a sure bet you'll end up "brining" some home—and trying one on the spot. Half-dill, please.

Le Choclatier Extraordinaire, 1822 Avenue M, off East 18th Street, 645-3481. Mon.–Wed., 10:30 A.M.–6 P.M.; Thurs. until 7 P.M.; Fri., 10 A.M.–2 P.M.; Sun., 10 A.M.–2 P.M.; closed Sat.

Perhaps the messiest chocolate shop this side of the Seine, Le Choclatier Extraordinaire is a study in contrasts: high-priced Godiva (yes, they are kosher) chocolates in a helter-skelter, ribbons-on-the-floor workshop environment. Most customers order gift baskets by phone.

Negev. 1211 Avenue J, between East 12th and East 13th streets, 285-2875. Sun–Thurs., 9 A.M.–6 P.M.; Fri., closes early; closed Sat.

A take-out kosher deli, Negev has smoked salmon, herring, and whitefish salads, kosher honey roast chickens and pastrami. The traditional cabbage, matzo ball, and kreplach soups are good. You can order special holiday dishes here.

Ostrowski Bakery. 1201 Avenue J, corner of East 12th Street, 377-9443. Sun.–Fri., 8 A.M.–6 P.M.; Fri., closes early; closed Sat.

Jewish European-style Ostrowski bakers turn out kosher chocolate rolls, babkas, cookies, and loaves of bread big enough to feed any army. For contemporary Americans who usually buy bread and cakes at the supermarket, just the tantalizing smells of freshly baked goods is enough to transport you to another time and place. This used to be Stern's Bakery.

Presser's Bakery. 1720 Avenue M, between East 17th and East 18th streets. 375-5088. Sun.–Fri., 8 A.M.–6 P.M.; Fri., closes early; closed Sat.

Ah, the chocolate rolls, brimming fruit pies, and babkas, all baked on the premises. In keeping with most of the neighborhood's shops, the food is kosher.

Avenue J Area Shopping

WOMEN'S CLOTHING

✪ **Miss Pauline's Bras and Girdles.** 1478 Coney Island Avenue, between Avenues K and L, 252-7310. Mon.–Thurs., 10 A.M.–4 P.M.; Fri., closes early; closed Sat. and Sun. No credit cards.

Don't be put off by the boxes piled in the window. After all, when was the last time you were *fitted* for a bra? This hole-in-the-wall shop has been in the business of fitting for forty years. Miss Pauline's inventory of American and European undergarments is discounted about 15 percent but it's the philosophy that permeates this shop that makes it special. If they had a motto, it would be "Make the best of what you've got!" So, in a couple of tiny dressing rooms the saleswomen patiently measure, test, and consult. Their on-site seamstress takes a tuck while you wait. Fan mail waxes enthusiastic and people call in from all over the country for mail shipments. You have to see this to believe it.

MENSWEAR

✪ **Crown Clothiers.** 1434 Coney Island Avenue, near Avenue J, 252-6666. Sun.–Thurs., 10 A.M.–6 P.M. Fri., closes early; closed Sat.

Crown has a complete line of medium- and high-quality menswear that includes a big selection of sports jackets and slacks, suits, sweaters, leather jackets, and accessories. The merchandise is discounted at least 15 percent off retail.

OTHER SHOPPING

✪ **Eichler's Religious Articles, Gifts and Books.** 1401 and 1429 Coney Island Avenue, 258-7643 and (800) 883-4245. Sun.–Fri., 10 A.M.–6 P.M.; Fri., closes early; closed Sat.

This is the largest of several New York City shops specializing in Judaica. There are tomes of the Talmud in Aramaic, Passover Haggadoth, holiday tapes in English and Hebrew, *tifilin*, and reference guides on how to teach your kid to be a Jewish mensch. Don't be surprised if there's a heated philosophical discussion going on between customers. There's another branch store in Borough Park.

Happy Home. Coney Island Avenue, between Avenues J and K, 692-2442. Mon.–Thurs., 10 A.M.–7 P.M.; Sun., 9 A.M.–5 P.M.; closed Sat.

Baruch, the bearded Israeli proprietor, is an old-fashioned guy, and so jokingly calls this a "toy store for women." Women—or men—who like their kitchenwork will enjoy browsing through cookbooks, trays, cups, utensils, pretty aprons, and other inexpensive and pragmatic items. The best is a Plexiglas teabag box like the ones restaurants use to offer customers a selection of teas (Baruch designed it himself, and people buy them by the half-dozen for house gifts). Happy Home has cake-decorating classes in the store on weekday evenings, taught by catering professionals.

Hecht's Hebrew Book Store. 1122 Avenue J, near Coney Island Avenue, 254-9696. Sun.–Thurs., 10 A.M.–6 P.M.; Fri., 10 A.M.–2:30 P.M.; closed Sat.

This is a pleasant Judaica store where you will find books, records, and religious items. You can order special things here such as imprinted skull caps for bar mitzvahs. There is a good gift selection as well.

Avenue M Area Shopping

WOMEN'S AND CHILDREN'S CLOTHING

Carole Block. 1413 Avenue M, between East 14th and East 15th streets, 339–1869. Mon.–Thurs., 10 A.M.–6 P.M.; Fri., 10 A.M.–2:30 P.M.; closed Sat.; Sun., noon–5 P.M.

Carole Block is known to carry one of the largest selections of fine leather handbags this side of Manhattan. Prices range from $50 to over $1,000. She has been in business for more than thirty years, and the service at the store is excellent.

Estee's. 2667 Nostrand Avenue between Avenues M and N, 258-8858. Mon.–Thurs,. 10 A.M.–6 P.M.; Fri. 10 A.M.–2 P.M.; Sun. 10 A.M–4 P.M.

You should see what is on the "wedding level" at this expensive (but discounted) women's clothing store geared to the religious community. There are lots of fancy dresses here, in traditional styles. Expect to find high cuts and long sleeves.

Head to Hose. 1717 Avenue M, near East 17th Street, 692-0820. Sun.–Fri., 10:30 A.M.–6 P.M.; Fri., closes early; Sun. noon-5 P.M. Closed Sat.

Good things come in small boxes. Head to Hose sells hair ornaments, hats, decorative stockings and socks for women and kids, including top brands. You can order for delivery by UPS.

Lavender Lace Lingerie. 1318 Avenue M, between East 13th and East 14th streets, 382-9349.

Pegnoir sets in silk, white delicate nightgowns, and thick terry robes are the specialty at this enticing lingerie shop. The selection is small, but prices are moderate and there is an interested and friendly staff.

Special Effects. 1914 Avenue M, near East 19th Street, 645-5119. Mon.–Fri., 10:30 A.M.–6 P.M.; Sun., 11 A.M.–5 P.M.; closed Sat.

An eclectic toy shop that parents and grandparents will love (and the only toy store on Avenue M), Special Effects specializes in the whimsical, imaginative stuff of childhood.

Tuesday's Child. 1904 Avenue M, between East 19th Street and Ocean Avenue, 375-1790. Sun.–Fri., 10 A.M.–6 P.M.; Thursday until 8 P.M.; closed Sat.

Exclusive, expensive, and elegant imported children's clothing ranging from layette through junior size for both girls and boys fill this upscale establishment. Many items are manufactured in Italy especially for the store and are not available even in the best Manhattan or suburban shops. Outfits start at $60. There's another Tuesday's Child "sale store" on 1429 Coney Island Avenue at Avenue J.

✪ **Yellow Door.** 1308 Avenue M, between East 13th, and East 14th streets, 998-7382. Mon.–Fri., 10 A.M.–5:45 P.M.; Sun., 11 A.M.–5 P.M.; closed Sat. and weekends in summer.

A woman of any age would love to have a gift or gift certificate from this shop. Perfect items for weddings, anniversaries, Mother's Day, or birthdays include fine crystal, unusual table linens, and decorative boxes. The Yellow Door also has a huge selection of high-fashion costume jewelry in the $50 to $800 range, all by well-known designers. They carry some antique silver items as well. Prices range from moderate to expensive, but many items are sold below retail prices (how else would they survive in this neighborhood?).

Zeldy's Place. 1815 Avenue M, near East 18th Street, 252-9313. Mon.–Fri., 10 A.M.–6 P.M.; Sun., 11 A.M.–5 P.M.; closed Sat.

Zeldy's stocks a full line of top- and middle-tier children's clothing from layette through junior boys and girls, with discounts of up to 30 percent on American and imported brands. The sales staff is helpful.

Kings Highway Shopping

SPECIALTY FOOD SHOPS

✪ **Highway Bagels Corp.** 1921–23 Kings Highway, between East 19th and East 20th streets, 336–9200. Daily, 24 hours.

Get 'em while they are hot—bagels, bialys, rolls, croissants, and more. Locals recommend this 24-hour bagel shop, which makes everything on the premises.

Mansoura's Oriental Pastry. 515 Kings Highway, between East 3rd and East 4th streets, 645-7977. Sun.–Thurs. 8 A.M.–7 P.M.; Fri., closes early; closed Sat.

A fifth-generation family business, run by Sephardic bakers from Aleppo, Syria, Mansoura's uses centuries-old recipes for their bird's nest honey-and-pistachio-filled pastry, Turkish delights, and other specialties.

Miller's Market. 914 Kings Highway, 336–8100. Sun.–Thurs., 8 A.M.–8 P.M.; Fri., closes early; closed Sat.

Reflecting the Eastern European bent of the neighborhood, this local supermarket sells Russian cheeses, blinis in six flavors, and cookies and cakes baked on the premises. You can pick up the fixings for dinner here after an afternoon of shopping.

WOMEN'S CLOTHING

✪ **Chuckies.** 1304 Kings Highway, near East 13th Street, 376-1003. Mon.–Sat., 10 A.M.–7 P.M.; Sun., noon–5 P.M.

Chuckies sells top-of-the-line imported shoes for both men and women. Don't expect to pound the pavement in them, though. No clodhoppers, these are knock-out, special-occasion fashion shoes, along with snazzy footwear for that dress-for-success look. After a few purchases here, you'll be better-shod but less well-heeled: prices are high, as is the fashion.

If you are wondering, this well-established Brooklyn store is a distant relative of the Chuckies in Manhattan.

✪ **Jimmy's.** 1226 Kings Highway, near East 13th Street, 645-9685. Mon.–Sat., 10 A.M.–6 P.M.; Sun., noon–5 P.M..

Jimmy's is in a class all by itself in Brooklyn. Their specialty is top-of-the-line, this-season fashion by European designers for both men and women, and accessories such as bags and shoes. What makes shopping here different from an upscale department store is the family-style service: regular customers are greeted on a first-name basis, and if you're in a pinch, tailoring can be done on the premises.

MEN'S CLOTHING

Clothing Connection. 508 Kings Highway, near East 2nd Street, 375-5893. Sun.–Thurs., 10 A.M.–6 P.M.; Fri., 10 A.M.–2:30 P.M.; closed Sat.

Updated classic Italian suits in fine lightweight wools are sold here at at least a 15 percent discount, including the top Italian brands.

✪ **Wasserberger.** 1709 Kings Highway, corner of East 17th and 18th streets, 998-2300. Mon.–Fri., 10 A.M.–6 P.M.; Tues.–Thurs, until 7 P.M.; Sat., 10 A.M.–5 P.M.; Sun., 11:30 A.M.–4:30 P.M.

The best of both worlds, Wasserberger stocks a huge selection of ready-made designer garments, and custom-makes suits, jackets, trousers, even tuxedo shirts, sewn on the premises by trusted tailors. A custom suit starts at $650; its off-the-rack counterpart costs from $250 to $650. As colorful as a tailor's thread box, the clientele runs the spectrum from judges and attorneys to blue-collar workers, from African-Americans to orthodox Jews to Russian immigrants, with a lot of businessmen and office professionals as well.

One of few remaining custom stores in Brooklyn, this three-generation business was started by a Holocaust survivor who arrived here in 1948.

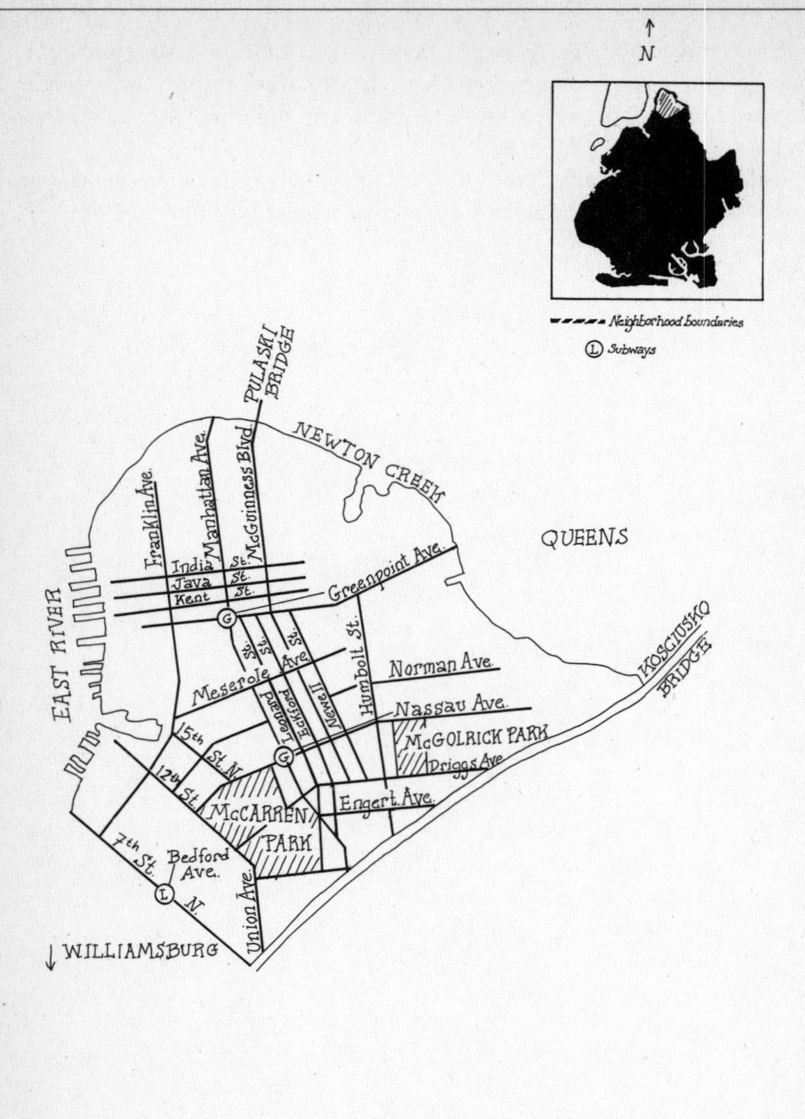
N
Neighborhood Boundaries
L Subways
PULASKI BRIDGE
NEWTON CREEK
QUEENS
EAST RIVER
Franklin Ave.
Manhattan Ave.
McGuinness Blvd.
India St.
Java St.
Kent St.
Greenpoint Ave.
Humbolt St.
Norman Ave.
Meserole Ave.
Leonard St.
Eckford St.
Newell St.
Nassau Ave.
McGOLRICK PARK
Driggs Ave.
KOSCIUSKO BRIDGE
15th St. N.
12th St.
McCARREN PARK
Engert Ave.
7th St. N.
Bedford Ave.
Union Ave.
WILLIAMSBURG

Greenpoint

Where it is: Northwest Brooklyn, bounded by Newtown Creek to the northeast, the BQE (Brooklyn-Queens Expressway), North 7th Street to the south, and the East River to the west.

What's nearby: Williamsburg is the contiguous neighborhood, with sometimes vague lines of demarcation. Greenpoint is on the border with Queens, right over the Pulaski Bridge. Manhattan is directly across the Williamsburg Bridge.

How to get to Greenpoint:

By car: From Manhattan, cross the Williamsburg Bridge and drive northeast along Bedford Avenue, turning left on Manhattan Avenue to enter Greenpoint.

From Brooklyn, if you are going north on the BQE, take exit 33 to McGuiness/Humbolt Boulevard, and take two lefts to Manhattan Avenue. If you are going over the 59th Street Bridge, go south on Jackson Avenue to Pulaski Bridge, to McGuiness Boulevard in Greenpoint, and, if you like, go one block over to Manhattan Avenue.

From Queens, take the Pulaski Bridge to McGuiness Blvd.

By subway: From Manhattan ride the L crosstown train from 14th Street to the Lorimer Street stop and transfer to the G subway heading north. Get off at the Nassau Avenue or Greenpoint Avenue stops.

(*Note*: The G train has no Manhattan stops.)

Cab service: Greenpoint Car Service (383-3737). About $10 to Brooklyn Heights, $12 to Grand Central Station.

Special events: Festival of Polish Culture and Polish film festival at Polish and Slavic Center (October–November). Phone 383-5290 for information.

How it got its name: Not surprisingly, Brooklyn's northernmost point was once covered in trees, hence "Green Point," now Greenpoint.

Historic district:

Within an area roughly bounded by: Java Street on the north, Leonard

Street on the east, Meserole Avenue on the south, and Franklin Street on the west.

ABOUT THE NEIGHBORHOOD

Greenpoint? Why bother? There are lots of reasons to explore here. Sociologists study Greenpoint as the American Dream in bloom. History and architecture buffs come because of Greenpoint's recently landmarked district. Americans come to live here because it is inexpensive and neighborly. Europeans come and stay, because, well, it feels like Europe.

A trip down Manhattan Avenue reveals a vibrant, ethnically authentic workingclass neighborhood with thriving businesses and shops.

Usually thought of as a Polish preserve (and that's what we focus on in the following listings), Greenpoint is in reality a multiethnic pastiche. The Polish area runs up **Manhattan Avenue** from about Nassau Street up to Java and India streets, beyond which the population becomes increasingly Hispanic, with a smattering of people from various parts of the Indian subcontinent. The Greenpoint Islamic Center, located on a side street, is testimony to religious diversity in the neighborhood. Being in Brooklyn, Greenpoint also has vestiges of Italian and Irish immigrations of earlier eras.

During the 1990s, Greenpoint (like the rest of the nation) enjoyed a period of prosperity. The population now includes increasing numbers of young Polish people, second- and third-generation Polish-Americans who have chosen to stay in ethnic Greenpoint, as well as spillover artists and others whose heart (or studios) may be in pricier, trendier Williamsburg, but whose pocketbook or need for solitude brings them here.

Imagine, for a moment, that you are visiting Krakow. The residential side streets exude a sense of orderly family life: neatly swept streets; small, freshly painted houses with lace curtains; and rows of well-kept cars parked in front. Take a quiet stroll through the architecturally significant area between Java and Calyer streets and Franklin and Manhattan avenues, an historic district. Chow down at the **Old Poland Bakery and Restaurant**, try a Polish donut at **Piekarnia Rzeszowska Bakery**, or pick up a pound of Polish sausage to take home from the **W. Nassau Meat Market**. There is, it seems, a babka in every kitchen, a kielbasa in every pot, with delis and small restaurants seemingly just around the corner of every residential street.

Greenpoint is a clean kind of place. Ask the jeweler to recommend a restaurant and he'll tell you about good little café—and, that it's clean. Ask the baker for a reference to a butcher, and you'll find out whose kielbasa is peppery or moist—and, made in a clean back room. The streets and sidewalks here may not be paved with gold, but they are swept daily, and so are devoid of ubiquitous New York litter.

Keep your eye peeled for crosscultural ironies. Karl Marx would have had a good chuckle at the Greenpoint store that advertises odd-couple wares: religious relics, chalices, vestments, rosaries—and cards, balloons, and party favors. Locals seem to have an insatiable appetite for sausage, yet they flock to buy fat-free cookware. Floor-length fur coats are displayed in storefronts in the summertime, despite sweltering 95-degree New York weather. It is fun to see how Greenpoint comfortably straddles two worlds.

From corners on the main shopping drag, Manhattan Avenue, you can see the Manhattan skyline like a distant mirage.

Historical Notes

Purchased by the Dutch in 1638 from the Indians, Greenpoint along with Williamsburg was part of the mid-seventeenth-century town known as *Bosijck* (Bushwick), meaning "the wooded district." Real development began only in the early and mid-1800s.

Greenpoint became a center for what were known as the "five black arts": glass and pottery making, printing, refining, and the manufacture of cast iron. Charles Pratt's Astral Oil Works refined kerosene here. In addition, a shipbuilding industry arose; the iron Civil War gunship, the *Monitor*, launched in 1862 from a site near the intersection of Oak and West streets, was fabricated in Greenpoint by Continental Iron Works at West and Calyer streets. Greenpoint's only better-known offspring, actress Mae West, was born here in 1893.

Greenpoint was settled by Northern Europeans, until the arrival of Polish, Russian, and eventually Italian immigrants in the 1880s and thereafter. Despite the downturn in local industry after World War II, immigration continued, and Greenpoint became the unofficial "Little Poland" of New York City. Immigrants from Puerto Rico also settled here.

We can't actually prove this bit of Greenpoint lore, but it is said that Brooklyn's famous and distinctive accent was born here in "Greenpernt." (It is linguistically similar sounding to the accent that developed in Flatbush, which also lays claim to having the original Brooklyn twang.)

An interesting note: the streets running roughly perpendicular to the East River are named alphabetically, from Ash to Box, Clay, Dupont, Eagle, Freeman, Green, Huron, India, Java, Kent, Greenpoint (which used to be Lincoln), Milton, Noble, and Oak streets.

Shopping Areas

Find your way to **Manhattan Avenue**, a narrow one-way street lined with well-kept, homey mom-and-pop shops in smallish old buildings.

If your stomach is growling, there's food sold everywhere in Greenpoint. Start with a particularly inviting concentration of shops along Manhattan

Avenue, between Greenpoint and Java avenues. Here you will find two excellent bakeries (**Piekarnia Rzeszowska Bakery** and **Poznanski's Bakery**), a couple of butchers who make their own sausages (**W. Nassau Meat Market** and **Steve's Meat Market**), a large, upscale health food market (**The Garden**), Polish restaurants (**Polska Restaurant, and Restauracja Rzeszowska**)—not to mention an outstanding Thai restaurant (**Thai Café**), and various newcomers. And if you like smoked fish and are driving, absolutely make a detour and stop at **Marshall's Smoked Fish** (open weekdays only).

Kidstuff

Point out the ethnic vigor of this neighborhood: the Polish magazines at newspaper stands, the menus in windows which list foods in English down one side and in Polish down the other. Young adolescents and teens can be surprisingly interested in why people emigrate to the United States. You can describe what they used to manufacture in this area. (see the Nitty-Gritty Then and Now box on page 300 in Williamsburg chapter) and how some buildings such as the imposing **Greenpoint Manufacturing and Design Center** down the street are being recycled into twenty-first-century uses. Kids are astonished, looking at the Astral Apartments, to think that indoor plumbing was once considered a luxury for workingclass people. Younger kids will enjoy playing in **Monsignor McGolrick Park** or tossing a ball in the larger **McCarren Park. Zapakone** specializes in folk art, and **BQ Sports** may also be of interest. If they can look and not touch, there are wonderful old cameras on display (but not for sale) at **Albert Photo Centrum**.

PARKS AND PLAYGROUNDS

Monsignor McGolrick Park. Along Nassau and Driggs avenues, between Monitor and Russell streets.

Monsignor McGolrick Park is reminiscent of a small, quiet European urban park. On a warm afternoon you will find moms strolling with babies, lovers holding hands, and gaggles of men sitting and talking.

History buffs will be interested in the **Winthrop Park Shelter Pavilion** in the center of the park (see p. 192). Note also the statue of the naked sailor pulling on his mooring rope, a memorial to the *Monitor*, a Civil War ship built locally.

For a game of soccer or baseball, go instead to nearby **McCarren Park**.

POINTS OF CULTURAL INTEREST

✪ **Astral Apartments.** 184 Franklin Avenue, between Java and India streets.

Like the "model tenements" of Cobble Hill, the Astral apartment complex represented an important step in socially progressive architectural planning. Charles Pratt's Astral Oil Works refined kerosene in Greenpoint, and this huge apartment house was built in 1886 to house Astral's workers. At the time it was built, the provision of light, indoor plumbing, and both hot and cold water were unusual amenities for laborers. Also note the patterned brickwork, brownstone lintels and arches, and multiple entrances. See also the **Home and Tower Buildings** (page 132).

Greenpoint Manufacturing and Design Center (GDMC). 1155–1205 Manhattan Avenue, at the northern end of Manhattan Avenue at Ash Street, 383-3935.

Williamsburg's craftsmen and artists have recycled a hulking old industrial complex that once housed a die works into New York State's largest industrial cooperative for artisans. It's a visionary project, based on the simple concept of community: many artists, craftspeople, and small businesses have similar needs for technical equipment, marketing and loans. GMDC (to whom they pay rent) helps provide it. Among the seventy or so tenants are painters, sculptors, jewelry makers, restorers, and other specialists. Interestingly, a number of Eastern European immigrants also work here, using Old World skills to make high-end furniture and other non–mass-produced products. This innovative project involved a multimillion-dollar renovation, financed in part by government funds. Although it has already won awards as an urban renewal project, it is still a work in progress.

Polish and Slavic Center. 77 Kent Street, off Manhattan Avenue, 349-1033 if you speak Polish, 383-5290 if you speak English.

A testimony to the local community's cohesiveness, this large social service center (located in what once was an Italian church) provides a host of facilities for new and established Polish residents, from an inexpensive cafeteria to training in English-language skills to a credit union. It serves both as a welcoming committee and a vehicle for acculturation.

Public School 34. 131 Norman Avenue, corner of Eckhart Street.

Public education was a major force in Brooklyn of the nineteenth century. Brooklyn established its first public education system as early as 1816. As the numbers of students increased, the bureaucracy also grew. This Early Romanesque Revival building, erected in 1867 with later additions, is one of the oldest schools in continuous use in New York City—and children still attend it.

✪ **Russian Orthodox Cathedral of the Transfiguration of Our Lord.** 122 North 12th Street, at Driggs Avenue.

Even though Brooklyn is considered the "city of churches," you won't want to miss this official landmark Greek Orthodox beauty, built in 1921. Its five copper-clad, onion-shaped domes, typical of Russian Byzantine style, tower over the neighborhood. When the structure was built, Greenpoint was one of several thriving industrial belts in Brooklyn, with a large Greek Orthodox population working in nearby factories. It is considered a monument to the importance of the Eastern European immigration to this area.

✪ **St. Stanislaus Kostka Church.** 607 Humboldt Street, corner Driggs Avenue, 388-0170.

The main church for Greenpoint's Polish community and a vital participant in community affairs. Come at Easter or Christmastime to get the full flavor of active European Christian worship. Many New Yorkers recall the visit here of Pope John Paul II when he was still a Cardinal.

Sidewalk Clock. 753 Manhattan Avenue, between Norman and Meserole streets.

Like the famous clock on Fifth Avenue and 23rd Street in Manhattan, this sidewalk clock was erected as an early form of advertising for jewelry and other stores. It is made of cast iron, and is a New York City landmark. There are only seven such clocks extant in New York City. This is the only one in Brooklyn.

Storage Tanks. If you are wondering what those enormous storage tanks visible from parts of Greenpoint are, they belong to Brooklyn Union Gas Company. They are an unofficial landmark, kind of a constant reminder that this part of Brooklyn is, and was, a gritty industrial area.

Winthrop Park Shelter Pavilion, Monsignor McGolrick Park. A New York City landmark, the lovely curved pavilion is reminiscent of eighteenth-century formal gardens. That's no accident; it was designed in 1910 after the Trianon at Versailles by Helmle and Hurberty, who were also the architects for the Prospect Park Boathouse and several other Brooklyn historic landmarks.

NOTABLE GREENPOINT RESTAURANTS

Christina's. 853 Manhattan Avenue, corner Milton Street, 383-4382. Daily, 8 A.M.–8 P.M. Cash only.

Ten booths and a counter are all there is to Christina's, and that intimacy, plus good-value and good-tasting food, are the reasons this little Polish diner is busy with local patrons during dinnertime. Try the Hungarian pancakes. You can get a substantial meal for less than $8 per person, and Sunday brunch is just $6.

Happy End/Polska Restaurant. 924 Manhattan Avenue, corner of Kent Street, 389-8368. Daily, noon–9 P.M. Cash only.

Not memorable, but filling; you can munch a pierogi or homemade kielbasa while the neighborhood regulars saunter in and out. Don't miss the blintzes or the borscht. Prices are rock bottom.

L&A Italian Ristorante and Pizzeria. 887 Manhattan Avenue, between Greenpoint and Milton avenues. 383-7183. Daily, noon–9:30 P.M.; closed Sun.

An Italian eatery from yesteryear, L&A cooks "stuffet calamari" better than it spells it in English. Unpretentious but good Italian food, for instance, "PotoBella mushroom," pork chops, escarole, and broccoli rabe are staples here. All is served in an old-fashioned white-tablecloth environment. Prices are moderate.

✪ **Old Poland Bakery and Restaurant, a.k.a. Restauracja Pierkrnia Staropolska.** 190 Nassau Street, corner of Humbolt Street, 349-7775. Daily 11 A.M.–9 P.M. Cash only.

A guy jumps out of the passenger side of a delivery truck and enters the restaurant. A mom pushing a stroller goes in. Two young men stop in. What's the attraction? Super-tasty homestyle foods: a dozen kinds of rich soups (fruit soup, sauerkraut soup, borscht, for starters) and an equal number of different fillings for blinis and pierogi; mounds of mashed potatoes and fresh vegetables, and cooked-to-a-T cutlets, dumplings, and meat loaf. Euro-deli style here; you wait in line to place your order, then sit down, and they will call you when your order is ready. A separate counter sells baked goods, such as whole rye breads, fruit babka—at low prices.

Polska Restaurant. 36 Greenpoint Avenue, near Manhattan Avenue 389-8368. Daily, noon–9 P.M.

Was the homemade food ever this good in the old country? Generous servings of entrées such as chicken cutlets, goulash with barley, and beefy Stroganoff cost less than $10. The $2 homemade soups—Russian borscht, sour soup, vegetable soup—are excellent, as are the potato pancakes.

Restauracja Rzeszowska. 931 Manhattan Avenue, near Java Street, 349-7501. Daily, noon–9 P.M.

When you want a step-up in decor, with the same hearty Polish fare, try this spiffy eatery. It's so cheery that they hang both chandeliers *and* fake flowers from the ceiling. The usual reliable Polish menu, heavy with meats, potatoes, stews, and soups, is produced nicely. And the desserts (made by their bakery across the street) are great. Good for a family get-together or, no jokes please, a Polish party with your friends.

Socrates Coffee Shop. 651 Manhattan Avenue, between Nassau and Norman streets, 389-2752. Daily, 8 A.M.–8 P.M. Cash only.

Snoops' delight: the terrace of this friendly Greek coffee shop overlooks the backyards of many Polish households: roses in bloom and neatly hanging laundry gives you an insider's sense of the neighborhood. It's a favorite stop of some Greenpoint tour guides.

✪ **Stylowa.** 694 Manhattan Avenue, between Nassau and Norman streets, 383-8993. Daily, 8 A.M.–8 P.M. Cash only.

Locals recommend the blinis, cheese rolls, and anything else rolled in dough at Stylowa's coffee shop. That's saying something in a neighborhood that cooks.

✪ **Thai Café.** 925 Manhattan Avenue, 383-3562. Mon.–Wed. 11:30 A.M. – 10:30 P.M.; Thurs.–Sat., 11:30 A.M.–11 P.M.; Sun., 1–11 P.M.

Owned by the same folks who brought you the fabulously popular **Plan Eat Thailand** (see page 314) in Williamsburg, this Thai restaurant has more tables, fewer crowds, the same great food, low prices, and for the time being, shorter lines. Try the chicken and mushroom in coconut soup, beef basil with chili sauce, garlic shrimp curry, and, of course, vegetable pad thai. Entrées are in the $6 range. Ask about the daily specials.

SHOPPING

Specialty Food Shops

Bakeries and Sausages. There are more sausage makers and bakeries in Greenpoint than you can shake your *paczki* at, and that's with or without the hole in the middle. And if you think that's Jabberwocky, that's because you haven't tried paczkis, the Polish version of the donut. The following lists a few bakeries and meat markets—and other food emporiums—that will transport you far from your diet into paczki and babka heaven.

Fortunato Brothers. 289 Manhattan Avenue, near Devoe Street, 387-2281. Daily, 8 A.M.–9 P.M.; Sun., 1–5 P.M. Cash only.

Classic Italian desserts are made here, from wedding cakes to spumoni to pastries. Stop in for a cappuccino or espresso, and enjoy!

✪ **Marshall's Smoked Fish.** 23 Anthony Street, near Vandervoort Avenue, on the Brooklyn side of Kosciusko Bridge, 384-4505. Mon.–Fri. 9 A.M.–5 P.M. Retail entrance on Meeker Avenue off Morgan Avenue.

They supply *Zabar's*, for heaven's sake. And other leading New York area stores, such as Murray's Sturgeon on Manhattan's Lower East Side, and Barney Greengrass on Manhattan's Upper West Side. They ship to Las Vegas, California, Chicago, to famous delis such as Nate and Als, and Junior's, no less, in Los Angeles. And you too can buy smoked fish at this world-class fish shop's little retail store. Cheaper, because this is THE source.

If you've ever driven north from Brooklyn on the BQE, you've seen their sign: MARSHALL'S. In business for decades on the border between Greenpoint and Williamsburg, Marshall's smokes about five tons of fish—that's *10,000 pounds*—daily, on the premises. You can buy fresh-smoked Nova Scotia salmon (sliced, presliced, full sides, packages), pickled herring, sturgeon, whitefish, baked salmon salad, chopped herring, whitefish salad, and more. The secret of their success? "We know what we are doing, and we are here watching it, every day."

✪ **Piekarnia Rzeszowska Bakery.** 948 Manhattan Avenue, corner Java Street, 349-7501. Mon.–Sun., 6 A.M.–9 P.M. Cash only.

Possibly the best cheese danish in Brooklyn are made at this cheery corner bakery—the cheese seems to erupt from the pastry. There are 18-inch-long, 5-inch-wide rolls of danish filled with apples, cherries, and cheese, oversized challahs and cheesecakes with fruit toppings. The bakery is owned by Helen and Jozef Waltos (who also run the restaurant across the street). And if pictures are truly worth a thousand words, then the shop's decorations speak volumes: a picture of an idyllic Kasprowy mountain scene on one wall, a tinselly Big Apple skyline on the other.

Poznanski's Bakery. 668 Manhattan Avenue, near Greenpoint Avenue, 389-5252, Daily, 8 A.M.–7 P.M. Cash only.

Poznanski's sells good, fresh babka (go for the cheese), challah and pastries. They also have just about the best hamentaschen (triangular pastries filled with prune, apricot, or poppyseed paste) in town.

Steve's Meat Market. 104 Nassau between Leonard and Eckhart Streets, corner of Leonard Street. 383-1780. Mon.–Fri., 8 A.M.–8 P.M.; Sat., 8 A.M.–6 P.M.; closed Sun. Cash only.

Steve's claims to have the best kielbasa in America. His salted, smoked sausages have won kudos from wiener-lovers, and the fact that there are a half-dozen different kinds of horseradish casually displayed in the window suggests that Steve takes his sausages seriously.

✪ **The Garden.** 921 Manhattan Avenue, between Kent and Greenpoint avenues, 389-6448. Mon.–Sat., 8 A.M.–8 P.M.; Sun., 9 A.M.–7 P.M. $15 minimum on credit cards.

The Dean & DeLuca of Greenpoint, the Garden is an upscale, health-oriented supermarket that sells a wide variety of foods, from fresh vegetables to prepared salads to dozens of different kinds of cheeses, to entire lines of packaged health food goods. And then there's the chocolate mousse. Cappuccino and an ATM on the premises make this a favorite meeting place for newcomers to the area.

✪ **W. Nassau Meat Market.** 915 Manhattan Avenue, near Greenpoint Avenue. 389-6149. Mon.–Fri., 8 A.M.–8 P.M.; Sat., 8 A.M.–6 P.M.; closed Sun. Cash only.

Don't be shy. Even if you don't know what something in the window is, wander in and ask. These Greenpoint butchers are so friendly you are likely to get several samples of their freshly made spicy meat loaf or some other Polish specialty. This shop is great for bacon, sausages, and kielbasa, plus things to go with them, such as huge loaves of fresh rye bread, imported mustard, horseradish, canned cherries, and other goodies.

Interesting Neighborhood Shops

✪ **Albert Photo Centrum.** 662 Manhattan Avenue, between Nassau and Norman streets, 383-1585. Mon.–Sat., 11 A.M.–8 P.M.; Sun., 11 A.M.–8 P.M.

One of New York's largest displays of vintage cameras graces the store window and shelves of this surprisingly upscale camera shop. The collection—which is *not* for sale—totals over one thousand old cameras, including two large antique "accordion"-style view cameras dating from the late 1800s. What you can buy are new cameras and equipment from top-line manufacturers such as Nikon, Leica, and Minolta, at low prices. The owner, a Polish-born photographer/collector whose shoulder-length hair and demeanor suggest the left bank of Paris more than Greenpoint, also has a commercial photo lab on the premises.

BQ Sports. 601 Manhattan Avenue, between Nassau and Driggs streets. 349-3528. Mon.–Sat., 10 A.M.–6 P.M.

Take me out to the ballpark—but first make sure I have the right uniform. For home-run prices and good service, check into this father-son operation that supplies customer uniforms to many Brooklyn youth sport teams. There are also good buys on basic sports equipment.

Chopin Chemists. 911 Manhattan Avenue, off Greenpoint Avenue, 383-7822. Daily, 9 A.M.–7 P.M.

Women will find an extensive line of preservative-free, all-natural Polish imported cosmetic products for all skin types in this otherwise fully Americanized pharmacy. There's an interesting line of natural products by a Dr. Irena Eris, and another called "Satysfakecja," plus herbal teas, chamomile, and other extracts.

Pop's Popular Clothing. 7 Franklin Street between North 15th Street and Meserole Avenue, 349-7677. Mon.–Sat., 10 A.M.–7 P.M. Cash only.

Smaller but more refined than Williamburg's Domsey's, Pops sells new and used clothing—rack after rack of quality winter coats ranging from $10 to $30. Authentic Navy pea coats, gas station jackets (many prepatched with names like "Ed" and "Larry" for those days you feel like being someone else), blue jeans, boots, belts, and a slew of thoroughly original shirts and ties. The perfect place to pick up rugged work clothes and those funny jumpsuits your dad used to wear in the garage. "Pop" can be cranky, but his amiable son is extremely helpful and has one of the most authentic Brooklyn accents you'd ever want to hear. (For more listings nearby, see page 319—**Williamsburg Vintage and Collectibles**).

Zakopane. 714 Manhattan Avenue, between Norman and Meserole streets, 389-3487. Daily, 11 A.M.–6 P.M. Cash only.

A woodcarver's paradise, the jumble of wooden bowls, jewelry boxes, and enormous carved eagles make this a must-stop in Greenpoint. Everything is imported from Poland. This is a good place to buy the kids a trinket they won't find in their local toy shop.

Zepter Showroom. 153 Nassau Street, corner Newel Street, 349-2406. Mon.–Sat., 10 A.M.–7 P.M.; Sun., 1–5 P.M.

You'll do a double take and suffer a mild case of cognitive dissonance when you pass by the shop windows here and see high-end Euro-designed cookware. Zepter is a Swiss-made brand of expensive cookware and tea sets, whose claim to fame is terrific modern design and a special cooking method that requires absolutely no fat or water, even for cooking vegetables.

The Hub

Brooklyn Heights and Atlantic Avenue

DUMBO, Fulton Ferry, and Vinegar Hill

Downtown Brooklyn and MetroTech

WHAT'S INCLUDED IN THIS CHAPTER

There really is no official "hub" of Brooklyn, but this chapter includes the areas first encountered when you enter Brooklyn via the Brooklyn or Manhattan Bridges: (1) Brooklyn Heights, (2) Atlantic Avenue, (3) DUMBO, Fulton Ferry, and Vinegar Hill, and (4) Downtown Brooklyn and Metro Tech. A brief word on shopping and parks is included below, but to get the historical background and points of cultural interest for each of these areas, turn to the appropriate section. And, by the way, you can walk through all four areas in under an hour.

Note: As delightful as Brooklyn's little neighborhoods are, the division of the borough into so many of them can be confusing for the tourist. Because we couldn't cover every neighborhood, informed readers are warned to expect oddities: bits of Cobble Hill are listed under Brooklyn Heights, whereas Boerum Hill shops are listed under Atlantic Avenue.

SHOPPING AREAS

The main shopping area in Brooklyn Heights is **Montague Street**, a charming four-block street with several restaurants and an increasing number of chains, including Waldenbooks, Banana Republic, GAP, Radio Shack, Starbucks, a new Pottery Barn, and more. On **Atlantic Avenue** you will find antiques, home decorating shops, and ethnic food stores; in **Downtown Brooklyn,** there's Macy's and a number of chain stores.

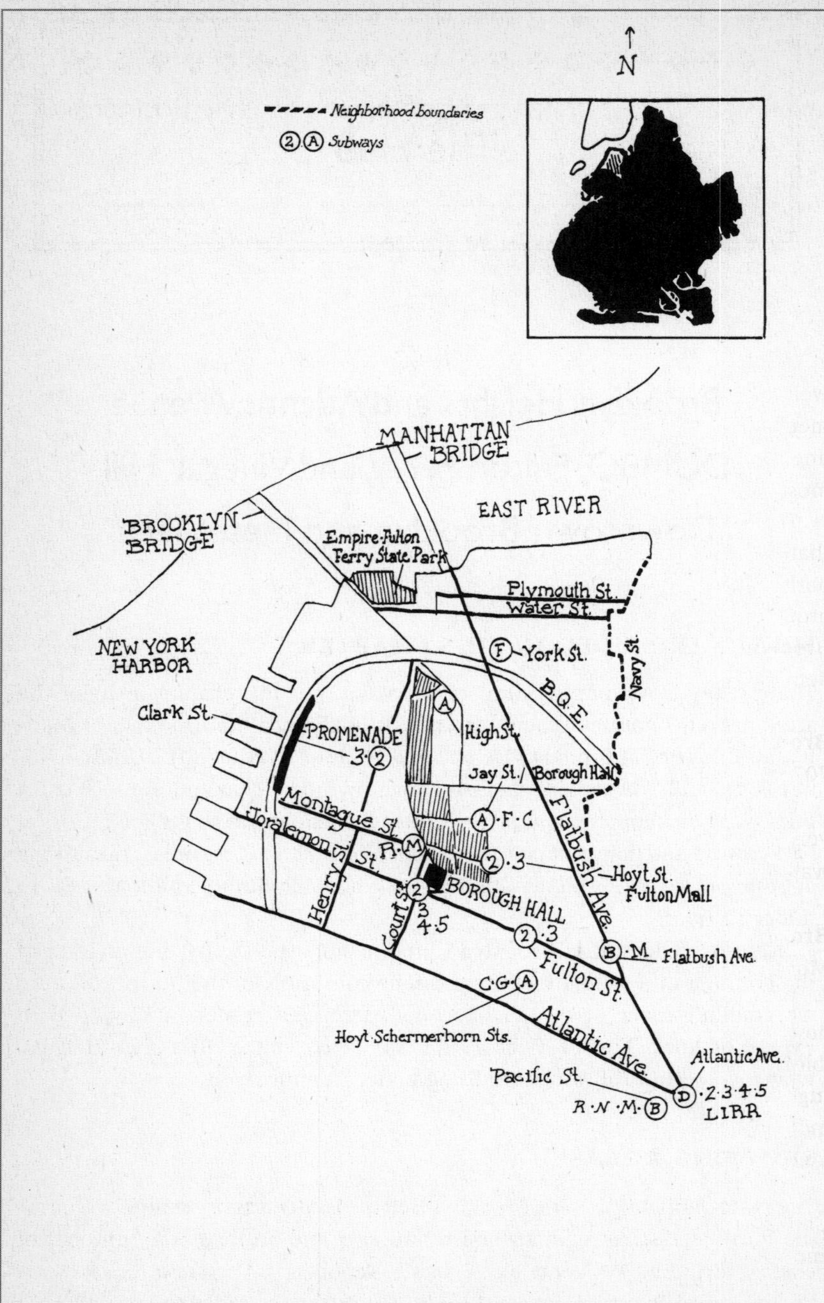
N
Neighborhood boundaries
2 A Subways
MANHATTAN BRIDGE
EAST RIVER
BROOKLYN BRIDGE
Empire-Fulton Ferry State Park
Plymouth St.
Water St.
NEW YORK HARBOR
F York St.
Navy St.
B.Q.E.
A High St.
Clark St.
PROMENADE
3·2
Jay St./Borough Hall
A·F·C
Montague St.
Joralemon St.
R·M
Flatbush Ave.
2·3
Hoyt St. Fulton Mall
2 3 4 5
BOROUGH HALL
Henry St.
Court St.
2·3
B·M
Flatbush Ave.
Fulton St.
C·G·A
Hoyt-Schermerhorn Sts.
Atlantic Ave.
Atlantic Ave.
Pacific St.
D·2·3·4·5
LIRR
R·N·M·B

ENTERTAINMENT, PARKS, AND PLAYGROUNDS

The following lists parks and playgrounds near *all* the neighborhoods included in this chapter.

✪ **Brooklyn Bridge.** Walkway entrance is at Adams and Tillary streets.

Walk it, drive it, bike it, or just admire it—the Brooklyn Bridge soaring over the East River is one of the greatest of New York City's bridges. An architectural beauty designed by John A. Roebling, it was at the time of its completion in 1883 the world's longest suspension bridge, connecting Manhattan at City Hall Park to Brooklyn's Cadman Plaza. It is an icon of the borough as well as the picturesque subject of paintings, photos, and movie sets, not to mention a few time-worn jokes. With spectacular views of Manhattan's skyline, the river, and the Statue of Liberty, the bridge is the place for one of the most romantic and inspiring strolls in all New York.

The opening of the Brooklyn Bridge was the first of several major changes that transformed Brooklyn from a rural farming area with scattered neighborhoods into a popular Manhattan suburb. Land speculators and developers brought new residents to established, if scattered, neighborhoods such as Brooklyn Heights, Fort Greene, and Bedford, and also carved out new residential areas in Carroll Gardens, Cobble Hill, and Boerum Hill.

Brooklyn Heights Cinema. 70 Henry Street, corner of Orange Street, 596-7070.

Cozy, old, and informal, this double-screen cinema is a local favorite. It is very close to **Henry's End** and **Noodle Pudding** restaurants, and within walking distance of Montague Street restaurants.

✪ **Brooklyn Heights Promenade.** Along the East River; access at the end of Montague and Orange streets, and streets in between.

Take a stroll here for what may possibly be the most spectacular view of downtown Manhattan to be had with your feet still on the ground. Also visible are the Statue of Liberty, the Brooklyn Bridge, and a constant flow of tugs, barges, and other harbor traffic. There are outdoor concerts in the summer, and an art show. Take a walk on the wild side; it's less than a half mile long.

Cadman Plaza. Bounded by Court Street, Cadman Plaza West, Joralemon and Adams streets.

Cadman Plaza is not really a plaza as such, but rather a stretch of green that runs several blocks in length. Don't be confused by the fact that the park and the adjacent street are called by the same name.

✪ **Empire Fulton Ferry Park.** New Dock Road, by Water Street and the East River.

You'll almost forget you're in New York City when you visit this sizable grassy meadow along the East River, sandwiched between the Brooklyn and Manhattan bridges. While the kids run around, you can treat yourself to a 360-degree view—of Manhattan in front, fabulous Civil War–era spice warehouses and turn-of-the-century industrial lofts behind, and the bridges on either side. Relatively undiscovered, this is a wonderful place for a picnic with or without kids. The park is at the end of the block on New Dock Street. You can walk, drive, or ride the B41 bus from Brooklyn Heights to the end of the line at the **Eagle Warehouse** apartment building (see page 228).

Harry Chapin Playground. Columbia Heights, along Middagh Street.

Like many of Brooklyn's best-kept secrets, this immaculate little playground is tucked away, almost unseen yet providing an enviable view of Manhattan across the East River. Go one-half block past the Eagle Warehouse apartment building and left up Everitt Street.

✪ **Pierrepont Playground.** Columbia Place, at the end of Montague Street.

Where else can a two-year-old play on a slide with a million-dollar view? This large, well-kept and safe playground is a classic, with climbing equipment and lots of sand for toddlers and older kids. A popular place for parents, baby-sitters, and grandparents, it is also one of the borough's "quiet zones," where radio playing is not allowed.

Brooklyn Heights

Where it is: "Brooklyn Heights" is bounded on the north and west by Columbia Heights and the BQE, Atlantic Avenue on the south, and Cadman Plaza West on the east.

What's nearby: Manhattan, Downtown Brooklyn, Cobble Hill, Carroll Gardens. Atlantic Avenue, and the Atlantic Center also are within a few minutes' drive, or a fifteen-minute walk of Brooklyn Heights.

How to get there:

By car: Coming from Manhattan over the Brooklyn Bridge, stay right to take the first exit to Cadman Plaza, staying in the left lane as you exit. To go to Montague Street, turn left onto Cadman Plaza, proceed several blocks (Cadman becomes Court Street), and turn right on Montague Street for Brooklyn Heights and the Promenade. For Cranberry Street and the North Heights, turn right a few blocks sooner, at Clark Street.

By subway: Brooklyn Heights is blessed with good public transportation. The following trains arrive at stations that are all within a ten-minute walk of each other, in and around the Heights: 2, 3, 4, 5, A, C, and F. The M, N, and R trains stop at Court Street nearby. However, if you want to get to a specific destination, use this guide:

North Heights (Cranberry, Orange Streets, etc.): Take the 2 or 3 to Clark Street.

Montague Streets: Take the 2, 3, 4, or 5 train to Borough Hall.

Special events: Art shows in Spring and Autumn (see DUMBO, page 223); summer concerts on the Promenade; a brownstone tour through the interiors of restored private landmark homes (May). See Events Calendar, page 331.

Historic District: The Brooklyn Heights historic area is bounded by Fulton Street on the north; Henry Street, part of Clinton, and part of Court Street on the east; Atlantic Avenue on the south, and Furman Street on the west. It was the first landmarked district in New York City.

ABOUT THE NEIGHBORHOOD

Given its proximity to Manhattan, the Heights is the one Brooklyn neighborhood that most Manhattanites have heard of. (After all, the Manhattan skyline is reassuringly visible from here.) Tourists weary of the bustle of midtown Manhattan marvel at the almost European nineteenth-century charm of Brooklyn Heights. Locals describe their small (by Brooklyn standards) neighborhood in similar terms: urbane in its sophistication, yet provincial in its neighborliness.

Whether shopping on the civilized "high" streets, soaking up the architectural treasures of well-kept brownstones and churches, or gazing at the enchanting Manhattan skyline at twilight from the **Promenade**, you will find that Brooklyn Heights has something to offer even the most itinerant visitor. Amid streets with names like Cranberry, Pineapple, and Orange, you can glimpse a backyard garden blooming in spring or sidewalks awash in the fallen leaves of autumn.

If you're seeking action, there is plenty here. **Arts at St. Ann's** offers an eclectic program including opera, jazz, and experimental theater; its sixty famous restored stained-glass windows, the first made in the United States, are rare treasures. Exhibits at **Brooklyn's History Museum** and lunchtime tours of **Borough Hall** shed light on interesting bits of Brooklynabilia.

Montague Street, a small four-block street that runs west toward the **Promenade**, has restaurants, outdoor cafés, and shops. Wandering the neighboring streets is a treat. On peaceful **Willow Street** are several Federal-style homes of architectural note (see particularly numbers 155, 157, and 159). **Grace Court Alley**, once used as a stable alley for fancy homes on Remsen Street, is a charming mews. **Pierrepont Street** is graced with some of New York City's most beautiful residences (numbers 2, 3, and 82), and Garden Place, Sidney Place, and Hunts Lane are pleasant detours from Joralemon Street.

Historical Notes

History has been kind to Brooklyn Heights. An aristocratic urban center in the nineteenth century, it deteriorated after the 1930s until a vigorous preservation movement during the 1960s led to the designation of some thirty blocks as New York's first historic district. The renaissance started by preservationists was completed by an influx of Wall Street lawyers and bankers during the late 1970s and 1980s. But for many lean years Brooklyn Heights was a bohemian haven. The young artists and writers who lived amid its slightly seedy, decaying elegance and subsequently became famous include Hart Crane, W. H. Auden, Walker Evans, John Dos Passos, Richard Wright, Thomas Wolfe, Arthur Miller, Norman Rosten, Alfred Kazin, Truman Capote, and Norman Mailer.

First settled by the Dutch, Brooklyn Heights dates to the mid-1800s. It was the civic and commercial heart of the then-independent city of Brooklyn. Secluded from Manhattan by lack of transportation other than the Fulton Ferry or private boat, Brooklyn Heights was developed by wealthy Protestant bankers, industrialists, and shipping magnates whose piers and ships were nearby. The Heights was the home of the activist nineteenth-century **Plymouth Church**, where Charles Dickens spoke and abolitionist Henry Ward Beecher preached; Walt Whitman, editor of the *Brooklyn Eagle*, first published *Leaves of Grass* here.

Many of Brooklyn's unique cultural institutions got their start here. The **Brooklyn Historical Society** was founded in the Heights under a different name in the 1860s, as were the **Brooklyn Philharmonic** and the original **Brooklyn Academy of Music,** first housed on Montague Street. **Packer Collegiate Institute,** housed in a fabulous Gothic building designed by Minard Lafever, and Borough Hall, which in the mid-nineteenth century was an elegant rival to Manhattan's City Hall across the river, were both built in this era. Among the prominent citizens who grew up here was Seth Low, who became mayor of Brooklyn, president of Columbia University, and finally mayor of New York City.

The opening of the Brooklyn Bridge in 1883 destroyed the exclusivity of this remarkable community. The elite retreated to fashionable Clinton Hill. Park Slope, or Manhattan's then-developing "Gold Coast" on upper Fifth

Avenue. Brooklyn Heights lost its status as an independent municipal civic center in 1898 when New York City incorporated the city of Brooklyn. Fortunately, Brooklyn Heights's early, aristocratic architecture has been preserved for later generations.

Kidstuff

Parents with kids in tow have a wide variety of choices in the Brooklyn Heights—Atlantic Avenue—Waterfront area. You can play along the **Promenade** or watch pizza being made at **Monty Q's**. The key is transportation, as many of these attractions are just far enough from each other to tire out small legs.

Speaking of transportation, kids can get their fill of all forms of locomotion. Combine a walk over the **Brooklyn Bridge** with a visit to the **New York City Transit Museum** or explore the **Atlantic Avenue Tunnel**. A trip to the piers to watch whatever huge ship is in port is always entertaining.

The littlest ones will find plenty to do just running up and down the many multistepped stoops. Try Hicks Street and the adjacent Garden Place mews just two blocks from Joralemon Street. As is the case in much of Brooklyn, the local firefighters are very friendly and open to showing curious children around their trucks.

POINTS OF CULTURAL INTEREST

BACA. 195 Cadman Plaza West, off Pierrepoint Street, 625-0080. Mon.–Fri. 10 A.M.–5 P.M.

BACA is a good place to start if you are interested in the art scene in Brooklyn. The Brooklyn Arts Council has brochures and information on local Brooklyn cultural events. It is a major conduit of governmental support for the arts in Brooklyn. Every year BACA sponsors several major events, such as the **Red Hook Spring Festival and Pier Show**. BACA is also forming a Collector's Club of serious art collectors who are interested in taking studio tours of Brooklyn artists.

BRIC (Brooklyn Information and Culture, Inc.) 30 Flatbush Avenue. 855-7882. Call for quarterly calendar of events and information.

Previously known as the Fund for the Borough of Brooklyn, this government-financed entity organizes several major events in Brooklyn, including the summer concerts in the parks and "Welcome Back to Brooklyn." They also run **Brooklynx** website (see page 367), the Brooklyn Tourism Council, organize the **Rotunda Gallery** (see page 207), and Brooklyn Community Access Television, **BCAT** (see page 117).

✪ **Brooklyn Heights Association Landmark House and Garden Tour.** 858-9193. House tours are given every May and cost about $25. Call for a schedule.

Maybe you're a landmarks buff, or are interested in seeing what brownstone mansions look like from the inside. Either way, join the many veterans of Brooklyn Heights house tours as they visit five houses and their extraordinary gardens dating from 1800 to 1890.

✪ **Brooklyn Heights Historic District.** This large, quaint, historic district—the first to be so designated in New York City—reads like a map of architectural history of early New York. The Heights was the first Brooklyn area to be settled after the Fulton Ferry made it easy to cross the East River, and in its row houses, brick buildings, old apartment buildings, and even a few old wooden homes, there are vestiges of almost every decade of the nineteenth century. A number of historically important buildings are listed in this book but for in depth-background on residences, pick up an architectural guide to New York City.

Brooklyn Historical Society and Museum 128 Pierrepont Street, between Clinton and Henry streets, 624-0890. Call for information.

The Brooklyn Historical Society is undergoing a $14 million building renovation and will reopen in 2001. This little-known gem of an institution houses the country's largest single collection of Brooklyn history in an elegant 1880 landmark building. Call for information on tours, alternative library research resources, and information about the museum (see below).

✪ **Brooklyn's History Museum** (at the Brooklyn Historical Society). 128 Pierrepont Street, between Clinton and Henry streets, 624-0890.

Take a tour here and you'll know more about Brooklyn than Ralph Kramden himself. You can revisit primal Brooklyn symbols such as the Brooklyn Bridge, Brooklyn Dodgers, and Coney Island. The four-thousand-square-foot museum includes imaginative displays of a model of the Brooklyn Bridge, a huge zinc eagle from the Brooklyn Daily Eagle, a mockup newsstand featuring ethnic papers in many languages, and remnants of Coney Island.

Heights Casino and Casino Mansion Apartments. 75 Montague Street and 200 Hicks Street, 624-0810.

Harking back to the first decade of the twentieth century, the once-exclusive Heights Casino is a remnant of genteel old Brooklyn Heights. In 1905, when it was first built, social clubs were an essential part of life for the moneyed classes and the Casino—located just a half block from the elegant

Promenade and enviable views of lower Manhattan and New York Harbor—catered to the classiest clientele in Brooklyn Heights society. The adjacent building, Casino Mansion Apartments, built in 1910, boasted only two apartments per floor and was considered one of the most prestigious addresses in Brooklyn.

Heights Casino is one of the few such buildings in Brooklyn to still be used as a private club. As the French say, the more things change, the more they stay the same: contemporary patrons play tennis, dine, and socialize, all for a hefty annual membership fee. (To learn the different fate of another Brooklyn social club, see **Montauk Club** in Park Slope, page 246.)

Orchestra of the SEM Ensemble. 25 Columbia Place. 488-7659.

Little known in Brooklyn, the SEM Ensemble is an important force in the performance of new (as in, post–John Cage) modern music. The ensemble, under the direction of Peter Kotik, has performed major concerts in New York (as in Carnegie Hall) and internationally.

Packer Collegiate Institute. 170 Joralemon Street, between Court and Clinton streets, 875-1644. Tours are by appointment.

It looks like an urban castle, with pinnacles, Gothic arches, and a tower. But look again, because Packer is one of Brooklyn's leading private schools. Conceived originally as an institute for young ladies, the lovely building dates from 1854 and was designed by Minard Lafever; inside are original Tiffany windows.

Rotunda Gallery. 33 Clinton Street at Cadman Plaza West, 875-4047. Call for a schedule.

An offshoot of the Brooklyn tourism and cultural association (BRIC), the Rotunda runs regular shows of established and emerging Brooklyn artists. There are guest curators, and shows cover a range of artwork.

✪ **The St. Ann Center for Restoration and the Arts.** 157 Montague Street, corner of Clinton Street, 834-8794. Call for a schedule.

There are two reasons to visit St. Ann's: the fabulous stained-glass windows, and the equally fabulous Arts at St. Ann's program of contemporary music.

The historic St. Ann's: St. Ann's is noted for having sixty of the first stained-glass windows made in the United States—nearly 8,000 square feet of figural glass, designed in the 1840s by William and John Bolton. It's being restored on-site in a state-of-the-art conservation studio. The building itself, now under renovation, was designed by architect Minard Lafever and is considered a fine example of Gothic Revival style.

Arts at St. Ann's: It's sexy and it's funky. All your senses come alive when you sit in this slightly decrepit, still-under-restoration nineteenth-century house of worship, and you look at the stained glass and exposed wiring, wonder if the rickety railings will hold, and listen to a rollicking, soulful, terrific concert. That's the experience at St. Ann's. Since 1980, Arts at St. Ann's has presented hundreds of concerts, from pop and jazz to blues and folk music, featuring performers such as David Byrne, Marianne Faithfull, Emmylou Harris, Bill Frisell, and Ron Sexsmith. There are two seasons, spring and autumn.

For kids, a program called **Kids & Jazz: No Jive!** features weekend shows with leading jazz musicians.

And, Arts at St. Ann's has embarked on something new: fostering the art of puppetry. It is home to the Lab, a cooperative puppetry studio for theater artists.

St. Ann's School. 129 Pierrepont Street, corner of Clinton Street, 522-1660.

St. Ann's is a prestigious private school with an enrollment of about a thousand students, preschool through grade 12. "Second Programs" evening courses are given for adults, and include literature, painting, and art classes, for about $200 per semester.

Churches

There are a number of noteworthy churches in Brooklyn Heights. Don't miss the following, many of which have Tiffany-made stained-glass windows.

Church of Pilgrims, now Our Lady of Lebanon Maronite Roman Catholic Church. Corner of Henry and Remsen streets.

The first Congregational church in Brooklyn was built by New Englanders who brought with them their Yankee sense of democracy and community. According to the *American Institute of Architects Guide to New York City Landmarks*, it was ". . . a radical design. The church is the first round-arched, Early Romanesque Revival Ecclesiastical building in America and became a model for many buildings erected by evangelical Protestant congregations in succeeding decades." The building now serves a Roman Catholic Lebanese congregation. For related history, see **Plymouth Church of the Pilgrims**.

First Presbyterian Church. 124 Henry Street, corner of Clark Street, 624-3770. Tours are by appointment.

Dating from 1846, the First Presbyterian Church is an early example of the many cultural, educational, and religious institutions built by the affluent mercantilists who first established Brooklyn Heights. It is located in an area settled because of its proximity to Fulton Ferry. Starting in 1814 the ferry provided fast boats from Fulton Street in Brooklyn to Fulton Street in Manhattan. First Presbyterian, which has six Tiffany windows, is across the street from the German Evangelical Lutheran Zion Church, built in 1840.

First Unitarian Church of Brooklyn. Pierrepont Street at Monroe Place.

New Englanders who came to live in Brooklyn in the 1840s built a number of Brooklyn Heights churches, including this lovely Gothic-style church designed by Minard Lafever. Both the church and its 100-year-old pipe organ have been restored. Note nearby Willow Chapel, on 26 Willow Place, which was built by Alfred Tredway White ten years later.

✪ **Grace Church.** 254 Hicks Street, corner of Grace Court, 624-1850. Tours are by appointment.

Detour a few short blocks from commercial Montague Street and you'll stumble upon this lovely 1847 church. It was designed by the prolific architect Richard Upjohn and it boasts several Tiffany windows. Even in the late twentieth century, tradition is carried on by a formidable Boys and Men's Choir.

If you visit, check out Grace Court Alley nearby—it was a true mews built for the mansions on Remsen and Joralemon streets.

✪ **Plymouth Church of the Pilgrims.** 75 Hicks Street, corner of Orange Street, 624-4743.

Few national historic landmarks are known for their association with progressive social causes. This one, dating back to the mid-nineteenth century, is called the "Grand Central Terminal of the Underground Railroad" and it was used by American slaves seeking asylum in the North and Canada. Suffragist and abolitionist Henry Ward Beecher was a pastor here for some forty years. Others who spoke here include Mark Twain, Clara Barton, Booker T. Washington, and Martin Luther King, Jr. Don't miss the original Tiffany windows or the sculpture of Beecher in the internal courtyard.

✪ **St. Ann's and the Holy Trinity Church.** 157 Montague Street, corner of Clinton Street, 834-8794.

An historic landmark, this church still has an active congregation as well as an active performing arts center. The humanist and religious aspects of St. Ann's have not always been harmonious, but St. Ann's is an important and vital part of Brooklyn's cultural community. (See pages 207–8 for information on the stained-glass restoration project, and performances.)

NOTABLE BROOKLYN HEIGHTS RESTAURANTS

Bistro 36. 36 Joralemon, Columbia Place. 596-2968. Tues.–Sat. 5:30–10 P.M.; closed Mon.

This cozy little neighborhood French bistro is a favorite among brownstone Brooklynites. Bistro 36 serves classics such as coq au vin, grilled fish and meats and nicely prepared vegetables. Children are welcome.

✪ **Heights Café.** 84 Montague Street, near Hicks Street, 625-5555. Daily, noon–3 P.M.; dinner, 5–11 P.M. American Express and cash only.

The eclectic, something-for-everyone menu includes favorites such as a hummus platter, seafood sausage, pizzas, pork chops, and Texas-style meat loaf. The Heights Café is a good place for a business meeting, a quick lunch while on a shopping spree, or a quiet dinner with a date. Upscale, modern, and big, it was designed by the same folks who brought you the Union Square Café in Manhattan. Dinner runs about $20 per person, without drinks.

✪ **Henry's End.** 44 Henry Street, corner of Cranberry Street, 834-1776. Mon.–Thurs. and Sun., 5:30–10:30 P.M.; Fri.–Sat., 11:30 A.M.–11:30 P.M.

Forever busy, forever noisy, forever crowded, Henry's End is one of the finest restaurants in the Heights. The menu often includes unusual entrées of game, as well as carefully prepared poultry and sensational seafood dishes. The chef assumes that you are really hungry, so light eaters should order half portions. There is an extensive wine-tasting menu and several dozen varieties of beer. Dinner runs about $28 per person, without drinks.

Las Tres Palmas. 24 Court Street, between Atlantic Avenue and State Street, 596-2740. Daily, 10 A.M.–10 P.M.

People have been giving Las Tres Palmas rave reviews for years. The menu offers well-spiced, well-cooked Cuban and Puerto Rican–style cuisine. Come when you are hungry or feeling broke; the portions are large and prices low. Most entrées cost less than $9, and are served with rice and beans, or plantains and salad.

✪ **Noodle Pudding.** 38 Henry Street, between Cranberry and Middaugh streets, 625-3737, Tues.–Thurs., 5:30–10:30 P.M.; Fri.–Sat., 5:30–11 P.M.; Sun. 5–10 P.M., closed Mondays. Cash only.

A light meal it's not, but Noodle Pudding is packed most nights. Families with kids, young couples, and retirees sometimes wait in line to eat at this storefront Italian eatery, for two reasons. First is the food: creative pasta dishes such as brasciola with mushrooms, rigatoni with broccoli rabe, a lively bruschetta, and grilled portobellos. Second is owner Tony Migliaccio's homespun charisma: he welcomes you personally and may even bring over a complimentary glass of wine to hasten your wait. Though the signature dish is not often served, you'll have plenty to choose from. Entrées range from $7 to $18.

✪ **Queen.** 84 Court Street, near Livingston Street, 596-5954. Mon.–Fri, 11 30 A.M.–11 P.M.; weekends, 2–11:30 P.M.

One of Brooklyn's best Italian restaurants, Queen is so low-keyed that even many gastronomically savvy Brooklynites forget it is there. Famous for drawing a big lunch crowd of lawyers and judges from the nearby Brooklyn courts, Queen is often pleasantly quiet—romantic even—at dinnertime. Despite its new location, the decor isn't quite up to the food, which is excellent. An average meal costs about $25, not including drinks.

✪ **Teresa's Restaurant.** 180 Montague Street, corner of Hicks Street, 797-3996. Daily, 7 A.M.–11 P.M. Cash only.

Located a block from the **Promenade,** Teresa's has been serving up inexpensive, hearty meals for a decade. A cross between a fancy diner and a simple restaurant, Teresa's serves Polish-Euro food: banana pancakes, apple fritters, chicken liver omelets for breakfast (served all day long), and borscht and other homemade soups, along with burgers, goulash, roast beef, and pork and great veggies at lunch and dinner. You can also get a milkshake and a tuna sandwich on rye. It is clean, airy, and the food is always satisfying. A favorite among senior citizens and kids alike.

Thai Grille. 114 Henry Street, off Clark Street, 596-8888. Mon.–Fri., noon–10:30 P.M.; Sat.–Sun., 3:30–11 P.M.

The discerning restaurant reviewers at the New York *Daily News* gave this pleasant neighborhood Thai restaurant three out of four stars, and with good reason: the spicing is good, ingredients are fresh, and the staff is helpful. Tucked away on a quiet residential street close to the Clark Street subway station, Thai Grille, with its welcoming bar, offers a good dining experience after a romantic walk over the nearby **Brooklyn Bridge** or seeing a movie at the **Heights Cinema**, just a block away. Try the curry noodle soup.

Bars, Cafés, Ice Cream Parlors, and Quick Meals

✪ **Fatoosh and Fatoosh Barbecue.** Fatoosh BBQ: 311 Henry Street, off Atlantic Avenue, 596-0030. Fatoosh Pitza: 330 Hicks and Atlantic, 243-0500. Daily, 11 A.M.–10 P.M.

With two little stores, Fatoosh has the best little Middle Eastern joints in

Brooklyn Heights. Fatoosh Pitza on Hicks Street is a tiny place that sells wonderful lentil soup, excellent appetizers, such as baba ghanoush and fool (which is fava bean salad), as well as falafel. Fatoosh BBQ on Henry Street sells the same, and also tasty chicken kebabs and good red pepper salad.

Monty Q's. 158 Montague Street, between Henry and Clinton streets, 246-2000. Daily, 11 A.M.–11 P.M.

This spiffy brick-oven pizza palace with colorful skylights and designer artwork not only looks great but its pizzas are superior. That's no surprise, because it was started in 1998 by the folks who brought us **Lassen & Hennings** (see below). You'll also find salads, pasta, rolls stuffed with chicken, and eggplant parmigiana, plus a selection of desserts.

Ozzie's. 136 Montague Street, corner Clinton Street. 852-1553. (See Park Slope listing, page 256.)

OTHER SHOPPING

Specialty Food Shops

Greenmarket. Cadman Plaza, near Court and Remsen streets. Tues. and Sat., 8 A.M.–6 P.M.

On Tuesday and Saturday you can find a refreshing contrast to the urban bustle of Brooklyn Heights as well as something good to eat at these outdoor stalls, which sell farm-fresh fruit and vegetables, fresh fish, and assorted baked goods. There are plenty of flowers and plants on sale as well. Other Greenmarkets nearby are held at Albee Square at Fulton Street and DeKalb Avenue on Wednesday, Grand Army Plaza in **Park Slope** on Saturday, and in summers in Williamsburg's **McCarren Park**.

✪ **Lassen & Hennings Deli.** 114 Montague Street, between Henry and Hicks streets, 875-6272. Mon.–Sat., 7 A.M.–11 P.M.; Sun., 7 A.M.–10 P.M.

Yes, it's the best upscale deli in brownstone Brooklyn, hands down. Get a picnic—homemade seasonal soups, gorgeous sandwiches, or your choice of several dozen health-packed salads—for a walk on the nearby Promenade, or a take-home dinner. There's imported chocolate, huge loaves of bread, and desserts you'd gladly die for here. If you come at lunchtime, arrive early to avoid the long lines.

✪ **Perelandra Natural Food Center.** 75 Remsen Street, between Clinton and Court streets, 855-0608. Mon.–Fri., 8:30 A.M.–8:30 P.M.; Sat., 9:30 A.M.–8:30 P.M.; Sun., 11 A.M.–6 P.M.

Named after the utopia described in C. S. Lewis' book by the same name, Perelandra is a big, clean, California-style health food supermarket. Along with the various healthy foodstuffs, fresh produce and breads, the store has a small juice bar that serves shakes and daily specials.

Interesting Neighborhood Shops

Brooklyn Women's Exchange. 55 Pierrepont Street, near Hicks and Henry streets, 624-3435. Mon.–Sat., 10 A.M.–4 P.M.; closed during the summer.

For a special gift that will look like you made it yourself, try the BWE selection of charming quilts, sweaters, mittens, hats, stuffed animals, and children's clothes. Almost everything is made by the elderly or disabled. A special section features gourmet foods.

✪ **Innovative Audio.** 77 Clinton Street, between Montague and Remsen streets, 596-0888. Mon.–Fri., 10:30 A.M.–7 P.M.; Sat., 10:30 A.M.–6 P.M.; Sun., noon–5 P.M.

Music aficionados with deep pockets will find high-end audio equipment, state-of-the-art theater multiroom systems, home theaters, and the like at whatever level of quality they desire. Brands include Nakamichi, Spectral, and Linn. There's a Manhattan location as well.

Seaport Flowers. 214 Hicks Street, near Montague Street, 858-6443. Tues.–Sat., 10:30 A.M.–7:30 P.M.; Sun., noon–5 P.M.; closed Mon.

No ordinary florist, Jane Roe's arrangements are often in demand by the Heights' most elegant drawing rooms. She specializes in a casual "cutting garden" Victorian look that is in tune with the area's marvelous nineteenth-century architecture.

✪ **Takes Two to Tango.** 145 Montague Street, between Clinton and Henry streets, 625-7518. Mon.–Fri., 10:30 A.M.–7 P.M.; Sat., 10:30 A.M.–6 P.M.; closed Sun.

One of the classiest boutiques in Brooklyn, Tango has a full line of women's clothing, including an excellent selection of fine shoes, dressy work clothes, casual wear, lingerie, and handbags. You'll find such brands as Max Mara and Emanuel here at department store prices—but without the crowds.

Atlantic Avenue

Where it is: Along Atlantic Avenue, from the East River to Flatbush Avenue.

How to get there:

By car: Take the first exit off the Brooklyn Bridge and proceed to Court Street. Follow Court Street to Atlantic Avenue.

By subway: 2, 3, 4, or 5 train to Borough Hall; or M, N, or R train to Court Street.

Cab service: Promenade (858-6666), Atlantic (797-5666), or Janice (797-5773). Cost is about $15 to Grand Central Station, $18 to Sheepshead Bay.

Special events: Atlantic Antic (October). Sidewalk Market, once a month, May–September, call 596-1866 (Atlantic Avenue Betterment Association) for information.

How it got its name: At the foot of Atlantic Avenue are the piers from which thousands of ships along Brooklyn's thriving waterfront sailed across the Atlantic Ocean.

Historic district: Atlantic Avenue cuts through the middle of a large historic district along the Brooklyn waterfront that includes landmarked areas in Downtown Brooklyn, Brooklyn Heights, Fulton Ferry, and Carroll Gardens. Slightly to the east of Court Street are two landmarked buildings, the **State Street Houses** and **Friends Meeting House**. Both are within two blocks of Atlantic Avenue, but not on it.

ABOUT THE NEIGHBORHOOD

Atlantic Avenue is famous for its concentration of Middle Eastern restaurants and shops, antique stores, and, in the late 1990s, trendy, offbeat retail establishments. In the past decade, a high-quality culinary corridor has also blossomed here, with small, interesting restaurants such as **La Bouillabaisse** and **Brawta Cafe** nestled in old, small storefronts.

The Middle Eastern enclave in the block between **Court** and **Clinton streets** is a colorful remnant of the days when Brooklyn's waterfront was a bustling international seaport. Today you can visit some of New York's best known Middle Eastern restaurants, grocers, and bakeries, specializing in traditional Lebanese and Syrian foods. Several outstanding establishments, including **Sahadi Importing Company, Damascus Bakery**, and **Oriental Pastry and Grocery** are two- and three-generation family businesses.

Since it is impossible to wander down Atlantic Avenue without wanting to try everything, following is a recommended menu.

Food for a Middle Eastern Feast

hummus and baba ghanoush spreads
pita bread
tabbouleh (grain and vegetable salad)
stuffed grape leaves
feta cheese (there are many varieties; ask for a taste)
spicy black and green olives
pistachio nuts
baklava, "bird's nest," or Turkish Delight for dessert
mint tea

If you are interested in Victoriana, oak furniture, reproductions and bric-a-brac, head east down Atlantic Avenue. The biggest concentration of antique stores is on the three-block strip between Bond and Smith streets. Two interesting shops are the **Upholstered Room**, a showcase store which carries plush, velvet-covered expensive Victorian furniture, and **Circa Antiques**, which specializes in dressers, dining room tables, and armoires of walnut and other fine woods.

A fraction of its former size, Atlantic Avenue's antique row now has only about twenty antique stores; funkier artifacts from the more recent past, say the 1960s, are more likely to be found a half-mile hike away on **Smith Street** in **Carroll Gardens**.

However, new life is blooming on this stretch. **Breukelen** and its counterpart, **Bark**, a sybaritic bed-and-bath shop, sell modern, sophisticated decorative wares for the home. Spare, angular stained-glass lamps at **Karl Lighting** are reminiscent of Frank Lloyd Wright.

POINTS OF CULTURAL INTEREST

✪ **Brooklyn Bridge Magazine.** 388 Atlantic Avenue, between Hoyt and Bond streets, 596-7400. To subscribe, send to above address, Brooklyn, NY 11217.

Brooklyn Bridge—the magazine, that is, not the bridge—is a new cultural landmark in Brooklyn on two counts. First, the editorial offices occupy a beautifully renovated edifice originally designed for the manufacture of cast-iron coin-counting machines, illustrating yet again how Brooklyn's old smokestack industrial economy has been transformed by the information age. More importantly, month after month, *Brooklyn Bridge*, in its own words, "celebrates the richness of life in Brooklyn" in articles and tidbits on culture and artists, food, history, trivia, ethnic communities, sports, nature, business, health care, and just about every aspect of Brooklyn, now and then.

Indeed, we are indebted to *Brooklyn Bridge* (which wasn't around for our first edition) for its in-depth Brooklyn reporting. Annual subscriptions cost $18—and if you like thumbing through this guidebook, chances are you'll love the magazine, too.

✪ **Brooklyn Historic Railway Association.** Atlantic Avenue Subway Tunnel utility hole, intersection of Court Street and Atlantic Avenue, 941-3160; 596-6849; 596-1866. Reserved tours, call for information. Cost is $15 for adults, $10 for children.

Bring a flashlight, and wear sturdy shoes for this most unusual adventure. It's a tour that is only given occasionally, by Robert Diamond, a trolley and urban transportation enthusiast who has the unusual distinction of having discovered a 150-year-old railway tunnel. Built in 1861 and then abandoned and sealed up in 1884, the Atlantic Avenue Tunnel was the city's first subway tunnel. Rediscovered by then-twenty-year-old Diamond in 1980 against the advice of various New York city bureaucrats and historians, the tunnel is now listed in the National Register of Historic Places. It's fun to see the old tunnel, but even more fun to share in Diamond's enthusiasm for his once-in-a-lifetime discovery. And, Diamond's discovery is a story that will enthrall children. "Nevah" say never, as they say in Brooklyn.

✪ **Islamic Mission of America.** 143 State Street off Bond Street, 875-6607.

A few blocks down from the historic State Street Houses the Islamic Mission of America has transformed a brownstone into what is now the oldest mosque in Brooklyn.

"That Billboard." Atlantic Avenue and Nevins Street.

You're driving down Atlantic Avenue toward Flatbush Ave. and suddenly there's a huge billboard with what looks like a color magazine ad from the 1950s or earlier. But it's not really an ad, it's more like an in-joke. This is the work of Jerry Johnson, sign painter and billboard guerrilla, who has been entertaining locals for the past ten years with his off-beat, social commentary message-on-a-billboard. Yes, it's legal. Yes, it's a little obscure. And yes, of course, he's a Brooklynite.

Shadowbox Theater. YWCA Memorial Hall. 30 3rd Avenue, between Atlantic Avenue and State Street, 875-1190. Call for a schedule.

With its original scripts and contemporary themes, this children's puppet repertory company has been a staple for New York City schools for over thirty years. The Shadowbox Theater performances have a range of small and large puppets, actors, and shadow puppets in shows that convey a social message, such as "Sing out for Peace." The theater is not far from the Heights, Carroll Gardens, and Park Slope.

State Street Houses. 291–299 and 290–324 State Street, between Smith and Hoyt streets.

Tucked away just one block from the bustle of Atlantic Avenue's antique stores is this lovely stretch of twenty-three neatly kept historic row houses. Built in the period from 1840 to 1870, they are New York City landmarks that reflect the evolving architectural styles of that era, from early Greek Revival to Italianate ornamentation. Built as homes for the prosperous merchants who "urbanized" this part of Brooklyn, today they are still private residences, lovely to walk by while conjuring up the past.

NOTABLE ATLANTIC AVENUE RESTAURANTS

✪ **Acadia Parish Cajun Cafe.** 148 Atlantic Avenue, between Clinton and Henry streets, 624-5154. Mon. and Wed.–Thurs.; 5–9 P.M.; Fri.–Sat., 5–11 P.M.; Sun., 4–9 P.M.

Welcome, ya'll, to a cozy corner of Louisiana, where hospitality reigns, the humor's down-home—and the cuisine is laced with Cajun spices. Fish lovers will enjoy the soupy gumbo, jambalaya, and grilled fish entrées. Cramped, casual, and BYOB, plan on spending about $15 per person.

✪ **Brawta Cafe.** 347 Atlantic Avenue, between Hoyt and Bond streets, 855-5515. Sun.–Mon., noon–10:30 P.M.; Tues.–Thurs., noon–11 P.M.; Fri.–Sat., noon–11:30 P.M.

This contemporary Caribbean joint is often crowded and with good reason. Try the "rasta pasta" plantains in spicy sauce, codfish cakes—and don't miss a special drink of ginger beer and sorrell or sea moss. There's Caribbean and Afro-centric art on the walls, and rave restaurant reviews hang in the window. No alcohol is served on the premises.

Caravan. 193 Atlantic Avenue near Court Street, 488-7111. Mon.–Sat., noon–11 P.M.; Sun., 2–10 P.M.

Even fussy food writers give a "thumbs up" to this restaurant, which is almost as small as the Middle Eastern nation from which its owners hail: Yemen. You can get a full, freshly prepared, and tasty meal of chicken, lamb, veal, or fish, along with rice, vegetables, and salad for two for about $28.

✪ **La Bouillabaisse.** 145 Atlantic Avenue, between Clinton and Henry streets, 522-8275. Mon.–Thurs., noon–10:30 P.M.; Fri., noon–11 P.M.; Sat.–Sun., brunch, 10:30 A.M.–3 P.M.

A meal at La Bouillabaisse is worth the occasional wait. They serve tastefully prepared French dishes, simple robust seafood entrées (including of course, a bouillabaisse) and zesty garden-fresh vegetables. Trekking to almost the end of Atlantic Avenue, sometimes waiting in line (there are no reservations here), and sitting elbow-to-elbow with your neighbor in a modest little room are all part of the adventure. Owner Neil Ganic is also a partner in the popular **Petite Crevette** restaurant on Atlantic Avenue.

Meson Flamenco. 135 Atlantic Avenue, 625-7177, Tues.–Sun., noon–11:30 P.M.; Sun., 4–11:30 P.M.

Olé! There's something new in Brooklyn: a real tapas bar and Spanish restaurant, featuring live entertainment—yes! flamenco dancing!—on weekends. Mouth-watering tapas—Spanish antipasti, heavy on garlic and seasonings—almost make a meal. Or, try the excellent shrimp dishes, tortilla de patatas, or seafood salad for a full dinner that will cost well under $20.

Mezcal. 151 Atlantic Avenue, between Henry and Clinton streets, 643-6000, Mon.–Thurs., noon–11 P.M.; Fri.–Sun., noon–midnight.

It's pretty tough to find anything better than run-of-the-mill Mexican these days. Most restaurants get by with frozen margaritas and chips, but Mezcal's food is both tasty and creative. For instance, the camarón ameyal is a garlic- and lemon-flavored mix of garbanzo beans and shrimp. And the pork cooked in adobo sauce is rich and hearty. Wash it down with tequila or with a cerveza (beer) served cold. Other locations: Bay Ridge and Park Slope.

Moroccan Star. 205 Atlantic Avenue, corner of Court Street, 643-0800. Daily, 1–11 P.M.

This simple restaurant hasn't changed much since the 1991 edition of our book, and even then the Moroccan Star was a fixed constellation on Atlantic Avenue. The place is in need of sprucing up, but the food is still honestly, authentically ethnic, and the staff timelessly friendly. Moroccan Star serves traditional North African Middle Eastern fare, such as lamb stew and chicken with vegetables, prunes, and almonds; stuffed kibbee and, of course, the standard hummus, baba ghanoush, tabbouleh, and stuffed grape leaves. Kids like the shish kebab. Bring your own wine. Entrées run about $9 to $14 on average.

Petite Crevette. 127 Atlantic Avenue, between Henry and Clinton streets, 858-6660. Daily, noon–11 P.M.

You can eat in, take out, or buy fish at the highly regarded European-style

Petite Crevette. The chowders and stews are fresh and wonderful, as are the fish cakes and seafood linguine. There's a children's menu with fish-and-chips, and a bargain lunch special for under $5.

Tripoli. 156 Atlantic Avenue, corner of Clinton Street, 596-5800. Mon.–Fri., 11 A.M.–11 P.M.; Fri.–Sat., 11 A.M.–midnight; Sun., 11 A.M.–10:30 P.M.

There's a ship sailing out of the Tripoli's huge windows. The restaurant's pleasant interior includes walls painted in a wonderful ocean motif, replete with lazy clouds, birds, and views of a rocky coastline along with heavy wooden seating and low lighting. The food is a very literal rendition of typical Middle Eastern fare—it is good, if not as imaginative as the decor. Entrées average $9 to $14.

Yemen Café. 176 Atlantic Avenue, between Court and Clinton streets, 834-9533. Daily, 10 A.M.–10 P.M. Cash only.

There's an Indian twist on the Middle Eastern food here. The cuisine of Yemen has elements of Indian cooking, including nan-like breads and mild curried dishes served with basmati rice. This restaurant serves the small, close-knit Yemeni community in the immediate vicinity.

Bars, Cafés, Quick Meals, and Ice Cream Parlors

Montero's Bar & Grill. 73 Atlantic Avenue, off Furman Street, 624-9799. Mon.–Sat., 10–4 A.M.; Sun., noon–4 A.M.

An innocuous local bar frequented by aging longshoremen and miscellaneous elderly locals, Montero's received a writeup in a 1998 *New York Magazine*, which said, "this place isn't just about nostalgia: some of the local literati come by to soak up stories for their next novel (along with some of the cheapest beer in town)."

✪ **Moustache.** 405 Atlantic Avenue, between Bond and Nevins streets, 852-5555. Daily, 11 A.M.–11 P.M.

Moustache is a wonderful small café, conveniently located on busy Atlantic Avenue. It serves very fresh hummus, tabbouleh, and other Middle Eastern standards, but is known for its unusual pizza (made of pita dough) with interesting toppings such as shrimp, and garlicky chicken. The back garden will snap you right back to the Middle East, if you've ever been there. There's a Moustache in Manhattan, too.

Peter's Ice Cream Café. 185 Atlantic Avenue, between Court and Henry streets, 852-3835. Sun.–Thurs., 11 A.M.–11 P.M.; Fri.–Sat., 11 A.M.–midnight; Sun., 11 A.M.–midnight.

If heaven is paved with rich, homemade ice cream, you've arrived. Peter's scoops up traditional favorite flavors plus some unbelievable chocolate concoctions. Call ahead to see what the specials are and whether the kids can watch it being made.

Peter's Waterfront Ale House. 155 Atlantic Avenue, between Clinton and Henry streets, 522-3794. Daily, 11:30 A.M.–1:30 P.M.; later on weekends.

This popular bar and eatery is a friendly local place with a good selection of new micro brews, single-malt scotches, small-batch bourbons, tequilas, and vodkas. It's the kind of place that families nip into with the kids for a quick, light dinner. Live music on weekends features jazz musicians, many drawn from local talent.

SHOPPING

Specialty Food Shops

✪ **Damascus Bakery.** 195 Atlantic Avenue, between Clinton and Court streets, 855-1456. Mon–Sat., 8 A.M.–5 P.M. No credit cards.

If you live in New York, you've probably seen packages of Damascus pita bread in your local supermarket. Inside this small shop is a vast selection of freshly baked plain, whole wheat, sesame, garlic, onion, and even oat bran pitas. The business was started in 1933 by grandpa Hassan Halaby, who hailed from Damascus.

El Asmar. 197 Atlantic Avenue, between Clinton and Court streets, 855-2455. Daily, 8:30 A.M.–9 P.M. No credit cards.

The late-night grocery of Atlantic Avenue, this father-and-son operation sells a panoply of Middle Eastern specialties that includes more than seven varieties of feta cheese, fifty different spices, dozens of beans, dried fruits, pickled vegetables, olives, hummus, and baba ghanoush, plus such desserts as baklava and Turkish Delight.

Oriental Pastry and Grocery. 170 Atlantic Avenue, between Clinton and Court streets, 875-7687. Daily, 10 A.M.–8:30 P.M. No credit cards.

The Syrians have been perfecting the sweet ancient taste of pistachio, honey, and dough for more than a thousand years, and here you'll benefit from all of that experience. Try the burma (shredded dough filled with honey and nuts) or the Turkish Delight. For something more substantial there is take-out hummus, lebany yogurt, and falafel mix, along with dozens of spices and other accoutrements of Middle Eastern cooking.

✪ **Sahadi Importing Company** 187–189 Atlantic Avenue, between Clinton and Court streets, 624-4550. Mon.–Sat., 9 A.M.–7 P.M.; closed Sun.

Part gourmet food store, part exotic deli, this is the largest and best stocked of the Middle Eastern food emporiums in New York City. There is an admirable selection of freshly prepared take-home foods, including soups, tabbouleh, stuffed vine leaves, imjadara (made of rice and lentils), apricot-currant chicken, hummus, curries, and couscous. Standard fare includes dried fruits, grains, beans, many kinds of olives, and feta cheese. Check for seasonal specials, such as Middle Eastern turkey stuffing and an edible almond Christmas wreath.

Antiques

The following antique and secondhand shops are listed in order of their addresses on Atlantic Avenue.

Horseman Antiques. 351 Atlantic Avenue, between Bond and Hoyt streets, 596-1048. Daily, 10 A.M.–6 P.M.

There's four floors of turn-of-the-century and Art Deco pine and oak furniture here, plus a fairly large collection of stained glass. In addition you will find an eclectic collection of new brass headboards and beds. Prices here are moderate, which may be one reason this store has been in business for some forty years.

In Days of Old, Limited. 357 Atlantic Avenue, near Hoyt Street, 858-4233. Wed.–Sat., 11 A.M.–5 P.M.; Sun., 1–5 P.M.

Lots of late Victorian oak, walnut, and mahogany pieces are sold here—armoires, desks, and tables—along with turn-of-the-century lighting fixtures. The friendly owner has restored several Brooklyn brownstones himself, and he has an eye for unusual pieces. This is a good place for people redecorating or renovating their own homes in period style.

Time Trader Antiques. 368 Atlantic Avenue, between Bond and Hoyt streets, 852-3301. Mon.–Fri., 11 A.M.–7 P.M.; Sat.–Sun., noon–6 P.M.

The excellent and fairly priced merchandise here spills over into no fewer than seven storefronts (308, 328, 368, 369, 373, and 443 Atlantic Avenue). This is one of the largest importers of English and European furniture in the tristate area. There are original armoires, sofas, chairs, and tables, Victorian to Deco, as well as less expensive reproduction pine and oak furniture. Delivery is available and they're open seven days a week.

✪ **Circa Antiques.** 374 Atlantic Avenue, between Bond and Hoyt streets, 5961866. Tues.–Fri., noon–5 P.M.; Sat.–Sun., 11 A.M.–6 P.M.

There are restored Empire tables, chairs, and beds of walnut, rosewood, and other fine woods here. Prices for sets range from $1,000 to $7,000. The store has been here for twenty-seven years, so you can be assured of its good reputation.

Upholstered Room. 412–416 Atlantic Avenue, between Bond and Nevins streets, 875-7084. Wed.–Sun., noon–6 P.M.; closed Mon. and Tues.

This is a classy collection of eighteenth- and nineteenth-century antique furniture. One room has high Victorian pieces, including high-quality tables, sofas, and chairs. The back room features period furniture perfect for that historically correct renovated brownstone. The styles range from American Federal to Empire. Everything is in mint condition and accordingly priced in the $1,000-and-up range.

Other Interesting Neighborhood Shops

✪ **Bark.** 369 Atlantic Avenue, between Hoyt and Bond streets, 625-8997. Tues.–Sun., noon–7 P.M.; closed Mon.

This high-end bath and linen shop is seductively luxurious. Thick cotton towels and robes, wonderful soaps, delightful bathroom ornaments and more ooze relaxation and delicious, harmless self-indulgence. And why not? Bark is definitely a great place to find a gift to pamper that someone special in your life—whether it's you or someone else you love.

✪ **Breukelen.** 369 Atlantic Avenue, between Hoyt and Bond streets, 246-0024. Tues.–Sun., noon–7 P.M.; closed Mon.

It looks a bit like the MOMA store, but much more laid-back. Breukelen (named after the borough's original Dutch name) sells artfully displayed, beautifully designed functional objects. Thomas Gibson and John Snyder have put together a terrific collection of classic and modern design objects for the home, ranging in price from $20 on up. Breukelen is straight out of Manhattan's Tribeca or SoHo—and there's nothing else like it in Brooklyn.

Karl Lighting. 396 Atlantic Avenue, between Bond and Hoyt streets, 596-1419. Sat.–Sun., noon–5 P.M. Call for a weekday appointment. No credit cards.

Beautifully crafted stained-glass custom lighting sells here for 25 percent less than prices at many upscale boutiques. You can spend from $300 to 3,000.

The Melting Pot. 492 Atlantic Avenue, near Nevins Street, 596-6849. Tues.–Sun., noon–7 P.M.; closed Sun.

An anachronism from the batik-crazy 1970s, this store has survived long enough to become fashionable again. It's a mother-daughter operation (started when the now-adult daughter was a small child) in which simple T-shirts, aprons, bibs, dresses, hats, baby quilts, and so on are hand-batiked in bright, cheery colors that will never run when washed. The folk art motifs include lots of stars, moons, polka dots, dinosaurs, and friendly flowers. These are great gift items, especially for children.

Scuba Network. 290 Atlantic Avenue, corner of Smith Street, 802-0700. Mon.–Fri., 11 A.M.–7 P.M.; Sat., 10 A.M.–6 P.M.; closed Sun.

Amid the antique dealers and Middle Eastern food merchants is this store catering to water lovers. You can get all the gear you'll need for snorkeling or scuba diving, or sign up for classes for your next trip south.

Two for the Pot. 200 Clinton Street, corner of Atlantic Avenue, 855-8173. Tues.–Fri., noon–7 P.M.; Sat., 10 A.M.–6 P.M.; Sun., 1–5 P.M.; closed Mon.

Savor the aroma of freshly roasted coffees here. While you are buying, check out the assortment of coffee makers, herbs, spices, and barbecue equipment. The personable owner, a former cartoonist, is ready with suggestions and information.

DUMBO (Down Under the Manhattan Bridge Overpass), Fulton Ferry Waterfront, and Vinegar Hill

Where they are: Along the waterfront of the East River, stretching from the area under the Brooklyn Bridge to the Brooklyn Navy Yard. Bounded by the water on the north, the Navy Yard on the east, the BQE on the south, and Main Street on the west/northwest.

DUMBO: The area bounded by the East River, Main, Bridge, and Sands streets, roughly from the Brooklyn Bridge underpass to slightly east of the Manhattan Bridge underpass.

Fulton Ferry: A historic district southwest of DUMBO, defined by the East River, Main Street, the end of Cadman Plaza West, and Furman Street.

Vinegar Hill: Northwestern Brooklyn, defined by the Brooklyn Navy Yard, East River, and Sands and Bridge streets.

How they got their names:

Fulton Ferry: Named after Robert Fulton's *Nassau*, the first steam-powered ferry, which first plowed the waters of the East River between Manhattan and a landing here. The ferries transported both people and produce; at their busiest, in the 1870s, they made about 1,200 crossings a day.

DUMBO: An acronym for Down Under the Manhattan Bridge Overpass (following in the tradition of SoHo (so-named because it is South of Houston Street) and Tribeca (Triangle Below Canal Street).

Vinegar Hill: Called Irishtown in the late 1700s, the area was renamed Vinegar Hill by a large landowner, John Jackson, in commemoration of a battle fought as part of the Irish revolution of that era.

Special events: Outdoor Sculpture Show, Brooklyn Waterfront Artists Coalition (May); DUMBO Art Center Festival (October).

How to get there:

Note that the entire area is about one mile square.

By foot: Walk over the Brooklyn Bridge, exit the footpath at Tillary Street. Turn right for DUMBO and Fulton Ferry; left for Vinegar Hill. Best to consult a map.

By car:

Fulton Ferry/DUMBO: Take the first exit off the Brooklyn Bridge, bear right onto Cadman Plaza West, quickly turn into right hand exit lane. Stay right, past the entrance to the BQE. With Eagle Warehouse on the left, Manhattan, River Café and Barge Music straight ahead, take a quick right under the Brooklyn Bridge.

Vinegar Hill: Take second exit off the Brooklyn Bridge, staying in left lane, turn left on Tillary Street, again left onto Jay Street, continue straight on Jay, ignoring a confusing mess of intersections located under the Manhattan Bridge, go several blocks and turn right on Plymouth or John Street.

By subway:

Fulton Ferry and DUMBO: Take the A or C High Street or the 2 or 3 to Clark Street.

Vinegar Hill: In order of proximity: closest train is F train to York Street stop; A or C to High Street, numbers 2 or 3 to Clark Street; a 20-minute walk from the numbers 4 and 5 stop at Borough Hall.

Cab services: Promenade (858-6666) or Atlantic (797-5666). Costs about $15 to Grand Central Station, $17 to Sheepshead Bay.

Historic Districts:

Fulton Ferry Historic District: Bounded by the east river to the north and northwest, Main Street to the east, Water Street and part of Fulton Street to the south.

Vinegar Hill Historic District: Two tiny areas that are difficult to describe, but roughly (1) along Navy Street bounded Front Street to the South, Plymouth Street to the north, and (2) a block on Front Street between Gold and Bridge streets.

ABOUT THE NEIGHBORHOOD

Whether you are interested in history, great views of Manhattan, Brooklyn's emerging art scene, or just a respite from the urban fray, a trip to the Fulton Ferry waterfront can be just what the doctor ordered. If you are traveling with children, the open spaces are wonderful for an urban romp. Among the notable sites on Old Fulton Street are the **Eagle Warehouse and Storage Company**, a huge 1893 redbrick factory converted into coops; **Bargemusic**, the **River Café**, and of course the Brooklyn Bridge itself.

There isn't much to "do" here other than gawk at the skyline and visit **Fulton Ferry Park**, perhaps fill one's tummy at the mouth-watering **Grimaldi's Pizza**. Studio tours of resident artists can be arranged in advance through BACA (see page 205).

Splendid Isolation

Since the 1980s a fair amount of abandoned industrial loft space underneath the bridges has been resuscitated by artists.

The architecture and scale of these buildings reflects their original use as sites for the construction of large metal units ordered by the nearby Navy Yard. For big-scale painters and sculptors, they offer ideal spaces.

Some say as many as 400 artists now populate the ten-block DUMBO area. Some live in lofts in various stages of renovation (some quite raw, some quite beautiful), or in early nineteenth-century houses on old cobblestone streets in nearby Vinegar Hill. A few artists and artisans moved here for the spectacular light, the views, the proximity to the bridges and the river. Most of the old-timers came for the low rent, and while enjoying the views, they also have endured inconvenience, rough conditions and desolation. Among them are up-and-coming artists, filmmakers, and musicians.

Renovation is a way of life. Some residents have contributed a tremendous amount of physical labor and skill to improving their buildings—they've built bathrooms, erected walls, and installed heating, even as renters. Inevitably, tensions between the big property owners and these renters escalated in the real estate boom of the

1990s. And, being New York, the question of how to develop the waterfront remains unresolved.

Unlike Williamsburg, very little commercial life has developed here. There are no trendy restaurants or crafts stores. The nearest supermarket is a hike away, though the stores and eateries of Brooklyn Heights suffice. However, it is interesting to look around the area and consider how extraordinary it is, in a city of 9 million and just a 30-minute walk from busy SoHo, that an artist can work in such splendid isolation.

Historical Notes

Fulton Ferry and DUMBO: Originally a waterfront hamlet, the Fulton Ferry area was the site from which Brooklyn's Dutch settlers embarked for Manhattan. In those days, boats were powered by oars, sails, or even horses walking on treadmills. The little hamlet became a bustling commercial and residential area in the nineteenth century, when steam ferries began transporting people and produce across the East River. Many historical figures lived here: Thomas Paine lived in a house at the corner of Sands and Fulton (now Cadman Plaza West). Talleyrand once lived in a Fulton Street farmhouse opposite Hicks Street. Walt Whitman set type for the first edition of *Leaves of Grass* in 1855 at 170 Fulton Street, on the corner of Cranberry. But with the completion of the Brooklyn Bridge in 1883 and the loss of ferry traffic, the neighborhood went into decline.

Vinegar Hill: Vinegar Hill evolved as a waterfront workingclass residential neighborhood. In the nineteenth century the row houses still standing today were built, and small industries thrived. (It was here that the New York Chewing Gum factory first put chicle on the map as a chewable treat.) It was a raucous boom town during the heyday of the adjacent **Brooklyn Navy Yard.** The area thrived through the end of World War II, but thereafter the Navy Yard itself declined, affecting the surrounding neighborhood. Since the 1980s Vinegar Hill has been on a gentle upswing, as increasing numbers of artists, some of whom work in nearby DUMBO, have moved into this predominantly low-income neighborhood.

POINTS OF CULTURAL INTEREST

Anchorage. Cadman Plaza West and Front Street, under the Brooklyn Bridge, 625-0080. Call for information.

Feeling cramped? For an adventure, visit the art gallery housed in eight fifty-five-foot-high stone chambers that hold the Brooklyn Bridge suspension cables. The chambers have been restored and provide a playful atmosphere for equally playful audio, visual, and performance artwork.

✪ **Bargemusic.** Fulton Landing, at the end of Cadman Plaza West, 624-4061. Call for the schedule of concerts. Tickets cost about $25.

The New York Times has written of Bargemusic: "Some of the finest chamber music around can be heard in a setting spectacular enough to be an event all its own." Since 1978 this renovated Erie-Lackawanna coffee barge has been the site of floating concerts on the East River. Noted performers play Mozart, Bach, Beethoven, Brahms, and the like year-round. The lovely wood-paneled hall has great acoustics, and since the boat is just 102 feet long, you virtually sit in the musicians' laps. Located to the left of the Brooklyn Bridge as you face Manhattan, and a short walk from several good restaurants, this little gem offers a uniquely romantic and musical evening. Reservations are a must.

"Between the Bridges" Outdoor Sculpture Show. Summer, Empire Ferry Park, 596-2507.

Every summer for about twenty years now, a most unusual sculpture garden is temporarily erected at the Empire Fulton Ferry Park between the Manhattan and Brooklyn bridges. If you happen to be in New York at the time, it's well worth a visit, or a picnic at this little-known park with world-class views.

Most of the sculptures are designed specifically for this venue. Would-be participants are asked to make sculpture that meets several criteria: for instance, that it will be displayed in a park across from Manhattan's world-famous skyline, it must be sturdy enough to withstand the vicissitudes of weather and be vandal-resistant, and be removable without a trace at the end of the show. Of the entries, only a handful are chosen for the show. One year, the sculptures were classified into categories such as "playful," "looking at Manhattan," "magical nature," and "nature." You get the gist.

✪ **Brooklyn Navy Yard.** Bounded by Hudson Avenue, Navy Street, Flushing Avenue, Kent Avenue, and the East River.

The colorful history of the Brooklyn Navy Yard reads like a roster of America's maritime adventures. Ships destined for raids against the Barbary Pirates were fitted out here. Similarly, seagoing vessels designed to encounter British merchant ships in the War of 1812 were built or overhauled here. Among the ships built or worked on at the Brooklyn Navy Yard were the oceangoing steamship pioneers *Fulton* and *Niagara,* and ships that fought in the Civil War (including the *Iron Monitor*). The Brooklyn Navy Yard was a key supply station during the Spanish American War.

In World War II the Brooklyn Navy Yard rapidly became the largest of the

U.S. Navy's construction facilities. Thousands of people were employed in its dry docks, piers, buildings, and railroads and related businesses. The booming population of Navy Yard workers created housing shortages in nearby residential neighborhoods such as Bedford-Stuyvesant.

During the mid- to late-twentieth century, after the end of World War II, the Brooklyn Navy Yard experienced severe cutbacks as shipbuilding moved to other centers. When the Navy finally closed the facility in 1966, selling the area to the New York City government, it closed a chapter on 150 years of shipbuilding at this location.

Today, light industrial businesses occupy the site. There has been talk of a movie studio being built on the premises.

The Navy Yard houses several landmark buildings: the Surgeon's House, the U.S. Naval Hospital, the Commander's House, and Dry Dock #1, which was considered one of the great accomplishments of nineteenth-century engineering.

✪ **DUMBO Arts Center.** 45 York Street, 624-3772. Thurs.–Monday, noon–6 P.M. Call for membership and schedule information, and for the website address.

Launched in 1998, the DUMBO Arts Center's mission is to foster creative expression in this part of Brooklyn, and to promote the work of local artists to a national and international audience. Located in a 10,000-square-foot space, the street-level gallery has plans to host shows curated by some of the nation's leading experts in emerging, contemporary international arts.

"DUMBO Art Under the Bridge" Festival and Open Studios. Sponsored by DUMBO Arts Center. October. 624-3772.

A new and promising annual festival, DUMBO Art Under the Bridge features over one hundred artists' studios open to the public, performance events, bands, and spontaneous happenings; one year a gang of people appeared in cardboard clothes, for instance. Thousands of people attend. Call for details or watch local listings.

✪ **Eagle Warehouse.** 28 Old Fulton Street, corner of Elizabeth Place, 855-3959.

In 1980 this elegant medieval-style warehouse was renovated into expensive cooperative apartments, many with spectacular views of Manhattan, the Brooklyn Bridge, and the East River. Built in 1893, it is one of Brooklyn's few remaining buildings by Frank Freeman, who was dubbed "Brooklyn's greatest architect" by the AIA Guide to New York. The arched entry bears large bronze letters reading EAGLE WAREHOUSE AND STORAGE COMPANY; atop the building is a huge clock, now situated in a studio loft. The Eagle does not stand alone as a reminder of the busy shipping past of the Fulton Street docks. The waterfront area is scattered with nineteenth-century warehouses; note the unusually large site occupied across the street by the circa 1885 Empire Stores, stretching from 53 to 83 Water Street.

✪ **Manhattan Bridge.** Spans the East River between Canal Street in Manhattan and Flatbush Avenue in Brooklyn. It is north of the Brooklyn Bridge, and south of the Williamsburg Bridge.

Built in 1909, this two-level suspension bridge with spectacular views of Manhattan was designed by Leon Moisseiff. It is over 2,000 meters long and carries cars, truck traffic, and a subway line. The upper deck has a pedestrian walkway. It leads directly into Canal Street, and Manhattan's Chinatown.

✪ **Watchtower.** 25 Columbia Heights, 625-3600.

The Watchtower and its Jehovah's Witness followers have large real estate holdings in Brooklyn Heights, although many residents prefer to turn a blind eye. Their properties include the prominent Watchtower building, visible from the bridge, at least one prime site on Montague Street, and various residences.

NOTABLE RESTAURANTS IN DUMBO

✪ **Patsy's, a.k.a. Patsy Grimaldi's, a.k.a. Grimaldi's.** 19 Old Fulton Street, between Front and Water streets, 838-4300. Daily, 11:30 A.M.–11:30 P.M.; weekends until 1 A.M.; closed Tues. No deliveries; cash only.

Yo, call it "Grimaldi's," not "Patsy's."

The pizza *tastes* like Patsy's: deliciously thin crust, topped with fresh sauce and toppings. And the joint *looks* like Patsy's: it's got the jukebox, red-checkered tablecloths, Sinatra photos, and a nice Brooklyn buzz. But there's been a legal tussle amongst pizzerias over the name Patsy.

So this one is now called G*R*I*M*A*L*D*I*'s—and it is still one of Brooklyn's best pizzerias.

Pete's Downtown. 1 Old Fulton Street at Water Street, 858-3510. Tues.–Thurs., noon–10 P.M.; Sat., noon–11 P.M.; Sun., 1–9 P.M.

Reserve a window-side table here: the Manhattan skyline is just across the river from this moderately priced Italian continental restaurant. The cooking style is adequate but unimaginative (although the portions are large). But with these views, the food hardly matters. Inside seating is dark and cozy. This is a good place for a tryst; unlike the River Café across the street, you probably won't meet anyone you know. Outside seating and parking is available.

✪ **River Café.** 1 Water Street, at end of Cadman Plaza West, 522-5200. Mon.–Sat., noon–2:30 P.M., and 6:30–11 P.M.; Sun, 11:30 A.M.–2:30 P.M., and 6–11 P.M.

Famous for its breathtaking views of the Manhattan skyline, the River Café has an excellent menu, lots of romantic ambience, and valet parking. Don't be put off by the whine of cars crossing the Brooklyn Bridge overhead; it's all part of the charm. This is the perfect place to celebrate a special occasion or have a drink before heading off to eat somewhere else (that's cheaper). Dinner at the River Café is fixed price and costs about $70; brunch and lunch are à la carte, with most entrées costing about $23. For the gents, jackets are required and ties preferred at dinner. Reservations are necessary.

Tin Room Café. 5 Front Street, corner Old Fulton Street, under Brooklyn Bridge, 246-0310. Tues.–Sun, 6 P.M.–midnight.

Like a pirates' getaway, this wonderful, quirky restaurant is tucked away behind an innocuous building near the foot of the Brooklyn Bridge (and within walking distance of a spectacular view of lower Manhattan). With an idiosyncratic Italian menu, opera solos on weekends, and a series of intimate rooms leading to a large back patio, the Tin Room Café is an enjoyable alternative to its better-known neighbors, the illustrious and pricey River Café, and the much-heralded, no-nonsense pizzeria, Grimaldi's.

Downtown Brooklyn and MetroTech Center

How to get there:

By car: Take the second exit off the Brooklyn Bridge. Turn left on Tillary Street and right on Jay Street.

By subway: Take the A, C, or F to Jay Street, or 2, 3, 4, or 5 to Borough Hall.

ABOUT THE NEIGHBORHOOD

If downtown Brooklyn seems transformed into Downtown Brooklyn, **MetroTech Center** is the reason why. Six million square feet of office space and research and other facilities have been constructed, along with the Commons, three-and-a-half acres of open parklike space. The renaissance brought about by this new development is still being felt throughout the Downtown Brooklyn area.

Brooklyn's first new hotel in decades, the **Marriott** opened in 1998 in a mixed-use office and hotel complex called **Renaissance Plaza**. Engineering hothouse **Polytechnic University** has moved into twenty-first-century facilities, and was recently the recipient of an enormous endowment. Not far away are famous eateries such as **Junior's** and **Gage & Tollner**, and the brilliantly quirky **New York Transit Museum**. In the future, look for the development of more office space, more retail stores, expansion of dorms and a gym for the colleges, and a bus loop that will transport passengers through the Downtown area.

POINTS OF CULTURAL INTEREST

Abraham & Strauss building—now Macy's. 420 Fulton Street, corner of Hoyt Street.

Macy's now occupies the historic Abraham & Strauss building, which was a 125-year old chain store with roots in Brooklyn's immigrant history. Abraham, a Bavarian immigrant, turned a small dry goods shop into a then-innovative concept in retailing: the one-stop department store. He chose this 1870s cast-iron building for his new store after correctly figuring that the area would flourish along with the opening of the new Brooklyn Bridge. The original store was fitted with stunning amenities and luxuries, such as lounging parlors for tired female shoppers, and a mineral spa. Renovated and enlarged in the 1920s, the Art Deco building boasted paned glass, twenty-foot ceilings, and brass-and-glass elevators.

✪ **Brooklyn Borough Hall.** 209 Joralemon Street, between Adams and Court streets. Mon.–Fri., 9 A.M.–5 P.M. Free tours are on Tuesdays, 1 P.M.; Call 855-7882, ext. 51 for details.

A New York City landmark, Borough Hall was built in 1846–51, and is one of New York's most fabulous Greek Revival buildings. Dating from the era when Brooklyn was a city separate from Manhattan (they merged in 1898), it is larger than City Hall and considerably more sumptuous. High points include a hammered brass cupola restored by the same French craftsmen who restored the Statue of Liberty, a spectacular courtroom, grand rotunda, and portico, and a gorgeous marble exterior. Today it is the office of Brooklyn's Borough President.

Brooklyn Friends School. 375 Pearl Street, near Willoughby Street. 852-1029.

Now located in the original Brooklyn Law School building, Brooklyn Friends School was started in 1867 by the descendants of early Quaker settlers, and was located in the basement of the **Friends Meeting House** (see page 232), still located on Schermerhorn Street. Today it is a highly regarded coed private school which continues to teach Quaker values, such as individualism and pacifism, to a diverse student body. An Academy Award–winning documentary, *Close Harmony,* captured the experience of a multigeneration chorus based at the school. It was also the birthplace of the **Brooklyn Youth Chorus**.

✪ **City of Brooklyn Fire Headquarters.** 365–367 Jay Street, between Willoughby and Myrtle avenues.

"This is a building to write home about" is what the late Elliot Willensky, Brooklyn's official historian and co-editor of the authoritative *AIA Guide to New York,* said about this little building. Go see for yourself.

First Free Congregational Church, now part of **Polytechnic Institute.** 311 Bridge Street.

From the mid-nineteenth century until the early twentieth century, this church was home to Brooklyn's oldest African-American congregation. After the congregation, known as the Bridge Street African Weslyan Methodist Episcopalian Church (A.W.M.E), moved to Bedford-Stuyvesant, the church was used as a factory. It was renovated by Polytechnic, and is now used as a student center. (See Bedford-Stuyvesant chapter, page 25.)

✪ **Friends Meeting House.** 110 Schermerhorn Street, off Boerum Place. 625-8705.

Quakers have been worshipping in Brooklyn since 1657. This landmark building reflects the values of Quakerism: simplicity and democracy. It is still used by the Brooklyn Monthly Meeting of the religious Society of Friends, which was founded in 1837, and has an affiliation with the progressive **Brooklyn Friends School** nearby, which was founded here in 1867.

Long Island University. University Plaza–Flatbush Avenue, between Willoughby and DeKalb avenues, 488-1015.

Just a few blocks down Flatbush Avenue from the Manhattan Bridge, LIU maintains a twenty-two-acre campus. More than forty nationalities are represented among the 11,000 students. Lectures and concerts are sometimes open to the public; to learn more, contact the Office of Public Relations, LIU, Brooklyn, NY 11201.

LIU houses one of the few remaining grand theaters from Brooklyn's past. Metcalf Hall, at the corner of Flatbush and DeKalb, was once the Brooklyn Paramount, which staged big-name shows with performers like Frank Sinatra. In 1933 scenes from the original *King Kong* movie were filmed here. The theater's 1930s vintage Wurlitzer organ, one of New York City's largest, is still used.

Marriott Hotel. Brooklyn Renaissance Plaza, 333 Adams Street, 246-7000 or (800) 228–9290.

Normally, a hotel wouldn't be listed as a "cultural attraction," but this spanking-new complex, which opened in 1998, is the first major hotel built in Brooklyn in *sixty years*—since the 1930s. An anchor in the revitalization of Downtown Brooklyn, the Marriott is a tremendous new amenity for American and foreign tourists, businesspeople, and Brooklynites. It is next to the **MetroTech** complex, and is located within a five-minute walk of the

Brooklyn Bridge. It has a restaurant, health club—and also a gift shop and some artwork featuring . . . what else? Brooklyn. The Marriott fills the gap left when the grand old St. George Hotel, now used as a residence, went out of business. Tours of Brooklyn now depart from the Marriott.

MetroTech Center. A sixteen-acre site bounded by Flatbush Avenue, Willoughby Street, Jay Street and Tech Place, 488-8200.

MetroTech is a large office and retail facility located in the heart of downtown Brooklyn, just minutes from the Brooklyn and Manhattan Bridges, and adjacent to the Marriott Hotel. Built in the 1990s, it is occupied by large corporate employers such as Bell Atlantic, Brooklyn Union Gas, Chemical Bank, Bear Stearns, and SIAC, whose employees, taken together, number about sixteen thousand. MetroTech is also the site of a leading engineering university, **Polytechnic University**.

There are summer lunchtime concerts, displays of public art, an urban garden festival, and other events in the MetroTech Commons.

Why is this particular office space noteworthy in a city which, after all, is filled with offices? MetroTech is more than just real estate; it has been a hard-won battle to reestablish commercial life in Downtown Brooklyn. The renaissance brought about by this new development, and the influence of MetroTech Business Improvement District and private investors has substantially improved the area for residents, workers, and visitors alike.

✪ **New York City Transit Museum.** Corner of Boerum Place and Schermerhorn Street, 243-3060. Tues.–Fri., 10 A.M.–5 P.M.; weekends, noon–5 P.M. Admission is $3 for adults; $1.50 for kids under 17 and seniors.

A must-see. Kids of all ages will love pretending they are passengers in this subway museum, authentically located underground in an obsolete subway station. Some of the beautifully restored old subway cars are open for visitors to walk through. The museum is home to a complete history of New York's mass transit system, the second largest in the world. It features fully restored cars of every maker type plus models of trolleys, fare collection boxes, memorabilia, and a scale model of the entire New York City system. Visitors can take a turn at the wheel of a MTA bus. The museum runs wonderful special events, such as the "Celebration of a Century of Buses," "Catch all the Trains You Missed," "Fare Collection," "Engineering in Transit: Past, Present and Future," and a photo exhibit of bus riders entitled "Personally, I Don't Like Cabs."

Polytechnic University—Center for Advanced Technology in Telecommunications. 333 Jay Street, near Flatbush Avenue, 260-3087.

Many Brooklynites aren't even aware that in our midst is one of the nation's leading engineering institutes. Polytechnic was founded in 1854 in

Brooklyn, and, as the nation's second oldest private engineering and science center, boasts over 37,000 alumni. Today it is training a diverse student body in telecommunications, information science, and technology management. Polytechnic was instrumental in spurring the development of **MetroTech**, a combined academic and commercial part that has significantly transformed part of downtown Brooklyn. In 1998, Polytechnic received from a retired faculty member a surprise endowment of more than $150 million, catapulting it into one of the top scientific schools in terms of its per capita endowment ratio.

U.S. Post Office and Court House, Brooklyn Central Office. 271–301 Cadman Plaza West.

Still in use after over a century of stamping, sending, and dispatching, this ornate Romanesque-style building is a Brooklyn landmark, and indeed an official New York City historic landmark as well. There's a terrific Philatelic Center inside that has interesting displays of commemorative stamps and offers a free booklet for kids on how to start a stamp collection.

NOTABLE DOWNTOWN RESTAURANTS

Archives Restaurant and Bar. Marriott Hotel, Renaissance Plaza, 333 Adams Street, 222-6543. Daily, 11 A.M.–3 P.M., and brunch on weekends.

It's more Miami than Brooklyn, and this large, carpeted dining room and bar makes the perfect meeting place for a Brooklyn version of the corporate hotel experience. An eclectic menu reflects the local culture, offering jerk chicken wings and "Sheepshead Bay fish chowder." It's a great place for a business meeting, or to bring out-of-towners, who can join in the fun with the "Brooklyn Borough Sampler" of smoked salmon with potato cake, prawn and caponata, mozzarella with eggplant tapénade and hummus with pita.

For kosher special events, there is a dedicated kosher kitchen and open chupah.

✪ **Gage & Tollner.** 372 Fulton Street, between Boerum and Smith streets, 875-5181. Daily: lunch, 11:30 A.M.–3:30 P.M., and dinner 5–10 P.M. Closed Sun. Valet parking. Lunch reservations required.

A New York City landmark, Victorian-style Gage & Tollner was established in 1897, when Brooklyn was a bustling port—and an independent city. Today, the restaurant draws people from all over for its turn-of-the-century ambience, with mahogany tables, gas chandelier lighting, old-fashioned mirrors, and old-time waiters. This old jewel has been restored and upgraded twice since the mid 1980s. Brooklyn's most-written-about restaurant is located just two blocks from the new Marriott Hotel, and just a hop, skip, and a jump from the **Brooklyn Bridge**. The shellfish dishes are the best thing on the menu.

✪ **Junior's.** 386 Flatbush Avenue, corner of DeKalb Avenue, 852-5257. Sun.–Wed., 6:30–12:30 A.M.; Thurs., 6:30–1 A.M.; Fri.–Sat., 6:30–2 A.M.

Roll across the Manhattan Bridge and up Flatbush Avenue on the Brooklyn side; you can't miss big, brightly lit Junior's. The menu lists just about every deli item your hungry heart could desire: cheese and cherry blintzes, hamburgers, corned beef, good pickles, and ice cream, sundaes. It is clean, urban, and bright, and at any time of day the customers might include cabbies, students from **Pratt Institute** and **Long Island University** across the street, artsy types from **BAM**, and people who just absolutely need a piece of Junior's famous cheesecake (best when plain). Entrées run about $12; cheesecakes to take home are $13 to $15, and you can FedEx a cheesecake anywhere in the country. If you get one of their huge deli sandwiches to go, plan to share it with a friend, unless you are a football linebacker or very, very pregnant.

Bars, Cafés, and Fast Food

Au Bon Pain. MetroTech Mall, 624-9598. Mon.–Fri., 6:30 A.M.–8 P.M. Closed weekends.

Bank executives, construction workers, and brainy engineers from nearby Brooklyn Polytechnic University rub shoulders while waiting on line for the unimaginative, but predictably decent salads, sandwiches, muffins, and coffee at this popular cafeteria. The breads are good, and sourdough bagels are baked fresh daily.

Flaming Embers. 52 Willoughby Street, near Lawrence Street, 403-9700, fax 403-0414. Mon.–Fri., 10:30 A.M.–11:30 P.M., weekends until 2 A.M.

Meat and potatoes, barbecue and fried shrimp—ordered by fax—are the specialties here. You may know Flaming Embers restaurant on 85th Street near Third Avenue in Manhattan; in their Brooklyn location, you can get homemade soups, or their #1 Seller: The "King" 14 oz. T-bone steak for under $10.

SHOPPING

Alpine Beauty Supply. 66 Willoughby Street, corner of Lawrence Street, 243-9121. Mon.–Fri., 8 A.M.–7 P.M.; Sat., 8:30 A.M.–7 P.M.; closed Sun.

Alpine Beauty Supply, a classic New York City multiethnic experience, sells an astonishing number of specialized hair products aimed primarily at an African-American market. Up front there's a huge inventory of wigs, and you'll also find imported (from the Dominican Republic) beeswax concoctions for braided hair and a collection of fabulous hair pieces made by Mo Town Tresses.

✪ **Barclay School Supplies.** 166 Livingston, off Jay Street, 875-2424. Mon.–Fri., 9 A.M.–5 P.M.

Parents of preschool through high school students, take note: Barclay's School supplies, located in the same building as the Board of Education of the City of New York, is where the teachers shop for their classrooms, and where you too can purchase durable, reasonably priced educational gear for your favorite youngster. Among the thousands of items they sell are maps and globes, flash cards for math and foreign languages, books, art supplies, wall calendars, English writing workbooks, and much more. This is one store that almost nobody but teachers know about, because it is located on the second floor of an office building.

Well worth a special trip. Call ahead if you are searching for a particular item; if it's not in stock, they might order it for you.

✪ **Bridge Street Fabric Shops.** Bridge Street, off Willoughby Street.

You'll have to look long and hard before you find a better collection of good, cheap fabrics and sewing notions. Some are 100 percent cotton (including eyelet in a half-dozen colors) and some are poly blends (with wool, satin, cotton) but the prices are all very low, ranging from $1 to $5 a yard. Among the half-dozen other fabric shops on this strip are: **Jay Fabrics** at 383 Bridge Street (624-3211) and **Fabric Discount Stores** at 392 Bridge Street (625–7200). **SewRite** at 388 Bridge Street (522-2525) sells $10-per-yard upholstery fabric.

Fulton Mall. Between Flatbush Avenue and Boerum Place, and Schermerhorn Street and the new MetroTech complex.

The Fulton Mall, anchored by Macy's (situated in what used to be the historic A&S building), includes two hundred stores, many of which are chain stores, such as Footlocker and Nobody Beats the Wiz (long gone are the old timers such as Namm's and Martin's) plus many small, low-price stores selling clothing, shoes, electronics, pharmaceuticals, and miscellaneous items. Fulton Mall is often disregarded because of a low-income, almost bazaarlike quality to the storefronts, but things may change in the twenty-first century: an improvement campaign is underway by the local business association and **MetroTech** to upgrade the Mall's image and to publicize to major retailers the extraordinary volume of shoppers who pass through here daily.

The Gallery at MetroTech: Flatbush Avenue and Willoughby Street.

A large indoor shopping mall is anchored by a Toys "Я" US store.

Save-A-Thon. 411 Bridge Street, off Willoughby Street, 852-5757. Mon.–Sat., 9 A.M.–7 P.M.

One of a chain, Save-A-Thon advertises itself as "New York's largest sewing machine, fabric and craft center." It's a handy, inexpensive place to go to get doll molds, fake flowers, baskets, T-shirt paints, and $3-per-yard juvenile print fabrics, foams, sewing machines, and related repairs and accessories.

Sid's Hardware and Home Center Corp. 345 Jay Street off Willoughby Street, 875-2259. Mon.–Fri., 8 A.M.–6 P.M.; weekends, 9 A.M.–5 P.M.

Some people just love hardware stores, and if you count yourself among them, stop in at Sid's. Long considered Brooklyn's best local hardware store, Sid's is the place to go when you need a wrench, garden hose, duct tape, and even a two-by-four piece of lumber. Some people have been known to buy Sid's gift certificates to give as birthday presents.

W.C. Art & Drafting Supply Co. 1 MetroTech Center, at Jay Street, 855-8078. Mon.–Fri., 9 A.M.–6 P.M.; Sat., 9 A.M.–5 P.M.; closed Sun.

One of the best all-purpose art supply stores in Brooklyn, W.C. sells fine art and drafting supplies, computer papers, and offers a ton of hobby and craft supply items that are often difficult to find elsewhere. And it is conveniently located next to **Sid's Hardware**, a long-standing Brooklyn institution.

Yolly Fabrics. 226 Livingston Street, between Hoyt and Elm streets, 875-0334. Mon.–Fri., 9 A.M.–6 P.M.; Sat., 10 A.M.–8 P.M.

Yolly Fabrics, located one block away from Macy's, sells fabric, notably a limited but highly unusual collection of imported African fabrics and exclusive screen prints. Some of the Senegalese and Nigerian fabrics cost an affordable $5 per yard. In addition, there are a half-dozen bolts of gorgeous decorative materials used for African ceremonial dress.

HOTELS

✪ **New York Marriott Brooklyn.** Brooklyn Renaissance Plaza, 333 Adams Street, 246-7000, or (800) 228-9900.

Brooklyn's only full-service upscale hotel, the Marriott has 376 guest rooms, huge meeting and ballroom spaces, and is spanking new. Look for the artwork reflecting Brooklyn themes. Call well in advance—lots of groups book here.

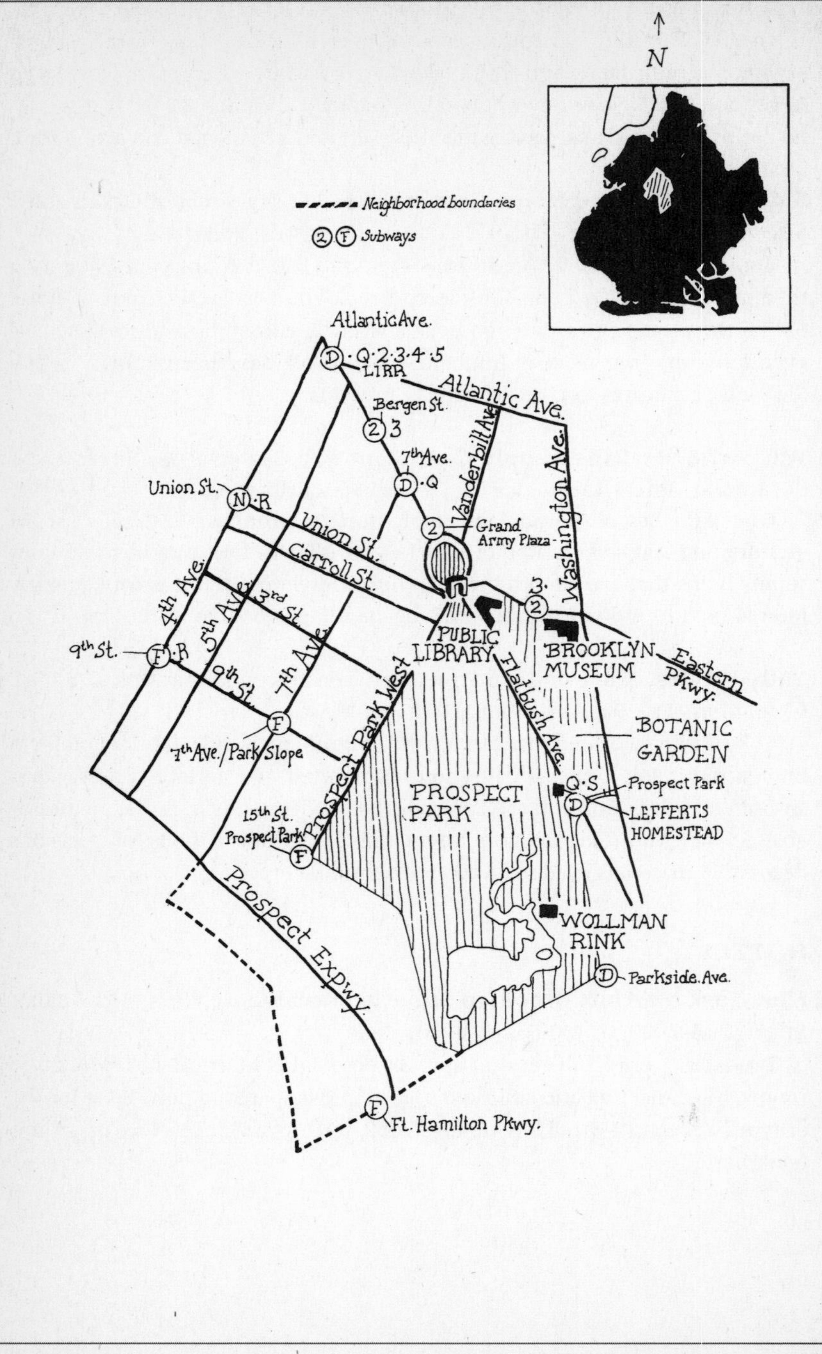

N
Neighborhood Boundaries
Subways
Atlantic Ave.
D·Q·2·3·4·5
LIRR
Atlantic Ave.
Bergen St.
2 3
7th Ave.
D·Q
Union St.
N·R
Vanderbilt Ave.
Washington Ave.
2
Grand Army Plaza
Union St.
Carroll St.
4th Ave.
5th Ave.
3rd St.
7th Ave.
3.
2
PUBLIC LIBRARY
BROOKLYN MUSEUM
Eastern PKwy.
9th St.
F·R
9th St.
F
7th Ave./Park Slope
Prospect Park West
Flatbush Ave.
BOTANIC GARDEN
PROSPECT PARK
Q·S
Prospect Park
D
LEFFERTS HOMESTEAD
15th St. Prospect Park
F
Prospect Expwy.
WOLLMAN RINK
D
Parkside Ave.
F
Ft. Hamilton PKwy.

Park Slope

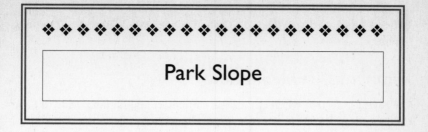

Where it is: Between Flatbush Avenue and 17th Street, sloping down from Prospect Park to 4th Avenue.

What's nearby: Carroll Gardens, Brooklyn Heights, Fort Greene, and Sunset Park.

How to get there:

By car: Take the Manhattan Bridge and continue on Flatbush Avenue approximately two miles, then turn right on 7th Avenue; turn right. Or take the Brooklyn Bridge: take the second exit and immediately turn left onto Tillary Street, then right onto Flatbush Avenue. Continue as noted above.

By subway: The 2 and 3 trains go to Grand Army Plaza and the D train goes to 7th Avenue, both at the north end of Park Slope. The F train will take you to the 7th Avenue stop at 9th Street, toward the southern end of the neighborhood. The M, N, and R stop at Union and 4th Avenue is closest to interesting shops and restaurants on 5th Avenue.

Cab services: Brownstone Cars (789–1536) or Denise Car Service (439-4943). Cost is about $17 to Grand Central Station and $8 to Brooklyn Heights.

Special events: Irish-American Parade (March); brownstone tour through the interiors of restored private landmark homes (third Sunday in May); Cherry Blossom Festival (May); Children's Halloween Parade, 7th Avenue (October); Fireworks (New Year's Eve). Call 788-0055 for year-round events in Prospect Park.

How it got its name: Any neighborhood that slopes downhill from Prospect Park could logically be known as Park Slope.

Historic District: Roughly defined by Flatbush Avenue, Grand Army Plaza, and Prospect Park West up to 14th Street. Bounded by 6th Avenue from Flatbush Avenue to Union Street, by 7th Avenue to 4th Street, and 8th Avenue from 2nd to 14th streets.

Official Landmarks: William B. Cronyn House; Public Bath No. 7, among others.

ABOUT THE NEIGHBORHOOD

The saying goes that when city-loving couples in Manhattan decide to have children they move to fertile Park Slope. Given the stroller gridlock that grips the neighborhood sidewalks on a sunny weekend, that probably is not far off the mark. What draws new residents and visitors alike are the well-preserved brownstones and town houses on Park Slope's many tree-lined streets, as well as the proximity to some of Brooklyn's grandest attractions: **Prospect Park**, the main branch of the **Brooklyn Public Library**, the **Brooklyn Museum**, and the **Brooklyn Botanic Garden**. (See next chapter, "Prospect Park and the Museums.")

The official *Guide to New York City Landmarks* calls Park Slope "one of New York City's most beautiful residential areas." It boasts twenty-four blocks of landmark buildings and charming shops. Huge **Prospect Park** is enticing, with its open fields, jogging paths, pedal boats, the **Wollman Skating Rink**, and the renovated **Prospect Park Carousel** and zoo, the **Prospect Park Wildlife Center**. Nearby, the **Brooklyn Museum** has world-class exhibits of Egyptian artifacts and nineteenth-century American paintings, among others. Visitors travel far and wide to the **Brooklyn Botanic Garden** for its renowned cherry blossom festival and to enjoy the acclaimed **Steinhardt Conservatory**. The imposing and decorative **Central Library**, which is wonderful to look at, has two floors of excellent collections. Elegant **Grand Army Plaza**, which joins Eastern Parkway and Prospect Park, successfully fulfills its designer's dreams that it beautifully mimic the Arc de Triomphe in Paris.

In contrast to Polish Greenpoint, Russian Brighton Beach, and Italian Bensonhurst, Park Slope does not have a predominant ethnic flavor—except perhaps yuppie. The style is casual, and the residents—count among them lawyers, writers, therapists, and businesspeople—tend to be well educated, liberal, and usually from somewhere in America other than Brooklyn. To suit their tastes, the neighborhood bristles with bookstores, nouvelle cuisine takeouts, upscale toy stores, handcraft specialty shops, and even a spectacular Victorian hostelry, **Bed and Breakfast on the Park**. Like a college town, Park Slope's trees and phone poles are papered over with notices announcing concerts, social action group meetings, lost dogs, and **stoop sales** (the vertical equivalent of yard sales).

You certainly won't go hungry in this neighborhood or its environs. There's Thai food at **Lemongrass Grill** and simple Latino dishes at **El Gran Castillo de Jagua,** great Italian food at **Cucina**, Mexican cuisine at the **Santa Fe Bar and Grill**. Along Fifth Avenue you can buy excellent fresh

Italian sausage and imported cheese at **A. S. Fine Foods**, and imported Eastern European specialty items at **Eagle Provisions**. Two local bakeries, **Little Red Hen** and **Cousin John's Cafe**, produce spectacular delicacies.

Architecture lovers will revel in the beautiful nineteenth-century homes and churches here. Amid spires, turrets, bay windows, and rows and rows of evenly matched brownstone stoops are architectural treasures reflecting Italianate and French Second Empire to Greek and Romanesque Revival styles. Among the most outstanding are the mock-Venetian palazzo **Montauk Club** and the parkside mansion in which **Brooklyn Poly Prep** is housed. Just walk along Montgomery Place, Carroll Street, or 6th Avenue to get a sense of the variety and beauty here. The landmark district goes from Park Place to Union Street between 6th and 8th avenues, then from Union Street to 4th Street between Prospect Park West and 7th Avenue.

5th Avenue

A frontier of gentrification, 5th Avenue between Flatbush Avenue and 9th Street sports new and interesting shops—while behind the scenes, a battle rages about keeping rents affordable. Over two dozen new stores opened on this strip between 1996 and 1998. You can easily identify some of the newcomers, including **Clay Play**, a paint-it-yourself pottery studio, and the **Rising Café**. Others, such as the immensely promising **Coco Roco** restaurant and the **Lopez Bakery** seem part of the fabric of this mixed Latino community.

A number of very good restaurants have been in the vanguard of this transition: **Cucina, Mike & Tony's, Aunt Suzie's**, and **Ozzie's**. The block near Cucina also boasts a wonderful Italian food store, **A.S. Fine Foods**, and across the street **Erica's Rugelach**. Stay tuned for more developments on the revitalization of 5th Avenue in Park Slope.

Whether you come by subway, car, or bicycle, you can walk through most of Park Slope in well under an hour. But don't come with expectations of a quick foray; the sights can keep you occupied for a full day.

For Brooklynophiles Only

Some of the listings in this chapter legitimately belong in the neighborhoods of Prospect Heights, Prospect Gardens, Windsor Terrace, or Crown Heights. We've included them here because they are relatively close to Park Slope and often are combined with visits to this neighborhood. Our apologies to purists.

Historical Notes

Settled in the seventeenth century by Dutch farmers, Park Slope remained the province of two large families until the mid-1800s, when developers began subdividing the area into neat rows of streets and avenues. The Litchfield family's mansion still presides over Prospect Park; today it is the headquarters for the Parks Department.

When developers first began selling homes here in the mid-1800s, German and English upper-middle-class families settled in the brownstones in what is now Park Slope's landmark district. The area came to be known as a "streetcar suburb," a pleasant place to live with easy access to Manhattan, just two miles away. (The description is still apt today.) Park Slope even gained its own version of Central Park: completed in 1873, Prospect Park was the masterwork of Calvert Vaux and Frederick Law Olmsted, the team that had collaborated on Manhattan's rural jewel. In the latter quarter of the nineteenth century Italian and Irish workingclass immigrants settled in more modest homes in what came to be known as the "South Slope" below broad, tree-lined 9th Street.

Just before the turn of the twentieth century the impressive new mansions being built across from Prospect Park on Prospect Park West and Plaza Street came to be dubbed "Millionaires Row" or "Brooklyn's Gold Coast." Development in the area continued after World War I with large apartment buildings rising on Plaza Street. After World War II the entire neighborhood went into decline—but, as with the rest of brownstone Brooklyn, a revival started in the 1960s that led to the renovation of many homes in Park Slope and the surrounding areas.

Kidstuff

Park Slope is a delightful place for children. **Prospect Park** has it all, from ball fields to a skating rink to tennis. The **Central Library** has an extensive children's book collection and video department. Toys and books abound at the **Brooklyn Museum Children's Shop, Brooklyn's Best Book and Toy Shop**, and **Little Things**. The **Botanic Gardens** and the **Brooklyn Museum of Art** cannot be beat for educational, interesting expeditions.

ENTERTAINMENT

BAM. While not in Park Slope proper, **BAM** (the Brooklyn Academy of Music) and its theater, movies, and other cultural programs, is within walking distance of Park Slope (see p. 116).

Brooklyn Commons. 12th Street and 2nd Avenue area. Under development on east side of Gowanus Canal.

Big changes may be underway here. In 1998, a private developer and New York City Mayor Giuliani announced plans to build a $65-million entertainment and shopping complex on this site. Preliminary plans include a 22-theater multiplex cinema, retail shops, restaurants, a large bowling alley, and a multistory 1,500-car parking garage. Stay tuned.

Pavilion Movie Theater. 118 Prospect Park West at 15th Street, 369–0838.

Opened in the late 1990s, this terrific renovated old movie house shows first-run flicks, and often has lines around the block. It is conveniently located across from Prospect Park, between Windsor Terrace and Park Slope. On weekends a small on-premises café serves light fare.

Plaza Twin Cinema. 314 Flatbush Avenue, near 7th Avenue, 636-0710. Call for show times.

Located virtually on top of the D and F trains' 7th Avenue subway stop, the Plaza Twin is one of Park Slope's two movie houses. With two screens, it shows plenty of first-runs and kiddie hits.

✪ **Puppetworks.** 338 6th Avenue, corner of 4th Street, 965-3391. Weekends; call for show times. Tickets cost $5 for children, $7 for adults.

The true art of puppetry might be lost if it were not for marionette makers and performers like these seasoned professionals who have helped create, among other things, Macy's annual Christmas and Easter puppet shows. The new 100-seat theater is air conditioned. For preschoolers through sixth-graders, the extensive year-round repertoire under the direction of Nicholas Coppola includes two dozen classics such as the *Wizard of Oz, Pinocchio,* and *Sleeping Beauty*. Productions run about forty-five minutes and are well reviewed by everyone from *The New York Times* to the *New York Post*. You can also have your child's birthday party here.

PARKS AND PLAYGROUNDS

Prospect Park. See pages 276–279.

POINTS OF CULTURAL INTEREST

Visitors will find it convenient to go to two major cultural institutions—the **Brooklyn Museum of Art** and the adjacent **Brooklyn Botanic Garden**—in the same trip. Both are a fifteen-minute walk or a five-minute car ride from the heart of Park Slope; see pages 274 and 272.

BAM—the **Brooklyn Academy of Music**—is also very close, a mere ten minutes' walk; see page 115.

Ansonia Clock Factory Coops. 420 13th Street, along 7th Avenue.

This four-story redbrick apartment building was once an abandoned clockworks factory that had employed many Polish and Irish immigrants in the nineteenth century. It is one of five hundred projects undertaken since the 1960s by the Brooklyn Union Gas Company through its "Cinderella" program to help revitalize Brooklyn neighborhoods. The program is still active in up-and-coming neighborhoods along 5th Avenue, and other Brooklyn locations. It has an impressive track record in aiding the revitalization of neighborhoods.

Brooklyn Conservatory of Music. 58 7th Avenue, corner of Lincoln Place, 622-3300. Call for schedule of classes, concerts, and other events.

If you hear music wafting down 7th Avenue, it's likely to come from the Brooklyn Conservatory of Music. Under new leadership by David Rivell (previously of Lincoln Center), the once-sleepy Conservatory has come to life on its 100th birthday in a way that reminds observers of Gepetto's impact on Pinnochio.

A sorely needed $2.5-million renovation is sprucing up the Conservatory's graceful 1881 Victorian Gothic mansion. Class acts, such as jazz saxophonists Jimmy Heath and Billy Harper (whose résumés respectively include stints with Dizzy Gillespie, Miles Davis, and John Coltrane; Max Roach and Gil Evans) have been booked; tickets are just $15. And if you need a musician for a special event, their "Find a Musician" referral service can help.

Founded in the nineteenth century by German-Americans in the model of a classical European conservatory, the twenty-first-century Conservatory offers instruction in Broadway melodies, jazz and gospel singing, Latin jazz, and African drumming. Together with its Queens division, it is one of the largest community music schools of the arts in the U.S. Stay tuned for more exciting developments.

✪ **Brooklyn Public Library, Central Branch.** Grand Army Plaza, corner of Flatbush Avenue and Eastern Parkway, 780-7810. Information and reference: 780-7700. Call for hours and location of other branches.

Brooklyn's library system is one of the largest in the United States. This is the main branch, housed in a 1930s landmark building that was part of a WPA project.

Inside, you will find Internet access service and related electronic services, part of a grant from Bill Gates' Microsoft, as well as excellent (if more traditional) librarian services. Kids love it too. There's a large reading room for preschoolers, and a study area for high school and grammar school students. Apart from this, there are also frequent readings and movies. The library café on the ground floor and the upstairs cafeteria are useful because the nearest shops and restaurants are a few blocks away.

The Brooklyn Collection includes the archives of the original *Brooklyn Eagle* newspaper, of which Walt Whitman was editor.

The Central Library is located within a five-minute walk of the **Brooklyn Botanical Gardens** and the **Brooklyn Museum of Art**, and within a ten-minute walk of Park Slope's 7th Avenue.

Coffee Smell . . .

Where does that wonderful aroma of roasting coffee that percolates through Park Slope come from? The Chock Full o' Nuts factory that takes up most of the block between 3rd and 4th avenues, between Baltic and Butler avenues, reportedly processes over 60 tons of coffee a day, and works an almost-24-hour shift.

DanceWave, Inc./Kids Café Festival. For information and locations, call 622-1810.

A nonprofit dance organization under the direction of Diane Jacobowitz that produces the work of children in Brooklyn and throughout the New York City area, including the popular Kids Café Festival. Performances are held at venues such as the **Brooklyn Music School.**

✪ **Gospel Choirs.**

Crowds galore—as many as 5,000 on a Sunday—attend the 250-person Grammy Award winning **Brooklyn Tabernacle choir**, so come early to get a seat; see listing on page 248.

Gowanus Arts Exchange. 421 5th Avenue at 8th Street, 832-0018. Call for schedule of events and classes.

One of the artistic treasures of Brooklyn, this spirited community arts institution offers a full range of programs in avant-garde dance, theater, performance art and music, with as many as seventy performances in a year. In operation for over a decade, the Gowanus (named after the nearby canal) is home to professional performances of works by an ethnically diverse, inventive crop of new artists from Brooklyn and beyond. Gowanus is also host to a range of programs for public school students, artists-in-residence, and other community-based arts groups.

Note for parents: Book early for the popular weekend "Groundhog Series" held during the winter doldrums months; music, puppetry, mime, and storytelling programs brighten up even the dreariest weekends.

✪ **Montauk Club.** 25 8th Avenue, corner of Lincoln Place, 638-0800. Not open to the public.

One of Park Slope's finest old buildings, the 1891 Venetian Gothic palazzo is surrounded by a thin moat of neatly trimmed green grass. The brass rails up the steps to the entrance are usually well buffed. The Montauk Club houses both a private social club (and it is often used as a set by film crews in need of a beautiful manor house interior) and five gorgeous apartments. In true Victorian tradition, the club once had a private parlor and separate entrance set aside for the female set.

Old Stone House Museum. J. J. Byrne Park, between 4th and 5th avenues and 3rd and 4th street (take F and R trains to 9th Street and 4th Avenue, respectively), 212 726-8062. Call for schedule.

Imagine cannons blazing and scruffy American troups in battle against the British—right here. Rebuilt in the 1930s using original stones from this Revolutionary War–era site, the Old Stone House museum celebrates Brooklyn's role in the American Revolution. A small exhibit features a diorama of the house is it was on August 27, 1776, during a bloody skirmish in the Battle of Brooklyn. There are regularly scheduled public programs and periodic special events to dramatize these historical events.

✪ **Park Slope Civic Council House Tour.** 832-8227. Fourth Sunday in May, noon-5 P.M.

Park Slope is one of Brooklyn's finest brownstone neighborhoods, an activist community, and the heart of the brownstone revival—so it's no surprise that the area's house tour, popular since 1959, is the oldest of its sort in all of New York City. Up to eight hundred people, many seeking ideas for their own renovations, sign up for the tour of the interiors of brownstone homes. History and architecture buffs are also big participants. Each of the ten to fifteen homes on the tour is staffed with knowledge volunteers to answer questions.

Poly Prep. Prospect Park West, corner of 1st Street, 768-7890.

Want to get an idea of how the true pioneers of Park Slope lived? Looking over Prospect Park, this fabulous 1883 Romanesque Revival mansion has a double outdoor staircase and turret windows and was originally the home of Henry Carlton Hulbertx, the vice president of the South Brooklyn

Savings Institution. Today it houses a private school, so plan to appreciate it mainly from the outside. As you walk the half-dozen blocks from Grand Army Plaza, you will pass a number of elegant mansions built in the same era.

Prospect Hall. 263 Prospect Avenue, between 5th and 6th avenues, 788-0777.

Built before the turn of the 20th century, this old opera house, restaurant, and speakeasy gradually fell into disrepair until its new owners restored it as a catering hall. They don't advertise it, but if you call ahead you may be able to convince them to take you on a tour. If not, walk in for a quick peek at the main staircase just inside the front door. The Grand Ballroom, complete with two balconies, holds up to fifteen hundred people and was the scene of a wedding celebration in the film *Prizzi's Honor*. The Men's Card Room, a former speakeasy, appears in the film *The Cotton Club*. The hall also contains the first elevator ever installed in Brooklyn (it still works). If ever there were an ideal place to throw a *big* party, this is it.

Public Bath #7 Theater and Gallery. 4th Avenue, corner of President Street.

Built in the 1911 as part of a city-wide campaign to improve public health, this old, interesting-looking bathhouse—an architectural landmark—sat empty for decades. In 1998 it was renovated to the tune of a half-million dollars, in the interest of transforming it into a performing arts and exhibition space. There's a 1947 trolley on the premises, and a new mural on the front of the building. Stay tuned.

✪ **Soldiers and Sailors Memorial Arch.** Flatbush Avenue, at Eastern Parkway, 788-0055. Sat. and Sun. only.

Known as America's "Arc de Triomphe," this imposing structure was built at a cost of $250,000 and unveiled in 1902 to celebrate the fallen heroes of the Civil War. From the top you'll get an idea of the urban vision that park designers Olmsted and Vaux had in 1860 for bringing European-style greenery and airiness into cramped city life. The view includes the landmark entrance to Prospect Park, the Manhattan skyline, the monumental **Brooklyn Central Public Library** (see page 244) and the first few blocks of Eastern Parkway, built in 1870 as the first American tree-lined promenade with benches and plantings. The six-story spiral staircase to the "Quadriga," the horse-drawn chariot sculpture at the top of the arch, is a fairly easy climb. Look for the bas-reliefs of presidents Lincoln and Grant on the inner sides of the archway.

Spoke the Hub Dancing. 748 Union Street, off 6th Avenue, 857-5158. Call for calendar of events and programs.

One of the neighborhood's creative whirling dervishes, Elise Long has created an eclectic, soul-warming institution here which gives classes, performances, and generally liberates the imagination. Spoke the Hub and the **Gowanus Exchange** were one institution many years ago, and now the Slope has the benefit of not one, but two highly regarded dance and performance outfits. Check it out.

William B. Cronyn House, 291 Ninth Street.

A stucco-covered house with a slate roof built in the 1850s in French Second Empire style. When built, the house was surrounded by farms; later it was transformed into the headquarters of an ink company, and today it is again in use as a private home.

Other Points of Interest

✪ **Brooklyn Tabernacle.** 290 Flatbush Avenue, near 7th Avenue, 783-0942. Sunday services are at 9 A.M., noon, 3 P.M., and 6 P.M.

Known for its contemporary gospel music, Brooklyn Tabernacle's nondenominational Sunday services have a huge 180-person choir with musical backup equipment that is so high-tech it looks like a recording studio. They won a Grammy Award in 1996 for best gospel choir album. The service is, to say the least, spirited. Come early; seats fill up fast.

✪ **Chassidic Art Institute (CHAI).** 375 Kingston Avenue, between Carroll and Crown streets in Crown Heights, 774-9149 or 778-8808. Sun.–Thurs., non–7 P.M.; Fri., closes early; closed Sat.

Not just Jewish, but specifically Hasidic folk art and paintings have been shown for twenty years in this unusual gallery located in nearby Crown Heights. Like Hasidic prayer, the art is fervent and emotional, exploring a Hasidic view of Jewish history, rituals, family life, and Jewish travail in the European ghetto. The nonprofit gallery was founded by community leaders after a 1977 **Brooklyn Museum** (page 274) show on Hasidic art drew ten thousand visitors. More than 100 artists are represented, including increasing numbers of Russian émigrés, who were prohibited from depicting religious themes in their work while living in the Soviet Union. Posters start at $10; paintings go up to $10,000.

NOTABLE PARK SLOPE RESTAURANTS, BARS, AND CAFÉS

al di la. 248 Fifth Avenue, off Carroll Street. 783-4565. Dinner only, Wed-Mon., 6 P.M.–midnight. Closed Tuesdays.

Comfortable and rustic, al di la has made a hit with its trattoria-style Northern Italian cuisine. Appetizers run about $6, pastas from $8 to $10, and other entrées up to about $15. They don't have a kids' menu but will happily accomodate with small portions or simplified dishes. Recommended for a casual or family dining experience.

Aunt Suzie's Kitchen. 247 5th Avenue, between Carroll Street and Garfield Place, 788-3377. Sun.–Thurs., 5–10 P.M.; Fri.–Sat., 5 P.M.–midnight.

The *New York Post* called this "one of the best under $15" meals in New York City. Not only is the Italian fare home-cooked, but the place feels like home. Specials change but are likely to include several fish dishes and items such as spinach manicotti. The high-ceilinged dining room is filled with wooden tables of different sizes and shapes. A small table at the front has a selection of plate-size games and kiddie books for the picking, making this a good place to take little ones.

Blah Blah Lounge. 501 11th Street between 7th and 8th avenues. 369-2524. Wed–Sun., 6 P.M.–1 A.M.

Relax on a sofa in this living room–like getaway, a nonsmoking lounge where you can hang out around a working fireplace, enjoy a few drinks, and *blah, blah, blah* with your pals, both old and new. The winter menu is likely to offer items such as angel hair pasta and shrimp or vegetable empañadas, with lighter fare in the summer; the crowd is young, professional, and artistic.

Bookstore and Museum Cafés

✪ **Brooklyn Museum Café.** 200 Eastern Parkway, corner of Washington Avenue, 638-5000. Wed.–Sun., 10 A.M.–5 P.M.; closed Mon., Tues.

Drink in the culture at BMA's moderately priced cafeteria, in a renovated space on the ground floor of the museum—and take in an exhibit while you're at it.

Café at Barnes & Noble (see page 264).

The standard B&N cafe, conveniently located near the Methodist Hospital and **Prospect Park**.

✪ **Café at Community Bookstore.** 143 7th Ave., 783-3075. Mon.–Fri., 9 A.M.–9:45 P.M.; Sat., 9 A.M.–10 P.M.; Sun., 10 A.M.–10 P.M.

A classy little café, with a postage-stamp garden with a dwarf-sized pond, make this bookstore nook a favorite meeting place for locals. They serve locally made breads and muffins, Southwest black bean salad, Provence pasta salad, sandwiches, and coffees. Check out the impressive calendar of author readings.

✪ **Terrace Café.** Brooklyn Botanic Garden, 622-4432. Tues–Sun., 10 A.M.–5 P.M.; closed Mon.

Lunch in May or June is heaven in this informal outdoor café in one of New York City's two major botanical gardens. Just getting there, walking past the Japanese gardens, Daffodil Hill, and rows of spring flowers in bloom is half the fun. It's jammed on the weekends, so try to come for a late breakfast or late lunch.

✪ **Christie's.** 334 Flatbush Avenue, one block east of 7th Avenue at the corner of Sterling Place, 636-9746. Mon.–Sat., 9 A.M.–7 P.M.; Sun., 10 A.M.–5 P.M.

This hole-in-the-wall take-out shop serves some of the best beef, chicken, and spicy vegetable Jamaican patties in all Brooklyn. And their sweet coconut turnovers will have you oohing and ahhing for more. Tourists often buy just a patty and a soda, but the regulars know that the best meal here is a patty laid inside one of their fluffy coco breads. Ask for a "patty sandwich."

✪ **Coco Roco.** 392 5th Avenue, between 6th and 7th streets, 965-3376. Mon.–Thurs., 12:30–10 P.M.; Fri.–Sat., 12:30–11 P.M.; Sun., noon–10 P.M.

Hmmm, what's Peruvian food like? Forget the passport, just take a quick trip to Park Slope's new rave-review restaurant, a startup powered by three young brothers from the mountainous Andes. Their menu reflects coastal tastes; for instance, ceviche papaya (red snapper marinated in papaya, ginger, and lime sauce) and *tacu-tacu con pescado,* a sweet potato–crusted fish with Peruvian rice-and-bean risotto, salsa, and yucca fritters. The beef and chicken dishes—some made with purple cornmeal crusts—are tasty. The chefs have toned down the spiciness for gringo palates, but will happily add more chilies upon request. Portions are huge, and the presentation is colorful. Entrées run about $12 per person.

Corn Bread Cafe. 434 Seventh Avenue between 14th and 15th streets, 768-3838. Mon.–Fri., 5–11 P.M.; Sat., 11 A.M.–11 P.M.; Sun., 11 A.M.–10 P.M.

For a change of pace go south, my friend. True to its name, Corn Bread Cafe serves homey meals with a Southern flair: butter-melting warm corn bread, tasty crab cakes, and authentic gumbos. You can make a meal of special side dishes, from collard greens to sweet yams. Entrees are in the $10–15 range.

Cousin John's Bakery. 70 7th Avenue, between Berkeley Place and Lincoln Place, 622-7333 or 768-2020. Sun.–Thurs., 7 A.M.–11 P.M.; Fri. and Sat., 7–1 A.M.

Chocolate lovers will think they've gone to heaven, and the smell of croissants, scones, and muffins will make your mouth water. The fruit pastries, such as kiwi and blueberry cream tarts, are both beautiful and tasty. Homemade ice cream and sorbet—try the cassis or champagne flavors—are sinful.

✪ **Cucina.** 256 5th Avenue, between Carroll Street and Garfield Place, 230-0711. Mon.–Thurs., 5:30–10 P.M.; Fri.–Sat., 5:30–10:30 P.M.; Sun., 5–10 P.M.

Cucina is one of Brooklyn's best modern Italian restaurants—and in a borough stuffed like a ravioli with great Italian food, that's saying a lot. You will be well taken care of at Cucina, which is why people come here for special occasions, with special guests, and when they need the comforts of good service. When you walk in, past the bar, a cornucopia of antipasti catch your eye. The specials are always excellent, and standard menu items—from a perfect penne to roasted chicken and carefully cooked fish dishes—satisfyingly tasty. Save room for the fabulous chocolate plate dessert. Like many of the brownstones around it, the ambience in this large, popular two-dining room restaurant is elegant but informal. If you see a white-haired gentleman looking like the proprietor, it's Anthony Scicchitano, who has given this area lots of food pleasures; he launched both **Mike & Tony's** and the **A. S. Fine Foods** on the same block.

Dizzy's. 511 9th Street, corner of 8th Avenue, 499-1966. Mon.–Fri., 6 A.M.–10 P.M.; Sat.–Sun., 9 A.M.–10 P.M.

A newcomer to the neighborhoods, Dizzy's, a "finer diner," is just that—a diner with better food (and a more limited menu). The French fries are hand-cut, the designer omelets use plum tomatoes and sweet onions, and the house salad is mesclun greens. Come early for Sunday brunch and grab the sofa seating.

El Gran Castillo de Jagua. 345 Flatbush Avenue, corner of Carlton Avenue, 622-8700. Daily, 7 A.M.–midnight.

There's almost always an urbane, working class crowd at the take-out counter for the authentic Dominican food at rock-bottom prices. You can also eat in at the restaurant section, which, with a jukebox and red plastic tablecloths, is unpretentious and fine for families. Food includes plenty of rice dishes, fried green plantains, shrimp soupy rice, fried chicken and chips, and paella. Breakfast specials are under $3, and average dinner entrées range from $7 to $12. It is conveniently located across from the **Plaza Twin** movie theater (see page 243). Free delivery is available.

✪ **Elora.** 272 Prospect Park West, off 17th Street, Windsor Terrace, 788-6190.

Just a stone's throw away from Prospect Park, Elora's is one of those ". . . but keep it a secret" restaurants. An extensive menu of Spanish and Mexican dishes includes a vegetarian platter, brochette with meat, or lamb and shrimp topped with a thick stewy brown sauce, plus lobster and broiled chops. If you haven't eaten for a month, try the tasty, outrageously oversized chicken fajita, brought to the table steaming hot in a skillet. Desserts are recommended—note the plural—especially the melt-in-the-mouth chocolate mousse cake. All this for a song; entrées range from $9 to $13. Café tables outside are the best bet, weather permitting.

Eva's Restaurant. 551 4th Avenue, corner 16th Street, 788-9354. Daily, 8 A.M.–8 P.M. Cash only.

Good seafood, Spanish style (Ecuadorian, actually), at low, low prices is why people come to Eva's. There are no menus and little English is spoken, but the fish stews, fresh daily soups, and shrimp dishes are very good.

Farrell's Bar. 215 Prospect Park West, at 16th Street, 788-8779. Daily, 11–1 A.M.

Farrell's was reputedly one of the first bars to open in Brooklyn after Prohibition was repealed, and it has stayed the way it was: an old-fashioned Irish saloon. Its decor is polished wood, mirrors, and brass, and it's strictly standing-room only. Run by Farrell family members, the place echoes with old memories, and is a favorite with cops, firemen, and old-timers.

Fava. 336 7th Avenue, corner of 9th Street, 788-2576. Sun.–Thurs., 11:30 A.M.–11 P.M.; Fri.–Sat., 11:30 A.M.–midnight. Cash only.

From Middle Eastern fare to individual pizzas, salads, and smoothies, Fava's portions are large, and tasty. Whether it's chicken couscous, falafel, or portobello mushrooms that you favor as your main course, you'll receive a hefty helping of rice, lentils, salad, or other sides along with a thick nan, the sour bread favored along the banks of the Euphrates River. Consider takeout, then tote your meal up to nearby Prospect Park.

✪ **Garden Café.** 620 Vanderbilt Avenue, corner of Prospect Place, 857-8863. Tues.–Sat., 6–10 P.M.; closed Sun.–Mon. Call for reservations; street parking available.

A wonderful place, the Garden Café is just a couple of blocks from Park Slope, tucked away on a mixed-income thoroughfare in Prospect Heights. There are just eight tables, and the owner-chef cooks in the nouvelle style, while his wife handles the clientele. The food is fresh, cooked and spiced with flair, and the wine list is substantial, so it is no surprise that this is a neighborhood favorite. Figure on spending $15 and up per entrée.

Gay/Lesbian Cafés and Bars

Park Slope has gained the reputation as being a gay-positive place to live. Whether or not this is true, the Slope does have a rich array of lesbian and gay-owned businesses and watering holes. Lesbian couples can be seen strolling along in the neighborhood, sometimes with babies in tow. And each June, the Brooklyn Gay Pride celebration parades down 7th Avenue and into Prospect Park, where local performers do their best Gloria Gaynor or Tina Turner imitations. Among the local hang-outs are **Rising Café, Sanctuary Lounge,** and **Carry Nation**.

Rising Café. 186 5th Avenue, near Sackett Street, 622-5072. Daily, 11 A.M.–11 P.M. Fri.–Sat., till midnight.

Women of all ages can be found sipping coffee or swigging a beer in this funky, lesbian hot spot. As if the place were your living room you can lounge in the cozy sofas and chairs up front, or head toward the back, where a pool table and TV set make for a lively spot to watch the NCAA finals. There is live music on Friday with a $3 cover. Otherwise, entrance is free and a jukebox provides tunes. The outdoor patio is an added attraction.

Sanctuary Lounge. 333 7th Avenue at 15th Street, 832-9800. Mon.–Thurs., 7 P.M.–3 A.M.; Fri.–Sat. 7 P.M.–4 A.M.; Sun., noon–3 A.M.

Have a drink in the early evening at the classic Sanctuary Lounge and enjoy a mellow mix of men and women, or come out on the first and third Tuesday of the month for a sampling of Brooklyn gay humor during the lounge's comedy nights. A pool table is the centerpiece in this small bar, but there is plenty of room to relax on the couch or a barstool. Large windows facing 7th Avenue give the Sanctuary an open, inviting feel.

Carry Nation. 363 5th Avenue, near 4th Street, 788-0924. Daily, 6 P.M.–4 A.M.

Opened in 1996, Carry Nation claims to be the first gay and lesbian bar in Park Slope. Its owners thought it would be funny to name the bar after the turn-of-the-century prohibitionist Carry Nation, who broke into bars with a hatchet to destroy the evil tonics. Her namesake bar admits women, of course, but the crowd is predominantly male. With a blue-tiled floor and drab mustard-colored walls, the bar slightly resembles an aging elementary school. The cartoons of happy gay couples on the walls however, quickly dispel that image. If the bar's patrons aren't squashed together by the narrow bar, they gravitate toward the pool table in the rear.

Contributed by Andrea Askowitz and Sue Fox.

Great Lakes. 284 Fifth Avenue, corner of 1st Street. 499-3710. Daily, 5 P.M.–A.M..

Come for the jazz and to hang, but don't plan on food. They only serve popcorn and drinks here. But Great Lakes serves up live music Monday through Thursday, often performed by recent music school grads. It's a twenty- and thirty-something scene. A good place to meet people.

Inaka Sushi House. 236 7th Avenue, between 4th and 5th streets. Mon.–Sat., noon–11:30 P.M.; Sun.,–10:30 P.M.

The best sushi in Brooklyn, according to many enthusiasts, is to be found at Inaka. The newly renovated restaurant (across the street from its old home) offers a modern, peaceful environment in which to enjoy made-on-the-premises maki, temaki, and various kinds of sushi, as well as tempura, teriyaki dishes, and udon soup noodles. Entrées average about $12.

✪ **Java.** 455 7th Avenue, corner of 16th Street, 832-4583. Mon.–Fri., noon–11 P.M.; Sat–Sun., noon–midnight.

This plain Jane Indonesian restaurant serves both mild and spicy delicacies. For a sampler, order the rijsttafel, which is a full dinner for two consisting of twelve or so dishes, plus dessert and coffee or tea, all for $27.50. Try the pastel appetizer, a patty stuffed with rice noodles and vegetables; it's light, tasty, and a wonderful starter. Also try the special drinks, like the Jakarta Green Light.

The same food with more sophisticated presentation and fancier digs would be a line-out-the-door smashing success—which is what makes this a real "find."

Lemongrass Grill. 61A 7th Avenue, near Lincoln Place, 399-7100. Daily, 11 A.M.–10 P.M.

Cramped and noisy, but *goood,* Lemongrass has been a hot spot since the first week it opened. Fiery Thai food and low prices keep hungry customers standing in line on Saturday nights. Try the *gai pad bai ga-prow* (spicy chicken with basil) for $8 or the *tao hu hor* (shiitake mushrooms vegetables and spinach in black bean sauce) for $9. On a warm night ask to be seated in the rear garden; or, if it's too busy, try **Nam** up the street (it's owned by the same family). Beer is available but no wine or hard liquor is served. For dessert or coffee, check out **Ozzie's** or **Cousin John's**, both within a block. There are Lemongrass Grills in Manhattan, too.

Mack's Room. 1114 8th Avenue, corner of 12th Street, 832-7961. Wed.–Sat., 5–11 P.M.; Sun. brunch, noon–3:30 P.M.; and dinner 5–10 P.M.

On a cold and rainy night, Mack's is a warm and cozy place to stop in for a meal, a drink, and refuge. The menu isn't extensive, but you're bound to find a fish or meat dish to suit your fancy. Good bets include the steamed dumplings in ginger sauce, pan-seared crab cakes or grilled fish, and an eggy prix-fixe brunch that costs about $10. Mack's is connected to **Johnny Mack's Bar and Grill** next door, so there's a better-than-average wine list here, and a better-than-average menu there.

✪ **Max and Moritz.** 428 7th Avenue, between 14th and 15th streets, 499-5557. Mon.–Fri., 5–11 P.M.; Sat.–Sun., 11 A.M.–4 P.M.

Considered one of the best restaurants in Park Slope, the decor is simple and the food exceptional. Dress casually but expect to be served with grace. While some would describe this as a French-American restaurant, let's call it eclectic nouvelle cuisine with its wild-mushroom ravioli, roasted duck, and salmon served on a bed of white beans. Anticipate that the menu will change over time, but always stay delicious.

✪ **Mike & Tony's Bar & Grill.** 239 5th Avenue, corner of Carroll Street, 857-2800. Mon.–Sat., 5:30–11 P.M.; Sun., 5–10 P.M.

If you come on Saturday evening, you are likely to be in the company of women in little black dresses and stockbrokers wearing suspenders and suits at this upscale restaurant on 5th Avenue, Park Slope's gentrification frontier. A substantial menu features serious food: hunter stew, steaks, fish, and stews. A full dinner for two with drinks can run $60.

And talk about skeletons in the closet: this site was an old funeral parlor in a previous life. These days, the large front parlor bar, adorned with stained glass, wood paneling, and elegant Victorian hues of paint, is especially lively on weekends. "Mike and Tony" by the way, are the owner and celebrated chef associated with the popular **Cucina**, across the street.

✪ **Nam.** 222 7th Avenue, corner of 3rd Street, 788-5036. Mon.–Thurs., noon–10:30 P.M.; Fri.–Sat., noon–11:30 P.M.; Sun., 1–10:30 P.M.

The Hann Low family, which hails from Malaysia, has created two ethnic taste sensations in Park Slope. One is **Lemongrass Grill,** which serves Thai food; Nam is its Vietnamese counterpart. If you like salmon, you'll love the *ca kho to,* with its salmon filet swimming in a spicy broth that includes carrots and sprouts. The *goi du du,* or green papaya salad with dried beef, calamari, and sesame seeds is also a unique and tasty dish. On warm days the sidewalk terrace is breezy and affords good people-watching.

New Prospect Café. 393 Flatbush Avenue, between 7th and 8th avenues, 638-2148. Mon.–Thurs., 11:30 A.M.–10 P.M.; Fri.–Sat., 11:30 A.M.–11 P.M.; Sun., 10:30 A.M.–10 P.M.

A very small restaurant with a homey atmosphere and good food, this is a favorite of many locals for dinner and Sunday brunch. It can be a little claustrophobic and pricey for small children, with dinners ranging from $12 to $18 per entrée. The menu tends toward fish, chicken, and vegetarian dishes. Reservations are recommended for three or more.

Olive Vine. 131 6th Avenue, between Park and Sterling places, 636-4333. Daily, 11 A.M.–11 P.M. Cash only.

Homemade lentil soup, superb falafel and hummus, and freshly made puffy pita bread beckon at this Middle Eastern café, located one block off the main shopping street. An individual pizza will satisfy an adult, or two children, for just $8. Owner Khaled Demis has another Olive Vine on 7th Avenue, but the back garden and quieter ambience here are extremely pleasant. Prices are rock-bottom.

✪ **Ozzie's Coffee.** 57 7th Avenue, corner of Lincoln Place, 398-6695 Daily, 8 A.M.–midnight. Also at 249 5th Avenue at Garfield Place and in Brooklyn Heights.

This gourmet coffee café is an "in" local hangout and meeting place for Slopers of all types. Ozzie's business reflects the pattern of the neighborhood: the early-to-work crowd gives way to moms with toddlers and writers with laptops, followed by high school students let out for lunch, and the post-work crowd again. Ozzie's serves coffees, muffins, and soups and sandwiches, and has a selection of quirky mugs for sale. There's live music on some weekends.

The big, new Ozzie's on Park Slope's 5th Avenue (right across from **Cucina**) has lured a chef from Manhattan's upscale Dean & Deluca to tempt customers with delicious soups, sandwiches, and salads, as well as pastries and sweets. Ozzie's also sells the yummy homemade sorbet and ices that locals know and love from Luna Park days, when this place was a popular ice cream parlor. And no question, the coffee is fresh! An on-site coffee roaster infuses the cafe with what a certain 1950s advertising campaign used to call "that *heavenly* aroma." Very informal; counter service only.

A third Ozzie's in Brooklyn Heights is a cozy café with overstuffed sofas, an outdoor patio, and a working fireplace.

Park Slope Brewing Company. 356 6th Avenue, corner 5th Street, 788-1756. Daily, 4–11:30 P.M.

The Park Slope Brewing company is a friendly neighborhood bar, with a pool table and a game room downstairs. It's a let-your-hair-down kind of place where corny gimmicks like twenty-cent chicken wings (only on weekday afternoons till seven) generate chicken wing competitions and a lot of jokes. And, there's always an interesting selection of brews. Outside tables in the summer add to the fun. There's another location in Brooklyn Heights (62 Henry Street).

Santa Fe Bar and Grill. 60 7th Avenue, corner of Lincoln Place, 636-0279. Mon.–Fri., 5–11 P.M.; Sat.–Sun., 3 P.M.–midnight.

Frozen margaritas, cold beer, and chips with salsa make this a popular hangout for young Slopers on weekends and after work. On cool nights the doors and windows are flung wide open, making the street scene almost a part of the dinner scene. The food is average Mexican, the atmosphere is lively.

2nd Street Café. 189 7th Avenue, corner of 2nd Street, 369-6928. Daily 8 A.M.–10:30 P.M.

Always humming, this is a kid-friendly place with paper table coverings and crayons to keep budding Da Vincis busy. The menu is a bit limited but locals like this diner-cum-bistro for its salads, burgers, and black bean soup. The most expensive entrée, a grilled rib eye in a red wine shallot sauce, is only $12.50. Sandwiches cost less than $7.

Tacos Nuevo Mexico. 491 5th Avenue at 12th Street. Daily, 10 A.M.–10 P.M.

This clean little place serves light Mexican fast food. There are authentic touches, such as the radish and lemon wedge added to your take-out taco. Try the vegetarian, steak, or chicken taco, and don't forget the homemade hot sauce. Beer, Mexican sodas, natural juices, and fruit shakes are all available. Cheap and good.

The Gate. 321 5th Avenue, off 4th Street, 768-4329. Hours.

So who's counting? Two dozen draft beers, 28 single-malt scotches, 20 American whiskeys, and half a dozen different bottlings in other categories is what pulls in the crowds at The Gate. Not to mention a spacious outdoor seating area, games of chess, backgammon, or darts—and a staff who know their customers well enough to take calls, hold keys, and the like.

Tofu on 7th Healthy Chinese Cuisine. 226 7th Avenue, between 3rd and 4th streets. Mon.–Thurs., 11:30 A.M.–10:30 P.M.; Fri.–Sat., 11:30 A.M.–10 P.M.; Sun., 1–10:30 P.M.

A large selection of vegetarian dishes, bamboo steamed specials, meatless tofu and vegetable specials, as well as traditional Chinese beef and chicken entrées makes Tofu on 7th Avenue stand-out.

Tom's Restaurant. 782 Washington Avenue, corner of Sterling Place, 636-9738. Mon.–Sat., 5 A.M.–5 P.M.

Just three long blocks past Flatbush Avenue is a former ice-cream parlor located in Prospect Heights that harbors one of the best breakfasts around. Since 1936 Tom, and now Tom's son, Gus, have been serving up inexpensive, tasty, and filling breakfasts and lunch. Three enormous apple pancakes cost just $4, a big bowl of grits is under $2, and the French toast is made of challah bread. The muffins are huge and the eggs and home fries are first-rate. Tom's also makes a mean egg cream—and likes kids. People come from afar for the 1950s style, warm and friendly feeling. *Note:* Washington Avenue is fairly run down.

12th Street Bar & Grill. 1123 8th Avenue, on corner of 12th Street, 965-9526.

12th Street Bar & Grill serves modern American-style cuisine with specials such as "grilled shrimp with a slightly spicy tomato jam, topped with leeks on an Israeli couscous salad," and a Brooklyn steak sandwich with "sautéed onions and peppers on French bread topped with Swiss and provolone," as well as grilled homemade duck saucisson, and sliced fennel and orange salad. It's a friendly, noisy, and usually fairly busy joint. The bar next door serves from this excellent kitchen.

✪ **Two Boots.** 514 2nd Street, just off 7th Avenue, 499-3253. Mon.–Thurs. and Sun., 11 A.M.–10 P.M.; Fri.–Sat., 11 A.M.–midnight.

Following in the footsteps of its fabulously popular Manhattan location, this zany, eclectic restaurant caters to the young at heart. It combines excellent, moderately priced food with kiddie accoutrements: coloring books and crayons, kid-level tables and coat hooks, and a pizza decorated like a face. It's not just a kids' place, though: items such as sweet potato and scallion omelettes with salsa verde will appeal to adults. The colorful outdoor patio is an extra plus. Sunday brunch is a family favorite.

✪ **Two Toms.** 255 3rd Avenue, corner of Union Street, 875-8689. Tues.–Sat., 5–9:30 P.M.; Sun., 3–7 P.M.

Some people love it, others hate it, but Two Toms is an undeniably Italian workingclass, family-oriented, no-nonsense restaurant. With huge portions of steak and chops, the meat dishes get raves. Ditto for the enormous antipasti. Good for kids, large groups, and low prices. Drive here if you can, since it's located in a somewhat isolated area between an auto body shop and a launderette near the Gowanus Canal. Weekend reservations are recommended.

SHOPPING

Specialty Food Shops

A. S. Fine Foods. 274 5th Avenue, between Garfield Place and 1st Street, 768-2728. Mon.–Sat., 7:30 A.M.–6 P.M.; Fri., 7 A.M.–7 P.M.; closed Sun.

For those seeking genuine Italian provisions from rolled veal with garlic to chicken stuffed with mozzarella and prosciutto, the people at A.S. have been perfecting the art of Italian cooking for more than fifty-five years. This is strictly a market; there's no seating. If you go on the weekend, pick up a couple of the focaccia, a small southern Italian pizza that's available only on Saturdays. This is one of many locations in the greater New York metropolitan area. Two others are at 8614 5th Avenue in Bay Ridge and 361 Avenue X in Gravesend near Sheepshead Bay.

Connecticut Muffin. 171 7th Avenue, corner of 1st Street, 768-2022. Mon.–Thurs., 6 A.M.–10:30 P.M.; Fri.–Sun., 6 A.M.–11 P.M.

There are 40 different muffins, cakes, and bagels to choose from, and on warm days the outdoor benches where the mix of singles, marrieds, and kids is an ever-evolving neighborhood movie.

There is also a branch at 206 Prospect Park West (965-2067, near the Pavilion movie house) and one on Montague Street in Brooklyn Heights (875-392).

✪ **Eagle Provisions.** 628 5th Avenue, corner of 18th Street, 499-0026. Daily, 6 A.M.–7 P.M.

This small, ultraclean supermarket with its international flavor and large selection of high-quality Eastern and Western European items seems to belong in Manhattan's Yorkville section instead of largely workingclass Latino 5th Avenue in Brooklyn. In addition to fresh produce, there are smoked meats made on the premises, from juicy hams to no-preservative sausages and oven-ready fresh stuffed chicken breasts and brisket. The store carries newspapers in Arabic, Spanish, and Polish alongside *Barron's* and the *Wall Street Journal*. The delicious breads are imported from a Lithuanian bakery. Other merchandise includes jars and jars of Hungarian red currants and gooseberries, Italian sour cherries, poppyseed filling for pastries, French chocolate and hazelnut sauce, Scottish soups, Italian polenta, German herring, imported chocolates, and so on.

Erica's Rugelach and Baking Company. 265 5th Avenue, between 1st and Garfield streets. Mon.–Fri., 9 A.M.–5 P.M.

They make mountains of rugelach here, and ship nationwide. You have to order a day ahead, but it's worth advance planning to get these fabulous rugelach, brownies, macaroons, linzer tarts, shortbread, and pies. The rugelach are made with all natural fruit juice sweetener and jam. It's located across the street from **A. S. Fine Foods**.

✪ **Fratelli Ravioli.** 169 Lincoln Place, just above 7th Avenue, 783-7833. Another branch at 169 7th Avenue, between Garfield Place and First Street, 369-2850. Open 7 days.

The original Carroll Gardens shop opened more than thirty years ago, and has since expanded into a small retail empire. Besides the classic (four-cheese, spinach) and eclectic (pumpkin, sun-dried tomato, and lobster in squid's-ink dough) ravioli and tasty homemade sauces (tomato vodka, pesto, marinara, etc.), olives, and other delicacies, you can get a great sandwich here for less than $6. With a day's notice, Fratelli's can produce fantastic hero sandwiches in lengths up to 6 feet!

La Bagel Delight. 252 7th Avenue, corner of 5th Street, 768-6107. Mon.–Thurs., 6 A.M.–7 P.M.; Fri.–Sun., 6 A.M.–10 P.M.

It isn't hard to find bagels in Brooklyn, but finding really *good* bagels is more of a challenge. Although there will always be those who disagree, many locals consider these baked-on-the-premises bagels the best round. You can pick up picnic fixings here before heading to nearby **Prospect Park**.

✪ **Lopez Bakery.** 435 5th Avenue and 8th Street, 852-5690. Open 24 hours. There's a second store at 6904 5th Avenue (491-9205).

What's bigger than a breadbox? Your appetite when you enter this enticing bakery. Park Slopers may argue about which is the best—seven-grain loaves, sourdough loaves, or the dynamite raisin cinnamon bread—but most agree that Lopez is the Slope's best bread bakery. And it is *very* inexpensive.

New Prospect at Home. 52 7th Avenue, between Lincoln Place and Sterling Place, 230-8900. Mon.–Fri., 7:30 A.M.–9 P.M.; Sat.–Sun., 8:30 A.M.–8 P.M.

When you don't want to sit down at the **New Prospect Café** (see page 256), head over to its take-out shop. It's a good place to pick up picnic supplies; choose from a wide variety of prepared dishes, including pasta and vegetable salads, fresh bagels, breads, and other baked goods. Many cheeses and natural juices are available as well.

✪ **Park Slope Food Co-op.** 782 Union Street, between 6th and 7th avenues, 622-0560. Mon.–Thurs., 10:30 A.M.–9:45 P.M.; Sat., 9 A.M.–7:30 P.M.; Sun., 8 A.M.–5 P.M. Checks accepted.

You can't shop here unless you are one of the more than 5,500 members that belong to this unique institution. This is the country's largest member-run food cooperative, in existence since 1973. Members do 80 percent of the work (paid employees handle the rest). The co-op caters to a wide range of tastes but specializes in healthy, natural foods. A big attraction is the extensive produce section, which includes many organic items, and low prices (just 17 percent above cost). Handwritten signs explain environmentally sound foods and staples to buy and to avoid.

Park Slope Seafood. 170 7th Avenue, corner of 1st Street, 832-2465. Mon.–Sat., 10 A.M.–8 P.M.; Sun., 10 A.M.–6 P.M.

You'd only buy fresh sushi from someone who knows what he's doing, right? Joung Un Tak is your man. With one store in exclusive Greenwich, Connecticut, and another in Greenwich Village, plus a master's degree in business, he runs a tight ship. You won't find a more immaculate fish store anywhere. If you take home this delicious sushi, dinner for two runs about $15. The store also features a beautiful selection of fresh fish to cook at home.

Pollio. 398 5th Avenue, between 6th and 7th streets, 768-6887.

Slopers who live on 7th Avenue probably aren't even aware of this great little Italian store, which makes fresh mozzarella, and sells sun-dried tomatoes and fresh basil, terrific sandwiches and homemade ravioli. Stop here and at **Lopez Bakery**, and you're all set for dinner.

Sweet Dreams Bakery. 455 7th Avenue at 16th Street, 768-3344, Mon.–Sat., 6 A.M.–7 P.M.

Low-fat scones and muffins made with fresh berries, apples, and bananas are made here. Muffins cost about $1.25 apiece, but they are worth every fruit-filled penny.

✪ **Terrace Bagels.** 224 Prospect Park West, between Windsor Place and 16th Street, 768-3943. Mon.–Fri., 6 A.M.–10 P.M.; Sat.–Sun., 7 A.M.–11 P.M.

Some of the best bagels in Brooklyn are made here (they supply the Park Slope Food Co-op, among other places).

Tropical Fruit Stand. 4th Avenue between 2nd and 3rd streets.

Like a tropical landmark in the heart of Brooklyn, in the summer there's always a parked truck loaded with fresh sugar cane, papayas, mango, small sweet bananas, and plantains at this corner. If you can't pull over fast enough, don't worry, there's a twin truck vendor at 4th Avenue and 35th Street. Rock-bottom prices.

✪ **Two Little Red Hens.** 1112 8th Ave. between 11th and 12th streets, 499 8108. Mon.–Fri., 7 A.M.–7 P.M.; Sat., 8 A.M.–7 P.M.; Sun. 8 A.M.–5 P.M.

Park Slopers line up on weekends for eat-in (if they can get a seat) or take-home goodies. The bestseller at this little gem of a bakery is the Brooklyn Blackout Cake, a dark chocolate confection filled with chocolate pudding and covered with chocolate icing and chocolate crumbs. If you aren't a chocoholic, go for the apple crumb pie or chocolate crinkle cookies. Pricey, but worth it.

Clothing and Shoes

✪ **Aaron's.** 627 5th Avenue, near 16th Street, 768-5400. Mon.–Sat., 9:30 A.M.–6 P.M.; closed Sun.

Their slogan says it all: "You won't do better unless your husband's in the business." Inside Aaron's innocuous, windowless storefront, you'll find discounts on leading designer sportswear, dresses, and coats at 25-to-50-percent savings. Look for labels like Harvé Bernard, Albert Nipon, Blassport, and Henry Grethel. There's parking across the street and the salespeople are quite attentive.

Almost New. 68 St. Marks Avenue, off 6th Avenue, near Flatbush Avenue, 398-8048. Mon.–Tues., noon–7 P.M.; Fri.–Sun., noon–6 P.M.; closed Wed.–Thurs.

Really great vintage jewelry, elegant suits and dresses, boas, furs, handbags, and other "finds" await at Almost New. Teenage girls who are into vintage will adore this store—and moms who want to play dress up will, too.

City Casuals. 223 7th Avenue, between 3rd and 4th streets, 499-5581. Mon.–Fri., 10 A.M.–7 P.M.; Sat., 10 A.M.–6 P.M.; Sun., noon–5 P.M.

Some working women will love this shop for its relaxed yet professional fashions. The specialty here is outfitting those women whose jobs don't call for suiting up and wearing a bow tie around the neck. Among the store's loyal customers are dentists, doctors, lawyers, writers, professors, and therapists. The dresses and two-piece outfits start at around $130. The shoes are good-looking and comfortable, with many imports ranging from $45 to $150.

Jamila's. 271-75 Flatbush Avenue, between Prospect Place and St. Marks Avenue, 398-6463. Tues.–Fri., noon–7 P.M.; Sat., 10 A.M.–6 P.M. Closed Sun.–Mon.

Beautifully displayed, fashionable casual wear is sold at this shop run by one of a handful of African-American women entrepreneurs in the area. Prices are moderate, given the strong sense of style here. Often the store has brochures on hand for various cultural events of interest, such as dance performances and concerts.

Treasures III. 443 4th Street, off 7th Avenue, 369-2529. Daily, 11 A.M.–7 P.M.

Thrift gone upscale. This pleasant and spacious thrift shop, complete with wood floors and skylights, was opened by the South Brooklyn Development Corporation in 1998. The project and proceeds help engage single mothers in job training. (There are two others in Carroll Gardens.)

Triangle Clothing. 182 Flatbush Avenue, corner of 5th Avenue, 638-5300. Mon.–Fri., 9:45 A.M.–6:30 P.M.; Sat., 9:45 A.M.–5:30 P.M.

In business since 1917, Triangle is a potpourri of sporting goods, work clothes, and sports clothes. There's a large inventory so ask for help. Prices can be lower than most chain stores; last year's $100 ice skates can be found here for as little as $60.

Shops for Children and Teens

✪ **Brooklyn's Best Book and Toy Shop.** 92 7th Avenue, between Union Street and Berkeley Place, 636-9266. Mon.–Sat., 10 A.M.–6:30 P.M., Sun., noon–6 P.M.

The em*PHA*sis here is on education and diversity. Husband-wife team Bill Hoblin and schoolteacher Sarai Nieves are the powerhouses behind this lovely, chockablock toy store specializing in multicultural and educational materials for babies to twelve-year olds. In addition to toys, there's a nice selection of books, videos, CD-roms, and serious equipment such as trikes and sandboxes.

With once-a-month weekend readings by famous children's authors, Cat-in-the-Hat–style hat-making workshops, and appearances by life-size favorite book characters such as Arthur, Clifford the Dog, and Angelina Ballerina, the store is a happening place for the younger set. Phone orders, shipping, and gift wrapping are available. An educational newsletter features topics such as why parents should read aloud to infants and why girls should play with blocks.

Jumpin' Julia's. 240 7th Avenue, between 4th and 5th streets, 965-3535. Mon.–Sat., 10 A.M.–7 P.M.; Sun., 11 A.M.–6 P.M.

Clothing for babies and small children in rainbow colors and practical styles are Jumpin' Julia's specialty.

✪ **Little Things.** 166–168 7th Avenue, between Garfield Place and 1st Street, 768-1014. Mon.–Fri., 10:30 A.M.–7 P.M.; Sat., 10 A.M.–6:30 P.M.; Sun., 11 A.M.–5 P.M.

The purple and yellow storefront is startling enough, but once inside Little Things, you may be so overwhelmed by the eclectic inventory that you miss the shop's best features. Forget the costume jewelry and T-shirts that crowd the front. Instead, head to the back for a good range of children's and babies' toys, educational toys, crafts, and knickknacks for party bags. There are two other branch stores at 135 and 145 Seventh Avenue.

✪ **Our Children's Enterprises.** Garfield Place, between 4th and 5th avenues, 788-4400. Mon.–Fri., 7 A.M.–4 P.M.; closed Sat. and Sun.

For basic educational toys—the kind you'll find in schools—this is one of Brooklyn's best-kept secrets. Primarily a wholesaler, this sizable store has a wide selection of puzzles, blocks, beads, paints, books, tapes, and name-brand toys geared to children of all ages. The selection is exclusively no-nonsense, durable equipment favored by teachers. Prices are not discounted, but many of the items here cannot be found in traditional toy shops.

Play It Again Sam. 732 Carroll Street between 6th and 7th avenues, 499-8589. Tues. and Thurs.–Sat., 10 A.M.–6 P.M.; Wed., 10 A.M.–8 P.M.

When owner Pamela Sherid's own children started to get too big for their britches, she came up with the entrepreneurial notion of transforming her brownstone basement into a secondhand children's shop. Nearly a decade later, the shop is booming. A great place to buy and sell children's clothes, equipment, shoes, maternity clothes, and to meet other moms to share information on schools, sitters, and activities.

Slang Betty. 180 Lincoln Place, off 7th Avenue, 638-1725. Sun.–Mon., noon–6 P.M.; Tues.–Sat., 11 A.M.–7 P.M.

"When a girl changes from bobbysox to stockings," as the old 1950s song went, is about when they begin to shop at Slang Betty's. A favorite among teens and young women, this little boutique specializes in feminine, fun, and inexpensive clothing and accessories. You won't find any name brands, but the styles are trend-setting. A summer top sells for $20; winter pants for $40. Donna, the personable owner, knows many of her young customers by name. Accessories include jewelry, handbags, occasional must-haves such as pink boas and purple hair dye, imported incense, and—what else—a rack of funky vintage clothing.

Interesting Neighborhood Shops

Barnes & Noble. 267 7th Avenue at 6th Street, 832-9066. Daily, 9 A.M.–11 P.M.

Café, books, and racks and racks of magazines—it's the standard Barnes &

Noble, and a popular addition to the neighborhood. Normally we wouldn't list a chain, but the Slope is a bookish place, and this has been a welcome addition.

Booklink. 99 7th Avenue, near Union Street, 783-6067. Mon.–Sat., 10 A.M.–9 P.M.; Sun., 11 A.M.–8 P.M.

Though small, Booklink packs a diverse selection onto its shelves, including a number of foreign and alternative journals you may not expect to find in a local bookstore. Not only is the children's section a good one, but it's in the back, where Junior won't disturb the peace. If you can't find the book you want, the owners will order it for you.

✪ **Clay Pot.** 162 7th Avenue, between Garfield Place and 1st Street (800) 989-3579 or 788-6564. Mon.–Fri., 11:30 A.M.–7:30 P.M.; Sat., 10:30 A.M.–6:30 P.M.; Sun., noon–5:30 P.M.

It's unusual to find a ceramics shop selling more than just the typical mugs and honey pots. Clay Pot carries real ceramic art (signed, handcrafted pottery) as well as jewelry, glass and wood crafts, and they specialize in handcrafted gold wedding rings, and represent over ninety goldsmiths nationwide, drawing customers from all over the tristate area. Prices for wedding bands range from $75 to upwards of $2,000. Clay Pot also features the work of hundreds of artisans in jewelry, pottery, weaving, lamps, and housewares.

✪ **Ecco Home Design.** 232 Seventh Avenue, at 4th Street 788-1088. Mon.–Sat., 10:30 A.M.–7:30 P.M.; Sun., A.M.–6 P.M.

Ecco is an elegant home furnishing store designed to make that brownstone apartment feel like the home you always wanted. They sell interesting designer lamps, rugs, picture frames, and a limited selection of lovely furniture. They will help design your room as well.

Eclipse Studio. 180 Lincoln Place, between 7th and 8th avenues, 783-7313. Mon.–Sat., 10 A.M.–7 P.M.

With all the stained glass that adorns homes in Park Slope, it's no wonder that Paul Solomon, Eclipse's owner and artist-in-residence, is busy. Customers come from far afield; one couple hired him to fix a broken window in a Long Island mausoleum. When Paul isn't repairing windows he builds beautiful hanging and standing lamps. The smallest cost about $150 and can be shipped—he guarantees—without breaking.

etc. . . . etc. . . . etc. 115 7th Avenue, between President and Carroll streets, 783-1706. Mon.–Fri., 11 A.M.–8 P.M., Sat., 11 A.M.–7 P.M.

When you need a quick gift for a tasteful woman, they've got it. When you want to treat yourself to a nice pair of earrings, Portuguese soap, unusual stationery, a hand-woven scarf or a hand-painted silk blouse, they've got it. "etc. . . . etc. . . . etc." is just the right name for this Slope long-timer because that's what they sell: miscellaneous lifestyle items that seem to fit Slope women like a great pair of gloves. Which, by the way, they also sell.

Hooti Couture. 179 Berkeley Place, off 7th Avenue, 857-1977. Daily, 11 A.M.–7 P.M.

Stylish secondhand stuff abounds here—old wooden bowls, *mahr*vellous vintage clothing, characterful garden furniture from the 1950s and '60s. You'll know the store by the wonderful outside displays and statuesque owner. Prices are good.

Journey. 158 Berkeley Place, off 7th Avenue, 638-3330. Daily, 11 A.M.–7 P.M.

Journey sells primitive, antique, and reproduction furniture and decorative items ranging from imported wooden benches, hand-woven baskets, to Indonesian puppets and colorful hand-painted dishes that will give your home that well-traveled, sophisticated look. The stock changes regularly, so come back and see what else is new. In fine weather, a Mehndi artist working outside draws a friendly crowd.

Last Exit Books. 447 6th Avenue at 9th Street, 788-6678. Tues.–Thurs., 1–8 P.M.; Sat., noon–10 P.M.; Sun., noon–8 P.M.

Used and scholarly books are bought and sold at Last Exit, which bills itself as "Brooklyn's only fine used book shop." Its hefty selection of serious titles, mostly in the humanities, make you think for a minute that you're in university town like Cambridge, Massachusetts, rather than in Park Slope, Brooklyn. If you are interested in a specific title, email allen@capanix.com.

✪ **Leaf 'N' Bean.** 83 7th Avenue, between Union Street and Berkeley Place, 638-5791. Mon.–Sat., 10 A.M.–6 P.M.; Sun., 11 A.M.–6 P.M.

This is a tastefully displayed shop selling a wide range of coffee beans and teas, plus attractive modern kitchenware, from cappuccino makers to oven mitts, mugs, tablewear, and more.

Nkiru Books. 68 St. Marks Place, between 5th and 6th avenues, 783-6306. Mon.–Sat., 11 A.M.–7 P.M.; Thurs., 11 A.M.–9 P.M.; Sun., noon–5 P.M.

A terrific resource, this tiny, densely packed bookstore is filled with the intellectual treasures of contemporary African-American and third-world cultures. The selection is a rare compilation of American, Latino, Caribbean,

South African, and African writers. Titles range from Afro-centric cookbooks and marvelous kids' books to novels by Achebe, biographies of Miles Davis, how-to career advice for minorities, and sociological studies of the Rastafarians. Some titles are in Spanish and other foreign languages, such as Vietnamese. If you're looking for books with a nonwhite perspective, a browse here is a good place to start.

PS 321 Flea Market. 7th Avenue between 1st and 2nd streets, 833-9864. Year-round, Sat.–Sun., 9 A.M.–6 P.M.

About fifty vendors sell vintage clothes, antiques, furniture, jewelry, postcards of Old New York, collectibles, and lovely junk at this popular weekend flea market.

Park Slope Barbershop. 223 Seventh Avenue, corner 4th Street, 965-4366. Mon.–Fri., 10 A.M.–6:30 P.M.; Sun., noon–5 P.M.

A local institution, this old-fashioned barbershop does its bit for Park Slope's cozy quality of life. It's been here since 1906, and is run by three jovial Italian brothers who snip, chat, and joke while Sinatra croons in the background (and they croon along, sometimes). They serve cookies and always put a great window display of electric trains at Christmas. Their shop, replete with antique fixings, has been used many times as a movie set to capture the mood of Old New York. You're as likely to see babies having their first locks snipped, as octogenarians who've been coming here for years.

Sew Brooklyn! 228 7th Avenue, between 2nd and 3rd streets, 499-7383. Mon.–Fri., 10 A.M.–7 P.M.; Sat., 10 A.M.–6 P.M.; Sun., noon–5 P.M.

Sew Brooklyn! has a wonderful selection of cotton fabrics and other sewing essentials. A fabric store with a mission, it offers sewing classes for adults and children, and also is at the center of an impressive folk-art renaissance in quilt making that has caught on like wildfire in Brooklyn. (Many of their quilt makers display their work at the annual quilt fair at the local PS 321.)

Sound Track. 119 7th Avenue, between President and Carroll streets, 622-1888. Mon.–Fri., 10 A.M.–7 P.M.; Sat.–Sun., 10 A.M.–5:30 P.M. (A branch store is located in Brooklyn Heights.)

Sound Track has been around Park Slope so long that its owners get quoted about neighborhood trends in *The New York Times* real estate section. This little local music store keeps pace with young musical tastes, and have a knowledgeable staff—about music, volleyball in Prospect Park, and, of course, about the neighborhood.

Stoop Sales

Brooklyn's answer to a yard sale, the stoop sale is a time-honored spring and fall tradition in much of Brooklyn, when people clean out their stuff to make way for growing families, moving, or eliminating clutter. These sales occur throughout Brooklyn, but Park Slope may have the best stoop sales for kids' stuff, housewares, and clothing. Prices can be as low as fifty cents for a book, or $2 for a shirt. A great opportunity for scavengers!

Stanley's Place. 329 5th Avenue, between 3rd and 4th streets, 832-0239. Mon.–Fri., 1.–7 p.m., Sat., 10 a.m.–7 p.m.

Tucked away on Park Slope's 5th Avenue, collectors will find interesting items from the era of the Negro Baseball League.

Third St. Skate Co. 207 7th Avenue, corner 3rd Street. Mon.–Fri., 11 A.M.–7:30 P.M., weekends, 10 A.M.–6 P.M.

Roller blade fanatics will love this store, located two blocks from Prospect Park. They were the first to distribute Hypno, and are a regular supplier of ice and hockey skates. They will match advertised prices. And, the owner himself does the ice skate sharpening, so you can trust that it will be a (sorry, readers) sharp job.

Zelda Victoria. 217 Garfield Place, off 7th Avenue, 398-6630. Wed.–Sun., noon–6 P.M., or by appt.

Mae West would have approved. Zelda's isn't Victorian at all; rather, they sell luxurious 1940s-style decorative items for the home, such as leopard-trimmed pillows. They also provide a full interior design service.

Zuzu's Petals. 81A 7th Avenue, between Union Street and Berkeley Place, 638-0918. Mon.–Sat., 10 A.M.–7:30 P.M.; Sun., 11 A.M.–7 P.M.

You don't have to buy anything to appreciate the tranquil beauty of this hole-in-the-wall flower shop. The owner, Fonda, has turned the tiny space into a floral wonderland. She and her staff can choose, arrange, and wrap one of the most elegant bouquets you'll ever buy. The flowers are always fresh and often unusual.

The following shops are within easy reach of Park Slope.

✪ **Brooklyn Botanic Garden Gift Shop.** 1000 Washington Avenue, along Eastern Parkway, 622-4433. Tues.–Fri., 10 A.M.–5:30 P.M.; Sat.–Sun., 10 A.M.–5:30 P.M.; closed Mon.

Even if you don't have a green thumb, you'll find something attractive in this spacious, bright gift shop located next to the **Steinhardt Conservatory** (page 273). There are plants, seeds, flowerpots, and some garden implements, of course, but you'll also find plenty of interesting and heavily illustrated coffee table books, unusual stationery, toys, books, and stuffed animals for kids, and even kitchenware with a floral motif. This is a wonderful place to find unusual souvenirs or small touches to make a place feel like home. Prices range from under $5 to $75 and more.

✪ **Brooklyn Museum Gift Shop.** 200 Eastern Parkway, corner of Washington Avenue, 638-5000. Daily, 10 A.M.–5 P.M.; closed Mon.–Tues.

Unusual among museum shops for its large collection of handmade items and antiques (rather than reproductions), this is a wonderful source for gifts. You'll find a stunning array of both contemporary and antique jewelry here, plus handmade African masks, quilts, rugs, and textiles, Japanese porcelain, and items that reflect the work shown in current exhibits. Among the extensive line of art books are some unusual remainders, often discounted. With plenty of items under $20, this is the place to shop for the holidays. A $40 museum membership entitles you to 25 percent off at the annual pre-Christmas sale.

There is also a special shop for children, ActSmart.

HOTELS

✪ **Bed and Breakfast on the Park.** 113 Prospect Park West, between 6th and 7th streets, 499-6115. Open daily, year-round.

One of New York's few European-style bed-and-breakfasts, this treasure of a getaway is tucked away in a row of 1890s landmark brownstones along what used to be called Brooklyn's Gold Coast. The wood-paneled bedrooms are decorated in lavishly feminine Victoriana. One has a canopy bed, another an outdoor patio with a breathtaking view of the Manhattan skyline, and a third has an old-fashioned dressing room. Breakfasts of homemade bread, homemade jam, fresh orange juice, and coffee, plus a main course of Belgian waffles, German pancakes, or stuffed omelettes are served in a beautiful Victorian dining nook. The entire house is homey and immaculate. Prices start at $125 per couple per night.

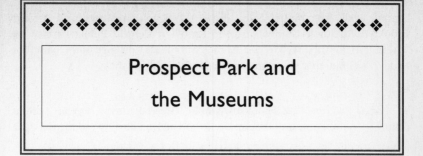

Prospect Park and the Museums

Brooklyn Botanic Garden, Brooklyn Children's Museum, Brooklyn Museum of Art, Prospect Park, Prospect Park Zoo

Where they are: All these destinations are located near each other, in west-central Brooklyn, near Park Slope.

Brooklyn Botanic Garden: 1000 Washington Avenue, along Eastern Parkway.
Brooklyn Children's Museum: 145 Brooklyn Avenue, corner of St. Marks Avenue.
Brooklyn Museum of Art: 200 Eastern Parkway, corner of Washington Avenue.
Prospect Park: Bounded by Eastern Parkway to the north, Washington and Ocean avenues to the east, Parkside to the south, and Prospect Park West and Prospect Park Southwest to the west.
Prospect Park Wildlife Center (Zoo): 450 Flatbush Avenue, near Empire and Ocean avenues.

What's nearby: Crown Heights, Ditmas Park, Park Slope, Prospect Heights, Prospect-Lefferts Gardens, Prospect Park South, Windsor Terrace.

How to get there: You can reach four of these five destinations (Brooklyn Museum of Art, Brooklyn Botanic Garden, Prospect Park, and Prospect Park Zoo) by hopping aboard the red **Brooklyn Trolley**, a free hourly shuttle service that runs weekends and holidays, noon to 5 P.M. (965-8999). The Brooklyn Children's Museum also has a summer trolley which runs on weekends from Grand Army Plaza. Call each institution for directions.

The main park entrance is at Grand Army Plaza, at the intersection of Flatbush Avenue, Prospect Park West, and Eastern Parkway. The zoo is a quarter-mile walk from Grand Army Plaza. The Brooklyn Museum of Art and Brooklyn Botanical Garden and the Brooklyn Central Public Library are within five minutes' walk of the Grand Army Plaza entrance of the park. The Brooklyn Children's Museum is a ten-minute car ride away.

By car:

To Prospect Park and Zoo: Flatbush Avenue, Ocean Parkway, Ocean Avenue, Coney Island Avenue, and Empire Boulevard all lead directly to Prospect Park.

To the Brooklyn Museum of Art and Brooklyn Botanic Garden:
Drive up Flatbush Avenue (or otherwise reach) to Grand Army Plaza, circle around onto Eastern Parkway and go several blocks to the east. The Botanic Garden and Museum entrances are both on the right side as you proceed up Eastern Parkway.

To Brooklyn Children's Museum: Follow directions to Brooklyn Museum of Art, and continue five blocks east on Eastern Parkway (heading away from Grand Army Plaza). Turn left on Brooklyn Avenue, and continue straight for six blocks. Street parking is available.

By subway:

To Prospect Park and Zoo: Take the 2 or 3 train to Grand Army Plaza, or the D train to 7th Avenue and walk five minutes up Flatbush Avenue. Or, for the zoo, you can also take the D train to Parkside Avenue.

To the Brooklyn Museum of Art and Brooklyn Botanic Garden: Take the 2, 3, or 4 train to the Eastern Parkway/Brooklyn Museum stop or, take the D or Q to the Seventh Avenue stop (four subway stops from SoHo), walk around Grand Army Plaza, and one block up Eastern Parkway.

To the Brooklyn Children's Museum: Take the 3, 2, C, or A train to Kingston Avenue (but be prepared to walk).

Cab Services: Family (596-0664) or Arecibo (783-6465). Costs about $15 to Grand Central Station, $7 to Brooklyn Heights.

Special events: All institutions have a busy schedule of cultural events. Call the main numbers, or watch listings in the newspapers and local magazines.

Official Landmarks: Brooklyn Museum, Lefferts Homestead, Litchfield Villa, Prospect Park, and Soldiers and Sailors' Memorial Arch, among others.

POINTS OF CULTURAL INTEREST

✪ **Brooklyn Botanic Garden.** 1000 Washington Avenue, along Eastern Parkway, 622-4433. Tues.–Sun., 8 A.M.–6 P.M.; Sat.–Sun., 10 A.M.–6 P.M.; closed Mon. Call for seasonal changes in hours. Adults 17 and over, $3; children age 6–16, 50 cents. The Garden is free to the public every Tuesday.

A refuge, a garden, a place of beauty and wonder: that's the Brooklyn Botanic Garden, located next to the Brooklyn Museum of Art.

Outside, there are over fifty acres of carefully designed and meticulously maintained environments: lilac and daffodil hills, rose gardens, a blossoming Japanese cherry orchard (and an annual festival with drumming and performances that's not to be missed) a children's garden, a fragrance garden, and a garden for the blind. A favorite is the enclosed Japanese Garden, with footbridges, paths, and a Shinto shrine. Kids will love feeding the ducks and fish or running along the walkways, including Celebrity Walk, which has names of famous Brooklynites inscribed on it. The summertime Children's Garden is a local institution.

Inside, the new and architecturally acclaimed **Steinhardt Conservatory** designed by Davis, Brody and Associates and completed in 1988 is a must-see. It houses the Trail of Evolution, the Aquatic House, a bonsai pavilion, and tropical, desert, and temperate environments. If you want to take some of this home with you, the well-stocked **Botanic Garden Gift Shop** sells gardening supplies, gift items, and house plants. For lunch or a snack, the **Terrace Café** is wonderful in warm weather (see listing page 250).

The Botanic Garden was founded in 1910, and is a New York City landmark. Call for information about the famous annual plant sale, tours, classes, and festivals.

✪ **Brooklyn Children's Museum (BCM).** 145 Brooklyn Avenue, corner of St. Marks Place, 735-4402. Wed.–Fri., 2–5 P.M.; weekends, 10 A.M.–5 P.M.; closed Mon. and Tues. but open on most school holidays. A free summer trolley transports visitors from Grand Army Plaza to the museum; weekends only. www.bchilmus.org

New York's best kept secret may be the Brooklyn Children's Museum. And that's not just because it is mostly underground.

Elementary school kids love it here. There's an exhibit called *Animals Eat,* a music studio where kids create their own music with electronic synthesizers; a plant-education area in which kids do things like to pretend to slither through soil and listen to trees talk about their lives, and a unit on sleep, called *Ready Set . . . Sleep,* in which kids search a giant bed for "sleep charms" from different cultures, and peek underneath looking for monsters. There's a new hands-on Greenhouse. And, BCM has launched a multicultural exhibit, *Take a Walk in My Shoes*, which will go on a national tour.

And parents will note that the kiddie clientele, a wonderful mix of races and backgrounds, is itself an education. BCM's inspired, exuberant, curiosity-provoking exhibits include multicultural artifacts, ethnomusical instruments, experiments that relate to concepts of space, measurement, and weight, and activities designed to teach peaceful collaboration between different cultural groups.

One of the few children's museums with a permanent collection, BCM has over 27,000 objects ranging from baskets and costumes to musical instruments. They are piloting an interactive data base of their collection, which is now stored in modern facilities built during a major renovation completed in 1998.

The Brooklyn Children's Museum was the world's first children's museum, and in 1999 it celebrates its centennial birthday. And there's a lot to celebrate: The Brooklyn Children's Museum pioneered a concept in the nineteenth century which has survived into the twenty-first century: hands-on, interactive installations. In other words, please, "DO touch!"

The museum's attendance is about 200,000 people a year. It's well worth a visit. Plan on spending a few hours here.

✪ **Brooklyn Museum of Art.** 200 Eastern Parkway, corner of Washington Avenue, 638-5000. Wed.–Sun., 10 A.M.–5 P.M.; closed Mon., Tues., and major holidays. Museum café open until 4 P.M. Museum libraries and archives open by appointment. Museum shops open 10:30 A.M. until museum closes. Admission is $4 contribution. www.brooklynart.org.

You won't believe what you will find here: a world-class museum in which you can prowl and browse in peace, to your heart's content. The blessing and the curse of the BMA is that it is a quiet refuge—which also means that it is undervisited. Why? Only because it is located in New York, the unofficial Museum Headquarters of the United States.

The BMA is *spectacular.* The Brooklyn Museum of Art is one of the premier art institutions in the world, with a permanent collection that represents almost every culture and includes more than one and a half million objects, from ancient Egyptian masterpieces to contemporary art. It ranks as the second largest museum in the United States, in terms of square footage of museum space.

The BMA is also an increasingly important venue for contemporary and emerging artists nationally. Some hail from New York City, including, of course, artists who live and work in Brooklyn, which has been called the nation's epicenter of new art. The curator of this department, Czechoslovakian Charlotta Kotik, is considered by many to be one of the most innovative curators of contemporary art in the United States.

BMA's collection of ancient Egyptian art is generally acknowledged to be one of the finest in the world, rivaling that of the Metropolitan Museum in terms of quality. It includes many objects excavated by museum-sponsored archeological expeditions.

And, to get an idea of how Americans lived in previous centuries, check out the extraordinary collection of nineteenth-century American paintings, and over two dozen period rooms.

The first museum in the U.S. to display African objects as art rather than as ethnological artifacts in 1923, the BMA today boasts a collection of African art that is particularly strong in works from central Africa, that is one of the largest and most important in the U.S. There are also arts of the Pacific, including Melanesia, and a collection of Andean textiles. The Asian art collection was started in 1903 and it includes the art of many cultures. And, there are small, specialized gems: the collection of Korean art is one of the most important in the U.S., while the art from Iran's Qajar dynasty is the only serious collection of its kind on display in the country.

Planned by its founders to be the largest museum in the world, the Brooklyn Museum would have surpassed the Louvre in size had it been completed. A recent renovation has been completed by the architectural firms of Arata Isozaki & Assoc. and James Stewart Polshek and Partners has expanded current facilities, but not yet to the scale of the original plans.

The origins of the Brooklyn Museum of Art go back to 1823, when it was founded as the Brooklyn Apprentices' Library Association. Walt Whitman was one of its first librarians. During the nineteenth century it occupied locations in downtown Brooklyn, and by 1890 it had evolved into the Institute of Arts and Sciences, with departments ranging from anthropology to zoology. The Brooklyn Museum of Art, Brooklyn Botanic Garden, the Brooklyn Academy of Music, and the Brooklyn Children's Museum arose out of the new institute, and by in the late 1970s, each of these institutions became separate corporate entities. Since the 1930s the BMA had established a new collecting policy focusing exclusively on art.

The museum has a strong track record as a social innovator, pioneering the field of museum education including interactive computer-based arts education programs. It helped the Adopt a School program, and made a significant investment of expertise in the creation of the innovative New York City Museum School, a public high school.

The BMA website features the museum's Ancient Egyptian collection and in-depth text about African art, art of the Americas, decorative arts, painting and sculpture, among other information.

✪ **Brooklyn Museum Café.** See Brooklyn Museum entry above.

It's the café that dared to be whimsical. The menu changes to reflect the cuisine of the museum's main show. That means that during the Jewels of the Romanov show, there was Russian food, including salmon and "Georgian chicken salad." Whatever the show, the food is tasty, and the art-food synergy is fun.

✪ **Prospect Park.** The main entrance is at Grand Army Plaza, at the intersection of Flatbush Avenue, Prospect Park West, and Eastern Parkway. 965-8999.

Special events: Summer concert series; summer fishing contest; park tours; historical events at Lefferts Gardens; Halloween walk. Call for information on races and special events.

Prospect Park is Brooklyn's second largest park (only **Marine Park** is larger). Frederick Law Olmsted and Calvert Vaux, who designed Manhattan's Central Park, said they considered Prospect Park to be their best work (experts say they didn't make the same mistakes twice). Designed in 1866, the 526 acres of rolling green lawns, wooded areas, streams, brooks, and lake make this a great environment for biking, in-line skating, walking, romancing, and relaxing. In winter there is ice skating at the outdoor Wollman Rink, and cross-country skiing, if there is snow, in Long Meadow. Year-round, there are soccer games, volleyball games, and dog walking. In the autumn the foliage is gorgeous, and the Urban Rangers put on a Halloween haunted walk for kids at Lookout Hill that follows a safe path into a ravine and across bridges and rocky ledges.

In the summer you can rent a pedal boat, listen to performances of the Metropolitan Opera, or attend a Celebrate Brooklyn concert at the bandshell every weekend. Car traffic is restricted in daytime hours along the park drive, making these good times to run or bike. And for little ones, there are good playgrounds at 3rd Street, 11th Street, Lincoln Road, and the award-winning Imagination Playground across from Wollman Rink.

Fishing Contest. Lakeside, near Wollman Rink, 965-8999. July.

R. H. Macy's sponsors an annual fishing contest in July. They provide the poles, but you have to find the fish. Kids age fifteen and younger are eligible to participate. Prizes include fishing gear and modest gift certificates from Macy's.

Kensington Stables. East 8th Street and Cullmit Place, near Park Circle–Coney Island Avenue, 972-4588. Daily, 10 A.M.–sunset. Call for rates.

There's a stable here with about twenty horses for rentals or lessons. It may seem incongruous to ride a horse in Brooklyn, but there are gorgeous trails through Prospect Park.

Pedal Boats. Lullwater Pond, near Wollman Rink, 965-8999. Open May.–Oct., weather permitting, daily noon–6 P.M. Cost is $10 per hour for a four-person boat.

You can't walk on water, but you can bike on it. The pedal boats in Prospect Park are good family fun. Kids under age sixteen must be accompanied by an adult.

Playgrounds. There's something for everyone in Prospect Park's playgrounds: sprinklers in the summer, climbing equipment and swings for grade-school kids, a sandbox and kiddie sings for preschoolers. Most playgrounds are located within walking distance of large ball fields as well. Major playgrounds are located as follows:

3rd Street off Prospect Park West: toddlers' area.

11th Street off Prospect Park West: slides, swings, sprinkler.

Imagination Playground. Corner of Park's Lincoln Road and Ocean Avenue entrance.

The award-winning Imagination Playground uses architecture to stimulate children's imaginations. Instead of slides and swings, there's an open stage, clusters of body masks in the shape of cats and ducks, and three playhouses decorated in black and white optical patterns.

Prospect Park Carousel. Near Empire Boulevard and Ocean Avenue, 965-8999. Call for hours of operation. Reservations for private parties.

A relic from the past, the Prospect Park Carousel reopened in 1990. For a mere 50 cents you can ride on this beautifully restored masterpiece, which cost more than a half million dollars to bring back to life. Choose from among fifty-one Coney Island–style horses, lions, giraffes, goats, and chariots, all restored according to original designs created in a Brooklyn shop around 1912. The Wurlitzer organ has been rebuilt too.

Prospect Park Tennis. Coney Island Avenue at intersection of Parkside Avenue. *For outdoor tennis April–November:* Contact Brooklyn Parks Department for hours, fees, and permit information, at 95 Prospect Park West, 965-8993 or 8914. Mon.–Fri., 9 A.M.–4 P.M.; closed most weekends. *For indoor tennis November–March*: **Parkview Tennis Center**, 436-4321. Daily, 7 A.M.–midnight. No credit cards; cash and checks only.

Parkview Tennis Center is the corporate entity that now runs the indoor "tennis bubble" at the far end of Prospect Park. Tennis pros here run adult and junior programs, and there are men's and women's leagues. Individual lessons run from $55 up, and group lessons from $20 up. Or, you can just rent a court for $20–40 per hour. Call in advance.

In the summertime, management of the courts reverts to the city, and you can play on the outdoor courts for free on a first-come, first-served basis after obtaining a tennis permit for a nominal fee from the Brooklyn Parks Department, in nearby Prospect Park. Word to the wise: Make sure to call ahead to check office hours and procedures, such as whether you need to bring photo ID, and whether you can obtain a permit for another family member.

Prospect Park Zoo (formally known as the Wildlife Center). 450 Flatbush Avenue, near Empire and Ocean avenues, 399-7339. April–Oct., Mon.–Fri., 10 A.M.–5 P.M.; until 5:30 P.M. on weekends and holidays. Nov.–March, daily, 10 A.M.–4:30 P.M. Admission is $2.50 for adults, $1.25 for seniors, 50 cents for kids ages 3–12.

Rain or shine, there's nothing better for kids than a trip to the zoo. This little 12-acre wonder run by the New York City Wildlife Conservation Society, a nonprofit conservation organization based at the Bronx Zoo, was reopened in 1993 after extensive renovation. Kids love the pop-up prairie dog display (they duck into and out of little gopher holes, and you can, too), the sea lions swimming in a circle, the baboons picking one another's fur, and the red panda, which is as nice as nice can be.

There's a cafeteria on the premises, and lots of special programs to attend.

Wollman Rink. Near Parkside Avenue, 287-6431. Open Thanksgiving to March, Mon.–Thurs., 8:30 A.M.–2 P.M.; Fri., 8:30 A.M.–8:30 P.M.; Sat.–Sun., 10 A.M.–6 P.M.

This outdoor skating rink draws a friendly crowd of kids and adults. There's parking right next to the rink, and pizza, hot chocolate, instant soups, and hot dogs are available. Weekdays are the quietest and least crowded times. A shuttle bus circles the park about once every fifteen to thirty minutes. Call for the bus schedule (287-5538).

There are two houses within Prospect Park that have been designated as historic landmarks: **Lefferts Homestead** and **Litchfield Villa**.

Lefferts Homestead Children's Museum. Flatbush Avenue, near Empire Boulevard, 965-8999. Call for schedule of special programs.

The Dutch were the first European settlers in Brooklyn. Outstanding among the several extant homesteads of this wealthy farming community is this 1777 traditional Dutch house which belonged to Peter Lefferts. Situated in Prospect Park, the house has period furniture and a garden planted with the herbs used during colonial times. To keep tradition alive, Lefferts Homestead offers terrific free holiday programs in the arts and crafts of yesteryear: sheep shearing, coopering, rag-rug making, broom and basket making, floorcloth painting, and more. Call the above number for the schedule.

Litchfield Villa. Prospect Park West, between 4th and 5th streets, 965-8999.

Ah, for the good old days when one's mansion had a commanding view! Built between 1855 and 1857 for land baron Edwin Clarke Litchfield by architect A. J. Davis, this lovely stuccoed mansion was only one of many estates built in "rural Brooklyn" by wealthy industrialists as a getaway from Manhattan. Shortly after the villa was completed, the city of Brooklyn paid the Litchfield family about $4 million for the more than five hundred acres that now constitute Prospect Park and acquired the mansion itself in 1892. The villa is now the Parks Department headquarters. You can wander inside, but to get a full sense of Park Slope's early history, the best bet is to take a guided tour (see page 335).

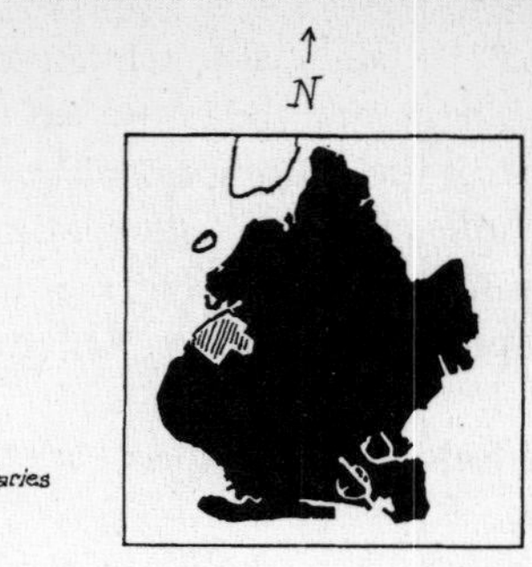
N

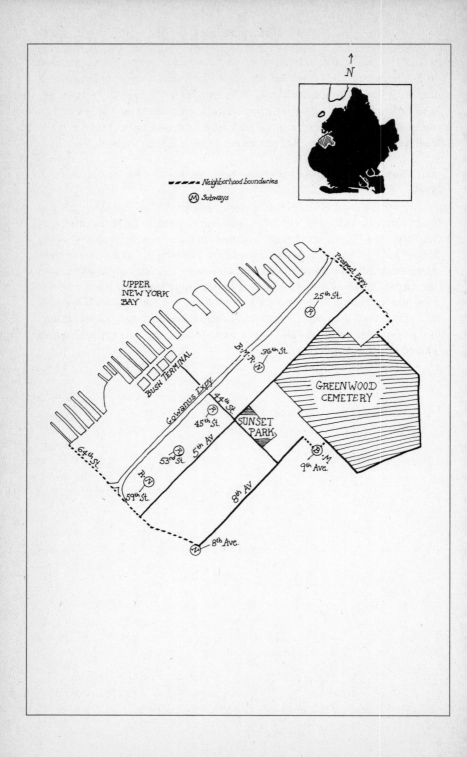

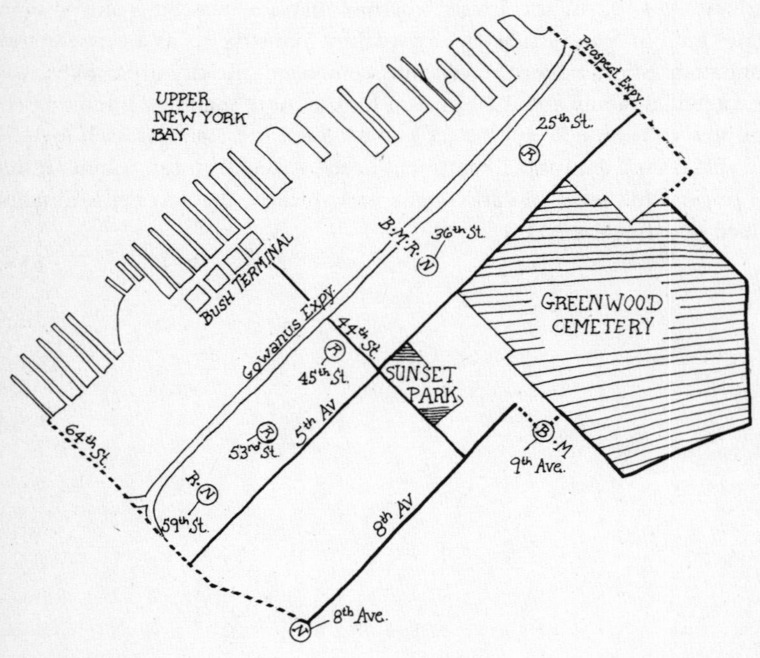
Neighborhood Boundaries
M Subways
UPPER
NEW YORK
BAY
Prospect Expy.
25th St.
R
B·M·R·N
36th St.
BUSH TERMINAL
Gowanus Expy.
44th St.
R
45th St.
SUNSET
PARK
GREENWOOD
CEMETERY
5th AV
53rd St.
64th St.
R·N
59th St.
8th AV
B·M
9th Ave.
N
8th Ave.

Sunset Park and Greenwood Cemetery

Where it is: Bounded by 65th Street to the south; Prospect Expressway to the north; 8th Avenue and Greenwood Cemetery on the east, and New York Bay on the west.

What's nearby: Park Slope, Bay Ridge, and Borough Park.

How to get there:

By car: Take the BQE (also known in this area as the Gowanus Expressway) to the 38th Street exit and proceed along 38th or parallel streets to either 5th or 8th avenues. To leave the area, re-enter the BQE on the Prospect Expressway or at 65th Street and 3rd Avenue.

By subway: R train to any stop between 25th and 59th streets, or the N train to the 36th or 59th Street stop. For Greenwood, use the 25th Street stop.

Cab services: Apple Car Service (363-9000) or Harborview Car Service (748-8800). Cost is about $10 to Brooklyn Heights, $22 to Grand Central Station.

Special events: Chinese New Year (Feb.) is celebrated with a parade, costumes, and firecrackers along 8th Avenue. Chinese restaurants are closed during the celebration. Finnish Celebration (June); Swedish Santa Lucia Festival (November). Also a Parade of Flags on 5th Avenue (October).

How it got its name: The area now known as Sunset Park took its name in the 1960s from a local park, which sits high above surrounding streets and commands a view of New York Bay. This area was previously known as part of Bay Ridge (the southern side) or simply called "South Brooklyn" (the shorefront area).

Official Landmarks: Weir Greenhouse (see McGovern Flowers listing), Greenwood Cemetery, 18th Police Precinct Station House.

ABOUT THE NEIGHBORHOOD

Greenwood Cemetery (although the official spelling includes a hyphen in Green-wood, most references leave it out) is reason enough to make the trek to Sunset Park. From a culinary angle, hungry visitors may be happily surprised to discover a small Chinatown as well as some remarkably good and inexpensive Polish and Latino restaurants in this unassuming slice of Brooklyn.

Fabulous, historic Greenwood Cemetery is a peaceful urban retreat set in 478 acres of rolling parklike hills. It is privately owned; you can take your chances on casually wandering in, but it's better to arrange a visit by calling in advance (see page 285). Your efforts will be rewarded. It is the burial site of the nineteenth and early twentieth century's rich and famous—actress Mae West, William Colgate of soap fame, Boss Tweed of Tammany Hall, abolitionist Henry Ward Beecher, and entrepreneur-philanthropist Peter Cooper, among others. Its elaborate Victorian mausoleums, obelisks, sculpture, and wonderful inscriptions offer an unmatched look at the history of old New York. Of Brooklyn's many historic sites, Greenwood Cemetery is the most evocative of the borough's partician heritage.

Contemporary Sunset Park, on the other hand, is an American melting pot par excellence. Built more than a century ago by workingclass immigrants, it is still a first stop for many newcomers to the United States.

About half of Sunset Park's 100,000 residents are Hispanic. They include a large number of Dominicans, as well as Ecuadorians, Nicaraguans, and Puerto Ricans, and most recently, Mexicans. Mexicans constitute the largest immigrant group in the U.S., but they are relatively new to New York City (estimates vary between 100,000 and 200,000 in all of NYC) and there's a rapidly growing contingent from the province of Puebla now living in Sunset Park.

Asians, including many immigrants from Canton province of China and increasing numbers from Hong Kong, represent over two-fifths of the Sunset Park community. Immigrants from Poland, India, Jordan, and Yemen as well as a contingent of fourth- and fifth-generation Norwegian Americans—descendants of Sunset Park's earliest nonnative settlers—round out an almost global cast. Since the 1970s a number of young American-born professionals have also moved into the area, seeking affordable brownstones.

Ethnic diversity is the watchword for explorers of Sunset Park. Within blocks there is a Buddhist temple, a mosque, and Brooklyn's largest Roman Catholic Church, Our Lady of Perpetual Help. There are Chinese acupuncturists, Latino *botánicas,* and *halal* butchers. And don't miss the view of the Verrazano-Narrows Bridge any time you're crossing 8th Avenue.

Hungry visitors can have octopus, fried plantains, and *morir soñando,* a fruit drink, on 5th Avenue, Chinese food at the **Ocean Palace Seafood Restaurant**, or sample Malaysian cuisine at **Nyonya** on 8th Avenue.

Historical Notes

Irish Catholics fleeing the potato famines of the mid-nineteenth century were among the earliest European pioneers to settle this part of Brooklyn. Polish immigrants followed in the 1880s, forming a community near the Czestochowa Church on 25th Street—now the site of a new wave of Polish immigration—and laboring in Greenwood Cemetery and Park Slope's Ansonia Clock Factory. Scandinavians found work at the shipyards in the late nineteenth century and created a "Little Norway" from 45th to 60th streets, where some of their descendants still live. The Finns here were the first in the nation to create cooperative housing, when in 1916 they joined together to build themselves affordable apartments, which are still in use today. Many of the Irish and Scandinavians moved into Bay Ridge by the 1920s. However, the slack was taken up by the huge Italian immigration that populated so much of Brooklyn and first settled in this waterfront area around the turn of the century. Saint Rocco's Chapel, at 27th Street, was a focal point of Italian life.

The neighborhood went into decline during and after the Depression. Like Carroll Gardens and Red Hook, Sunset Park's economic base suffered as construction of the Gowanus Expressway in the 1940s cut a swath through the neighborhood and again in the 1950s when a shift to containerized shipping rendered the Brooklyn waterfront facilities obsolete. The suburbs lured residents, and housing prices plummeted. Sunset Park's recent revival has been led by immigration, community activists and the local Lutheran Medical Center. It remains a workingclass neighborhood, and the housing stock has largely been repaired and refurbished, the 5th and 8th Avenue commercial strips are vibrant, and even the waterfront area is rebounding.

ENTERTAINMENT

Melody Lanes. 461 37th Street, off 5th Avenue, 832-2695. Sun.–Thurs., 9 A.M.–11 P.M.; Fri.–Sat., until 2 A.M.

A long-standing favorite, if you like bowling. Children three and up can bowl here, to seventies-generation disco beat—and it's a great place for kid birthday parties.

PARKS AND PLAYGROUNDS

Sunset Park Pool and Recreation Center. 7th Avenue, between 41st and 44th streets, 965-6578. Call for hours.

This enormous Olympic-size pool run by the New York City Parks Department is located alongside an elegant old building, which also houses a community center that holds arts and crafts and aerobics classes. The quietest time for a swim is early on a weekday; it is extremely busy during weekends. Lockers are available, but bring your own locks. You'll find an urban crowd from the surrounding neighborhoods.

POINTS OF CULTURAL INTEREST

Bush Terminal and Brooklyn Army Terminal. Along the waterfront, between 28th and 65th streets.

Bush Terminal. Use your imagination if you visit this large industrial site. Irving T. Bush first opened this area to industrial development in 1890. It had once been the site of Wild West shows, and later it was the location of Irving's father's oil business. With some foresight, Mr. Bush anticipated the development of the huge shipping industry and related heavy industry and manufacturing jobs that would keep Brooklyn's economy going for decades. The waterfront declined after World War II. Today the area including Bush Terminal and the new Harborside industrial complex is again being marketed as a viable area for small and large businesses.

Brooklyn Army Terminal. The whole story here is in its original name: the New York Port of Embarkation and Army Supply Base. The terminal was built in 1918, after World War I, but in time for World War II. In fact, if you know someone who fought in Europe in World War II, he most likely left from this terminal.

18th Police Precinct Station House. 4302 Fourth Avenue, corner 43rd Street.

Now the Sunset Park School of Music, this landmark was designed by police department architect George Ingram in 1890. It looks like a medieval fortress.

Fatih Camii Mosque. 5911 8th Avenue, at 59th Street, 438-6919.

This Turkish mosque was constructed in 1980 from an old Irish and Norwegian dance club—adding yet another layer in Brooklyn's archaeology of immigration. One of New York's most beautiful mosques, inside is a dim, pervasive calm. The first thing you will see is the *sadirvan*, a large and decorative tile fountain with several low faucets, a ritual bath in which Muslims wash their feet and hands prior to prayer. The large inner prayer room, used by up to 600 people on Friday nights for prayers, is plain (according to Muslim custom) with a large wall made of decorative handmade tile imported from Kutahya, Turkey. The Mosque is open to the public except at prayer times; ask for a tour. The bookstore on the premises sells prayer rugs, and religious texts and objects.

Finding History on 37th Street.
The **Brooklyn Historical Society** publishes wonderful educational packages, including a Sunset Park walking tour for schoolchildren. Among the things they point out are "seashells mixed in with the concrete," at 37th Street on 4th Avenue, explaining that "the shells are left over from the days when oysters were one of the biggest boom trades in this part of Brooklyn." The booklet instructs you to look west (toward 3rd Avenue) to see the area inhabited by the Canarsie Indians. And, set in the sidewalk in front of 441 37th Street, note several bluish bricks, like the kind used in Spain about 500 years ago.

✪ **Greenwood Cemetery.** The main entrance is on 5th Avenue, at the end of 25th Street, 768-7300. Mon.–Fri., 8:30 A.M.–3:45 P.M.; weekends, 8 A.M.–4 P.M.

World-famous Greenwood Cemetery is a vast parklike and entirely manmade environment of rolling hills, paths, and lakes. The Victorian Gothic gate at 5th Avenue and 25th Street is just one of the architectural masterpieces here, along with enormous mausoleums and ornate Victorian monuments. You can roam the serene setting or hunt for the tombs of the rich and famous. The roster of Greenwood's nineteenth-century inhabitants goes on and one: pharmaceutical giants Edward Squibb and Charles Pfizer; *New York Times* founder Henry Raymond; James Merritt Ives of lithographers Currier and Ives; Henry E. Steinway of piano fame (whose mausoleum has room for more than one hundred bodies); Charles Tiffany, founder of the Tiffany store; Louis Comfort Tiffany, the stained-glass artist; Charles Ebbets, after whom the Dodger's ballpark was named: Samuel Morse, of the code by the same name; plus the inventors of, respectively, the safety pin, carbonated water, the sewing machine, and the steam locomotive. Also buried here are the following: James Renwick, Jr., architect of the Smithsonian Institution; Richard Upjohn, architect of Trinity Church in Manhattan; Peter Cooper, inventor of Jell-O and founder of Cooper Union; Henry Bergh, founder of the American Society for the Prevention of Cruelty to Animals (ASPCA); Lola Montez, companion to composer Franz Liszt, novelist Alexandre Dumas, and others;

and William Marcy Tweed, also known as Boss Tweed. Plain folk also are buried here, as told by tales like the following on simple, old headstones: "Nelly, age 2, leaving an empty hearth and broken hearts."

Still a lovely place to roam today (and quite safe, due to extensive security), the 478-acre Greenwood was used as a park in the 1850s by locals and tourists, according to historical accounts. In fact, the popularity of Greenwood's open spaces was one of the reasons used to justify the creation of Manhattan's Central Park in 1856.

If you want a tour, your best bet is to call the **Brooklyn Center for the Urban Environment**, 788-8500, or Mr. J. Cashman or Frank Mescall at 469-5277.

Wier-McGovern Florist. See page 293.

NOTABLE SUNSET PARK RESTAURANTS

Hispanic 5th Avenue

International. 4405 5th Avenue at 44th Street, 438-2009. Daily, noon–9 P.M.

International is a popular, inexpensive American-Spanish restaurant where you can get a reliable meal of beans and rice, steak and roast pork chops and stuffed tortillas. The seating upstairs can easily accommodate groups of six or more—which is one reason why the International is often used for community and political gatherings, and has even played host to New York City's mayor.

✪ **Ricos Tacos.** 505 51st Street, corner 5th Avenue, 638-4816. Daily, 10 A.M.–9 P.M. Cash only.

Intrepid (and preferably Spanish-speaking) travelers will be rewarded by venturing into this busy, crowded little workingclass joint on a side street. Nose-tingling sauce, fresh tamarind juice ladled out of a vat, a mini-taco filled with meat and an abundance of freshly diced vegetables are the reasons there are so many people chowing down here. There's no menu in English, and, in fact, not much English at all is spoken. You will feel like an outsider, but what the heck, you are. If you strike up a conversation, don't be too snoopy; there may be undocumented immigrants in this neighborhood.

Asian 8th Avenue

Tip: Dim sum is served from 8 A.M. until about 2 P.M. at many local restaurants.

Bay Palace Seafood Restaurant. 5810 Eighth Avenue, corner 58th Street, 439-0652. Daily, noon to midnight.

A favorite dim sum restaurant, Bay Palace also has a reputation for great bowls of steaming, filling soups and outstanding spareribs and bean curd dishes. Entrées start at $8.

Chinese Ocean Restaurant. 5606 8th Avenue, corner 56th Street, 587-8686. Daily, 8–2 A.M.

If you are a twosome or foursome, come to this family-sized Cantonese restaurant sporting festive pink tablecloths which, if you've ever been there, will immediately remind you of Hong Kong. Gently cooked tofu, poultry, and seafood are nicely turned out, and the portions are more than adequate. The menu doesn't indicate whether dishes are spicy (most customers are Asian, and probably can tell from the Chinese names). Entrées cost $8 and up. If you don't want MSG, say so.

Eva's Coffee Shop. 4902 8th Avenue, corner of 49th Street, 854-2700. Daily, 7 A.M.–9 P.M.

Clean, cheap, and delicious, this Polish-American coffee shop is a local mainstay. The menu offers both standard coffee shop fare, including eggs, pancakes, and bagels on one side, and on the other side lists a mix of Polish ethnic treats, including potato pierogi, cabbage soup, noodles with cheese, apple fritters, and goulash.

✪ **Jade Plaza.** 6022 8th Avenue, between 60th and 61st streets, 492-6888. Daily, 8–2 A.M.

For about $20 you can get a terrific seafood dinner, or a multi-dish dim sum. This is one of the better known of Sunset Park's several good restaurants. It has a slightly nicer-than-average ambience and decor.

✪ **Nyonya Malaysian Cuisine.** 5323 54th Street, corner 8th Avenue, 633-0808, or 972-2943. Daily, 11 A.M.–11:30 P.M.

If you love Asian foods—Chinese, Indian, or Thai—make sure you visit this excellent and very authentic Malaysian restaurant whose chefs hail from Penang, reputedly the food capital of Malaysia. Here, you will find unique dishes that are artfully presented, extremely tasty, and very fresh. You can try homemade roti in a tangy brown sauce, pearl noodle soup served in a clay pot, steamed sea bass in *teo chow* style—that is, brought to the table in a beautiful, vegetable-packed fish steamer. There are interesting drinks such as watermelon juice, and desserts wonderfully served in a half coconut shell. While most of the customers are Asian, the friendly waiters speak English and will help you with your selection from an extensive menu. The wood-paneled decor is meant to be reminiscent of Malaysian outdoor food stands, adding to the general sense that you are in a foreign outpost. A three-course dinner for two runs under $40.

✪ **Ocean Empire.** 5418 8th Avenue, near 58th Street. Daily, 8–2 A.M.

The discerning *Brooklyn Bridge* magazine cited this restaurant's steaming chicken, turnip cakes, and steamed spareribs as "tasty and inexpensive" (entrées start at $8). The Cantonese food is generally good, and your little kids can keep busy until the food comes, watching the huge tanks of crabs and wide-eyed fish here. Note the hours that this, and other nearby restaurants, are open; Ocean Empire is a good bet for a late-night snack.

✪ **Ocean King Seafood Restaurant.** 5606 8th Avenue, corner 56th Street, 587-8686. Daily, 8–2 A.M.

Like its neighbors, Ocean King serves a full menu of Cantonese cuisine. Dim sum roll out of the kitchen all day long—egg custard and dumplings to rolls and pineapple buns—and you could probably eat it all day, the prices are so low. Entrees cost at $8 and up.

✪ **Ocean Palace Seafood Restaurant.** 5423 8th Avenue, near 55th Street, 871-8080. Daily, 8–2 A.M.

If you want to eat dim sum with a large crowd, this is the place to go. It's one of two frequently mentioned Chinese restaurants on the same block and it serves the full complement of dim sum specialties like vegetarian dumplings, pork buns, and spareribs, as well as regular menu items. Early on a Saturday morning the place is already half full of hungry local residents. Entrées start at $8. There's another Ocean Palace in Sheepshead Bay (at 1418 Avenue U).

Cafés, Ice-Cream Parlors, and Quick Meals

Vega Deli. 5417 5th Avenue, near the corner of 54th Street. Open 9 A.M.–10 P.M.; closed Sundays. Cash only.

"It's not really good for you, but *oh* it's delicious—and just like in Puerto Rico!" is what the pretty lady in the nearby bakery said about Vega Deli—and she's right. Jose Colon, the deli proprietor, makes a few classic Latino fried foods: *mafongo, pastelillos de guava y yuca,* and *alcapurrias* (meat-filled, elongated savory dumplings). Snag an extra napkin because these deep-fried treats are greasy.

Taqueria Mexicana. 4818 18th Avenue, near 48th Street, 492-7572. Daily, 9 A.M.–9 P.M. Cash only.

This little taqueria, popular among local residents, serves up fresh, thickly stuffed tacos that will put meat on your bones. Prices are rock-bottom.

Sunstone Tortillas Express. 5411 5th Avenue, corner 54th Street, 439-8434. Mon.–Thurs., 1 A.M.–10 P.M., Fri.–Sun., 1 A.M.–10:30 P.M. Cash only.

Despite the glossy colored photos in the window, which just about screams "fast food!" the menu claims that food here is "fresh, without artificial spices, chemical spices, MSG, lard, or preservatives." You can get fabulous made-from-scratch flour tortillas filled with chicken and beef, and vegetarians say this is the best place in the neighborhood for a fresh, veggie-laden taco.

SHOPPING AREAS

This section takes you to two key shopping areas of Sunset Park: Latino 5th Avenue, and Chinese 8th Avenue.

5th Avenue: For a taste of Hispanic Sunset Park, go to 45th Street and 5th Avenue. Within a few blocks you will find **La Lachanga**, a music store with the latest in Dominican and Mexican hits; **Zapateria Mexico II**, a fabulous Mexican-owned cowboy boot shop, and **La Gran Via Bakery**, a diet-crasher that sells delicious cakes and has an extravagant window display of wedding cakes.

You're still in Brooklyn, but you'll feel like you are in another country.

Stroll up 5th Avenue on a weekend or late in the afternoon on a weekday to get the flavor of this bustling, workingclass neighborhood. Note the wall mural on the side of the building at 47th Street off 5th Avenue; its sunrise colors give you the feel of the street—warm and vibrant. Along a half-mile stretch of shops selling inexpensive merchandise, you can't miss the displays of oversized valises, bikes piled high, backpacks hanging off shop awnings, tin taco warmers for sale, and signs in both English and Spanish for "RECKLESS FASHION," "TODA MODA" and "SEÑORITA" above racks of skimpy outfits for women, costing under $15. Street vendors on the corners sell peeled oranges in bags and churros (a donutlike sweet). If you wander into **Juns Market** you'll discover otherwise hard-to find ingredients for an authentic Latin American meal.

Both Mexican and Dominican restaurants abound. They are not upscale like the ones you might find in Manhattan's tourist areas, nor are they sanitized like many of the "Tex Mex" chains at suburban malls. Expect small cafés like **Taqueria Mexicana** or **Ricos Tacos** to be noisy, with big-screen televisions blaring Mexican news or Spanish soap operas, and a jukebox playing as well. Not much English is spoken, the meat is served in small pieces on jagged-cut bone, and you can see big, battered old pots on the stove, but the food is authentic—and when it's good, it's delicious.

8th Avenue: The most concentrated Chinese and Asian retail area is along 8th Avenue from about 53rd to 60th streets marked, again, by telling store signs: "ORIENTAL AND MEDICAL," "DRAGON HOUSE GIFT SHOP," "GET WELL PHARMACY," and "SWEET HOME FURNITURE." The food stores are overflowing—fresh fish markets brimming with glassy-eyed fish, and produce stands piled high with exotic vegetables and roots. Peking ducks hang in the restaurant windows. There are Chinese nail salons, Chinese record stores, and ginseng and tea shops such as the upscale **Ten Ren's Tea Time**. Neatly dressed, well-organized families, with children in tow, purposefully head to the stores, a restaurant, or home.

When it comes to food, you can shop at the huge **Hong Kong Supermarket** or less overwhelming **Lien Hung Supermarket**. Dim sum, or a conventional dinner, can be had at more than a dozen Chinese restaurants ranging from the large **Ocean Palace Seafood Restaurant** to a more family-style **Chinese Ocean Restaurant**. For Middle Eastern food, stop in at the marvelous **Birlik Oriental Food/Halal Meat Market**, which is just a few blocks away from a Turkish mosque.

SHOPPING

Specialty Food Shops

5TH AVENUE

✪ **Juns Market.** 4921 5th Avenue, corner 49th Street, 435-9078. Daily, 24 hours.

Owned by Koreans, this overflowing vegetable market serving a Latino community has an unusual selection of tropical fruits and vegetables. Here you can find special ingredients such as guava, sour oranges, chayote, *mamey*, Dominican eggplant, cactus leaves, green *guajes*, corn husks, slabs of guava jelly, dried ground shrimp, and, of course, many kinds of dried peppers and tortillas. There's the usual run of fresh vegetables as well.

✪ **La Gran Via Bakery.** 4516 5th Avenue, between 45th and 46th streets, 853-8021. Daily, 8 A.M.–8 P.M..

You can't miss this spot. The display window is chockablock with kiddie birthday cakes featuring cartoon characters; there are also spectacular, three-tiered wedding cakes. For a snack, try one of the traditional Latino specialties, like coconut pudding, pastries, or sweet breads made of corn or coconut.

✪ **Mas Que Pan Bakery.** 5401 5th Avenue, corner 54th Street, 492-0479. Mon.–Sat., 7 A.M.-7 P.M.; Sun., 8 A.M.–5 P.M.

The wedding cakes with edible flying buttresses displayed in the window would turn the eye of the most dedicated bachelor. Stop inside this airy bakery for tembleque (coconut pudding), pastelillos with guava and powdered sugar or pineapple or coconut confections. There are a few seats for coffee if you have to nibble right then and there. And, they deliver. There's another store at 179 Smith Street near Bergen Street.

8TH AVENUE

Birlik Oriental Food/Halal Meat Market. 5919 8th Avenue, near 60th Street, 436-2785. Daily, 8 A.M.–10 P.M.

Turkish, Middle Eastern, and Asian foods make for an eclectic mix at Birlik's, which covers almost half a block along 8th Avenue. Feast your eyes and taste buds on the olives, cheeses, more than fifty fresh herbs and spices. There is a wonderful fresh fruit and vegetable market here, too. Birlik's is close to the **Faith Camii Mosque** (page 284).

Golden Harvest Trading Company. 5315 8th Avenue, near 53rd Street, 633-0985. Open daily, 10 A.M.–8 P.M.

There's a fascinating array of roots, plants, teas, dried flowers, and other kinds of Chinese herbal remedies in this store, as well as a knowledgeable staff and an acupuncturist on the premises. If you are unfamiliar with this brand of alternative medicine, ask a lot of questions. The acupuncturist, for instance, is not licensed by New York State but was trained in a Chinese institute of acupuncture.

✪ **Hong Kong Supermarket.** 6013 8th Avenue, corner 60th Street, 438-2288. Daily, 9 A.M.–9 P.M. Parking lot on the premises.

Busy, crowded, brash, and commercial—like Hong Kong itself—this block-long, suburban-style supermarket carries every conceivable item you might want to make a Chinese meal at home: condiments; utensils; mixes; fresh fruits and vegetables; and canned, salted, pressed, and vinegared ingredients you may never have heard of before. It is educational just to browse, so bring the kids. Hong Kong Supermarket is the largest Oriental ethnic supermarket in Brooklyn.

Kolawster Bakery. 5804 8th Avenue, near 58th Street, 439-8545. Daily, 7 A.M.–7 P.M.

Don't let the name "Kolawster" fool you; this is a indeed a Chinese bakery and nobody quite remembers how or why it kept the previous owner's name. The selection is vast and the prices are low for mixed nut rolls, mini-mooncakes with lotus seed paste, yellow egg bean cakes, and shrimp chips. Try one of the enormous walnut or almond cookies, or grab a bag of red bean curd chips.

Lien Hung Supermarket, Inc. 5705 8th Avenue, corner 57th Street, 435-3388. Daily, 9 A.M.– 8:30 P.M.

A family-owned Chinese supermarket, Lien Hung serves a Cantonese clientele. Roam the isles and consider delectables such as shrimp sauce, fermented turnips, pickled ginger, spiced preserved bean curd, fresh fish, twenty-five-pound bags of rice, and more. Browsing here is an inspiration to go home and cook.

✪ **Ten Ren's Tea and Ginseng Company.** 5817 8th Avenue, near 58th Street, 853-0660. Daily, 10 A.M.–8 P.M.

Natural herbs have been used in Chinese diets for thousands of years. Decide for yourself if they really improve sexual deficiencies, decrease blood fat and cholesterol, stave off baldness, and cure headaches, depression, and all kinds of diseases.

A tea and ginseng international marketing consortium, Ten Ren's Tea and Ginseng Company has locations from Manhattan to Los Angeles, Canada to the Far East. It's as homey as an airport duty-free shop (in contrast to the family businesses surrounding it), but well-trained staff do offer visitors a taste along with an informative lecture about the health benefits of green tea. They will help you select from among the hundreds of types on display. Ginseng tea starts at $24 for 10 ounces, and prices soar as high as $128. Don't forget to pick up one of the glossy recipe brochures that describe—what else?—how to prepare a good cup of tea.

OTHER SHOPPING

Costco Wholesale Club. 37th Street and 3rd Avenue, 832-9300. Mon.–Fri., 11 A.M.–8:30 P.M.; Sat., 7:30 A.M.–7:30 P.M.; Sun., 10 A.M.–6 P.M. For information, call 965-7610.

This national discount store attracts every possible nationality in Brooklyn. If you are a card-carrying member you can shop here for the discounted prices, but another reason to come to Costco is the human parade: it's a microcosm of the tremendous ethnic diversity in Brooklyn.

East Coast Beer Company. 969 3rd Avenue at 37th Street, 788-8000. Mon.–Sat., 8 A.M.–9 P.M.; Sun., 10 A.M.–7 P.M. (Beer sold only after noon on Sundays.)

You'll count a lot more than 99 bottles of beer on the wall at this newly established distributor of brew, both Brooklyn-made and imported. They carry about 400 brands of beer, and you can buy it by the keg or case as well as sodas. While you are here, check out the nearby super store **Costco Wholesale** at 37th and 3rd Avenue, or go uphill to Sunset Park's Latino (5th Avenue) and Chinese neighborhoods (8th Avenue) for some fine ethnic food.

Frankel's Discount Store. 3924 3rd Avenue, near 39th Street, 768-9788 (across from Lutheran Ambulatory Surgery). Tues.–Sat., 10 A.M.–7 P.M.; closed Sun.–Mon.

Specializing in overruns and closeouts, Frankel's sells Nike and other brand-name sneakers for at least 20 percent off the retail price. Brand-name cowboy boots for men and women are also discounted, and you'll find top-of-the-line Ray Ban sunglasses, jogging suits, outdoor gear, hiking boots, Timberland and Red Wing shoes, and more—for less! (*Note*: There's easy parking right under a constantly rumbling BQE.)

✪ **La Lachanga.** 4424 5th Avenue, at 45th Street, 972-5261. Daily, 10 A.M.–7 P.M.

There's one whole wall here of Mexican pop hits, and another of Dominican at this Latino record store. One stop here and you will be dancing the night away to the sounds of some of salsa and merengue's biggest stars, such as Los Hermanos Rosario, Chichi Peralta, and Tito Nieves.

McGovern's Florist. 750 5th Avenue at 25th Street, (800) 734-9494. Mon.–Fri., 8 A.M.–6 P.M., weekends, 8 A.M.–4 P.M.

This four-generation family business is famous for its beautiful antique glass-encased display area, which is a New York City landmark. They sell indoor and outdoor plants and provide many flowers and arrangements for **Greenwood Cemetery**, across the street. There's another store at 240 Prospect Park West.

Tien Wei Aquarium. 5822 8th Avenue, between 57th and 58th streets, 567-7176. Daily, 10:30 A.M.–8:30 P.M.

The kids will love this well-kept aquarium store, open since 1994. There are at least six dozen different sizes of goldfish and other low-maintenance pet alternatives.

✪ **Zapateria Mexico II.** 4505 5th Avenue at 45th Street, 851-4074. Daily, 10 A.M.–8 P.M.

Did you know that Mexicans invented the cowboy? They did, and the cowboy culture is still going strong. Maybe that's why there's an incredible display of imported cowboy boots and related gear from Mexico, priced between $100 and $170. Women can purchase smaller sizes of the men's boots. If you get into it, try a cowboy shirt for about $45 or an authentic sombrero. The store owner is thinking about organizing a Mexican rodeo in Sunset Park. Stay tuned.

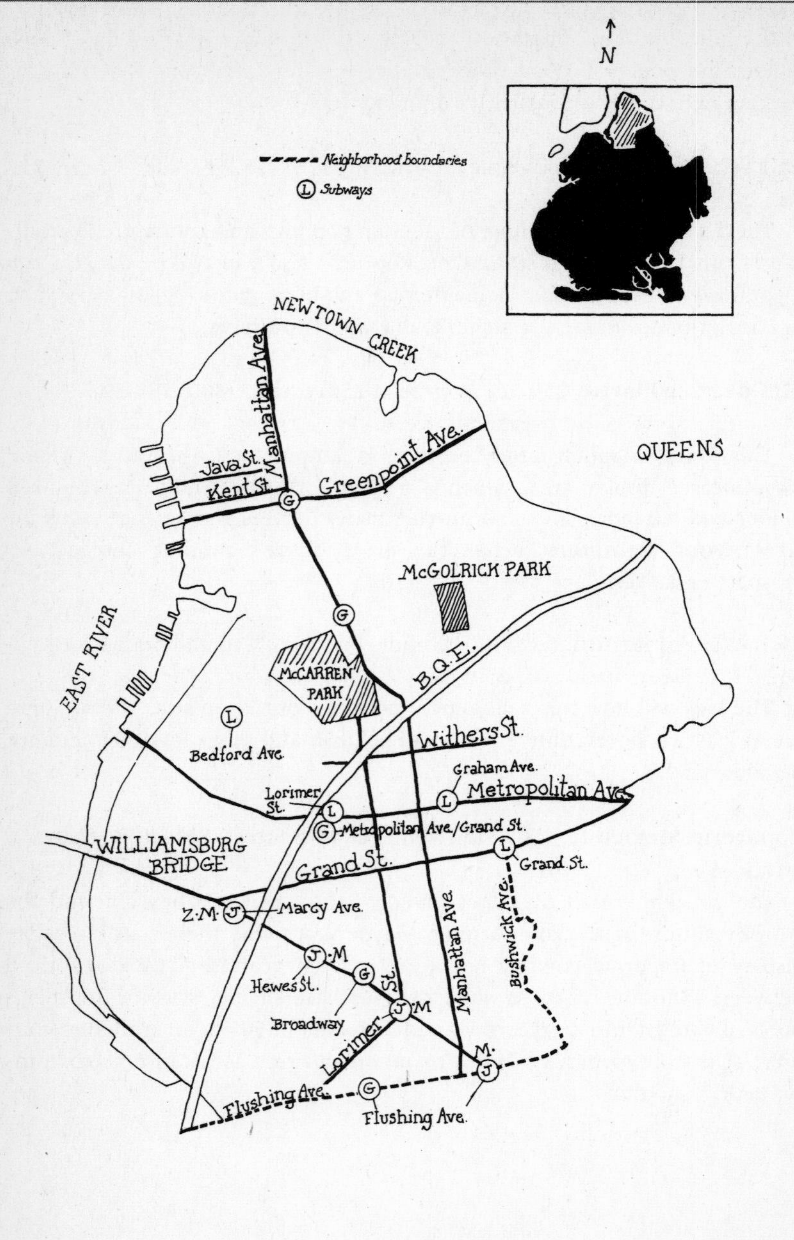
N
Neighborhood Boundaries
Subways
NEWTOWN CREEK
QUEENS
Manhattan Ave.
Java St.
Kent St.
Greenpoint Ave.
McGOLRICK PARK
EAST RIVER
McCARREN PARK
B.Q.E.
Bedford Ave.
Withers St.
Graham Ave.
Lorimer St.
Metropolitan Ave.
Metropolitan Ave./Grand St.
WILLIAMSBURG BRIDGE
Grand St.
Grand St.
Z.M
Marcy Ave.
Hewes St.
Broadway
Lorimer St.
Manhattan Ave
Bushwick Ave.
Flushing Ave.
Flushing Ave.

Williamsburg

Quotable Quote

"We don't consider ourselves part of Brooklyn. It's Williamsburg, *Manhattan.*"

—Williamsburg artist

Where it is: Williamsburg covers a large area bounded by North 7th Street to the north, Queens County line to the east, Flushing Avenue to the south, and the East River to the west.

Williamsburg is divided on most geographic maps into Northside, Southside, and East Williamsburg. Grand Street divides North and South Williamsburg. Bushwick Avenue Divides East Williamsburg from both the North and South sides.

A demographic map would show "new Williamsburg" (where the artists live and work) as centered in North Williamsburg and parts of Southside. The Hasidic area is in the Southside, centered around Wythe Avenue, Broadway, and Heyward Street, and along Bedford by Lee, Marcy, and Division avenues. Latino Williamsburg is East Williamsburg, and parts of Southside. Confused yet?

What's nearby: Manhattan is directly across the Williamsburg Bridge. Greenpoint is contiguous with Williamsburg. Queens is over the Pulaski Bridge.

How to get to Williamsburg:

By car: From Manhattan, cross the Williamsburg Bridge, accessible from Delancey Street. At the end of the bridge, make a hard right onto Broadway. Go two blocks to Bedford Avenue.

From downtown Brooklyn, take the BQE to exit 32, Metropolitan Avenue. Go left under the BQE onto Metropolitan Avenue. Head toward Berry Street or Bedford Avenue and go left.

From Queens, take the Pulaski Bridge to McGuinness Boulevard in Greenpoint.

By subway: To Northside Williamsburg (most of our "new Williamsburg" listings), from 14th Street in Manhattan, take the L train to Bedford Avenue and North 6th. Or, the G train to Metropolitan Avenue and transfer to the *Manhattan-bound* L train, one stop to Bedford Avenue. To Southside Williamsburg (most of our listings under "Old Williamsburg"), take the Z, J, or M train to Marcy Avenue, exit at Broadway.

By foot: Take a 15-minute walk across the Williamsburg Bridge from Delancey Street in Manhattan (it's best go to on weekends or go with friends). Walk over the Williamsburg Bridge to Washington Plaza. Broadway is right there; if you want the north side of Williamsburg, walk west on Broadway to Bedford Avenue and north along Bedford.

Within Williamsburg: The B61 bus runs north on Bedford Avenue and south on Driggs Avenue. Be prepared to wait.

Cab services: Greenpoint Car Service (383-2727), Havemeyer Cars (486-6060), Northside Car Service (387-2222). About $12 to Brooklyn Heights, and $15 to Grand Central Station.

Special events: San Genario, the Feast of the Giglio, Our Lady of Mount Carmel Church (July). BARC Dog Parade, (September). Simchas Torah, religious festival of Hasidic Jews (Spring). Open Studio tours occur, but not on a scheduled basis.

How it got its name: Williamsburg was named in 1810 after the man who surveyed the area, Colonel John Williams, reputedly a grandnephew of Benjamin Franklin. The original spelling included an "h" at the end; only a few places, such as the Williamsburgh Savings Bank, still use the old spelling.

And on the subject of names: Almost every street from Wythe to Ellery streets (north of the park) is named after one of the fifty-six American patriots who signed the declaration of Independence.

Landmark sites: New England Congregational Church, Williamsburgh Savings Bank, Kings County Savings Bank.

ABOUT THE NEIGHBORHOOD TODAY

If you haven't visited Williamsburg since 1996 or so, you are in for a surprise. The pulse of this old industrial section of Brooklyn is quickening with the influx of young artists, musicians, performers, and other creative spirits.

New Yorkers who have witnessed other neighborhood makeovers quickly recognize the telltale signs—old buildings turned into residences and workspaces; word-of-mouth networking; the arrival of enthusiastic urban pioneers.

"Artists' Williamsburg" (see page 297) accounts for a fraction of the area's estimated 100,000 residents. To find out about the rest of Williamsburg, talk to the Latino community activists at **El Puente Community Center**, visit such old Jewish shops as **Nathan Borlan**, or attend the famous **Italian Feast of the Giglio, Our Lady of Mount Carmel**.

A political struggle is underway for future use of waterfront property in this area. State authorities and USA Waste Stations, Inc., want to put a waste transfer station on a 20-acre site along Kent Avenue, through which would pass about 5,000 tons of residential garbage a day. Locals want parks and housing. As you can see from the newly renovated **Grand Ferry Park**, a lot can be done with these Manhattan views and waterfront. As in Red Hook and DUMBO, the struggle for the Williamsburg waterfront is a struggle for the soul of the neighborhood.

Williamsburg: Brooklyn's East Village?

Less ritzy and less radical than SoHo or the Village, Williamsburg is often seen as an extension of the Lower East Side/East Village art scene. But unlike anywhere in Manhattan, Williamsburg is almost, well, cozy. Two-story brick buildings, narrow streets, and a no-nonsense industrial environment define the physical terrain. There is lots of art (not all of it great) on the walls of cafés. The shops are small and inexpensive; in Williamsburg, gross commercialism is out, and secondhand is stylish.

Community as well as art is being created. A woman casually rides her bike—the wrong way—down the main street, Bedford Avenue. A passerby waves to the waitress in a coffee shop. Two creamy-cheeked youths return from the tennis courts in nearby McCarren Park, racquets in hand. Signs advertising art studio spaces for rent ($450), futons for sale, and roommates needed are pasted on shop doorways. Manhattan seems light-years away—except that you can see its spectacular skyline just by looking down a side street.

A tourist advisory: You'll be disappointed if you come here expecting to see SoHo or even Tribeca. The epicenter of the art renaissance is North 7th Street and Bedford Avenue, but most of the life of the artists in Williamsburg happens in private lofts. The truly adventurous hipster can discover by word-of-mouth any number of parties and art installations that flicker from the windows of warehouses after dark. Inside, you could find yourself dancing to salsa, big-band, or techno music just by hopping from one roof to another late into the night. Or, tamer or older souls can see the work of Williamsburg artists at local galleries—**Pierogi 2000, Momenta,**

57 Hope, or the **Williamsburg Art & Historical Society**. If you are a serious art collector, arrange for a studio tour (see end of this chapter).

Who are the Williamsburg artists? There are enough artists and musicians in this neighborhood to populate a Vermont village, and, as in any small town, there's a range of people, from serious to whimsical, obscure to well-known. For instance, Israeli-born sculptor Boaz Vaadia, whose work appears in private collections and is sold by the prestigious O.K. Harris Gallery in SoHo, works in a studio here, sculpting huge rocks, some unearthed in Williamsburg by utility street workers. There's Andy Levine, the artist-entrepreneur who invented those cute clocks-in-tin-cans sold in gift shops nationwide. And perhaps you've seen the work of muralist Mason Nye, whose large zodiac murals decorate major public spaces, from the construction barricades at Grand Central Station, to Macy's main restaurant. Coyote Recording Studio clients range from obscure musicians to Dion of Dion and the Belmonts; rumor has it that Philip Glass had a recording studio on North 7th Street. And, lots of support services—welding, packing, shipping, supplies—have cropped up around this creative "industry."

To get an idea of where people live in Williamsburg, walk down the choice residential streets such as **North 7th Street,** funky **Dunham Place** between Wythe and Kent, and prim **Ellmore Place**, between Driggs and Roebling. Or, look at the renovation at 64 Havemeyer between North 5th and 6th streets, a former convent-turned-co-op that was derelict for a century until the recent artist-driven boom in Williamsburg real estate.

Williamsburg's renaissance reiterates what Brooklyn has always had to offer: a livable corner of New York City. As real estate prices increase, some artists are exploring adjacent neighborhoods. Watch for the transformation of streets east of the current artistic center—especially near to other subway stops in Williamsburg and Greenpoint.

For the latest information on "new Williamsburg," look for the free local weekly *Waterfront Week* (398 Wythe Avenue, Brooklyn, NY 11211), available at the **L Café** and **Plan Eat Thailand** on Bedford Avenue.

And A Word About the L Train

The lifeline to Williamsburg is the L subway (you may be surprised to learn that it even exists). It dumps you right onto Bedford Avenue, the hub of Williamsburg's small commercial center. Going toward Manhattan, the L transverses 14th Street. Jam-packed into the wee hours of the morning with young people returning from Manhattan clubs and nightlife to Williamsburg, the L is also jam-packed again at 7 A.M. with workers on their way to Manhattan jobs. (Sometimes it's the same people.)

Historical Notes

Question: What do Rabbi Teitelbaum, Henry Miller, Commodore Perry, and Captain Kidd have in common? Answer: Williamsburg.

The tale is told that Captain Kidd, the famous pirate, frequented a dock belonging to the seventeenth-century farmer Jean Mesurolle, a pioneer in this part of the Brooklyn woods. Whether or not it is true, Williamsburg was settled as early as the 1660s by Northern European farmers and their African slaves. The area began to develop under the influence of David Dunham, the so-called father of Williamsburg, who opened a steam ferry and helped finance the building and incorporation of the Village of Williamsburg in 1827. By the 1850s, there was some industry and a resident population of about thirty thousand people here.

In the mid-nineteenth century, parts of Williamsburg were a suburban retreat popular among rich New Yorkers of German and Irish backgrounds. Commodore Perry and William W. Whitney transversed the East River by Fulton Ferry to come to fancy restaurants and hotels in the area. **Peter Luger Steak House**, founded in 1887, saw some of this carriage trade. At the same time, heavy industry located here, including businesses whose names later became household words: Astral Oil (which became Standard Oil), Brooklyn Flint Glass (which became Corning Glassware), and the Pfizer Pharmaceutical Company.

The upstairs-downstairs demographics of Williamsburg changed radically with the opening of the **Williamsburg Bridge** in 1903. Workingclass immigrants, mostly Jews escaping overcrowding on the Lower East Side of Manhattan, poured into Williamsburg—indeed, the *New York Tribune* of that era refers to the bridge as "Jews Highway." Italians settled in the area between Union and Bushwick avenues. Lithuanians, Polish, and Russian Orthodox immigrants established small communities. With the influx of Manhattan refugees, the area's population doubled in record time. The recently spruced-up **Metropolitan Pool**, built in 1922, served those immigrants, as did one of New York's earliest and still-finest low-income housing complexes, the **Williamsburg Houses**, dating from the 1930s. Many famous Brooklynites, Henry Miller among them, got their start here. And, of course, the upper crust fled to more exclusive resorts.

In the economic crash of the 1930s, most of the middle class, including Williamsburg's original Jewish families, moved away. Today a different, but highly visible, Jewish presence remains—about fifty thousand Satmar Hasidim from over a dozen sects, who arrived as Holocaust refugees in 1946.

From the 1950s through the 1980s, Latinos settled here in numbers, first Puerto Ricans and more recently Dominicans and Mexicans. The destruction of low-income housing and resultant social unrest occasioned by the building of the Brooklyn-Queens Expressway in 1957 was a turning point in the area, which remained stagnant, poor, and overcrowded for several decades. Considerable tension built up between the Latino and Hasidic communities, mostly over real estate and housing.

In the 1990s, young artists fleeing Manhattan's staggeringly high rents have breathed new life into the half-dozen streets approaching the waterfront, again transforming Williamsburg. Latinos, orthodox Jews, Italian Americans, and well-educated European and American artists reside in Williamsburg today.

Remarkably, all these layers coexist in a perfectly odd mix.

Nitty-Gritty, Then and Now

Lest one be tempted to think of Williamsburg/Greenpoint as trendy art centers, here's a reminder of the area's nitty gritty manufacturing side, past and present:

Penicillin: Pfizer, the giant pharmaceutical conglomerate has long had a presence in Brooklyn. Penicillin wasn't discovered here, of course, but it was first mass-produced in a Williamsburg area plant.

Chinese food: "BoBo Poultry" was for many years a producer of Buddhist-style chickens, supplying the bulk of Chinatown's chickens. And, if you've eaten a fortune cookie recently, there's a chance it was made in East Williamsburg by Wonton Foods, a forty-year-old business specializing in feel-good, good-luck fortunes.

Woven goods: In the mid-twentieth century, Brooklyn was home to many weaving mills, supplying New York's famous rag trade. Most of that business has since moved to the Far East, but Newcastle Fabrics on Wythe Avenue remains, spinning out specialty fabrics for uses as diverse as covering stereos and long-range military missiles.

Passover goodies: Spilkes and Oberlander's, two local kosher bakery wholesalers, whip up tons of kosher Passover macaroons, and several hundred thousand dollars' worth of Passover cakes, cookies, and sweets.

—*Excerpted in part from profiles in* Brooklyn Bridge *magazine.*

Kidstuff

McCarren Park is an enormous expanse of green, with all of the urban amenities—playground, ball fields, sprinklers, and concerts in the summertime. Bring a bat and ball and a picnic. And there are lots of eateries and funky shops on Bedford Avenue that teens will think are "cool."

ENTERTAINMENT

Because Williamsburg is one short subway stop from Manhattan, many residents take the L train into town for entertainment. People coming *into* Williamsburg might check out the following:

Brooklyn Brewery and Tours/Events. 79 North 11th Street, 486-7422. Free tours Saturdays, noon–5 P.M. Call for calendar of other special events.

Drop by for a free tour of the plant and quaff the stuff fresh from the vat. The brewery also hosts monthly public events, nothing stodgy, more in the way of a Polkafest featuring Polish food or a world-beer tasting, which is both fun and benefits a scholarship fund. See Brooklyn Brewery listing, page 306.

BARC Dog Parade. September. For information, call 486-7489.

The annual BQE pet parade, better known as "BARC," is a Brooklyn Mardi Gras with a doggie theme. Costumed pets, and their owners dressed like dogs, march through the main streets of Williamsburg. Music is provided by the local Italian marching band known for its more serious performances during the religious Giglio festival. A carnival atmosphere takes over as streamers and confetti fly, and one imaginative float after another, some made by local artists, create a hipsters' extravaganza.

For $1, you can enter "Pet and Owner Look-Alike," "Best Butt Contest," and "Best Dressed Dogs" contests. The parade, conceived in 1987, starts at the sponsoring organization, the **BQE Pets** at 253 Wythe Avenue (corner North 1st and Wythe streets) and ends at **McCarren Park**. Proceeds go to the dog shelter.

Ocularis Films. 70 North 6th Street, between Wythe and Kent avenues, 388-8713. Call for schedule and times; only occasional showings. Cash only.

Ocularis is housed in an old mayonnaise factory (there are still vats overhead). It is a kind of homemade movie theater that runs first-rate independent, cult, and classic films—but only on Sunday nights—and also enables local filmmakers to screen their fresh, often experimental material. It was started by a young Irishman who started showing movies on his roof, and discovered a market. There's sometimes live music beforehand, and a BYOB policy.

You can't tell that this is a movie theater from the street, by the way; the signal is orange traffic cones placed outside the door on show nights. To say that this place is informal would be putting it mildly.

Music

Tons of musicians live in Williamsburg, and music of all types is being played, but most of it is casual and unadvertised. The following lists a few formal venues, but if you are really interested, come and get the inside scoop by chatting with the people who work in music stores or restaurants that play music, and read the local newspapers.

Williamsburg Music Center. 367 Bedford Avenue, at South 5th Street, 384-1654. Cash only.

Every Saturday afternoon, from 2 to 6 P.M., you can catch a jazz performance workshop featuring local singers and instrumentalists working out their latest riffs.

See also: **Williamsburg Arts and Historical Society** and listings of restaurants such as **Charleston Bar and Grill**, and **Vera Cruz**, featuring live music.

Night Scenes

Coyote Recording Studio Rock Club North 5th Street between Berry and Wythe avenues, 387-7958.

Coyote's got connections in the rock business—they've been a recording studio in Williamsburg for over a decade, so their long-anticipated bar-stage combo venue is likely to draw some great acts. Their recording studio is on North 6th Street; call there to get the scoop on this as-yet-unopened club.

✪ **Galapagos Performance Art Space.** 70 North 6th Street, between Wythe and Kent avenues, 782-5188. Sun.–Thurs., 6 P.M.–2 A.M.; Fri.–Sat., 6 P.M.–4 A.M.

Galapagos, a multimedia warehouse space opened in 1988, is the brainchild of Robert Elms, whose idea for the nondescript building is to mix it up with rock and DJ music, and edgy dance, theater, and various hybrids of performance art. Come for movies, music, beer, and sushi. It's a scene!

The following places host weekend parties and events. Part of their success has been that they are *not* advertised, so only those privy to word-of-mouth communication know what's happening where and when. All this may have been changed forever by a 1998 *Time Out New York* magazine article citing the following as "Underground Clubs," so call before you go to see if they are still there—or where the party has moved to.

Eleven Hope. 11 Hope Street, between Roebling and Havemeyer streets, 486-9116.

Gargoyle. 97 South 6th Street, between Bedford Avenue and Berry Street, (212) 228-8356; ask for "Cleat."

Rubulad. 141 South 5th Street, between Bedford and Driggs avenues, 782-8523.

PARKS AND PLAYGROUNDS

Grand Ferry Park. Grand and River streets, on the waterfront, between the Domino Sugar Factory and the Con Ed factory (about a 10-minute walk to the Williamsburg Bridge, and 20 minutes to the L train stop at Bedford Avenue.)

The views! There's an open cobblestoned area, a stone footbridge, and a nice picnic area. Manhattan looms right across the water. Climb up to the viewing mound to get a sweeping view of the East River. The seventy-foot smokestack remains, a relic from the Pfizer Chemical Company that once had big plants here.

Between 1800 and 1918, Grand Ferry Park served as a ferry landing for boats shuttling passengers every five minutes between Brooklyn and Manhattan's Grand Street on the Lower East Side. In 1974, **El Puente** Williamsburg community youth organization created an open public space at the landing, which eventually led to the establishment of this lovely riverside park, opened in 1998. It's a small, sweet victory for locals who for twenty-five years have been trying to expand public access to Williamsburg's industrial waterfront.

McCarren Park. Bounded by Manhattan Avenue, Berry Street, North 12th Street, and Bayard Street.

A large, well-used urban park that is home to *serious* soccer and baseball games, extended family BBQs, and very sociable dog walking, McCarren Park is the dividing line between Williamsburg and Greenpoint, and is used by residents of both communities. There is a **Greenmarket** here in summer months.

✪ **Metropolitan Pool.** 261 Bedford Avenue, corner Metropolitan Avenue, 599-5707. Call for times.

This beautiful, copper-ceilinged indoor public pool underwent a multimillion-dollar renovation, reopening in 1997. Originally called Metropolitan Bathhouse, it was built in 1922 when public bathing facilities were high on the priority list for improving the health of poor immigrant communities. The original architect was Henry Bacon, who also designed Washington, D.C.'s Lincoln Memorial. Today it is gleaming new, and one of only ten city-owned indoor pools in the Big Apple. In an unusual arrangement, members of the public can pay a $10 membership fee to join and use the weight room upstairs.

POINTS OF CULTURAL INTEREST

Art Galleries and Performance Arts Spaces

Stay abreast of local listings for shows and gallery openings and closings.

Crest Hardware Show. 558 Metropolitan Avenue, between Lorimer and Union streets, 388-9521.

Crest is just a hardware store, not a gallery, but it gained some fame in the late 1990s as the host to the zany once-a-year "Crest Hardware Show," curated and conceived by Gene Pool, known as the man who wore a suit made of grass on national television. As you walked through the store, you would suddenly happen upon some gizmo among the saws, or an atomic frog or film reel in the paint section. The hardware store remains, but the show may or may not go on. Call to find out.

Momenta Art. 72 Berry Street, 218-8058.

A small, stark, and "edgy" nonprofit space where you're likely to find anything from video installations to pen-and-ink. Momenta has gained a strong reputation in the last few years. It is definitely worth a visit.

✪ **Open Studio and Garden Tours.** 596-2507. Call for dates, locations and hours.

Artists from Williamsburg and Greenpoint (and other Brooklyn neighborhoods) open their working studios to visitors on a given weekend. There are lots of opportunities for first-time collectors to view and purchase paintings, sculpture, and other works of art ranging in price from $100 to $5,000. It is organized by the **BWAC** (the Brooklyn Waterfront Artists Coalition) and local artists.

✪ **Pierogi 2000.** 177 North 9th Street, 599-2144. Open by appointment, and weekend afternoons.

Founded in 1994 by California-born artist Joe Amrhein, this tiny art gallery is at the heart of what's happening in the neighborhood, and its shows are occasionally reviewed enthusiastically by *The New York Times, Time Out New York,* and other New York City publications. Joe shows what he calls "cutting edge" work which sells from $50 up to $1,500. This is a good place to buy affordable art.

✪ **WAH: Williamsburg Art & Historical Society.** 135 Broadway, underneath the Williamsburg Bridge, 486-7372. www.wahcenter.org. Call for hours, a schedule of events, and to get on the mailing list.

Located in a beautifully renovated 1868 bank building, WAH is a neighbor to Peter Luger Steak House—but instead of steaks or greenbacks it is hoping to serve up the latest in Williamsburg art. The nonprofit gallery space, opened in 1997, has showcased everything from wild Coney Island poster art to the work of celebrated photographer Kim Iacono.

An informal, friendly crowd turns out for such events as a monthly music series, seasonal art shows, readings, and even a funky Halloween party. The driving force behind this space is Japanese-born painter Yuko Nii, who is a Williamsburg resident.

Complete with meeting rooms, poetry readings, performance art space, and high-tech facilities, WAH is a work-in-progress with fundraising and renovations still underway.

First-timers: It's about sixteen city blocks from the L train stop at Bedford and North 6th Street to this location.

Other Galleries: Other artist-run galleries that seem to be here to stay are listed below. Most are open only on the weekend, so call ahead. Don't be surprised if you get a home answering machine.

Art Moving. 166 North 12th Street, between Berry Street and Bedford Avenue, 302-9314.

Brooklyn Art Gallery. 283 North 6th Street, near Meeker Avenue, 486-0946.

Cave. 58 Grand Street, 388-6780.

Everything Is Everything. 245 South 3rd Street near Havermeyer Street, 388-3947.

Eyewash. 143 North 7th Street, 387-2714.

Flipside. 84 Withers Street, 389-7108.

4 Walls. 138 Bayard Street, 388-3169.

Holland Tunnel Art Projects. 61 South 3rd Street, 384-5783.

Momenta Art. 72 Berry Street, 218-8058.

MWMWM. 65 Hope Street, near Meeker Avenue. 599-9411.

N3 Project Space. 85 North 3rd Avenue, at Wythe Avenue, 599-9680.

Roebling Hall. 65 Roebling Street, between North 7th and North 8th streets, 599-5352.

Sideshow. 319 Bedford Avenue, 486-8180.

Velocity Gallery. 281 North 7th Street, 302-1709.

Points of Contemporary Interest

✪ **Brooklyn Brewery.** 79 North 11th Street, 486-7422. Free tours Saturdays, noon–5 P.M. Call for calendar of other special events.

It's not just beer, its a beer *culture*. The pride of Brooklyn, this eleven-year-old brewery pumps out hearty brews such as Brooklyn Weisse, Blanche de Brooklyn, Black Chocolate Stout, Pennant Ale (the original Brooklyn lager), and special Monster barley wine. You'll find these and other craft-brewed beers all across New York City. That thirst-quenching fact is due in part to Steve Hindy and Tom Potter (respectively a former banker and a former foreign correspondent), who founded Brooklyn Brewery and also have spurred the New York distribution of "world-class" beers imported from Belgium, Holland, Britain, and Germany.

Founded in Park Slope (where the two entrepreneurs were neighbors), Brooklyn Brewery opened the Williamsburg facility in 1996, marking Brooklyn's first commercial brewery in twenty years. Company material notes that pre-Prohibition Williamsburg was home to many breweries; one ten-block area with eleven breweries was known as Brewers Row. The Brooklyn Brewery's very modern brew house and tanks are set in at 1860s-era former steel foundry.

Hasidic Community. You can't miss them in the blocks on Bedford below Broadway, the men in long black coats and earlocks and women in modest, long-hemmed, long-sleeved styles. Their lives are built around Torah study, prayer, and adhering to the rigorous disciplines laid out in early and medieval Judaic scholarly writings.

Travel along Rutledge Road to view synagogues and yeshivas of the Satmar Hasidim housed in nineteenth-century mansions, like that built by the founder of the company that became the Jack Frost sugar empire, or take note of the low-income housing on Kent Avenue populated mostly by Hasidim. Known for their strongly held anti-Zionist views, they have counterparts living in Jerusalem who do not acknowledge the hegemony of the state of Israel, claiming that nationalism is a false route to the messianic era.

Almost by definition, the inward-looking, closed community of Satmar Hasidim are not overly interested in becoming a tourist attraction. And it is best not to disturb this pious community on holidays or during their Friday night–to–Saturday night weekly Sabbath.

El Puente Community Center. 211 South 4th Street, 387-0404.

This community center has been instrumental in improving living conditions in the poor areas of Williamsburg—for instance, in reclaiming the new **Grand Ferry Park,** and in smoothing tensions that arise between different ethnic groups residing here.

Rabbi J. Teitelbaum Place. Williamsburg St. E and Marcy Avenue.

This picturesque Old-World intersection, a retail area peppered with small Jewish stores located under the BQE, is named after the religious leader of the Satmar Hasidim, Rabbi Joel Teitelbaum.

✪ **San Genario Festival of the Giglio.**

The highlight of this June festival is a procession in which several hundred men reenact an early medieval procession, complete with bands and dancing in the streets, by carrying a sixty-five-foot painted wooden spire for a mile and a half. There's always an accompanying street fair. If you are interested in religious festivals or ethnic celebrations, don't miss this one.

Slicks Motorcycle Repair. Wythe Avenue and North 1st Street.

No, that long row of motorcycles is not a bikers' club, just an idiosyncratic long-time resident and entrepreneur, "Slick," who runs his TV outside on warm summer nights while he fixes motorcycles. He must be good at it; people come here from all over.

Points of Historical and Architectural Interest

Domino Sugar Refinery. Kent Street from South 1st to 5th streets.

The dark, hulking factory that dominates Kent Street has been sweetening the Williamsburg waterfront for more than one hundred years. Today a meager staff of several hundred workers run a 24-hour-a-day automated operation, offloading sacks of sugar from boats that arrive at the refinery's docks. Kids like to learn that here's where they turn out the sugar they buy at the supermarket, as well as honey, cinnamon, and peanut-butter-flavored sugars for the wholesale market.

Kings County Savings Bank. 135 Broadway.

A New York City landmark, the Kings County Savings Bank, built in the 1860s, is "one of New York's most magnificent French Second Empire buildings," according to the *Guide to New York City Landmarks.* Today it houses the avant-garde **Williamsburg Art and Historical Society** (see page 305).

New England Congregational Church. 79 South 9th Street.

Built in the 1850s in New England style by settlers from that region of the U.S. the New England Congregational Church represents an unusual combination of brownstone materials and Italianate style. It is a New York City landmark.

Our Lady of Mount Carmel Church. 275 North 8th Street, 384-0223. By appointment.

This church organizes the **Giglio**, one of New York City's most famous Italian festivals/street fairs; it is held every July.

✪ **Williamsburg Bridge.** Walkway entrance on Brooklyn side is at Williamsburg Bridge Plaza, Driggs and Broadway; on the Manhattan side, at Delancey Street.

The views of Manhattan are spectacular.

And, oh, is there history. Immigrants escaped tenement life to the fresh air of Brooklyn via this bridge.

Jazz great Sonny Rollins spent much time playing atop the bridge's footpath, and in 1962 released an album called, appropriately, *The Bridge*.

Bikers, strollers, runners, and walkers, the subway J, M, and Z lines also cross regularly.

Renovations are scheduled for completion in 2002. Until 1994, when cracks were discovered in the span, the more secluded sections of the Bridge were a favorite site for not-quite-legal birthday parties, rock band concerts, Halloween parades, and other rollicking festivities.

Tip: If you are want to walk or bike across, go on the weekends when there is likely to be more pedestrian traffic; there's not much of a police presence on the bridge.

Williamsburg Houses. Maujer Street to Scholes Street, Leonard Street to Bushwick Avenue.

This public housing project, built in 1937, was the first of many in New York City. Many experts still consider it to be the best, with its low, four-story buildings with courtyards, columned entrances, and other visual amenities.

Williamsburgh Savings Bank (now Republic National Bank). 175 Broadway.

The lovely Williamsburgh Savings Bank, located at the foot of the Williamsburg Bridge, is an Italian Renaissance–style building from the early twentieth century.

NOTABLE WILLIAMSBURG RESTAURANTS, BARS, AND CAFÉS

Old Williamsburg

✪ **Bamonte's.** 32 Withers Street, between Union and Lorimer streets, 384-8831. Wed.–Mon., noon–10:30 P.M.; Sat., till 1 A.M.; sun., 1–10 P.M.; closed Tues.

Classic Italian fare is served at this big, popular, old-fashioned family restaurant known for its white-shirted waiters, dim lighting, and big portions. You'll feel right at home, and the kitchen is glass-enclosed, so you can see what's cooking. Meat entrées cost $16 on average, and the pasta, which is excellent, costs somewhat less.

✪ **Cono and Sons O'Pescatore.** 301 Graham Avenue, corner of Ainslie Street, 388–0168. Mon.–Thurs., 11 A.M.–11 P.M.; Sat., until midnight; Sun., 11 A.M.–10 P.M. Takeout is available.

If it were in Manhattan rather than tucked away in Williamsburg, Cono's family fish restaurant would be packed every night. You can't go wrong here.

The broad selection includes shellfish (try the mixed seafood dish, tornido di pesci) and the specials are excellent, as are the veal scaloppine ala piccata. The prices range from $12 to $20 per entrée. And, you can order takeout.

✪ **S. Cono's Pizzeria.** 303 Graham Avenue, 782-3199. Daily, 7 A.M.–10 P.M., closed Sun. Cash only.

This terrific little eatery is worth a detour. The menu offers pastas with a choice of no fewer than fifteen different sauces, from scungilli marinara to primavera to seasonal broccoli rabe. As for the pizza, the cheese is thick, the crust is hard, and if you like vegetable toppings you can have a choice of sun-dried tomatoes, spinach, mushrooms, and olives. The "fresca" has an inch-thick toping of tomatoes, onions, and zucchini.

Galleria Pastry Shop and Pizzeria. 600 Metropolitan Avenue, 782-3777. Daily, 8 A.M.–9 P.M.; Sun., 1–5 P.M. Cash only.

This slick *pasticceria* has a cappuccino-espresso bar, great brick-oven pizzas, lots of mirrors. It's near the trendy **Moon Dog Café** and across the street from the famous **Tedone Latticini**, one of the best and oldest mozzarella makers in the city. The pastries are okay, but the pizza is really satisfying.

Giando on the Water. 400 Kent Avenue, 387-7000. Mon.–Thurs., noon–10 P.M.; Fri., noon–midnight; Sat., 4 P.M.–midnight; Sun., 3–10 P.M.

Giando's view is extraordinary—you can gawk at New York's famous skyline from midtown to the tip of Manhattan island. A favorite among busloads of Japanese tourists, according to some old-timers Giando is almost "too nice for the neighborhood." But the dress code spans informal to dressy, and the Italian food and service are excellent. Bring your parents and try the sunset dinner, it's a full gourmet meal. This large, glitzy restaurant set back from austere Kent Avenue is one of the area's unofficial landmarks.

✪ **Gottleib's Restaurant.** 352 Roebling Street corner of Division Street, 384-9037. Mon.–Thurs., 10 A.M.–6 P.M.; Fri., 10 A.M.–2:30 P.M.; Sun., noon–5 P.M.; closed Sat.

One of Brooklyn's best kosher delis, Gottleib's is a pleasant sit-down restaurant with great corned beef and other traditional Jewish meat dishes. It is conveniently located near the Williamsburg Bridge, just a stone's throw away from that other famous meatery, **Peter Luger**.

✪ **Green & Ackerman Dairy Restaurant.** 216 Ross Street, between March and Lee avenues, near the Williamsburg Bridge, 625-0117. Sun.–Thurs., 11 A.M.–7:45 P.M.; closes early on Fri.; closed Sat.

Vhat's on the menu at this large kosher dairy restaurant, you *vant* to know? It changes every day. But always, there are three kinds of soup, blintzes, fish, rice, sandwiches of all kinds. And endless amounts of Eastern European advice dispensed along with it. A meal here is spiced with the flavor of old Jewish Williamsburg.

✪ **La Laconda.** 32 Graham Avenue, between Withers and Frost streets, 349-7800. Mon.–Sat. 11 A.M.–11 P.M.; closed Sun. Cash only. Weekend reservations are recommended.

Slightly off the beaten track, come here for Neapolitan homestyle cooking of the Old World school. Portions are hefty, so you can rely on a light meal of soup or pizza, or if you are starving, go for a full main course of veal, chicken, or pasta.

✪ **Peter Luger Steak House.** 78 Broadway, between Bedford and Driggs avenues, 387-7400. Mon.–Thurs., noon–10 P.M.; Fri.–Sat., noon–10:45 P.M.; Sun., 1–10 P.M. Cash only. Parking lot and valet. Reservations necessary.

You don't have to step too far into Brooklyn to get to Peter Luger; just pop over the Williamsburg Bridge and you're there. In business since 1887, one of New York's most famous restaurants deserves a visit from everyone who loves steaks. The portions are enormous, the atmosphere is noisy and informal, with oak floors and tabletops, and the waiters can be a classic pain in the neck. Aged porterhouse steaks, grilled on the bone, are considered the absolute best of the genre. Plan to spend $40 to $50 a person. Bring cash.

Sal's Pizza and Hot Plates. 544 Lorimer Street, between Devoe and Anfeli streets, 388-6838. Cash only.

One of the Williamsburg's several popular pizzerias, Sal's makes a great pie. Try the Sicilian, and, if the weather is right, treat yourself to a homemade ice.

New Williamsburg

The Abbey. 536 Driggs Avenue, between North 7th and 8th streets 599-4400. Daily, noon–4 A.M.

Long, spacious bar, big pool room, great jukebox: all the makings of a hopping neighborhood watering hole. There's hip-hop and techno DJs on Sunday nights, occasional rock music scheduled throughout the month. When it's 2 A.M. and everything else is shutting down except your partying spirit, try The Abbey, which is open till 4 A.M.

Amarin. 617 Manhattan Avenue, between Driggs Avenue and Nassau Street (closer to the G Nassau Street stop than the L train), 349-2788. Daily, 11 A.M.–11 P.M. Cash only.

A new Thai restaurant with light, very fresh food, started by folks who used to work at Plan Eat Thai. As of this writing, it's too new to really tell, but Amarin looks like a great addition to the area's restaurants.

Anna Maria Pizza. 179 Bedford Avenue, near North 6th Street, 599-4550. Mon.–Fri., 11 A.M.–10 P.M.; usually closed Sat. and Sun.

Cheap Latin food—yucca, overcooked chicken, and rice-and-beans are sold here, along with pizza. It has a workingclass ambience. People come here to *eat.*

✪ **Bean.** North 8th Street off Bedford Avenue, 387-8222. Daily, noon–11 P.M.; weekends, 3 P.M.–midnight.

It's tiny, busy, and cool. This small restaurant serves up tasty Mexican food, and the burritos in particular are *deliciosa.* Try the jicama salad or fried bacalao served with chipotle cream and pico de gallo, and top it off with a homemade fruit cobbler of the day. The owner is also one of the entrepreneurs behind **LadyBird**, the highly publicized antique store on Bedford Avenue. Dinner costs under $10.

Black Betty. Corner Havemeyer and Metropolitan avenues. No phone at time of writing.

Black Betty's aims to add not just a bar, but an entire riff to the music-and-food scene in W'burg. It wasn't quite open yet at the time this book went to print, but it is slated to appear on the site of the former "Don Diego" restaurant. Stay tuned.

Bliss. 191 Bedford Avenue between North 6th and 7th streets, 599-2547. Mon.–Fri., 8 A.M.–midnight; weekends, 11–1 A.M. Cash only.

For organic vegan cuisine, come to this tiny, upbeat café decorated with the work of local painters. Heaping salads, marinated tofu sandwiches, and various combinations of healthful foods, plus freshly juiced combos of fruits and vegetables are the draw here. Takeout.

✪ **Brooklyn Alehouse.** 103 Berry Street, corner North 8th Street, 302-9811. Daily, 3 P.M.–4 A.M.

A popular bar that attracts Manhattan crowds, the Brooklyn Alehouse serves a full range of **Brooklyn Brewery** brews. With chunky wood benches and tables, stained-glass windows, and a beautiful mahogany bar, this is a great place to gear up or down.

✪ **Charleston Bar and Grill.** 174 Bedford Avenue, between North 7th and 8th streets, 782-8717. Open 3 P.M.–2 A.M.

The Charleston offers live rock music every weekend, featuring bands from the Williamsburg and the tristate area. There's lots of atmosphere here. Founded (officially) at the end of Prohibition, Charleston still sports a Depression-era mahogany bar, red bar stools, and an old fireplace mantle dating from when it was a malt-and-hops place. No cover, one-drink minimum; the action starts at 9 P.M.

Diner. 85 Broadway, off Berry Street, 486-3077. Lunch, noon–4 P.M.; dinner, 6 P.M.-midnight. Cash only.

Things are jumping at this new Williamsburg hot spot, a restored 1922 diner with a retro feel and booth seating for an intimate crowd of about forty-five people. You can find good food with a French flair here—cassoulet, mussels, French fries, and steak—or down-home fried or roast chicken with sides of spinach, mashed potatoes, and other comfort foods. The sole dessert is Kate's killer chocolate cake. Entrées are under $12.

Like the Empire Diner in Manhattan, the bar serves wine, beer, and hard liquor, and it is open—and busy—all day until 2 A.M.

Despite its street address, *don't* confuse this upscale Williamsburg restaurant, named Diner, with the **Broadway Diner**, which is a soulfood joint in Bushwick, a nearby low-income neighborhood.

✪ **Kasia.** 146 Bedford Avenue, corner North 9th Street, 387-8780. Mon.-Fri., 6 A.M.–9 P.M.; closed weekends. Cash only.

A Polish-American diner, Kasia is a staple of neighborhood life. Breakfast here is great, and locals say Kasia's chicken soup and other steamy, home-cooked food are just like mom's: cheap, homemade, and delicious.

✪ **L Café.** 189 Bedford Avenue, near the L train stop, 388-6792. Daily, 9 A.M.–midnight; weekends, open at 10 A.M. Cash only.

The unofficial hub of the artists' Williamsburg, the L Café is *the* place to take in the menagerie of artists in the area: You could be looking at a future Harte Crane or Georgia O'Keeffe. A shady outdoor dining area in back is the perfect place to enjoy bagels, foccacia sandwiches, and endless coffee as you wile away an afternoon reading the paper or simply planning your next move. Inside, the tables are close, chairs unmatched, and the walls are adorned with the work of local talent. See the free fliers and newspapers here for current happenings in the area.

Miyako. 143 Berry Street at North 6th Street, 486-0837. Mon.–Sat., 11:30 A.M.–11:30 P.M.; closed Sun.

Williamsburg's new Japanese restaurant, Miyako, serves tofu salads, sushi, and other Japanese specials.

Mugs Ale House. 125 Bedford Avenue at North 10th Street, 384-8494. Daily, 2 P.M.–4 A.M.

You can test beers to your heart's content here, chugging through a satisfyingly large variety of on-tap ales and brews. Mugs is a big, airy bar with cozy booths up front and lots of seating in back, plus the usual bar menu. Local artisans who get hungry doing physical labor like carpentry commend the burgers, but say Mugs' portions are not overly generous.

Northside Café. 119 Kent Avenue at North 7th Street, 388-9000. Daily, 11:30 A.M.–11 P.M.

In contrast to most of Williamsburg's cram-packed eateries, this spacious restaurant with a brass and mahogany bar and quiet patio out back is an appealing spot, especially for large groups and families (there is also a "family" price available). The setting is more memorable than the food, so stick to the simple menu choices.

What's unique is the mixed clientele: Italians and Poles catching a Yankees or Mets game at the bar and a sprinkling from the thirty-something end of the artist population. There's also an impressive selection of single-malt scotches and—count 'em—fourteen microbrews on tap.

✪ **Oznot's Dish.** Corner of North 9th and Berry streets, 599-6596. Open for brunch, lunch, and dinner. Mon.–Fri., 10 A.M.–midnight; Sat.–Sun., 11 A.M.–midnight.

Surely one of the most unique and delightful eateries in North Brooklyn, the artful Indo-Moroccan decor (think Hindu Mondrian) is only the beginning at this wonderful establishment. Oznot's takes traditional fare (steak and eggs, huevos rancheros, salmon steak, even chicken) and turns it on its ear by adding Mediterranean, Moroccan, and Indian flavorings, christening brunch dishes with quirky titles like "camel boy eggs" and "gulabi's French toast." The chef is clearly an experimenter who rarely fails. The sunny patio is perfect for those relaxing, bottomless-coffee brunches. Friendly, hip service. Your waiter or waitress is probably an artist or musician. Ask about their extensive, top-notch wine and beer selection.

✪ **Plan Eat Thailand.** 133 Berry and 115 North 7th Street, off Bedford Avenue, 599-5758. Daily, 11 A.M.–midnight. Cash only.

Voted by the *New York Press* readers as the best Thai food in the city, this simple restaurant is a Williamsburg hot spot—which is why it moved in the spring of '99 to much bigger digs around the corner from its original, cramped quarters. Although it's always crowded at dinner with trendy Manhattanites, and although the service is frantic at best, the food is absolutely delicious and stunningly cheap: the average entrée costs $6.00. If all the seats are taken, eat at the counter and watch the masterful chef whirl, sizzle, and steam as he juggles thirty orders with a beatific smile. Expect local art on the walls, local artists at the tables.

As for the name, Plan Eat Thailand used to be called Planet Thailand until Planet Hollywood apparently became apprehensive over name infringement. Overshadowed by this little Bedford Avenue eatery across the river, they pressured the proprietors into adding an 'a.' If Plan Eat Thailand is just too crowded, head over to **Amarin** or **Thai Café.**

Right Bank. 409 Kent Avenue, corner of Broadway, 388–3929. Daily 10–2 A.M. Cash only.

A Williamsburg pioneer, this spirited bar and restaurant serves a light menu of big sandwiches and brunch on weekends. There's a garden and an upstairs gallery that has occasional art shows. A crooner resurrects the sounds of Sinatra and Nat King Cole or blues and rock on weekends. The eclectic clientele includes locals, artists, and bridge workers, Domino Sugar factory workers from across the street, and visiting Europeans. The original owner is an ex-fireman, Lieutenant Keri Smith.

✪ **Seasons.** 556 Driggs Avenue, corner of North 6th and North 7th streets, 384-9695. Tues.–Thurs., 5–11 P.M.; Fri.–Sat., 6 P.M.–midnight; Sun., noon–midnight. Reservations are recommended on weekends.

Seasons is a knockout bistro located just about a block from the L train stop. For about $30 you will feel like royalty as attentive waiters bring you bread warmed to perfection, full-bodied meals of meats and vegetables, and indulgent desserts. It is an intimate experience, reminiscent of a small, good restaurant in France or Italy. Like the neighborhood, the restaurant has been transformed; it used to be a diner. See if you can spot the vestiges.

✪ **Teddy's Bar and Grill.** 96 Berry Street, corner North 8th Street, 384-9787. Daily, 11 A.M.–midnight; weekends until 2 A.M. Cash only.

For a great bar scene with live entertainment on Thursdays and Saturdays, pop into this welcoming neighborhood joint. The front section of Teddy's has the atmosphere up the wazoo (it was established in 1894, before the Bridge was built) with Brooklyn-made stained-glass windows and an old-fashioned ceiling. There's also a modern back room. The crowd is a mix of visitors, blue-collar end-of-the-bar types, and local artisans. Depending on the evening, you may catch some jazz, funk, or country music. On Saturday night Teddy's livens up with a DJ who spins good music for dancing. Festivities gear up around 9:30 P.M. The beer is fresh (Brooklyn Brewery is nearby) and the chips delicious, but if you are really hungry, try the burgers, the surprise BLT, or just skip straight to dessert. Brunch is good, too, and Teddy's Bloody Marys are dynamite.

Vera Cruz. 95 Bedford Avenue, between North 5th and 6th streets, 599-7514. Daily, 11 A.M.–midnight; later on weekends. Reservations are recommended.

This hip little Mexican joint—decorated not with sombreros but with retro photos of Marilyn and Greta, thank you very much—is jumping with a young, happy crowd of residents, European tourists, and miscellaneous New Yorkers. The stick-roasted corn con queso and cactus salad appetizers are delicious, but many main courses—fajitas, enchiladas, and the like—are standard fare. But it's the ambience you come here for: the sidewalk bar scene and cozy garden dining in the summer, the friendly chat among locals, and sometimes extraordinary live music with, say, leading Afro-Cuban musicians (they don't advertise; this is word-of-mouth). Good service; costs about $20 per person.

Villa de Mexico Azteca. 280 Bedford Avenue, between Grand and North 1st streets, 384-8787.

The Villa is a mix of old and new Williamsburg—a local family-run Mexican joint that local artists patronized so regularly that in 1998 they renovated and expanded. The new Villa will boast a new garden, a 24-hour schedule, and seafood, a juice bar, and American dishes—as well as their fan-winning chilies rellenos and tamales.

SHOPPING

Specialty Food Shops

OLD WILLIAMSBURG

✪ **Bruno's Bakery.** 602 Lorimer Street, between Conselyea and Skillman Avenue, 349-6524. Daily, 7 A.M.–8 P.M. Cash only.

If you haunt Greenwich Village, surely you know "the other" Bruno's, on LaGuardia Place. The Williamsburg location is where these traditional Italian breads and pastries—sourdough and olive and herb breads and fine chocolate confections—are baked. Bruno's chocolate pear royale, and cake of chocolate mousse, hazelnut, and pear mousse won accolades from the retail bakers trade association of New York. Their seasonal specials, like an edible chocolate cornucopia at Thanksgiving, are legends-in-the-making. You can buy these goodies here, cheaper, and get a wake-me-up cuppa coffee to go.

✪ **Tedone Latticini.** 597 Metropolitan Avenue, between Lorimer and Leonard Streets, 387-5830. Mon.–Sat., 8 A.M.–5:30 P.M.; closed Sun. Cash only.

Talk about authenticity. For over seventy-five years Tedone has been making excellent homemade cheeses and antipasti here. The sole owner, Georgia

Tedone, is now an elderly lady who continues to work her special brand of magic turning out 60 pounds of fresh warm mozzarella every morning, and more on weekends.

NEW WILLIAMSBURG

Greenmarkets: Havemeyer and Broadway (mid-July–Oct.) and McCarren Park in the summer (mid-July–Oct.).

Joe's Busy Corner Deli. 552 Driggs at North 7th Street, 388-6372. Mon.–Sat., 6:30 A.M.–6:30 P.M.; closed Sun. Cash only.

"Like having your auntie around the corner," is what locals say about Joe's, but the big-hearted guys behind the counter look more like football linebackers. They sell fresh ravioli, cold cuts, and freshly prepared foods such as stuffed artichoke hearts, string bean salad, fritatta, chicken cutlets, olives, hot peppers and mushroom salads, roasted potatoes, and made-on-the-premises mozzarella.

Laura Bamonte's Bakery. 263 North 6th Street, corner Havemeyer Street, 384-9662. Tues.–Fri., 7 A.M.–6 P.M.; Sat.–Sun., 8 A.M.–6 P.M.; closed Mon. Cash only.

The daughter of the family that owns the famous Bamonte's restaurant opened this delightful new bakery in 1995, and when you come to pick up a croissant, apple pie, or tiramisù she and her husband are likely to be the friendly folks behind the counter. In nice weather you can sit outside under an umbrella and soak up the Williamsburg vibes.

✪ **Mosha's Bread.** 170 Wythe Avenue, at North 7th Street, 387-5816. Sun.–Fri., 9 A.M.–10 P.M.; Sat., 9 A.M.–9 P.M.; closed Sun. Cash only.

If you're within a couple blocks of this famous shop, you'll certainly know it. In business since 1890 this five-generation bread bakery started on the Lower East Side and has kept Williamsburg wafting with the smell of freshly baked breads and rolls for the past half-century. Before walking into the shop on Wythe, swing around to the North 7th Street side and watch the bread being made. Sourdough, challah, sunflower, and seven-grain, pumpernickel, sweet breads, and the specialty they've made all these years, European corn bread. Fifth-generation co-owner Judy Farkas likes the rye raisin walnut and bestseller rye bread the best; these recipes go back 85 years.

Interesting Neighborhood Shops

OLD WILLIAMSBURG

✪ **Nathan Borlan.** 157 Havemeyer Street, near South 2nd Street, 782-0108. There's a parking lot near the Williamsburg store; call to hear a tape for travel directions. Sun.–Thurs., 10 A.M.–5 P.M.; Fri., closes mid-afternoon; closed Sat. Checks accepted.

Nathan Borlan is right over the Williamsburg Bridge from Manhattan. It is Williamsburg's most famous store, and you shouldn't miss it, especially if you are looking for boys' and girls' clothing in classic styles—at discount prices. This family-run business is in its sixth decade of operation. Some of the same high-quality merchandise you'll find here is sold at Manhattan's better department stores for 30 percent more—which is why shoppers flock here when looking to purchase big-ticket items such as winter coats.

The annex at 575 Kings Highway specializes in boys' wear. Both stores have a wide range of styles and prices, from children's through preteen sizes.

NEW WILLIAMSBURG

✪ **BQE Pet Supply and Grooming.** 253 Wythe Avenue, 486-7489. Mon.–Sat., 10:30 A.M.–7 P.M.; closed Sun.

Like NPR's radio stars Click and Clack, BQE is run by gregarious locals who effortlessly keep up an informative patter about Williamsburg, both old and new. People who have moved to Williamsburg from elsewhere actually bring their visiting parents and friends here to meet and greet, it's that homey.

There seem to be a lot of dog owners (and dogs) in Williamsburg—where else do they hand you a business card for the dog walkers club?—and they congregate at this incredibly friendly, somewhat zany, extraordinarily busy neighborhood dog supply store. Don't trip over the dozen or so dogs and cats underfoot; the strays from BQE's dog shelter freely hang out in the store. And, please, *do* notice the lovely gate outside the door, with the animal motif.

Clovis Press. 229 Bedford Avenue, off North 4th Street. 302-3751. Mon.–Fri., 8 A.M.–8 P.M.; Sat.–Sun., noon–8 P.M.

The only book shop in Williamsburg (to date), Clovis sells new and used fiction, classics, art books, and contemporary international art magazines. Come and settle in for an hour or so on one of the sofas, sip a cup of coffee, and nibble a fresh scone; it's that friendly. The store's name, by the way is not in honor of France's Ol' King Clovis, but after a pooch belonging to Amanda, the young New York–born artist and entrepreneur who opened this lovely bookstore. Occasional readings are scheduled.

Main Drag Music. 207 Bedford Avenue, between North 5th and 6th streets, 388-6365. Mon.–Sat., 11–7 P.M.; Sun., noon–6 P.M.

Two young entrepreneur musicians run this friendly hole-in-the-wall shop that sells vintage guitars for working musicians. It's well known among both residents and visiting artists.

Max and Roebling. 89 Bedford Avenue, between North 5th and North 6th streets, 387-0045. Daily, noon–9 P.M.; open later on weekends.

Women's clothing and accessories are sold at this quirky, centrally located little store. Owner Eva Maura shows the work of local artists on consignment. The goods include sheer, funky summer tops, colorful handbags, and jewelry. It's a favorite among European tourists.

Sarkana Classic Art Materials. 208 Bedford Avenue, between North 5th and 6th streets, 599-5898. Mon.–Sat., 11 A.M.–6 P.M. Closed Sun.

Artists who lived in Williamsburg in the true pioneering era, in the 1980s, suffered for lack of a traditional art store (though local hardware stores have done their best). This tiny, high-end store specializes in handmade or hand-ground art supplies.

Vintage and Collectibles

Vintage and collectible shops are scattered throughout the area. **Domsey's** is perhaps the most famous local clothing store. And there is a small cluster of antique and junque stores nearby, on Wythe Avenue and South 1st Street, including, appropriately, a store called **Junk** (388-8580).

There are lots of new places as well, such as **Furniture Charles** on Grand Street, who advertises as "complete home remedies," and **Bazaar Bizarre** on Grand between Bedford and Driggs avenues.

Beacon's Closet. 110 Bedford Avenue, corner of North 11th Street, 486-0816. Daily, noon–7 P.M.

If you are a mid-twenty-something hipster, check out this savvy secondhand consignment clothing, music, and book store. Vintage 1940–1970s meets the 1990s.

✪ **Domsey Outlet Warehouse.** 431 Kent Avenue, corner of South 9th Street, 384-6000. Mon.–Fri., 8 A.M.–5:30 P.M.; Sat., 8 A.M.–6:30 P.M.; Sun., 11 A.M.–5:30 P.M. Cash only.

A dream come true for thrift-shop buffs and bargain hunters: three stories of secondhand clothes, army surplus apparel, and dirt-cheap necessities like hangers, socks, batteries, light bulbs, and assorted knickknacks. Whether you're in the market for a $15 tuxedo, a ten-pack of blank tapes, or corduroy Levis in every color ever made (five bucks a pop), you'll love the free-for-all shopping heaven that is Domsey's (as it's affectionately called by locals). No salespeople whatsoever, so be ready to spend some time mixing, matching, and sorting.

✪ **Lady Bird.** 136 Bedford Avenue, between North 9th and North 10th avenues, 599-9300. Wed.–Sun., 1–6 P.M., or by appointment.

Hipper than hip, with more edge than a switchblade, Lady Bird has a display of great Americana. Outrageously spiky high heels, cool patio furniture, and wonderful gems from the early days of rock'n roll, *Leave It to Beaver* TV shows and other quaint mid-twentieth-century foibles fill both the store and back garden. The staff are friendly, and well connected to the local "scene." In case you didn't get the reference, the store is named after 1960s Lady Bird Johnson, who ran a "Make America Beautiful" campaign during her husband, Lyndon Baines Johnson's, presidency.

Moon River Chattel. 62 Grand Street, between Wythe and Kent avenues, 388-1121. Wed.–Sat., noon–7 P.M.; Sun., noon–5 P.M.; closed Mon.–Tues.

Whether you're meticulously restoring a brownstone to nineteenth-century splendor or searching for an interesting architectural artifact for your modern apartment, Moon River Chattel is dedicated to salvaging the goods to make it possible: doors, windows, spindles, handrails, et cetera. Precious (and expensive) antiques, but nevertheless a Williamsburg original and the most unique of the shops on the neighborhood's "antique row." Old claw-footed bathtubs and barber's chairs, funky Art Deco chairs, beautiful table sets, light fixtures, antique bird cages, and an assortment of fifties-style sleds right out of *The Saturday Evening Post.* Ornately framed mirrors and shelves of antique books lend the place a musty charm. The crafts of local artisans (candles, clocks) are also available. And although the nude mannequins are $200 a pop, they are for sale.

✪ **"R" 20th Century Design.** 326 Wythe Avenue at South 1st Street, 599-4385. Wed.–Sun., noon–7 P.M., or by appointment.

Far more expensive than most of its neighbors, "R" is a vintage furnishing shop featuring post–World War II furniture and home paraphernalia. Some items are in the $100 range, but there's also chic, retro, and über-cool furniture at jaw-dropping prices: Alvar Aalto armchair ($2,700), an Edward Wormley sideboard ($4,500), an orange vinyl Florence Knoll sofa ($2,000).

Two Jakes. 320 Wythe Avenue, between Grand and South 1st streets, 782-7780. Wed.–Sun., 11 A.M.–7 P.M.; closed Mon.–Tues.

The less quaint but entirely practical neighbor of Moon River Chattel, Two Jakes is a perfect place to begin assembling a home office or to start fitting out an upstart business: desks, chairs, filing cabinets, bookcases, lamps, coat trees, and typewriters of varying vintage, from clunky Underwoods to electric

Smith-Coronas, and a generous assortment of prints and original art as well. The downsizing of some corporate enterprise across the river can be your gain: For about $400, you can look like a CEO behind an executive desk.

Ugli Luggage. 214 Bedford Avenue, between North 5th and 6th streets, 384-0724. Daily, noon–7 P.M.

A humorous collection of tasteful flea-market finds is sold here. The collection varies, of course, but the price is right and the store's owners have an eye for comfy, old-fashioned kitsch. If you like it, you'll love it.

Used Clothing and Furniture, a.k.a. "Sidney's." North 11th Street and Driggs Avenue. No phone.

This is a great place to buy used props, for theater or for life. The stuff is beat-up but there's lots of it—books, kitchenware, belts, computer monitors, stuffed chairs, kitchen chairs, rocking chairs, crutches, golf clubs, sofas, sewing machines, vintage clothing, coats, shoes, and you-name-it. The Hasidic gentleman who runs the place, Sidney, is a local legend.

Studio Tours of Local Artists

If you want to see what kind of art is being created in Williamsburg, contact the **Brooklyn Arts Council (BACA**; 625-0080) or the **Brooklyn Waterfront Artists Coalition (BWAC**; 596-2507). For individualized tours for serious collectors, call Annie Heron, an independent consultant (782-7853) or the **Williamsburg Art and Historical Society** (486-7372).

Contributed in part by Joe Hagen.

Brooklyn's Best Bets for Children

Brooklyn offers great outings for kids, from museums to parks to fishing boat trips. Here we've listed some highlights. In this section you'll find museums, zoos, parks, special outdoor fun, live entertainment, places to see how things are made, and more. (For trips on what Brooklyn Heights, Park Slope, and other neighborhoods offer children, see individual neighborhood chapters. For listings of child-friendly restaurants, and toy and clothing shops, refer to the Kidstuff Index (pages 344–347).

ESPECIALLY FOR KIDS

Brooklyn Botanic Garden and Children's Garden (see full description on page 273). 1000 Washington Avenue, along Eastern Parkway, 622-4433. Tues.–Fri., 8 A.M.–6 P.M.; Sat.–Sun., 10 A.M.–6 P.M.; closed Mon.

There's plenty to do here, from wandering the Japanese garden to feeding ducks to serious nature study at the **Steinhardt Conservatory** (page 273). From April to August school-age children tend their own garden plots in the Children's Garden. Call early in the season to reserve a plot for the little green thumbs in your household.

Brooklyn Children's Museum. 145 Brooklyn Avenue, corner of St. Marks Avenue, 735-4432 or 4402. Wed.–Mon., 2–5 P.M.; weekends and holidays, 10 A.M.–5 P.M.; closed Tues. The suggested contribution is $2 per person.

Founded in 1899, the world's first children's museum has always been dedicated to hands-on learning. It is exuberantly interdisciplinary, multiethnic and multimedia—kids absolutely love it. Larger than the Manhattan Children's Museum and much more whimsical, the Brooklyn Children's Museum has wonderful, curiosity-provoking exhibits of cultural and technological artifacts; ethnomusicological instruments; and concepts of space, measurement, and weight. At the entrance, there is an unusual corrugated steel tube through which a constant stream of water flows. The current museum, rebuilt on its original site but partially underground to preserve park space above, opened in 1977 and recently was renovated to include new exhibits. Weekend concerts or special performances are held frequently.

Coney Island (Astroland Amusement Park and **Deno's Wonder Wheel).** See full description on page 88. Surf Avenue, at West 12th Street.

You'll find plenty of rides, noise, and hot dogs here; the famous Coney Island Boardwalk and the New York Aquarium are nearby.

Nellie Bly Amusement Park. See full description on page 42). 1824 Shore Parkway, near Toys "Я"Us, 996-4002.

This petite, relatively clean amusement park is just a couple minutes' drive from Toys "Я" Us. Not only is it a little bit of heaven for toddlers and preteens, it's also pretty easy on parents.

New York Aquarium. See full description on page 89. Surf Avenue, at 8th Street West, 265-3474 (265-FISH).

Located along the Boardwalk in Coney Island, the New York Aquarium was the first public aquarium in the United States. Today it is a world-class educational center for environmental conservation, with more than twenty-one thousand living specimens, a popular dolphin and sea lion show, and spiffy new exhibits.

New York City Transit Museum. See full description on page 233. Schermerhorn Street, corner of Boerum Place, 243-3060.

Built in an old subway station, this underground museum, with its full-size trains to look at and wander through, is perfect for children of all ages.

Prospect Park Carousel. See full description on page 277. Prospect Park, near Empire Boulevard and Ocean Avenue, 965-8999.

Few things are more fun for kids than a ride on an old-fashioned carousel.

LEARNING HOW THINGS ARE MADE

Anchorage. See full description on page 226. Cadman Plaza West and Front Street, under the Brooklyn Bridge, 625-0080. Call for a schedule.

Kids will love the space, and parents will probably enjoy the art shown here. How often can you actually walk inside the mammoth structures that support a bridge?

Brooklyn Terminal Market. See full description on page 165. The main gate is on Foster Avenue, near 85th Street East. Daily, 8 A.M.–6 P.M. Cash only.

Show your kids where the store owners go shopping, at this bustling food and garden wholesale marketplace.

Cousin John's Bakery. 70 7th Avenue, between Berkeley Place and Lincoln Place, 622-7333. Open daily at 7 A.M.

Watch the bakers at work here: just take a seat at a couple of small tables perched upstairs, almost in the kitchen.

Lefferts Homestead. See full description on page 278. Prospect Park, Flatbush Avenue, near Empire Boulevard, 965-8999.

This historic homestead conducts terrific free holiday programs in the arts and crafts of yesteryear, such as sheep shearing, coopering, rag-rug making, broom and basket making, and floorcloth painting. Call for the schedule.

UrbanGlass. 647 Fulton Street, near Flatbush Avenue, 625-3685.

Kids like to see things being made, and this nationally recognized stained- and art-glass workshop offers a perfect opportunity. Call to make arrangements for a visit.

LEARNING ABOUT BROOKLYN

Borough Hall Tour. See full description on page 231. 209 Joralemon Street, between Adams and Court streets, 855-7882, ext. 51.

Bring a brown-bag lunch in the summertime, take a stroll through the nearby Greenmarket, and give your kids a Civics 101 course here.

Brooklyn Center for the Urban Environment Tours. See full description on page 336. 788-8549 (recording) or 788-8500.

Older kids may enjoy these tours of Greenwood Cemetery, the Brooklyn Bridge; and industrial sites, such as Bush Terminal, Water Tunnel 3, and the Coney Island subway repair yards.

Brooklyn Historical Society and Museum. See full description on page 206. 128 Pierrepont Street, between Clinton and Henry streets, 624-0890. Call for hours.

Although not specifically for children, this museum in the Brooklyn Historical Society offers lots to discuss with school-age kids.

Brooklyn Historic Railway Association. See full description on page 216. Atlantic Avenue Subway Tunnel utility hole, intersection of Court Street, 941-3160. Reserved tours are usually on Saturday.

You need a group of about ten to tour this fantastic underground tunnel. Call to get on the waiting list.

Greenwood Cemetery. See full description on page 285. The main entrance is on 5th Avenue, at the end of 25th Street, 768-7300. Call in advance for permission to visit.

Peruse the tombs of the rich and famous here and let the kids happily run and jump among the rolling hills.

Soldiers and Sailors Memorial Arch. See full description on page 247. Flatbush Avenue, at Eastern Parkway, 965-8999.

If you're ready for a climb, the view from the arch is fabulous.

Weeksville (Hunterfly Road) houses. See full description on page 33. 1968–1708 Bergen Street, between Rochester and Buffalo roads, 756-5250.

The museum provides a chance to talk with your kids about the history of African-Americans in the United States or about urban archeology. Either way, it's an unusual and enriching trip.

LIVE ENTERTAINMENT

"Family Time." See full description on page 163. Brooklyn College Performance Center, Whitman Hall–Brooklyn College, intersection of Hillel Place and Campus Road, 951-4500.

From *Cinderella* to puppet shows to musical concerts, this is a wonderful program for children and parents. Subscriptions are available.

Gowanus Arts Exchange. See full description on page 245. 421 5th Avenue at 8th Street, 832-0018.

Dozens of programs in avant-garde dance, theater, performance art and music are performed by an ethnically diverse, inventive crop of new artists from Brooklyn and beyond.

Puppetworks. See full description on page 243. 338 6th Avenue, corner of 4th Street, 965-3391.

There are wonderful puppet shows here for preschoolers through sixth-graders.

Shadowbox Theater. See full description on page 216. YWCA—Memorial Hall, 30 3rd Avenue, between Atlantic Avenue and State Street, 875-1190.

Shadowbox stages puppet shows with original scripts and contemporary themes from October through June.

Spoke the Hub Dancing. See full description on page 248. 748 Union Street, off 6th Avenue, 857-5158.

Call this local dance and movement center for their calendar of events and programs.

Young People and Family Series at the Brooklyn Academy of Music. Lafayette Avenue, corner of Ashland Place, 636-4120. Call for a schedule.

From December through May BAM sponsors over twenty professional musical, acrobatic, and dramatic programs for children ranging from pre-kindergarten through high school. Programs are scheduled both for weekday and weekend family performances.

MUSEUMS

Brooklyn Children's Museum. See page 273. 735-4402.

Brooklyn's History Museum. See page 206. 624-0890.

Brooklyn Museum of Art. See full description on page 274. 200 Eastern Parkway, corner of Washington Avenue, 638-5000.

The twenty-eight full-scale rooms on the museum's fourth floor are a child's delight. An outdoor sculpture garden, a good cafeteria, a special children's gift shop, and the proximity to the Brooklyn Botanic Garden make this a super outing for children.

Harbor Defense Museum at Fort Hamilton. See full description on page 8.

If your child loves military stuff, at Fort Hamilton you'll find cannons, barracks, and a fortlike stone house that now encases a military museum.

Magnolia Tree Earth Center Grandiflora. See full description on page 32. 679 Lafayette Avenue, opposite Herbert Von King Park, 387-2116.

The George Washington Carver Gallery is worth a visit to teach kids about environmental issues. Hours vary, so call ahead.

New York City Transit Museum. See page 233. 243-3060.

Wyckoff House Museum. See full description on page 167. Clarendon Road and Ralph Avenue, at East 59th Street, 629-5400.

The craft sessions, kiddie story hours, and outdoor programs held on a large lawn area are excellent. Call for current programs.

OUTDOOR FUN

Fishing and Boating

Fishing Boats. See full description on page 97. Emmons Avenue, between Ocean and Bedford Avenues.

You can just look at these boats, or actually go on a half-day fishing expedition in one. For older kids only.

Macy's Fishing Contest, Prospect Park. See full description on page 276. Lullwater Pond, near Wollman Rink, off the Parkside–Ocean Avenue entrance, 965-8999.

For years the Urban Rangers have organized this July fishing contest sponsored by the department store.

Pedal Boats. See full description on page 277. Prospect Park, next to Wollman Rink, 965-8999. May–Oct. (weather permitting).

Take a pedal boat out in the Lullwater in Prospect Park. Kids under sixteen must be accompanied by an adult.

Horseback Riding

Jamaica Bay Riding Academy. See full description on page 99. 7000 Shore Parkway, between exits 11 and 13, 531-8949.

There are wonderful trails here spread over three hundred acres of birdwatching country, including three miles along the beaches of Jamaica Bay.

Kensington Stables. See full description on page 276. East 8th Street and Cullmit Place, near Park Circle–Coney Island Avenue, 972-4588.

Your kids will love a horse ride through Prospect Park. It's the perfect thing for autumn or spring. Call for fees and information.

Ice Skating

Wollman Rink. See full description on page 278. Prospect Park, near Parkside Avenue, 287-6431. Open Thanksgiving to March.

This outdoor skating rink has equipment rentals, a food concession, and parking on the premises.

Tennis. See listings in index, page 362.

Other Sports

Gateway Sports Center. See full description on page 98. 3200 Flatbush Avenue, across from Floyd Bennett Field, 253-6816.

The golf range, tennis courts, and batting cages, plus an eighteen-hole miniature golf facility, are open year-round.

PARKS

Empire Fulton Ferry Park. See full description on page 202. New Dock Road, by Water Street and the East River.

There's a big grassy space here with views of the East River, Manhattan, fabulous Civil War–era industrial lofts, and both the Brooklyn and Manhattan bridges.

Marine Park. See full description on page 99. Between Flatbush and Gerritsen avenues, exit 11 off the Shore Parkway, 965-8900.

This huge park has tennis courts, playgrounds, kite flying, bird watching, biking, and the usual park-related activities, as well as summertime concerts and a golf course.

Owl's Head Park and **Shore Road Park.** See full description on page 6. Shore Road, between 68th Street and Colonial Road, 965-8900.

With almost thirty acres of green overlooking the harbor, this breezy point is a popular place for family picnics. Around 97th Street there are ball fields, two lovely playgrounds, and tennis courts (call 965-8993 for permit information).

Prospect Park. See full description on page 276. Main entrance is at Grand Army Plaza, at the intersection of Flatbush Avenue, Prospect Park West, and Eastern Parkway; 965-8999 for special events or 965-8900 for park information.

This park offers more than five hundred acres of rolling hills and meadows, plus playgrounds, a carousel, and facilities for pedal boating, biking, and wintertime outdoor ice skating.

Prospect Park Zoo (a.k.a. the Wildlife Center). See full description on page 278. 450 Flatbush Avenue, near Empire and Ocean avenues, 399-7339.

A small, fun zoo featuring such attractions as prairie dogs, sea lions, baboons, and other entertaining animal friends.

Red Hook Parks. See full description on page 154.

Fishing, soccer, and room to ride a bike—but read about it first.

Shore Parkway Promenade. See full description on page 7. From Owl's Head Park at 69th Street to Bensonhurst Park at Bay Parkway.

Take the kids for a bike ride or run along the waterside here. Along the route are several popular places to fly kites.

OTHER PLACES TO WALK AND WANDER

Boardwalk. See full description on page 90. Along the Atlantic Ocean, between Coney Island and Brighton Beach.

There's plenty of room to run, bike, and cavort along this forty-foot-wide boardwalk, which extends through Coney Island to Brighton Beach. The breezes are fresh, and the ocean views can't be beat. And it is a quiet zone, so loud radios are prohibited.

Brooklyn Bridge. See full description on page 201. The walkway entrance is at Adams and Tillary streets.

Walk it or bike it for a good breeze and a spectacular view of Manhattan's skyline, the East River, and the Statue of Liberty.

Brooklyn Heights Promenade. See full description on page 201. Along the East River, access at end of Montague, Orange, and streets in between.

This is an ideal vantage point for observing harbor traffic, the Statue of Liberty, and various bridges. There's a beautiful little playground here as well.

PLACES TO GO IN BAD WEATHER

Brooklyn Public Libraries. It may seem old-fashioned in the age of Nintendo, but books are still a favorite diversion for kids. Every neighborhood has at least one library, and each library has a special section for children. If you have a New York City library card, you can take books out and return them to any Brooklyn library. Some libraries also have movies, game times, and story readings for children. Call the neighborhood library for information.

Movies. See the listing for movie theaters located in neighborhoods included in this book.

Indoor Sports

Bowling. Try **Lee Mark Lanes** in Bay Ridge, 423 88th Street between 4th and 5th avenues, 745-3200 (see full description on page 5), **Maple Lanes** at 1570 60th Street, near 15th Avenue in Bensonhurst, 331-900 9000 (see full description on page 42), or **Melody Lanes** on 37th Street in Sunset Park (see full description on page 283).

UNUSUAL STORIES FOR KIDS

(See also Kidstuff Index on page 344.)

ArtSmart. Brooklyn Museum, 200 Eastern Parkway, 638-5000. Call for hours.

A wonderful museum shop for children, ArtSmart is crammed with unusual toys, books, games, and art materials for toddlers to teens. The themes reflected in the merchandise are in sync with the museum's exhibits. If specialty items like books about the Great Pyramids or kits for backyard archaeological digs exist, you'll find them here—the museum has an outstanding Egyptology division—alongside tribal dolls, stenciling materials, and corn-cob doll kits. Neither stuffy nor esoteric, this is a shop that makes kids love going to the museum. Prices range from under $1 to over $50.

Brooklyn Gallery of Coins and Stamps. See full description on page 18. 8725 4th Avenue, near 87th Street, 745-5701.

Children as young as six can start collecting stamps, coins, and antique toys here.

Train World. See full description on page 69. 751 McDonald Avenue, near Ditmas Avenue, 436-7072.

You'll find hundreds of trains, pieces of scenery, miniature figures, and lots of track at this store.

U.S. Post Office. Brooklyn Central Office, 271–301 Washington Street, 271 Cadman Plaza, 834-3600 Mon.–Fri., 9 A.M.–5 P.M.

The terrific Philatelic Center has interesting displays of commemorative stamps and also offers a free booklet for kids on how to start a stamp collection.

Calendar of Festivals and Events

For up-to-date listings obtain a calendar of events from organizations of interest, such as **Prospect Park,** the **Brooklyn Museum of Art, Brooklyn Children's Museum, Brooklyn Historical Society, Brooklyn Botanic Gardens, Brooklyn Academy of Music**, etc.

JANUARY

Polar Bear Club Atlantic Ocean swim. January 1. CONEY ISLAND.

Chinese New Year (sometimes February). Call Brooklyn Chinese American Association for information, 438-9312. SUNSET PARK.

FEBRUARY

Black History Month. Call the Brooklyn Borough President's office for schedule of events, 802-3800.

MARCH

Women's History Month. For schedule of events call the Brooklyn Borough President's office, 802-3800.

APRIL

Irish American Parade. PARK SLOPE, 786-6798.

Pesach Spectacular. BOROUGH PARK, 851-5300.

MAY

Big Apple Circus. PROSPECT PARK, 780-0055.

Cherry Blossom Festival (Sakuri Matsuri). BROOKLYN BOTANIC GARDEN, 662-4433.

Historic House Tour. FLATBUSH, 859-3800; BEDFORD-STUYVESANT, 574-1979.

Craft Series. LEFFERTS GARDENS, PROSPECT PARK, 965-8999.

Cultural Crossroads Fair. FORT GREENE, 638-6700.

DanceAfrica Bazaar. Brooklyn Academy of Music, FORT GREENE, 636-4119.

Historic house tours: BROOKLYN HEIGHTS, 858-9193; CLINTON HILL, 624-1712; PARK SLOPE, 832-8227; PROSPECT HEIGHTS, 284 6210.

Norwegian Constitution Day Parade (first Sunday after May 17). BAY RIDGE, 836-6700.

Outdoor Sculpture Show. DUMBO, 596-2507.

Sidewalk Market (antiques). ATLANTIC AVENUE, 596-1866.

You Gotta Have Park Day. PROSPECT PARK, 965-8999.

JUNE

DanceAfrica at BAM. FORT GREENE. 636-4119.

Fulton Art Fair. BEDFORD-STUYVESANT, 636-6900.

House and Garden Tour. FORT GREENE, 237-9031.

June Balloon. BROOKLYN CHILDREN'S MUSEUM, 735-4402.

Lesbian and Gay Pride Parade. PARK SLOPE, 832-9800.

Mardi Gras on Avenue M. MIDWOOD, 469-8990.

Mermaid Parade. CONEY ISLAND, 372-5159.

Outdoor Concerts. *Celebrate Brooklyn* series in Brooklyn Parks, 965-8999.

Sidewalk Market (antiques). ATLANTIC AVENUE, 596-1866.

Smith Street Sunday Fun-Day. CARROLL GARDENS, 825-0328.

Welcome Back to Brooklyn Festival. PROSPECT PARK, 855-7882/965-8999.

JULY

Fulton Art Fair. BEDFORD-STUYVESANT, 636-6900.

International African Arts Festival. BEDFORD-STUYVESANT, 638-6700.

Macy's Fishing Contest. PROSPECT PARK, 965-8999.

Nathan's Hot Dog Eating Contest (July 4). CONEY ISLAND, (516) 338-8500.

Outdoor Concerts. *Celebrate Brooklyn* series in Brooklyn Parks, 965-8999.

Procession of St. Fortunata. BENSONHURST, 331-6532.

San Genario, the Feast of the Giglio, Our Lady of Mount Carmel Church. WILLIAMSBURG, 394-0223.

Sidewalk Market (antiques). ATLANTIC AVENUE, 596-1866.

AUGUST

Brighton Jubilee. BRIGHTON BEACH, 891-0800.

Outdoor Concerts. *Celebrate Brooklyn* series in Brooklyn Parks, 965-8999.

Pakistan Independence Day Parade. FLATBUSH, 802-3800.

Sidewalk Market (antiques). ATLANTIC AVENUE, 596-1866.

SEPTEMBER

Atlantic Antic. ATLANTIC AVENUE, 875-8993.

BARC Dog Parade. WILLIAMSBURG, 486-7489.

Coney Island Air Show. CONEY ISLAND, 266-1234.

Court Street Crawl. CARROLL GARDENS, 858-0557.

Flatbush Frolic. FLATBUSH, 859-3800.

Great Irish Fair. CONEY ISLAND, 266-1234.

Open Studio Tours. WILLIAMSBURG, 596-2507.

Santa Rosalia Festival. BENSONHURST, 331-6532.

Sidewalk Market (antiques). ATLANTIC AVENUE, 596-1866.

Succos SimchaThon. (Sometimes Oct.) BOROUGH PARK, 851-5300.

West Indian American Day Parade. EASTERN PARKWAY, 773-4052 or 802-3800.

OCTOBER

DUMBO Art Center Festival. DUMBO, 624-3772.

Festival of Polish Culture/Polish film festival. GREENPOINT, 383-5290.

Halloween Parades/events. CARROLL GARDENS, 825-0328. PARK SLOPE, 636-8736. WILLIAMSBURG, 486-7372.

Monster Mash. BROOKLYN CHILDREN'S MUSEUM, 735-4402.

Parade of Flags. SUNSET PARK.

Ragamuffin Parade and Third Avenue Festival (first weekend in October). BAY RIDGE, 836-6700.

NOVEMBER

Thanksgiving Programs. PROSPECT PARK, 965-8999.

DECEMBER

New Year's Eve Fireworks. PROSPECT PARK, 965-8999.

St. Nicholas Day Celebration. PROSPECT PARK, 965-8999.

Tours

Tours can be a wonderful way to find out about Brooklyn as a whole, to explore a neighborhood in depth, or to focus on a specific interest, be it art, food, architecture, or urban transportation. Here are a number of organizations and individuals to choose from. As with all tours, your experience will depend a lot on a number of variables, including your guide and fellow travelers. Please consider the following as suggestions, not recommendations or endorsements. *Tip*: Call for up-to-date information, including price and itinerary, as tours change frequently.

The following is, to our knowledge, the most comprehensive list of Brooklyn tours to be published to date. They are listed alphabetically, by category: commercial tours; tours by nonprofit organizations; general Brooklyn tours; specialized ethnic and architectural tours; do-it-yourself tours; house-and-garden tours; and art-scene tours.

Jolly Red Trolley

On weekends, get a free ride on the red "Day in Brooklyn Trolley," which provides hourly shuttle service on a circuit including: Prospect Park and Zoo, the Victorian carousel, the Brooklyn Museum of Art, the Brooklyn Botanic Garden, and Grand Army Plaza. 965-8999. Noon–5 P.M.

COMMERCIAL TOUR COMPANIES

Sponsor: New York Apple Tours. (212) 944-9200.
Specialty: The largest double-decker-bus tour company in New York City runs a "hop on, hop off" tour that enables you to stop for awhile at a site, then take a later bus. The route includes over a dozen stops, including Metro Tech Center, Junior's, Atlantic Avenue's Middle Eastern stores, the Brooklyn Museum of Art, the Brooklyn Children's Museum, and the Brooklyn Botanic Garden.

MAJOR NONPROFIT ORGANIZATIONS

Sponsor: Brooklyn Center on the Urban Environment (BCUE). 788-8500.
Specialty: Top-notch tours are run of ethnic neighborhoods, Greenwood Cemetery, Gowanus Canal, and other central points in Brooklyn by a roster of professional Brooklynophiles, all of whom live in Brooklyn. Past trips have included "Noshing Tour of Brooklyn's Ethnic Neighborhoods," "Canal Boat on the Gowanus Canal," and "Ecology Sails in Jamaica Bay." The sponsoring organization is based in Prospect Park, and is known for its smart, educational programs. Highly recommended. Call for schedules or to discuss customized group tours.

Sponsor: Brooklyn Historic Railway Association. 941-3160.
Specialty: Built in 1861 and then abandoned and sealed up in 1884, the Atlantic Avenue Tunnel was the world's first subway tunnel. Rediscovered in 1980, it is now listed in the National Register of Historic Places. Robert Diamond conducts tours—you enter through a utility hole—for groups of ten or more. An unusual experience; call to get on a waiting list. See listing, page 216.

Sponsor: Brooklyn Historical Society Tours. 624-0890.
Specialty: A rich program of tours and walks are sponsored by the most likely of all institutions, the local historical society. In-depth walking tours focus on specific neighborhoods, with titles such as "Spotlight on Cobble Hill," and "Greenpoint: Architecture of a Small Town." Call for a schedule. Cost is about $5 for members, $12 for non-members. Highly recommended for history buffs.

Note that the Historical Society started a major renovation in 1998, and so programs may be temporarily disrupted.

Sponsor: New York Transit Museum (in Brooklyn). 234-8601. (www.mta.nyc.ny.us/nyct/Museum/musmain.htm)
Specialty: Scheduled tours focus on interesting bits of Brooklyn life from the perspective of transportation and the train system, for instance "By Subway to Brighton," "The City Transformed," "The Park the Parkways and the Emerald City," and others. Top-notch and an unusual slant. Call to see which tours are appropriate for kids. See listing, page 233.

Sponsor: 92nd Street Y Tours. (212) 996-1100.
Specialty: Group tours are conducted, usually on Sunday. Past tours have included: "Brighton Beach: The Russian Experience," "Coney Island Revisited," "Brooklyn Heights South," "Jewish Williamsburg," "Williamsburg's

Burgeoning Art Scene," "Inside Private Homes of Park Slope," "Flatbush: Past and Present," "Victorian Brooklyn Heights," "Inside Private Homes of Fort Greene," "The Experimental Glass Workshop," "Art and Architecture of Brooklyn's Vinegar Hill," and many others. The Y has an excellent reputation for informative tours.

Sponsor: American Museum of Natural History. (212) 769-5200.
Specialty: Geology, history, ecology.
Note: These are run infrequently, only several times a year.

Sponsor: Municipal Art Society. (212)439-1049.
Specialty: Walking tours organized by this leading art institution have examined Park Slope brownstone architecture.

GENERAL TOURS

The following vary in price, focus, and duration. Try to pick a theme or area that is of interest to you. Some run scheduled tours only; others can build a tour around an individual or group.

Sponsor: Big Onion Walking Tours. (212) 439-1090 (www.bigonion.com).
Specialty: A twilight walking tour with background on the history and architecture of the Brooklyn Bridge and Brooklyn Heights, including of literati Walt Whitman, Truman Capote, Henry Miller, and Thomas Wolfe. Call to see if other destinations have been added.

Sponsor: Brooklyn Attitude Tours. 398-0939.
Specialty: Bus and walking tours in French, Italian, English (and possibly German) of architecture, food, landmarks in numerous ethnic neighborhoods. It's organized by Park Slope resident Elliot Niles. Join a group or make your own.

Sponsor: History Tours of New York. (212) 242-5762.
Specialty: Joyce Gold, experienced tour guide, leads neighborhood walking tours. Join a group or make your own.

Sponsor: NYC Discovery Walking Tours. (212) 465-3331.
Specialty: Ethnic neighborhoods, architecture, and history. Join a group or make your own.

Sponsor: Urban Explorations. 721-5254.
Specialty: Patricia Olmstead, who also teaches at the New School for Social

Research, leads neighborhood explorations in walking tours of Brooklyn. Join a group or make your own.

Sponsor: VIP Tours. (800) 300-6203 or (212) 247-0366.
Specialty: A service that custom designs tours for individuals or groups, offering "an in-depth view of architecture and culture" that is staffed by experts in theater and architecture, and musical actors. VIP Tours works with groups such as the National Trust for Historic Preservation and nonprofit theater companies who come to New York.

SPECIALIZED, ETHNIC, AND ARCHITECTURE TOURS

Sponsor: Braggin' About Brooklyn. 297-5107.
Specialty: African-American history, including a tour of 17 African-American historical sites. Join a group or make your own.

Sponsor: Brooklyn Brewery. 486-7422.
Specialty: Saturday tours of the Brooklyn Brewery plant.

Sponsor: Brooklyn Center on the Urban Environment (BCUE.) 7888-8500.
Specialty: Gowanus Canal Tours.
See listing on page 336.

Sponsor: Discover New York. (212) 337-1321.
Specialty: Architecture, Horticulture, and Food of Brooklyn's Neighborhoods

Walking or bus tours of Brooklyn neighborhoods with emphasis on architecture and history; horticulture; foods; and fine arts. To be arranged in advance; minimum of 12 for walking tour; minimum of 16 for bus tour.

Sponsor: First Battle Revival Alliance. (212) 726-8062.
Specialty: This nonprofit, volunteer organization is dedicated to Revolutionary War history and its members give occasional tours of related Brooklyn sites. Call for schedule.

Sponsor: Friends of Gateway. (212) 352-9330.
Specialty: Free walks along Brooklyn's shore from Sheepshead Bay to Rockaway by Neighborhood Open Space Coalition. In season, you can go swimming and picnic.

Sponsor: Gravesend Historical Society Tours. 375-6831.
Specialty: Brooklyn History. Call well in advance for information and schedule.

Sponsor: Greenwood Cemetery Tours. 469-5277.
Specialty: Greenwood Cemetery.

John Cashman, a senior citizen and retired police officer, will lead you in a town around Greenwood Cemetery. He used to mow the lawn here as a kid and knows where the skeletons are buried, from Horace Greeley's grave to Leonard Bernstein's. There are five different two-hour walking tour, $5 per person; parking is available within the cemetery. September–November; April–June. Call for a flyer, and information on other guides and tours.

Sponsor: Hasidic Crown Heights Tours. 953-5244.
Specialty: An "insider's view" of Crown Heights, home of the worldwide Lubavitcher movement. Two-and-a-half-hour walking tours start in a Hasidic community library, proceed through a Hasidic synagogue, and include other sites. Join a group or make your own. Please do not call on Friday night or all day Saturday.

Sponsor: Israelowitz tours of Jewish Brooklyn. 951-7072.
Specialty: Occasional Sunday tours of Jewish Brooklyn by Oscar Israelowitz, a guidebook author who specializes in this topic.

Sponsor: Mary Ann DiNapoli. 522-1916.
Specialty: A walking tour of Brooklyn's Arabic Middle Eastern quarter by a licensed tour guide. Tours last 90 minutes.

DO-IT-YOURSELF QUICK LANDMARK VISITS

Sponsor: BRIC.
Specialty: Grand Army Plaza Rooftop Tour. (718) 855-7882.

Offered continuously from 1 to 5 P.M. every summer weekend, you climb up to the top of top of Soldiers and Sailors Memorial Arch and get a bird's-eye view of Prospect Park, Eastern Parkway, and Park Slope.

Sponsor: Brooklyn Borough Hall. 875-4047.
Specialty: Brief tour of 1848 "town hall," Tuesdays at 1 P.M. Free.

Sponsor: Coney Island.
Specialty: Self-guided visit to Cyclone and Wonder Wheel rides (in season).

See the Coney Island chapter, page 86.

HOUSE AND GARDEN TOURS

House Tours. Half-day, self-guided tours through privately owned historic brownstones homes, opened to the public for one day only. Call for dates, cost, and details on how to purchase a ticket.

Bedford-Stuyvesant historic house tour (April; 574-1979).

Brooklyn Heights historic house tour (April; 858-9193).

Fort Greene historic house tour (May; 237-9031).

Park Slope historic house tour (April; 832-8227).

Victorian Flatbush house tour (April; 469-8990).

GARDEN TOURS

Brooklyn Botanic Gardens. 622-4433. The Brooklyn Botanic Garden is an extraordinary resource; call for information on tours.

Brownstone Brooklyn Garden District. Private and community gardens in Fort Greene, Clinton Hill, and Prospect Heights, with a concurrent indoor/outdoor exhibit of garden-inspired works by members of the Brooklyn Watercolor Society (June; 852-9423).

Fort Greene Garden Tour. (May; 237-9031).

ART SCENES

The following are not necessarily licensed as New York City tour guides, but can help visitors interested in the Brooklyn art scene. If one doesn't work out, don't hesitate to call another. All require advance arrangements.

Sponsor: Brooklyn Arts Council Association 625-0080.
Specialty: Group tours for "serious collectors" organized by this government-financed organization. Schedule in advance.

Sponsor: BWAC—Brooklyn Waterfront Artists Coalition. 596-2507.
Specialty: This nonprofit organization of artists mounts exhibits and special events; call for information about open studio tours.

Sponsor: Clinton Hill Simply Art Gallery. 857-0074.
Specialty: Not a tour per se, this is a gallery that specializes in African-American emerging artists (including Brooklynites, but not exclusively so) for the new collector.

Sponsor: DUMBO Arts Center. 624-3772.
Specialty: Art in DUMBO area; studio tours can be arranged. Call in advance. See listing, page 228.

Sponsor: Annie Heron. 782-7853.
Specialty: Williamsburg art studios.

Annie Heron, an experienced art dealer, arranges private studio tours for experienced and novice collectors interested in the Williamsburg art scene. She will custom-design the tour to a collector's area of interest, or help new collectors choose. Minimum two hours at $75 per hour. Book at least one week in advance.

Sponsor: WAH Society. 486-7372.
Specialty: It is not a tour company, but the WAH Society can arrange customized tours of Williamsburg galleries in advance for small groups or interested individuals. Call well ahead. See listing, page 305.

Accommodations

BED-AND-BREAKFASTS

Akwaaba Mansion Bed & Breakfast. 347 McDonough Street, Bedford Stuyvesant. 455-5958. A gorgeous renovated Victorian mansion; a favorite among honeymooners. Located in historic black neighborhood of Bedford-Stuyvesant. Rates from $100–$125 per night.

Baisley House Bed & Breakfast. 294 Hoyt Street, between Union and Sackett streets. 935-1959.

A Victorian brownstone with garden in Carroll Gardens. Prices range from $85 to $125.

Bed and Breakfast on the Park. 113 Prospect Park West, between 6th and 7th streets. 449-6115.

Elegant mansion across from Prospect Park. Rates from $125 to $280.

Foy House Bed & Breakfast. 819 Carroll Street, between 8th Avenue and Prospect Park West, 636-1492. $125 for two with private bath; two-night minimum.

A classic, small bed-and-breakfast located in Park Slope.

Homestay New York. 434-2071, fax 434-2071.

For foreign visitors only: If you want to stay with a Brooklyn family, call Homestay to be placed in a real home setting, with "real New Yorkers!" Homestay has two price levels. Budget travelers can stay in a "working class neighborhood" and for $75 to $95 get a breakfast and dinner along with a MetroCard for public transportation. Homestay in a "middle/upper class neighborhood" with breakfast, dinner, use of the phone, and a Metro Card costs from $100 to $120.

HOTELS

New York Marriott in Brooklyn. Brooklyn Renaissance Plaza, 333 Adams Street, 246-7000, or (800) 228-9290.

Brooklyn's finest hotel, this Marriott opened in 1998 and offers a full range of guest services. About $180–240 per night; prices vary.

Comfort Inn. 8315 4th Avenue, off 83rd Street. 238-3737.

A newly renovated 70-room hotel located in residential Bay Ridge. About $160 per night.

Park House Hotel. 1206 48th Street, near 12th Avenue. 871-8100.

Caters to religious Jewish clientele, located in Borough Park. About $90 per night.

Avenue Plaza Hotel. 47th Street and 13th Avenue. (As of this writing, no phone number was available.)

A new luxury hotel is being designed for Orthodox Jewish customers, with special features for their religious needs. Rates will be about $170 per night.

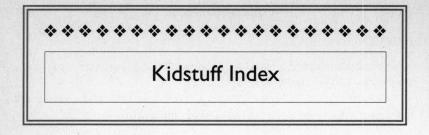

Kidstuff Index

Here's a quick index of child-friendly restaurants and stores specializing in children. (See also the general index, starting on page 367, and Brooklyn's Best Bets for Children, starting on page 322.)

KID-FRIENDLY STORES

Kids' Clothing

Books and Music

Educational Material

Toys

Italian

Jewish

Mexican/Spanish/Latino

Middle Eastern

Pizza

Polish

Where to Find It

This subject index indicates in parentheses the neighborhood in which a listing is described, and the page number on which you will find it. The icon ✪ indicates a Brooklyn Best Bet. Please note that this is a very subjective list; don't hesitate to try them all!

FOOD AND DINING

Here you will find restaurants, cafés, and bars, as well as lists of food stores that sell ethnic specialties, fresh produce, etc.

Dining by Cuisine

African

American Eclectic

From burgers to steaks to tuna sandwiches.

Delis (eat-in)

See page 354 for take-out deli food stores.

Restaurants with Other Special Features

This includes a selective list of restaurants with music, outdoor seating, and nineteenth-century ambience. Family-friendly restaurants are listed in the Kidstuff Index on page 345.

Restaurants with Music

Selected List; see also Nightlife

Outdoor Seating

Selected list

Nineteenth-Century Ambience

Child-Friendly Restaurants

See Kidstuff Index, page 345

Nightlife

Ethnic Food and Grocery Stores

Bagels

Baked Goods

Beer

Candy and Ice Cream

Deli (take-out)

✪ Adelman's Family Restaurant (kosher; Flatbush), 178
Cangiano's Italian Deli (Italian; Bensonhurst), 48
D'Amico Foods (Italian; Carroll Gardens), 145
✪ Defonte's Sandwich Shop (Italian; Carroll Gardens/Cobble Hill), 145
Delicatessen at Verandah Place (eclectic; Carroll Gardens/Cobble Hill), 145
✪ Edna's Glatt Kosher Delicatessen (kosher; Flatbush), 174
Essex on Coney (kosher; Flatbush), 178
Gottlieb's Restaurant (kosher; Williamsburg), 310
Joe's Busy Corner Deli (Italian; Williamsburg), 317
✪ Junior's (eclectic; Downtown Brooklyn), 235
✪ Lassen & Hennings Deli (eclectic; Brooklyn Heights), 212
New Prospect at Home (eclectic; Park Slope), 260
Pollio (Italian; Park Slope), 261

Discount Food Stores

Costco (Sunset Park), 292
✪ Flatbush Food Cooperative (Flatbush), 174
✪ Marshall's Smoked Fish (Williamsburg), 195
✪ Park Slope Food Co-op (Park Slope), 261

Ethnic Foods

Selected list; see also Baked Goods, Deli, Pizzerias, *and* Ethnic Restaurants

A & S Greek American Meat Market (Greek American foods; Bay Ridge), 16
A & T Turkish Halal Meat Market (Mediteranean/Turkish foods; Bay Ridge), 17
A. S. Fine Foods (Italian foods; Park Slope), 259
A Touch of Spirit (kosher wines; Borough Park), 63
Astoria European Foods (Russian foods; Bay Ridge), 18
B & A Pork Store (Bensonhurst), 48
Bari Pork Store (Italian foods; Bensonhurst), 50
Birlik Oriental Food/Halal Meat Market (Middle Eastern foods; Sunset Park), 291
Cangiano's Italian Deli (Italian foods; Bensonhurst), 48
Cheffy's Jamaican (Caribbean foods; Flatbush), 174
Christina's (Caribbean foods; Park Slope), 250
✪ Eagle Provisions (Eastern European imports; Park Slope), 259
EFE International (dried fruits; Brighton Beach), 83
El Asmar (Middle Eastern foods; Atlantic Avenue), 220
Esposito Pork Store (Italian foods; Carroll Gardens/Cobble Hill), 146
✪ G. Fratelli Ravioli (Italian foods; Park Slope), 260
Gus' Pickle Look-Alike (pickles; Flatbush), 179
Hellas American Food Market (Greek American foods; Bay Ridge), 16
✪ Hong Kong Supermarket (Asian foods; Sunset Park), 291
✪ International Food (Italian foods; Bensonhurst), 50
Juns Market (Latino foods; Sunset Park), 290
Lien Hung Supermarket (Sunset Park), 291
M & I International (Russian foods; Brighton Beach), 84
Marshall's Smoked Fish (Greenpoint), 195
Mejlander and Mulgannon (Nordic foods; Bay Ridge), 17
Miller's Market (Russian/Jewish foods; Flatbush), 184
Mrs. Stahl's Knishes (fresh knishes; Brighton Beach), 84
Negev (Israeli/kosher foods; Flatbush), 180
✪ Nordic Delicacies (Nordic foods; Bay Ridge), 17
North Carolina Country Kitchen (Southern foods; Bedford-Stuyvesant), 35
Oneg Take-Home Foods (kosher Jewish fare; Borough Park), 63
Oriental Pastry and Grocery (Middle Eastern foods; Atlantic Avenue), 220
Ossie's (Jewish fare; Borough Park), 63
Paradise (Russian foods; Bay Ridge), 18
Park Slope Food Co-op (health and vegetarian; Park Slope), 261

✪ Pastosa Ravioli (Italian foods; Carroll Gardens/Cobble Hill), 50
✪ Produtti Alimentari Italian, Giordano and Sons (Italian Foods; Bensonhurst), 51
Punjab (Pakistani and Indian spices and foods; Flatbush), 170
Queen Ann Ravioli (Italian pasta and foods), 51
✪ Sahadi Importing Company (Middle Eastern and gourmet foods; Atlantic Avenue), 221
Sbarro (Italian foods; Bensonhurst), 51
✪ Schmura Matzoh Factory (matzoh; seasonal; Borough Park), 61
✪ Schwartz Appetizing (Jewish fare; Borough Park), 64
Steve's Meat Market (Polish foods; Greenpoint), 196
✪ Sybil's Bakery and Restaurant (Caribbean; Flatbush), 174
✪ Ten Ren's Tea Time (imported ginseng and teas; Sunset Park), 292
Tony's Foccaceria (Italian foods; Bensonhurst), 51
✪ Trunzo Brothers (Italian foods; Bensonhurst), 52
W. Nassau Meat Market (Polish meats; Greenpoint), 196

Fresh Produce, Fish, and Meats

B & A Pork Store (Bensonhurst), 48
B and H Fruit and Vegetable (Flatbush), 173
✪ 18th Avenue Fruits and Vegetable Market (Bensonhurst), 50
Fish Tales (Carroll Gardens/Cobble Hill), 146
Flatbush Food Cooperative (Flatbush), 174
✪ Garden, The (Greenpoint), 196
Greenmarkets (Brooklyn Heights, Park Slope, Greenpoint), 212, 317
✪ Jim & Andy Fruit and Produce Market (Carroll Gardens/Cobble Hill), 146
✪ Jordan's Lobster Dock (Sheepshead Bay), 100, 105
✪ Juns Market (Latino specialty fruits and vegetables; Sunset Park), 290
✪ #1 Fish Market (Brighton Beach), 84
✪ Park Slope Food Co-op (organic/health food; Park Slope), 261
Park Slope Sea Food (Park Slope), 261
✪ Perelandra Natural Food Center (health food; Brooklyn Heights), 212
✪ Staubitz Market (Carroll Gardens/Cobble Hill), 147
Steve's Meat Market (Polish foods; Greenpoint), 196
Tropical Fruit Stand (Park Slope), 261
Vegetable stands (Brighton Beach), 82
✪ W. Nassau Meat Market (Polish meats; Greenpoint), 196

Fresh Roasted Coffee

D'Amico Foods (Carroll Gardens/Cobble Hill), 145
J &A Espresso Plus (Bensonhurst), 48
Two for the Pot (Brooklyn Heights), 223

Mozzarella *(homemade)*

If you've never tried homemade mozzarella, you are in for a treat. It's soft, warm, and only lasts a day—but what an experience!

A. S. Fine Foods (Park Slope), 259
✪ Aiello Brothers Cheese Company (Bensonhurst), 49
Fratelli Ravioli (Carroll Gardens, Park Slope), 260
✪ Latticini-Barese (Carroll Gardens/Cobble Hill), 146
✪ Lioni Latticini Mozzarella (Bensonhurst), 48
✪ Pastosa Ravioli (Italian foods; Carroll Gardens/Cobble Hill), 147
Pollio (Park Slope), 261
✪ Tedone Latticini (Williamsburg), 316

CULTURE & HISTORY

Includes the following: Arts, Gallery Spaces, Arts Organizations; Architecture, Education and History; Bridges; Brooklyn-Specific Culture; Historic Churches and Religious Institutions; Historic Districts; Museums and Visual Arts; Other Points of Cultural Interest; Performances and Live Entertainment.

Arts, Gallery Spaces, Arts Organizations

See also Museums and Visual Arts *listings*
Anchorage Gallery (DUMBO), 226
Art Moving (Williamsburg), 306
✪ Arts at St. Ann's (Brooklyn Heights), 207
BACA (Brooklyn Heights), 205

Architecture, Education and History

The following are either official New York City landmarks or have played an important role in the history of Brooklyn.

Historic Districts

Museums and Visual Arts

Also see listings under Arts, Gallery Spaces, Arts Organizations

Other Points of Cultural Interest

Performances/Live Entertainment

Music

Theater and Dance

Movies

Brooklyn Heights Cinema (Brooklyn Heights), 201
Cineplex Odeon Alpine Theater (Bay Ridge), 5
Cobble Hill Cinema (Carroll Gardens/ Cobble Hill), 131
Kent Triplex (Flatbush), 163
Kingsway RKO Cinema (Flatbush), 163
Ocularis Films (Williamsburg), 302
Pavilion (Park Slope), 243
Plaza Twin Cinema (Park Slope), 243
Rose Cinemas (*see* BAM Rose Cinemas)
UA Cinema Complex at Sheepshead Bay (Sheepshead Bay), 78
United Artists Marboro Quad (Bensonhurst), 42

Note: Two new theaters are planned, one for Court Street off Atlantic Avenue and another at Brooklyn Commons in Park Slope; neither built yet as of this writing.

Amusement Parks

Astroland Amusement Park, "Home of the Cyclone" (Coney Island), 88
✪ Buzz-a-rama (Flatbush), 173
✪ Deno's Wonder Wheel Amusement Park (Coney Island), 88
Fun Time, USA (Sheepshead Bay), 95
✪ Nellie Bly Amusement Park (Bensonhurst), 42

OUTDOOR RECREATION

Batting Cages

Fun Time, USA (Sheepshead Bay), 95
Gateway Sports Center (Sheepshead Bay), 98

Beaches

Coney Island Beach, 90
✪ Manhattan Beach Park, 97

Biking

Boardwalk at Coney Island (6–10 A.M. *only*), 90
Floyd Bennett Field (Sheepshead Bay), 98
✪ Ocean Parkway bike path (Flatbush), 164
Prospect and Marine parks (Prospect Park; Sheepshead Bay), 165
Shore Parkway Promenade (Bay Ridge), 7

Boating/Fishing

Emmons Avenue fishing boats (Sheepshead Bay), 97
Coffey Street Pier (Red Hook), 154
✪ Plum Beach (Sheepshead Bay), 97
Prospect Park pedal boats (Prospect Park), 97
✪ Sebago Canoe Club (Sheepshead Bay), 99
Sheepshead Bay Sailing School (Sheepshead Bay), 97

Boccie Courts

Carroll Park (Carroll Gardens), 135
Marine Park (Sheepshead Bay), 99

Cross-Country Skiing

Bring your own equipment.

✪ Marine Park (Sheepshead Bay), 99
Prospect Park (Park Slope area), 165

Golf

Dyker Beach Park and Golf Course (Bensonhurst), 43
Gateway Sports Center (Sheepshead Bay), 98
Marine Park Golf Course (Sheepshead Bay), 99

Horseback Riding

Jamaica Bay Riding Academy (Sheepshead Bay), 99
Kensington Stables (Prospect Park), 276

Ice Skating

Abe Stark Ice-Skating Rink (limited hours; Coney Island), 88
Wollman Rink (Prospect Park), 278

Kite Flying

Prospect, Marine, and Fort Greene parks, 114, 276
Shore Parkway Promenade (Bay Ridge), 7

Miniature Golf

✪ Gateway Sports Center (Sheepshead Bay), 98

SCUBA

Scuba Network (Atlantic Avenue), 223

Swimming

Selected. In addition, there are various health clubs and private organizations with pools.

Red Hook Pool (Red Hook), 155
Sunset Park Pool (Sunset Park), 284
Metropolitan Pool (Williamsburg), 304

Tennis

The following are public courts. Call the parks department for permit information (965-8993).

Windsurfing

At your own risk.

Zoos

Parks and Playgrounds

A selected list of parks, playgrounds, and green spaces.

SHOPPING

The following listings detail neighborhood shops.

A Word on Malls

There are several malls in Brooklyn with major stores such as Macy's and Sears:

Atlantic Center (BAM/Fort Greene area)
Kings Plaza (Flatbush)
Fulton Mall (Downtown Brooklyn)

In addition, there are many chain stores in Brooklyn, including Costco, Staples, Home Depot, etc., all listed in the phone book.

APPAREL

See also Antique, Collectible, and Vintage

Women's Apparel (general)

Art and Art Supplies

The following lists galleries, art shows and other venues where art can be purchased. Some are seasonal events.

Books and Music

listed here are listed because they reflect something interesting about their neighborhoods. For complete lists, see the Yellow Pages.

Alpine Beauty Supply (Downtown Brooklyn), 235
Bania Spa (Flatbush), 170
✪ Hollywood Car Wash (Flatbush), 170
M and H Cosmetics (Borough Park), 66
Park Slope Barbershop (Park Slope), 267
PJS Cosmetics (Sheepshead Bay), 107

Sports and Hobby Gear

Bicycle Land (Flatbush), 170
BQ Sports (Greenpoint), 197
BQE Pet Supply (Williamsburg), 318
Panda Sports (Bay Ridge), 22
Royale Sporting Goods (Bay Ridge), 22
SCUBA Network (Atlantic Avenue), 223
Third St. Skate Co. (Park Slope), 268
Tien Wei Aquarium (Sunset Park), 293

Selected Brooklyn Websites

Brooklyn Cultural and Tourism Information, www.brooklynx.org
Alliance for the Arts, www.allianceforarts,org:80/brookhome1.html
Brooklyn Botanic Garden, www.bbg.org
Brooklyn Brewery, www/brooklynbrewery.com/brewer
Brooklyn Children's Museum (BCM), www.bchilmus.org
Brooklyn Historical Society, www.brooklynhistory.org
Brooklyn Museum of Art, www.brooklynart.org
Brooklyn Public Library, www.brooklyn.lib.ny/us/world
Brooklyn Bridge magazine, www.brooklynbridgemag.com
Courier Life newspapers, Brooklynny.com
Prospect Park, www.prospectpark. org
Williamsburg "scene," billburg.com
Williamsurg Art and Historical Society, www.wahcenter.org

General Index

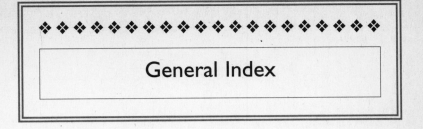

This general index indicates in parenthesis the neighborhood in which a listing is described, and the page number on which you will find it. The icon ✪ indicates a Brooklyn Best Bet.